PAUL THE MISSIONARY

1. J.A. Loader, *A Tale of Two Cities, Sodom and Gomorrah in the Old Testament, early Jewish and early Christian Traditions*, Kampen, 1990
2. P.W. Van der Horst, *Ancient Jewish Epitaphs. An Introductory Survey of a Millennium of Jewish Funerary Epigraphy (300 BCB-700 CE)*, Kampen, 1991
3. E. Talstra, *Solomon's Prayer. Synchrony and Diachrony in the Composition of 1 Kings 8, 14-61*, Kampen, 1993
4. R. Stahl, *Von Weltengagement zu Weltüberwindung: Theologische Positionen im Danielbuch*, Kampen, 1994
5. J.N. Bremmer, *Sacred History and Sacred Texts in early Judaism. A Symposium in Honour of A.S. van der Woude*, Kampen, 1992
6. K. Larkin, *The Eschatology of Second Zechariah: A Study of the Formation of a Mantological Wisdom Anthology*, Kampen, 1994
7. B. Aland, *New Testament Textual Criticism, Exegesis and Church History: A Discussion of Methods*, Kampen, 1994
8. P.W. Van der Horst, *Hellenism-Judaism-Christianity: Essays on their Interaction*, Kampen, Second Enlarged Edition, 1998
9. C. Houtman, *Der Pentateuch: die Geschichte seiner Erforschung neben einer Auswertung*, Kampen, 1994
10. J. Van Seters, *The Life of Moses. The Yahwist as Historian in Exodus-Numbers*, Kampen, 1994
11. Tj. Baarda, *Essays on the Diatessaron*, Kampen, 1994
12. Gert J. Steyn, *Septuagint Quotations in the Context of the Petrine and Pauline Speeches of the Acta Apostolorum*, Kampen, 1995
13. D.V. Edelman, *The Triumph of Elohim, From Yahwisms to Judaisms*, Kampen, 1995
14. J.E. Revell, *The Designation of the Individual. Expressive Usage in Biblical Narrative*, Kampen, 1996
15. M. Menken, *Old Testament Quotations in the Fourth Gospel*, Kampen, 1996
16. V. Koperski, *The Knowledge of Christ Jesus my Lord. The High Christology of Philippians 3:7-11*, Kampen, 1996
17. M.C. De Boer, *Johannine Perspectives on the Death of Jesus*, Kampen, 1996
18. R.D. Anderson, *Ancient Rhetorical Theory and Paul*, Revised edition, Leuven, 1998
19. L.C. Jonker, *Exclusivity and Variety, Perspectives on Multi-dimensional Exegesis*, Kampen, 1996
20. L.V. Rutgers, *The Hidden Heritage of Diaspora Judaism*, Leuven, 1998
21. K. van der Toorn (ed.), *The Image and the Book*, Leuven, 1998
22. L.V. Rutgers, P.W. van der Horst (eds.), *The Use of Sacred Books in the Ancient World*, Leuven, 1998
23. E.R. Ekblad Jr., *Isaiah's Servant Poems According to the Septuagint. An Exegetical and Theological Study*, Leuven, 1999
24. R.D. Anderson Jr., *Glossary of Greek Rhetorical Terms*, Leuven, 2000
25. T. Stordalen, *Echoes of Eden*, Leuven, 2000
26. H. Lalleman-de Winkel, *Jeremiah in Prophetic Tradition*, Leuven, 2000
27. J.F.M. Smit, *About the Idol Offerings. Rhetoric, Social Context and Theology of Paul's Discourse in First Corinthians 8:1-11:1*, Leuven, 2000
28. T.Y. Horner, *Listening to Trypho. Justin Martyr's Dialogue Reconsidered*, Leuven, 2001
29. D.G. Powers, *Salvation through Participation. An Examination of the notion of the Believers' Corporate Unity with Christ in Early Christian Soteriology*, Leuven, 2001
30. J.S. Kloppenborg, P. Hoffmann, J.M. Robinson, M.C. Moreland (eds.), *The Sayings Gospel Q in Greek and English with Parallels from the Gospels of Mark and Thomas*, Leuven, 2001
31. M.K. Birge, *The Language of Belonging. A Rhetorical Analysis of Kinship Language in First Corinthians*, Leuven, 2003
32. P.W. van der Horst, *Japheth in the Tents of Shem. Studies on Jewish Hellenism in Antiquity*, Leuven, 2002
33. P.W. van der Horst, M.J.J. Menken, J.F.M. Smit, G. van Oyen (eds.), *Persuasion and Dissuasion in Early Christianity, Ancient Judaism, and Hellenism*, Leuven, 2003

L.J. LIETAERT PEERBOLTE

PAUL THE MISSIONARY

PEETERS

LEUVEN — PARIS — DUDLEY, MA

2003

Library of Congress Cataloging-in-Publication Data

Lietaert Peerbolte, L.J.
    Paul the missionary / L.J. Lietaert Peerbolte
    p. cm. -- (Contributions to biblical exegesis & theology; 34)
    Includes bibliographical references and index.
    ISBN 90-429-1326-6 (alk. paper)
    1. Paul, the Apostle, Saint. 2. Missions--Biblical teaching. I. Title. II. Contri-
    butions to biblical exegesis and theology; 34.

    BS2506.3.P44 2003
    225.9'2--dc21

                                                            20030468648

© 2003 — Peeters, Bondgenotenlaan 153, B-3000 Leuven

ISBN 90-429-1326-6
D. 2003/0602/80

PREFACE

Some books take their time, and the present volume is such a book. I started my research in 1996, on a scholarship granted by the Theological University of Kampen. At the origin of the project stood the Leiden New Testament Seminar (*Nieuwtestamentisch Werkgezelschap*) on Paul, run by Henk Jan de Jonge and Harm W. Hollander. The discussions in that Seminar encouraged me to take up this subject. The project accompanied me for a long time: I took it along with me from Leiden and Kampen to Utrecht where I taught during the fall of 1999 and the spring of 2000. And after that *Paul the Missionary* accompanied me back to Kampen. As a result the present volume became influenced by the theological climate of all three universities mentioned. All in all the process of working out solutions to the problems I encountered was like a journey in the Alps: after each climb you expect a valley, but find another mountain. Now the journey has come to an end. Looking back on the expedition as a whole I find the journey fully worth the effort.

At this place a brief remark should be made on the specific approach I chose for the questions this volume deals with. I have first and foremost tried to interpret Paul as part of his religious context, so that from this perspective the main characteristics of his ministry and ideas would emerge. Of course, the question asked prevented me from giving a reconstruction of 'the theology of Paul'. Neither that nor a full blown reconstruction of Paul's ministry and the chronology pertaining to it is at stake here. The subject of this book therefore is not Paul as a whole, but the question: to which extent can we label Paul's ministry as 'missionary' and how can we account for his endeavour? It is up to the reader to determine whether my answers are convincing or not.

The classes I was allowed to teach on Paul, on Acts, and on the Synoptic Gospels, have through the years changed my views. This was mainly thanks to the critical questions asked by my students. Next to them there are two colleagues whom I would like to mention in particular: Marinus de Jonge and Pieter W. van der Horst. Marinus de Jonge (Leiden) inspired me to take up the New Testament at all and specialise in this field, and commented upon a previous version of this book. Pieter W. van der Horst (Utrecht) introduced me to his approach of the *Umwelt* of the New Testament, and recently accepted this volume in the present series. I thank them both for their continuing support.

Finally, I want to dedicate this book to my wife Liesbeth, and our children Esther and Martin, who helped me to stay in touch with the real world outside Paul, and taught me to keep up the faith at times when that was difficult.

L.J. Lietaert Peerbolte
Kampen/Leiderdorp, November 2002

TABLE OF CONTENTS

ABBREVIATIONS

A. *Sources*

1 Chron	1 Chronicles
1 Clem.	*1 Clement*
1 Cor	1 Corinthians
1 Kgs	1 Kings
1 Macc	1 Maccabees
1 Sam	1 Samuel
1 Thess	1 Thessalonians
1 Tim	1 Timothy
1QH	Hodayot (= *Thanksgiving Psalms* from Qumran)
1QM	Milhama (= *War Scroll* from Qumran)
1QpHab	Pesher Habakkuk
	(= *Commentary on Habakkuk* from Qumran)
1QS	Serek hayyahad
	(= *Community Rule* from Qumran)
2 Apoc. Bar.	*2nd (Syriac) Apocalyse of Baruch*
2 Clem.	*2 Clement*
2 Cor	2 Corinthians
2 Kgs	2 Kings
2 Macc	2 Maccabees
2 Pet	2 Peter
2 Sam	2 Samuel
2 Thess	2 Thessalonians
3 Apoc. Bar.	*3rd (Greek) Apocalypse of Baruch*
3 Macc	3 Maccabees
4 Macc	4 Maccabees
Adv. haer.	*Adversus haereses*
Ant.	*Antiquitates Iudaicae* (Josephus)
Apoc. Abr.	*Apocalypse of Abraham*
Apoc. Ezra	*Apocalypse of Ezra*
Apoc. Sedr.	*Apocalypse of Sedrach*
Apol.	*Apology* (Justin Martyr)
As. Mos.	*Assumption of Moses*
Bib. Hist.	*Bibliotheca Historica* (Diodorus Siculus)
BJ	*De Bello Judaico* (Josephus)
c. Ap.	*Contra Apionem* (Josephus)
Cato Minor	*Photion and Cato the Younger = Vitae Parallellae* VIII (Plutarch)
c. Cels.	*Contra Celsum* (Origen)
CD	Damascus Document
c. Gal.	*Contra Galilaeos* (Julian)

Col	Colossians
Dan	Daniel
De Civ. Dei	*De Civitate Dei* (Augustin)
De Conf. Ling.	*De Confusione Linguarum* (Philo)
De Div.	*De Divinatione* (Cicero)
De Gig.	*De Gigantibus* (Philo)
De Mut. Nom.	*De Mutatione Nominum* (Philo)
De Virt.	*De Virtutibus* (Philo)
Deut	Deuteronomy
Did.	*Didache*
Diss.	*Dissertationes* (Epictetus)
Div. Inst.	*Divinae Institutiones* (Lactantius)
Ep. Aris.	*Epistle of Aristeas*
Eph	Ephesians
Exod	Exodus
Ezek	Ezekiel
Gal	Galatians
Gen	Genesis
Geogr.	*Geography* (Strabo)
Heb	Hebrews
Herm., *Sim.*	Hermas, *Similitude*
Herm., *Vis.*	Hermas, *Vision*
Hist. Rom.	*Historicae Romanae* (Dio Cassius)
Hist.	*Historiae* (Tacitus)
Ign.	Ignatius
In Flacc.	*In Flaccum* (Philo)
Isa	Isaiah
Jdg	Judges
Jer	Jeremiah
Jos. Asen.	*Joseph and Aseneth*
Jos.	Josephus
Josh	Joshua
Jub.	*Jubilees*
Jud	Jude
Just.	Justin Martyr
LAB	*Liber Antiquitatum Biblicum* (Ps.-Philo)
Leg. All.	*Legum Allegoria* (Philo)
Lev	Leviticus
LXX	Septuagint
Magn.	*Letter to the Magnesians* (Ignatius)
Matt	Matthew
m Mak	Mishna Makkoth
Num	Numbers
Pelop.	*Pelopidas and Marcellus* = *Vitae Parallellae* IV (Plutarch)
PG	*Patrologia graeca* (ed. Migne)
Phil	Philippians
Philop.	*Philopoemen and Flaminius* = *Vitae Parallellae* X (Plutarch)

Phld.	*Letter to the Philadelphians* (Ignatius)
Phlm	Philemon
Pliny, *Ep.*	Pliny the Younger, *Epistles*
Praep. Ev.	*Praeparatio Evangelica* (Eusebius)
Prov	Proverbs
Ps-Crates, *Ep.*	Pseudo-Crates, *Epistles*
Ps-Diog. *Ep.*	Pseudo-Diogenes, *Epistles*
Ps	Psalms
Ps.-Just.	Pseudo-Justin
Pss. Sol.	*Psalms of Solomon*
Rev	Revelation
Rom	Romans
Sat.	*Saturae* (Juvenal)
Serm.	*Sermones* (Horace)
Sib. Or.	*Sibylline Oracles*
Sir	Ecclesiasticus or Wisdom of Jesus ben Sira
Synesius, *Ep.*	Synesius, *Epistles*
T. Ash.	*Testament of Asher (TestXIIPatr)*
T. Ben.	*Testament of Benjamin (TestXIIPatr)*
T. Job	*Testament of Job*
T. Jos.	*Testament of Joseph (TestXIIPatr)*
T. Jud.	*Testament of Judah (TestXIIPatr)*
T. Naph.	*Testament of Naphtali (TestXIIPatr)*
T. Reub.	*Testament of Reuben (TestXIIPatr)*
TestXIIPatr	*Testaments of the Twelve Patriarchs*
Tit	Titus
Tob	Tobit
Tusc.	*Tusculanae Disputationes* (Cicero)
Vita	*Vita* (Josephus)
Vit. Ad.	*Vita Adae et Evae*
Vit. Ap.	*Vita Apollonii* (Flavius Philostratus)
Vit. Mos.	*De Vita Mosis* (Philo)
Vit. Proph.	*Vitae Prophetarum*
Vit. Phil.	*Vitae Philosophorum* (Diogenes Laertius)
Wis	Wisdom of Solomon

B. *Bibliography*

AB	Anchor Bible
ABD	*Anchor Bible Dictionary*
ABRL	The Anchor Bible Reference Library
AGAJU	Arbeiten zur Geschichte des antiken Judentums und des Urchristentums
AJ	Acta Jutlandica
ANRW	*Aufstieg und Niedergang der römischen Welt*
ASMS	American Society of Missiology Series

ATANT	Abhandlungen zur Theologie des Alten und Neuen Testaments
BAFCS	The Book of Acts in its First Century Setting
Bauer, *Wörterbuch*	W. Bauer, K. Aland, B. Aland (eds.), *Griechisch-deutsches Wörterbuch zu den Schriften des Neuen Testaments und der frühchristlichen Literatur* (Berlin, New York: De Gruyter, 6th ed., 1988).
BBB	Bonner biblische Beiträge
BCH	*Bulletin du correspondance hellénique*
BDF	W. Blass, A. Debrunner, R.W. Funk, *A Greek Grammar of the New Testament and other Early Christian Literature* (Chicago: University of Chicago Press, 1961).
BDR	W. Blass, A. Debrunner, F. Rehkopf, *Grammatik des neutestamentlichen Griechisch* (Göttingen: Vandenhoeck & Ruprecht, 15th ed., 1979).
Beginnings	F.J. Foakes Jackson, K. Lake (eds.), *The Beginnings of Christianity* 5 vols. (London: MacMillan, 1922-1939).
BeTh	Beiträge zur evangelischen Theologie
BETL	Bibliotheca Ephemeridum Theologicarum Lovaniensum
BhTh	Beiträge zur historischen Theologie
BibS	The Biblical Seminar
BKP	Beiträge zur klassischen Philologie
BNTC	Black's New Testament Commentaries
BS	Bollingen Series
BT	Bibliothèque théologique
BtS	Biblisch-theologische Studien
BUS	Brown University Studies
BZ	*Biblische Zeitschrift*
BZNW	Beihefte zur Zeitschrift für die neutestamentliche Wissenschaft
CBET	Contributions to Biblical Exegesis and Theology
CBNTS	Coniectanea Biblica New Testament Steries
CBQ	*The Catholic Biblical Quarterly*
CLS	Clarendon Law Series
CNT	Commentaire du Nouveau Testament
CP	Calwer Paperback
ClR	*Classical Review*
CRINT	Compendia Rerum Iudaicarum ad Novum Testamentum
EAC	Entretiens sur l'antiquité classique
EHS	Europäische Hochschulschriften
EKK	Evangelisch-katholischer Kommentar zum Neuen Testament

EMZ	*Evangelische Missionszeitschrift*
EPROER	Études préliminaires aux religions orientales dans l'Empire romain
EvQ	*Evangelical Quarterly*
EWNT	H. Balz, G. Schneider (eds.), *Exegetisches Wörterbuch zum Neuen Testament*, 3 vols (Stuttgart: Kohlhammer, 1980-1983).
ExpTim	*Expository Times*
FRLANT	Forschungen zur Religion und Literatur des Alten und Neuen Testaments
FS	Festschrift
GLAJJ	M. Stern, *Greek and Latin Authors on Jews and Judaism*, 3 vols. (Jerusalem: Israel Academy of Sciences and Humanities, 1974-1984).
GNS	Good News Studies
GNT	Grundrisse zum Neuen Testament
GTA	Göttinger Theologische Arbeiten
HABES	Heidelberger althistorische Beiträge und epigraphische Studien
HAW	Handbuch der Altertumswissenschaft
HNT	Handbuch zum Neuen Testament
HThK	Herders theologischer Kommentar zum Neuen Testament
HTR	*Harvard Theological Review*
HTS	Harvard Theological Studies
ICC	International Critical Commentary of the Holy Scriptures
JAC	*Jahrbuch für Antike und Christentum*
JBL	*Journal of Biblical Literature*
JRS	*Journal of Roman Studies*
JSHRZ	Jüdische Schriften aus hellenistisch-römischer Zeit
JSNT	*Journal for the Study of the New Testament*
JSNTSS	Journal for the Study of the New Testament Supplement Series
JSOTM	JSOT Manuals
JThS	*Journal of Theological Studies*
KEK	Kritisch-exegetischer Kommentar über das Neue Testament
KuD	*Kerygma und Dogma*
LCL	Loeb Classical Library
LPS	Library of Pauline Studies
MNTS	McMaster New Testament Studies
Moulton-Turner, *Grammar*	J.H. Moulton, *A Grammar of New Testament Greek*, 4 vols. by J.H. Moulton [vols. 1-2] and N. Turner [vols. 3-4] (Edinburgh: Clark, 3rd ed., 1957-1976)
MS	Mnemosune Supplements

NCB	New Century Bible
NIC	New International Commentary on the New Testament
NT	*Novum Testamentum*
NTD	Das Neue Testament Deutsch
NTG	New Testament Guides
NTOA	Novum Testamentum et Orbis Antiquus
NTS	*New Testament Studies*
NTTS	New Testament Tools and Studies
OTKNT	Ökumenischer Taschenbuch Kommentar zum Neuen Testament
OTPseud	J.H. Charlesworth (ed.), *The Old Testament Pseudepigrapha*, 2 vols. (New York: Doubleday, 1983).
PG	*Patrologia Graeca*
PM	Past Masters
PRS	*Perspectives in Religious Studies*
PRSA	Problemi e ricerche di storia antica
QD	Quaestiones Disputatae
RGG	*Religion in Geschichte und Gegenwart*
RGRW	Religions in the Graeco-Roman World
RHPR	*Revue d'histoire et de philosophie religieuses*
Robertson, *Grammar*	Robertson, A.T., *A Grammar of the Greek New Testament in the Light of Historical Research* (New York: Hodder & Stoughton, 3rd ed., rev. and enl., 1919).
SAC	Studies in Antiquity and Christianity
SANT	Studien zum Alten und Neuen Testament
SB	Studi biblici
SBL	*The Society of Biblical Literature*
SBLDS	SBL Dissertation Series
SBLSBS	SBL Sources for Biblical Study
SBS	Stuttgarter Bibelstudien
SCHNT	Studia ad Corpus Hellenisticum Novi Testamenti
Schürer *et al.*, *History*	G. Vermes, F. Millar, M. Black, P. Vermes, revision and edition of: E. Schürer, *The History of the Jewish People in the Age of Jesus Christ (175 B.C. – A.D. 135)*, 4 vols. (Edinburgh: Clark, 1973-1987).
SG	Sammlung Goschen
SGRR	Studies in Greek and Roman Religion
SJSJ	Supplements to the Journal for the Study of Judaism
SNT	Supplements to Novum Testamentum
SNTSMS	SNTS Monograph Series
SO	Symbolae Osloenses
SPB	Studia Post-Biblica
Strack-Billerbeck	H.L. Strack, P. Billerbeck, *Kommentar zum*

	Neuen Testament aus Talmud und Midrasch, 6 vols. (München: Beck, 1922-1961).
SUNT	Studien zur Umwelt des Neuen Testaments
T&T	Tekst & Toelichting
TANZ	Texte und Arbeiten zum neutestamentlichen Zeitalter
TBN	Themes in Biblical Narrative
TD	Texts and Documents
TEH	Theologische Existenz Heute
TF	Theologische Forschung
ThHK	Theologischer Handkommentar zum Neuen Testament
ThWNT	G. Kittel, G. Friedrich, *et alii* (eds.), *Theologisches Wörterbuch zum Neuen Testament*, 10 vols. (Stuttgart: Kohlhammer, 1933-1979).
Translator's Handbook	The *Translator's Handbook* series, United Bible Societies
TTPS	Texts and Translations Pseudepigrapha Series
TynB	*Tyndale Bulletin*
UB	Urban Bücher
VD	*Verbum Domini*
VigChr	*Vigiliae Christianae*
WBC	World Biblical Commentary
WMANT	Wissenschaftliche Monographien zum Alten und Neuen Testament
WUNT	Wissenschaftliche Untersuchungen zum Neuen Testament
ZB	Zürcher Bibelkommentare
ZMR	*Zeitschrift für Missionskunde und Religionswissenschaft*
ZNW	*Zeitschrift für die neutestamentliche Wissenschaft*
ZTK	*Zeitschrift für Theologie und Kirche*

INTRODUCTION

THE QUESTION AND ITS HISTORY

Many people today, Christians and non-Christians alike, know Paul as the Apostle to the Gentiles. Paul himself uses this designation when he addresses the congregations of the Galatians and the Romans (Gal 2,8; Rom 11,13). In these passages it seems that Paul states a clear view of himself and his task: he is an apostle and his mission is directed at the Gentiles. Paul makes no secret of the fact that he was called directly by God, and thus the picture is clear: Paul was called to be a missionary, to be an apostle, in order to bring the gospel to the Gentiles.

With some modification, the Book of Acts presents the same view of Paul. He is the one commissioned with the task of converting Gentiles to the Christian way. Although Acts appears to have great trouble in calling Paul an 'apostle', the book does picture him as the one whose activities resulted in the spread of Christianity across the entire Mediterranean world. Paul is the restless missionary, compelled to preach the gospel, and urged on by God himself.[1]

At first sight it would seem that from the beginning of his Christian existence Paul saw himself and his call from this perspective.[2] Paul would have had a consciously planned strategy for missionising the Gentile world and he would have hastened to fulfil his plan before the *parousia*.[3]

---

[1] G. Bornkamm, *Paulus* (UB 119D; Stuttgart [etc.]: Kohlhammer, 1969), p. 74: 'Denn das große Ziel, das Evangelium bis an die Enden der Erde zu bringen, hielt ihn in Bewegung und Unruhe.'

[2] G. Lüdemann, *Paulus und das Judentum* (TEH 215; München: Kaiser, 1983), p. 21, is clear on this: 'Paulus wurde vor Damaskus zum Heidenapostel berufen.'

[3] P. Wernle, *Paulus als Heidenmissionar* (Leipzig, Tübingen: Mohr, 1899), pp. 17-18; see also e.g. M. Dibelius, W.G. Kümmel, *Paulus* (SG 1160; Berlin: De Gruyter, 4th ed. 1970), pp. 61-77; K.G. Kuhn, 'Das Problem der Mission in der Urchristenheit', *EMZ* 11 (1954), pp. 161-168, esp. p. 166. Among others O. Cullmann, 'Le caractère eschatogique du devoir missionaire et de la conscience apostolique de S. Paul. Étude sur le κατέχον (—ων) de 2 Thess 2,6.7', *RHPR* 16 (1936), pp. 210-245 has argued that Paul saw his task to proclaim the gospel throughout the entire world as a necessary precondition for the coming of the *parousia*. The restraining force or person of 2 Thess 2,6-7 would thus have been Paul himself. A better solution is offered by the present author: 'The κατέχον / κατέχων of 2 Thess 2:6-7', *NT* 39 (1997), pp. 138-150; also: L.J. Lietaert Peerbolte, *The Antecedents of Antichrist. A Traditio-Historical Study of the*

Thus, P. Wernle, a New Testament scholar from Basel, in 1899 described Paul's missionary strategy as follows:

> Mit einem wahren Adlerblick schaut er aus freier Höhe auf die Missionskarte und zeichnet längst zum voraus seine Zukunftsrouten in sie ein. Trotz Angst und Trübsal ist es ihm, als führe ihn Gott als seinen Gefangenen im Triumphzug durch die ganze Welt.[4]

Recent studies of Paul's religious context show that there is every reason to ask two central questions in this respect. Firstly: did Paul indeed perform a proselytising mission? And secondly: which specific contribution did Paul make to the development of Christianity as a missionary movement?

During the last century scholarly views of Paul have changed profoundly. Nevertheless, many students of the early Christian movement have remained under the influence of the classic description by A. Harnack. In his *Die Mission und Ausbreitung des Urchristentums*[5] Harnack described the birth of the early Christian mission, to put it bluntly, as little more than a shift of content within Jewish mission. According to Harnack all that the Christian missionaries had to do was take their new, Christian message and follow the wake of Jewish missionaries who had cleared the way.[6]

Earliest Christian Views on Eschatological Opponents (SJSJ 49; Leiden [etc.]: Brill, 1996), pp. 63-95: the notion of the κατέχον and κατέχων has been introduced by the deutero-Pauline author who is responsible for 2 Thessalonians as part of a literary fiction. By means of this vague notion he suggests a common knowledge between Paul and his readers, whereas he himself does not know the true reason for the delayed *parousia* either. H.-J. Schoeps, *Paulus. Die Theologie des Apostels im Lichte der jüdischen Religionsgeschichte* (Tübingen: Mohr, 1959), pp. 231-242, even argued that Paul shared the pharisaic idea (sic!) that missionary zeal would accelerate the coming of the Messiah, and that therefore in Paul's Christian ministry the mission to convert the gentiles was a necessary precondition for the *parousia*.

[4] Wernle, *Heidenmissionar*, p. 21.

[5] A. Harnack, *Die Mission und Ausbreitung des Christentums in den ersten drei Jahrhunderten* (Leipzig: Hinrich, 2nd rev. ed. 1906, [1]1902), 2 vols.

[6] Many have followed Harnack's views. See e.g. F.M. Derwacter, *Preparing the Way for Paul. The Proselyte Movement in Later Judaism* (New York: Macmillan, 1930); E. Lerle, *Proselytenwerbung und Urchristentum* (Berlin: Evangelische Verlagsanstalt, 1960). The same point was also made by K. Axenfeld, 'Die jüdische Propaganda als Vorläuferin und Wegbereiterin des Christentums', in: idem *et alii*, (eds.), *Missionswissenschaftliche Studien* (FS Warneck; Berlin: Warneck, 1904), pp. 1-80. Axenfeld's views are typical of the intellectual climate in Germany at the beginning of the twentieth century: 'Endlich leistete die jüdische Mission der urchristlichen Mission ihren letzten, großen Dienst, daß sie zur rechten Zeit das Feld räumte' (sic!). A comparable reconstruction of Jewish mission is given by H. Gressmann, 'Jüdische Mission in der Werdezeit des Christentums', *ZMR* 39 (1924), pp. 169-183. Gressmann is even worse with his biased, almost nazistic evaluation of Judaism in the Graeco-Roman period: 'Die weltweite Seele des israelitischen Prophetentums, die im Begriff gewesen war, alles Jüdische von sich abzustreifen und sich auf das rein Menschliche zu besinnen, war wieder in die Enge eines echtjüdischen

The only new element in Paul's appearance as a Christian missionary was the Christian gospel.[7]

Harnack's perception of the development of the early Christian movement, impressive as it may be in its great mastery of sources, was influenced too much by the missionary movement of the nineteenth century. Nonetheless, it has obtained a lasting influence. At present the debate on the missionary character of the Jewish religion in the Graeco-Roman period is still going on. Its outcome is of course of great interest to anyone trying to reconstruct Paul's position within the early Christian movement, for to a high degree it defines the origin and context of the Christian movement. Harnack's view that the Jewish religion at the dawn of the Common Era was a missionary movement that purposely converted Gentiles to Judaism is still shared by many scholars.[8] For a long period all Jewish literature written in Greek was considered missionary in character, simply because of the language.[9] Harnack's view of Judaism as a missionary movement has however been contradicted by a number of scholars.[10]

Leibes gezwängt und konnte ihr Schwingen nicht mehr frei entfalten.' Also more recently Harnack's views have been influential: see e.g. T.L. Donaldson's conclusion to his article 'Israelite, Convert, Apostle to the Gentiles: The Origin of Paul's Gentile Mission', in: R.N. Longenecker (ed.), *The Road from Damascus. The Impact of Paul's Conversion on His Life, Thought, and Ministry* (MNTS 2; Grand Rapids: Eerdmans, 1997), pp. 62-84, who states: '... if Gal 5:11 refers to a pre-Damascus stage in Paul's life, then Paul's Gentile mission may be understood as the christological transformation of a proselytizing concern already present in his pre-conversion days.' (p. 81). The same view is presented by Donaldson in his *Paul and the Gentiles. Remapping the Apostle's Convictional World* (Minneapolis: Fortress, 1997), esp. pp. 275-284.

[7] The same thought has been stated by E. Barnikol, *Die vor- und frühchristliche Zeit des Paulus* (Kiel: Mühlau, 1929), pp. 18-24, who argues that before his conversion/call, Paul had been a Jewish missionary proclaiming the necessity of circumcision.

[8] Several authors have defended the existence of a Jewish proselytising mission. See e.g. B.J. Bamberger, *Proselytism in the Talmudic Period* (New York: KTAV, 1968 = Hebrew Union College Press, 1939); W.G. Braude, *Jewish Proselyting in the First Five Centuries of the Common Era, the Age of the Tannaim and Amoraim* (BUS 6; Providence: Brown University, 1950); M. Simon, *Verus Israel: étude sur les relations entre chretiens et juifs dans l'empire romain (135-425)* (Paris: Boccard, 2nd ed. 1964, [1]1948). In the present debate the existence of a Jewish proselytising mission is advocated most clearly by L.H. Feldman, in e.g. his *Jew and Gentile in the Ancient World. Attitudes and Interactions from Alexander to Justinian* (Princeton: Princeton University Press, 1993); also by D. Georgi, cf. below.

[9] See for instance P. Dalbert, *Die Theologie der hellenistisch-jüdischen Missionsliteratur unter Ausschluss von Philo und Josephus* (TF 4; Hamburg-Volksdorf: Reich, 1954).

[10] The strange perception of Jewish literature in Greek as evidence for the missionary character of the Jewish religion was effectively challenged by V. Tcherikover, 'Jewish Apologetic Literature Reconsidered', *Eos* 48 (1956), pp. 169-193 – cf. below, p. 22.

Two recent publications in particular have re-opened the discussion. In 1991 S. McKnight challenged Harnack's view of Judaism as a missionary movement.[11] McKnight argues that 'Jews were integrally related to the non-Jewish society in which they were living.' In their perception, they integrated this society into the universal view of the world as created and governed by the one God. And yet, McKnight concludes, 'Judaism never developed a clear mission to the Gentiles that had as its goal the conversion of the world.' McKnight is ready to admit that 'Jewish missionary activity may have existed at times in Rome', but firmly denies that Judaism was 'a missionary religion'.[12]

In 1994 it was the Oxford scholar M. Goodman who in a compelling monograph defended the theory that a proselytising attitude was lacking in Jewish religion before the turn of the first and second centuries CE.[13] Goodman takes the argument one step further. He questions the existence of proselytising mission altogether in the pre-Christian era. According to him, mission understood as proselytising is a phenomenon more or less invented by the Christian movement.[14] Traces of this form of mission are found in Jewish writings only after 100 CE, and according to Goodman this new religious attitude probably developed under the direct influence of Christian activities. Pagan cults did promote their deities but proselytising mission aimed at converting people was neither a pagan nor Jewish habit before the Christian era.

Goodman's analysis has been of great help for the present study that, different as it may be in scope and character, will in part state some of the same views. The main point in which Goodman's theories have influenced the present volume is in the perception of mission. How should the

---

For a critical attitude towards the existence of Jewish proselytising mission, see K.H. Rengstorf, *ThWNT*, vol. I, p. 418; J. Munck, *Paulus und die Heilsgeschichte* (AJ 26,1; Koebnhavn: Munksgaard, 1954), pp. 259-265 (= *Paul and the Salvation of Mankind* [London: SCM, 1959], pp. 264-271 – p. 265: 'Judaism neither posessed any missionary theory nor felt any call to receive the gentiles into the chosen people.'); A.D. Nock, *Essays on Religion and the Ancient World* (Oxford: Clarendon, 1972), vol. 2, p. 929.

[11] S. McKnight, *A Light among the Gentiles. Jewish Missionary Activity in the Second Temple Period* (Minneapolis: Fortress Press, 1991).

[12] The quotations have all been taken from *Light*, pp. 116-117.

[13] M. Goodman, *Mission and Conversion. Proselytizing in the Religious History of the Roman Empire* (Oxford: Clarendon Press, 1994).

[14] This is also argued by e.g. Rosenkranz, in: *RGG³*, vol. 4, p. 969. Pesch's objection – 'Freilich läßt sich die inzwischen eingebürgerte Begriffsbildung kaum rückgängig machen...' – does not mean that one should not make a very careful distinction between the various forms of mission that Goodman describes. Cf. Pesch, 'Voraussetzungen', p. 13 (full title below).

phenomenon of 'mission' be adequately described? Goodman's distinction is useful: he defines four different categories of mission, only one of which is aimed at conversion. Because of the importance of this distinction, Goodman's words are quoted here at some length. Goodman describes three forms of non-proselytising mission:

> Three attitudes in particular are worth isolating as involving considerably less than a mission to win converts, despite the fact that they are often described simply as missionary by historians of religion. Thus there is much evidence that some people in antiquity felt that they had a general message which they wished to impart to others. (…) Such an attitude might be termed informative mission. (…) Secondly, some missionaries did intend to change recipients of their message by making them more moral or contended, but did not require that the novel behaviour and attitudes of their auditors be recognized by those auditors as part of the belief system espoused by the missionary. Such a mission to educate is easily distinguished from a desire to win converts. (…) Thirdly, some missionaries requested recognition by others of the power of a particular divinity without expecting their audience to devote themselves to his or her worship. Such a mission was essentially apologetic.[15]

Then Goodman describes the phenomenon that is usually presupposed when scholars speak of 'mission':

> Information, education, and apologetic might or might not coexist within any one religious system, but all three can individually be distinguished from what may best be described as proselytizing. Those who approved of a proselytizing mission believed that, as members of a defined group, they should approve of those within their number who might choose to encourage outsiders not only to change their way of life but also to be incorporated within their group.[16]

The distinction advocated by Goodman is indeed useful. It points out that, unlike with the three other types of mission, the aim of proselytising is to make converts who would not only change their views, but also leave their social group with its own particular values to join a new group whose views they had come to share. Of course, the types mentioned are 'ideal types'.[17]

The present study focuses on the part Paul played within the developing proselytising Christian mission.[18] Its point of departure lies in the

---

[15] Goodman, *Mission and Conversion*, pp. 3-4.
[16] Goodman, *Mission and Conversion*, p. 4.
[17] Goodman, *Mission and Conversion*, p. 4.
[18] For a description of the period after Paul had been active, see the excellent descriptions by R. MacMullen, *Christianizing the Roman Empire (A.D. 100-400)* (New Haven,

observation that the surrounding religious context – Jewish and pagan religions – did not know this type of proselytising mission. By implication, the pre-Christian Paul cannot be seen as a 'missionary' in the traditional way. And yet, after the great change he experienced, he did travel, he did proclaim the gospel wherever he went, and he did found Christian congregations. How should Paul's ministry be accounted for in this light? The question becomes all the more relevant if we are ready to consider Matt 28,16-20 as being the first explicit example of the proselytising missionary attitude. It would go too far to describe the Christian movement at the turn of the first and second centuries as a fully proselytising movement, but certainly the proselytising attitude was present in some Christian circles at that time.

The two elements mentioned are indicative of the problem: the absence of a proselytising mission from the religious context of early Christianity and the fact that Matt 28,16-20 proves that such a mission did exist within post-Pauline Christianity. Sometime in its early history Christianity must have developed this attitude. Since there is no single Christian author from the earliest period who has left us so many sources as Paul did, while at the same time contributing so much to the spread of Christianity, the question to be asked is: what contribution did Paul make to the development of Christianity as a proselytising religion?

Previous Studies

This book is neither the first nor will it be the last volume in which the early Christian movement is examined from the perspective of its missionary activities. A number of scholars in the past have described the early Christian missionary movement or the religious climate in which it originated.[19] In 1963 F. Hahn wrote his *Habilitationsschrift* on the understanding and theological foundation of mission in the New Testament.[20]

London: Yale University Press, 1984), and R. Lane Fox, *Pagans and Christians in the Mediterranean World from the Second Century AD to the Conversion of Constantine* (London: Penguin, 1986 = New York: Knopf, 1986), esp. pp. 265-335.

[19] This survey of literature on early Christian mission is, of course, not exhaustive. Only the most important scholars and publications are mentioned.

[20] F. Hahn, *Das Verständnis der Mission im Neuen Testament* (WMANT 13; Neukirchen-Vluyn: Neukirchener Verlag, 1963). Hahn correctly observes that the literature of the preceding decades had produced few explicit examinations of the subject and mentions just two highlights: R. Liechtenhan, *Die urchristliche Mission. Voraussetzungen, Motive und Methoden* (ATANT 9, 1946); and Kuhn, 'Problem'. Hengel's verdict on Liechtenhan is applicable to Kuhn as well: a 'wenig befriedigende Untersuchung' – Hengel, 'Ursprünge' (full title: below), n. 2.

Hahn's study focuses on the theology, not the origin of mission, and rests upon the hypothesis that Hellenistic Judaism was characterised by strong missionary activity.[21] In this respect, Hahn does not differ too much from Harnack.[22] In his analysis of Paul's position within the early Christian movement, Hahn is also more interested in Paul's theology than in his history.[23] In Hahn's view Paul acted as a missionary: the apostle was called to proclaim the gospel to the Gentiles. Hahn's interpretation denies any development that Paul may have gone through, does not question the phenomenon of Christian mission as such, and thus gives no answer to the question asked above.

The scholar, whose influence is present in every publication on early Christian mission or propaganda of the past few decades, is D. Georgi. In 1964 he published his dissertation on Paul's opponents in 2 Corinthians, and the way in which they were embedded in the religious propaganda of the period.[24] Georgi is also greatly indebted to Harnack. He bases his view on Harnack's observation that the number of Jews in the Diaspora increased during the last two centuries before and first century of the Common Era to such an extent that Jewish mission must have been one of the causes.[25] In Georgi's reconstruction the most important vehicle for mission was the synagogue service. Here the interpretation of the Law that formed the core of Jewish identity throughout the Roman Empire was given. Georgi mentions a number of examples in which pagans were apparently drawn to the synagogue,[26] and adds that missionary attempts by Jews were not organised in a central way by a supervisor in

---

[21] Hahn, *Mission*, p. 15: 'Ein umfangreiches und intensives Werben für den jüdischen Glauben ist offensichtlich von dem hellenistischen Judentum ausgegangen.' On p. 18 Hahn makes a distinction between religious propaganda, that was made to win God-Fearers, and proselytising mission ('Proselytenwerbung'), that aimed at converting pagans to Judaism.

[22] See Hahn, *Mission*, p. 18: 'Die Erfolge dieser Bestrebungen waren nicht gering und es steht außer Zweifel, daß damit der Mission des Urchristentums in hohem Maße der Weg gebahnt worden ist.'

[23] Hahn, *Mission*, pp. 80-94.

[24] D. Georgi, *Die Gegner des Paulus im 2. Korintherbrief. Studien zur religiösen Propaganda in der Spätantike* (WMANT 11; Neukirchen-Vluyn: Neukirchener Verlag, 1964); also available in English: *The Opponents of Paul in Second Corinthians* (Edinburgh: Clark, 1987). To this translation Georgi added an epilogue (pp. 333-450) in which he brought his book up to date and presented a criticism of his own work, but did not substantially alter his views.

[25] Georgi, *Gegner*, pp. 83-87; cf. p. 87: 'die massenhafte Gewinnung von Heiden setzt einen entsprechenden Werbewillen der Juden voraus!'

[26] An important example is the description by Josephus of the Jewish community in Antioch that attracted large crowds of pagans – Josephus, *BJ* vii,45.

Jerusalem.[27] The most interesting element in Georgi's analysis is the fact that he claims that Jewish preachers travelled throughout the Empire acting as interpreters of the Mosaic Law. These preachers could act as *divine men* (θεῖοι ἄνθρωποι), and were thus in a far better position to be heard because audiences were eager to meet such men. They also acted in the way of Cynic-Stoic philosophers by leading a wandering existence and providing for their livelihood by begging.[28]

A second way in which, according to Georgi, Jewish preachers sought converts was the use of magic. Georgi argues that there were preachers who acted as spiritualists and thus tried to lead people to the one true God. Their magical actions were representations of the greater spiritual riches that could be obtained in the synagogue.[29] Georgi concludes his survey of the organisation of Jewish mission with the statement that all these activities, both inside and outside the synagogue, aimed at interpreting scripture and that this in itself was proselytising.[30]

After Georgi had thus analysed the organisation of Jewish mission, he described the 'theological foundation of Jewish mission'.[31] This survey of Jewish theological views is influenced by Georgi's perception of Jewish mission to such an extent, that we can leave it aside in the present volume. What is more interesting is the fact that Georgi subsequently describes pagan mission as a great competition of individual cults searching for new adherents.[32] Within this competition the role of θεῖοι ἄνθρωποι and the importance of tradition are considered as crucial. In Georgi's opinion pagan messengers who brought news of a certain cult acted as divinely inspired men who professed to proclaim a deity standing in a long tradition.[33] The first Christian missionaries did the same thing, according to Georgi, because they too acted as spiritualists and

---

[27] Georgi, *Gegner*, p. 93.

[28] Georgi decides that Jewish preachers lived itinerant lives, since Cynic-Stoic philosophers did the same thing: 'Wie schon das Bild des Bettlers an sich so deuten auch die Parallelen aus dem Bereich der kynisch-stoischen Propaganda darauf hin, daß die angeblichen jüdischen Bettler nicht seßhaft waren, sondern wanderten.' (*Gegner*, p. 111).

[29] Georgi, *Gegner*, p. 130: 'Alle außergottesdienstliche Tätigkeit der jüdischen Pneumatiker war Werbung für den Gottesdienst selbst, als den Ursprungs- und Sammelort der einzelnen pneumatischen Kräfte.'

[30] Georgi, *Gegner*, p. 131.

[31] Georgi, *Gegner*, pp. 138-187.

[32] Georgi, *Gegner*, pp. 187-192 ('Mission als Konkurrenz'). It is against this image of the competition between various cults that Goodman turned in his *Mission and Conversion* – cf. p. 1, where Goodman speaks out against the 'presupposition of a competitive attitude among adherents of religions other than Christianity.'

[33] Georgi, *Gegner*, pp. 187-205.

proclaimed Jesus as a new Moses, thereby placing him in an old and long tradition.[34]

Georgi's presentation of the material has been very influential. Many of the parallels Georgi mentions are indeed present. Nonetheless, this book endeavours to offer an alternative. It will contradict Georgi's conclusions by arguing that proselytising mission was absent from both Judaism and pagan cults. On the basis of this observation a new question arises, viz.: how did the Christian proselytising mission emerge? And more especially: what was Paul's role in this process?

A few years after Georgi, G. Schille presented the early Christian movement as an antique *collegium* (1967).[35] In his treatise Schille does make a number of interesting observations but on the whole his study is not very useful. His perception of the material is pre-judged, and no arguments are given for his equation of Christian congregations with *collegia* – the identity of the two is simply taken for granted.[36] The comparison with Roman and Egyptian *collegia* especially is not entirely without merit, but nowhere does Schille really prove that the early Christian congregations he writes about understood *themselves* as *collegia*. Two observations he made do however have some importance for the present subject. Firstly, Paul would not have been as interested in founding communities as he was in preaching the gospel.[37] This observation will play an important part in the present analysis of Paul's ministry. And secondly, although the interpretation of the early Christian missionary development as *Kollegialmission* may have been made too easily, the fact is that Paul and Barnabas did apparently act on behalf of the congregation of Antioch. The commissioning of envoys by congregations to proclaim the gospel elsewhere was indeed

---

[34] Georgi, *Gegner*, pp. 205-213.

[35] G. Schille, *Die urchristliche Kollegialmission* (ATANT 48; 1967). See also his *Anfänge der Kirche. Erwägungen zur apostolische Frühgeschichte* (BeTh 43; München: Kaiser, 1966).

[36] Apart from that, a serious objection against this book is that the process of reading it is an utter torment to the reader. Furthermore, Schille's reconstruction of the 'fellow-workers' is rendered out of date by W.-H. Ollrog, *Paulus und seine Mitarbeiter. Untersuchungen zu Theorie und Praxis der paulinischen Mission* (WMANT 50; Neukirchen-Vluyn: Neukirchener Verlag, 1979) – cf. below, p. 230.

[37] Schille, *Kollegialmission*, p. 82: 'Erste Aufgabe des Wanderapostels war die Verkündigung. So kümmert sich Paulus im allgemeinen weniger um die Ausbreitung der Ortsgemeinschaften als um die der Botschaft.'

an important element within the spread of the early Christian movement.

In 1969 H. Kasting published a monograph on the origin of the early Christian mission.[38] According to Kasting, the early Christian mission originated in the Easter appearances: Jesus commissioned his followers to proclaim the gospel when he appeared to them after his resurrection.[39] Kasting does assume some continuity between the movement during Jesus' life and the church that he considers to be founded after the resurrection, but he advocates a post-Easter commissioning event as the moment at which the Christian mission was born.[40] Kasting's work has to face one serious objection in particular: it lays too much emphasis on an event that cannot be reconstructed by the methods of historical research. What can be relied upon is the perception the first Christians had of their own tasks and that of the resurrection appearances. Within this perception we have to assume a greater continuity between the Jesus movement before and after Jesus' death. Therefore, Kasting's attempt to answer the question of the origin of Christian mission should be considered as fruitless in this respect. In two other aspects, however, Kasting's work did progress beyond previous studies. Firstly, Kasting denied the existence of any organised Jewish mission.[41] In his perception it was the monotheistic message itself that resulted in a Jewish awareness of religious superiority. Jews, in contrast to pagans, did proclaim the one universal God and because of this the synagogues in the Diaspora were missionary in character, but this mission was not expressed in a worldwide plan or scheme.[42] Although Kasting refuses to characterise this Jewish mission as 'religious propaganda',[43] he maintains the idea that Jews in the first century were filled with a missionary consciousness.[44] Secondly, Kasting removes the myth of Paul as the great missionary travelling around day and night in order to proclaim the gospel to the entire world

---

[38] H. Kasting, *Die Anfänge der urchristlichen Mission. Eine historische Untersuchung* (BeTh 55; München: Kaiser, 1969).

[39] Kasting, *Anfänge*, pp. 80-81, 126.

[40] 'Anlaß und Grundlage (der urchristlichen Mission; LP)... bot erst die in den österlichen Christophanien ergangene Sendung.' – Kasting, *Anfänge*, p. 126.

[41] Kasting, *Anfänge*, pp. 11-21.

[42] Kasting, *Anfänge*, p. 20: 'Nirgends stößt man in der Überlieferung auf eine organisierte Mission und auf den wandernden Missionar, der wie ein hellenistischer Popularphilosoph oder ein urchristlicher Apostel die Welt durchzog, um für seine Botschaft zu werben.'

[43] Kasting, *Anfänge*, p. 30.

[44] Kasting, *Anfänge*, p. 29: 'Aus den angeführten Stellen geht hervor, daß die Juden zur Zeit Jesu von einem bedeutenden Sendungsbewußtsein erfüllt waren.'

before the *parousia*.[45] Instead, Kasting describes Paul as one who concentrated on founding congregations in a number of provincial capital cities.[46]

Kasting's reconstruction of the origin of Christian mission is a careful but inadequate attempt. His evaluation of Jewish religious propaganda is unbalanced and his emphasis on the post-Easter commissioning is not consistent with the view of the historian. The analysis offered of Paul's ministry is too short and too limited to answer the question posed in the present enquiry.

M. Hengel published an important essay on the origin of Christian mission in 1971.[47] Hengel also starts with the observation that Jewish missionary activities had paved the way.[48] Paul was a missionary from the moment of his call and his theology is missionary in that it proclaims the universal rule of Christ as the *kyrios*.[49] Hengel traces the direct origin of Paul's proclamation of Christ to the Gentiles to a group of 'Hellenists'.[50] They formed the bridge between Jesus, the earliest Christian community in Jerusalem, and Paul. Hengel's study is a careful and important step, but it leaves out a number of issues. The first and most important of these is the meaning of 'mission'. Like so many others Hengel uses the word without clarifying what he understands by it. Secondly, Hengel is not critical enough with regard to the existence of a Jewish mission. Since he does not define the word, he fails to observe the true character of Jewish religious propaganda. And thirdly, Hengel remains closely attached to the picture given by the book of Acts.[51] A debate with Hengel will be evident throughout the present study.

[45] Kasting, *Anfänge*, pp. 107-108.
[46] Kasting, *Anfänge*, p. 107: 'Paulus hat sich seines Auftrages zur Heidenmission nicht in überstürzter, sondern in wohldurchdachter Weise entledigt. Allem Anschein nach hat er schwerpunktmäßig gearbeitet: Damaskus, Antiochia, Tarsus, Thessalonich, Korinth, Ephesus. Er suchte vor allem die Provinzhauptstätte auf, in denen er sich mitunter jahrelang aufhielt und Missionszentren bildete.'
[47] M. Hengel, 'Die Ursprünge der christlichen Mission', NTS 18 (1971-72), pp. 15-38; English translation in *Between Jesus and Paul. Studies in the Earliest History of Christianity* (London: SCM, 1983), pp. 58-64.
[48] Hengel is very careful in his analysis, but still remains close to Harnack: 'Die jüdische Mission hatte im Schutze der augusteischen pax romana ihren Höhepunkt erreicht. (...) Es ist deshalb damit zu rechnen das der "Hillelit" Paulus, bevor er Christ wurde, bereits mit der jüdischen Mission vertraut war.' (p. 23).
[49] Hengel, 'Ursprünge', pp. 17-24.
[50] Hengel, 'Ursprünge', pp. 24-30; cf. also Hengel, 'Zwischen Jesus und Paulus', ZTK 72 (1975), pp. 151-206 (= *Between Jesus and Paul*, pp. 1-29).
[51] In later publications Hengel started something like a war against those interpreters who critically question the book of Acts; cf. below, pp. 100-103.

In a more recent article P. Bowers has pictured Paul's ministry from the missionary point of view.[52] Bowers considers the religious context in which Paul operated as one in which many forms of religious propaganda existed side by side. One of these forms was that of proselytism. Thus, in Bowers' view also, Paul and the early Christian movement did not really create anything entirely new. In this analysis of Paul's ministry Paul operated according to a clearly planned geographic programme. Yet according to Bowers, it was not the programme that was exceptional, but the fact that Paul carried it out. In the present study both elements in Bowers' interpretation will be contested. It will be argued that neither the theory that a proselytising mission already existed nor the notion that Paul directed his own ministry on the basis of an all-encompassing plan can be upheld.

In an essay on the origin of Christian mission published in 1982 R. Pesch provides a survey of the terminology used in the various writings of the New Testament within a missionary context.[53] In a helpful distinction Pesch defines a mission to other Jews as a *missio interna* and one to the Gentiles as a *missio externa*.[54] According to Pesch, the early Christian movement originated in the *missio interna*, i.e. in an inner-Jewish movement started by Jesus who proclaimed the nearness of eschatological salvation and aimed at the renewal of Israel.[55] Based on the universal interpretation of Jesus' death and the Easter-commissioning, the early Christian movement proclaimed the nearness of the end and the salvation that could be obtained through Christ.[56] This proclamation was eventually also directed at Gentiles. Pesch mentions a number of constituent factors for the new *missio externa*, among which the Jewish missionary attitude towards Gentiles plays an important role. In his evaluation of Paul's ministry as the apostle to the Gentiles Pesch explains that Paul gradually acquired this role.[57] According to Pesch it was at the Apostolic Council that an agreement was made on the status of the mission to the Gentiles, but Paul put this agreement aside due to the incident at Antioch.[58] Finally,

---

[52] P. Bowers, 'Paul and Religious Propaganda in the First Century', *NT* 22 (1980), pp. 316-323.

[53] R. Pesch, 'Voraussetzungen und Anfänge der urchristlichen Mission', in: K. Kertelge (ed.), *Mission im Neuen Testament* (QD 93; Freiburg [etc.]: Herder, 1982), pp. 11-70.

[54] Pesch, 'Voraussetzungen', p. 17.

[55] Pesch, 'Voraussetzungen', pp. 24-26.

[56] Pesch, 'Voraussetzungen', pp. 26-32.

[57] Pesch, 'Voraussetzungen', p. 63: 'Zum "Apostel der Heiden" (Röm 11,13) ist Paulus *geworden!*'

[58] Pesch, 'Voraussetzungen', pp. 65-67.

the concept of a worldwide missionary programme emerged and thus the birth of Christian mission was accomplished.

Pesch's reconstruction has great advantages but it is also characterised by a number of limitations. In the first place, it does not give an analysis of Jewish and pagan religious propaganda. Secondly, it lacks the clear distinction between proselytising mission and other types of religious propaganda as made by Goodman. And finally, it is too brief in its description of Paul to really contribute to a better understanding of his ministry within the context of the development of the early Christian movement. Nevertheless, the analysis by Pesch contains a number of elements that will reappear in the present volume.

Two recent publications do consider Paul from a missionary perspective. In his *Preaching to the Nations*, A. Le Grys describes the growth of the concept of mission in the early Christian movement.[59] The focus of this publication is more on the theological impetus of first century developments than that of the present volume. Le Grys depicts the theological structures of these developments, but fails to adequately relate the Christian movement to its Jewish and pagan contexts. Since Paul is not the main subject of the book – it rather aims at describing the growth of the Christian movement as a whole – it leaves open many questions in regard to his exact contribution to the growth of Christianity as a proselytising movement. Nevertheless, the outcome of Le Grys' analysis of Paul is somewhat similar to the one offered in the present volume: Le Grys, too, argues that the concept of a proselytising mission originates in the gradual growth of Christianity from its Jewish origins into a state of independence.

W. Reinbold offers a rather different approach in his *Propaganda und Mission im ältesten Christentum*.[60] Reinbold chooses a 'prosopographic' angle to study the first-century developments. He extensively discusses the roles of all those involved in the spread of the Christian movement, and still traceable through the writings of the New Testament. From this perspective Reinbold gives a detailed analysis of the main characters of this first stage of the Christian missionary movement. His discussion of Paul is detailed and valuable: throughout the following chapters various references to Reinbold can be found. A major limitation of Reinbold's

---

[59] A. Le Grys, *Preaching to the Nations. The Origins of Mission in the Early Church* (London: SPCK, 1998).

[60] W. Reinbold, *Propaganda und Mission im ältesten Christentum. Eine Untersuchung zu den Modalitäten der Ausbreitung der frühen Kirche* (FRLANT 188; Göttingen: Vandenhoeck&Ruprecht, 2000).

monograph is, however, that he does not discuss Paul's ministry within the context of Jewish and pagan propaganda. This blurs the perspective on Paul to a certain degree. Nevertheless, the main characteristics of Paul's ministry, as Reinbold reconstructs them, will return in our discussion: Paul practiced 'Weltmission' (the gospel should be proclaimed throughout the world), 'Zentrumsmission' (he would settle in a certain place and attract new believers by his message), and 'Mitarbeitermission' (he did not work on his own, but with a group of fellow workers). Furthermore, Reinbold's detailed research enables us to leave the prosopographic matters aside here.[61]

In Pauline scholarship the missionary character of Paul's work is sometimes treated explicitly, but more often it is passed over as a silent presupposition. Major publications of the last decades like E.P. Sanders' *Paul and Palestinian Judaism*,[62] C.J. Beker's *Paul the Apostle*,[63] J.D.G. Dunn's *The Theology of Paul the Apostle*,[64] T. Engberg-Pedersen's *Paul and the Stoics*,[65] or J.G. Gager's *Reinventing Paul*[66] focus on Paul's thoughts rather than on his deeds.[67] Nevertheless, his missionary practices undoubtedly formed the *Sitz im Leben* for his

---

[61] For a survey of literature on mission within early Christianity, see Reinbold, *Propaganda und Mission*, pp. 4-5. Remarkably enough a recent study on early Christianity in Syria is missing: A. Feldtkeller, *Identitätssuche des syrischen Urchristentums. Mission, Inkulturation und Pluralität im ältesten Heidenchristentum* (NTOA 25; Göttingen: Vandenhoeck&Ruprecht; Freiburg Schw.: Universitätsverlag, 1993). Feldtkeller so much focuses on Christianity in the syrian region, that he appears to overlook Paul's importance.

[62] E.P. Sanders, *Paul and Palestinian Judaism. A Comparison of Patterns of Religion* (London: SCM, 1977); Sanders did write about Paul's missionary endeavours in his *Paul, the Law, and the Jewish People* (Philadelphia: Fortress, 1983), pp. 171-206.

[63] J.C. Beker, *Paul the Apostle: the Triumph of God in Life and Thought* (Philadelphia: Fortress Press, 1980).

[64] J.D.G. Dunn, *The Theology of Paul the Apostle* (Edinburgh: Clark; Grand Rapids: Eerdmans, 1998).

[65] T. Engberg-Pedersen, *Paul and the Stoics* (Louisville: Westminster John Knox; Edinburgh: Clark, 2000).

[66] J.G. Gager, *Reinventing Paul* (Oxford: Oxford University Press, 2000).

[67] Many other publications can be mentioned; to name but a few important ones: J. Becker, *Paulus. Der Apostel der Völker* (Tübingen: Mohr, 2nd rev. ed. 1992, [1]1989); E. Lohse, *Paulus. Eine Biografie* (München: Beck, 1996); J. Murphy-O'Connor, *Paul. A Critical Life* (Oxford [etc.]: Oxford University Press, 1996); C.J. Roetzel, *Paul. The Man and the Myth* (Columbia: University of South Carolina Press, 1998). For an extensive biobliography on Paul see H. Hübner, 'Paulusforschung seit 1945. Ein kritischer Literaturbericht', in: W. Haase (ed.), *ANRW 2 Principat* 25/4 (1985), pp. 2649-2840.

ideas as well as *vice versa*. The interaction between Paul's ideas and his missionary endeavour has not been sufficiently analysed. As a result, the view of Paul as one who worked on the basis of a consciously planned missionary scheme as described for instance by Wernle (cf. above) is still often found as a presupposition in many studies on either Paul's ministry or other elements within the early Christian movement.[68] The present volume, however, argues that Paul's significance for the early Christian movement is to be found in the specific interaction of his ideas and his missionary actions rather than in such an all-encompassing theological programme. His ministry did not originate in a specific missionary plan that would account for the whole of Paul's activities, but in the interaction between his specific context and his perception of the significance of Jesus Christ. As a result of this specific interaction, it was Paul's genius that legitimised the community of believers from Jews and Gentiles and thereby created the *Sitz im Leben* as well as the actual practice of Christian mission.

The Outline of this Book

The question asked above can be subdivided into six questions, which will be answered in the six chapters of this book: 1. Was there any such thing as a Jewish proselytising mission before or during the period in which Paul acted? 2. Was there any such thing as a pagan proselytising mission in that period? 3. What contribution did pre-Pauline Christianity make to the development of the Christian mission? These three questions regard the Jewish, the pagan, and the pre-Pauline Christian context of Paul's ministry. They will have to be answered before we can look into that ministry itself. Subsequently, three questions concerning Paul himself will have to

---

[68] See e.g. S.G. Wilson, *The Gentiles and the Gentile Mission in Luke-Acts* (Cambridge: University Press, 1973), p. 261, who speaks of a 'planned, gradual progression'. A clear expression of the view that Paul consciously planned his activities to fulfil a programme is given by A. Schweitzer, *Die Mystik des Apostels Paulus* (Tübingen: Mohr, 1930), pp. 180-181. For more recent elaborations of this idea, see R. Riesner, *Die Frühzeit des Apostels Paulus* (WUNT 71; Tübingen: Mohr, 1994), pp. 207-234, and J.M. Scott, *Paul and the Nations. The Old Testament and Jewish Backgrounds of Paul's Mission to the Nations with Special Refernce to the Destination of Galatians* (WUNT 84; Tübingen: Mohr, 1995). According to Riesner it was the prophecy in Isa 66,18-21 that Paul tried to fulfil, whereas Scott 'explores the possibility that in developing his missionary strategy, the former Pharisee and Hebrew of Hebrews appropriated the OT and Jewish tradition of the Table of Nations (Genesis 10; 1 Chr 1:1-2:2)' – Scott, *Paul and the Nations*, p. 216.

be addressed: 4. What were the effects of the great change in Paul's life: his 'call'? 5. What evidence do we have on Paul's perception of his task as an 'apostle for the Gentiles'? And finally: 6. How did Paul perform his task as such an 'apostle for the Gentiles'? Let us briefly take a look at the various chapters.

Chapter 1 deals with the phenomenon of Jewish religious propaganda. L.H. Feldman has restated Harnack's theory on the existence of active Jewish proselytising. In this chapter the evidence for the Harnack-Feldman thesis is surveyed and it is argued that there is insufficient evidence for the existence of active Jewish proselytising in the period up to 70 CE. A number of features of Jewish religious propaganda are studied. It appears that idolatry was one of the main charges by Jewish authors against pagan cults. Yet these charges are made in apologetic writings aimed at Jewish readers rather than in missionary literature aimed at a Greek audience. In a number of passages Judaism is depicted as an ancient religion with a very high moral standard. The aim of this presentation of Judaism was to inform pagan authors who misunderstood Jewish customs and therefore mocked and misrepresented them. A number of passages on Judaism by pagan authors are examined. Here it appears that the two main reproaches against Jews were those of atheism and misanthropy. Finally, the expulsions of Jews from Antioch and Rome are dealt with.

In chapter 2 pagan religious propaganda is considered by evaluating the spread of a number of important pagan cults (Isis and Sarapis, Asclepius, and the Emperor cult) as well as the ministries of Apollonius of Tyana and Alexander of Abonouteichos. It appears that cults did spread owing to various factors, but also that none of them was actively proselytising in Goodman's sense. It is due to the great appeal of these oriental cults that they spread so easily. The only group that appears to have had a more or less missionary attitude is that of the Cynic-Stoic philosophers. A number of features of these philosophers are discussed, resulting in a comparison with Paul.

After the religious context of the early Christian movement has thus been explored, chapter 3 deals with the movement itself by analysing the proclamation of the gospel by the early Christian communities in Palestine and the Hellenistic mission. The method used is a traditio-historical and literary-critical reconstruction of the early Christian proclamation. First the synoptic traditions on the commissioning of disciples by Jesus are scrutinised. Then pre-literary formulae in Paul's letters and the description of the earliest spread of the Christian movement in Acts are looked into. Finally, the missionary command of Matthew 28 is presented as evidence that first century developments did indeed lead up to a specific form of proselytising mission among Christians at the end of the first century.

After the stage has thus been set for the description of Paul's ministry and method, chapter 4 deals with the picture Paul gives of himself in his letters. These letters contain a number of passages where Paul explicitly deals with the great change in his life: Rom 11,1; 1 Cor 9,1; 15,1-9; 2 Cor 11,22-23; Gal 1,13-16; Phil 3,4-6. It is argued that in all of these passages Paul is looking back on his life prior to what he perceived to be his call, from the perspective of the time of writing his letters. Secondly, the evidence from Acts is taken into account. The thesis of this chapter is, that Paul came to interpret his call through the paradigm of his preaching activities, and that for a correct understanding of Paul's ministry, it is important to realise that he thought of his own call as that of a prophet.

Chapter 5 deals with Paul's perception of his ministry as focused on the Gentiles: Paul considered himself as an apostle, whose task it was to bring the gospel to the uncircumcised. The various elements that are necessary to understand Paul from this perspective are treated: his view of his own task as that of an 'apostle', his idea of 'being sent', and his perception of the Gentiles to whom he considered himself sent.

After all preliminary matters have thus been discussed in the first five chapters, the final chapter deals with Paul and his missionary endeavour: How did Paul relate to 'his' Churches? How did he maintain his independence, and what is the meaning of his manual labour? Who worked together with Paul in his mission? Who were his audiences? And finally: which theological notions were so basic to Paul's mission, that they shaped his ministry? In this last chapter great stress will be laid on Paul's view of the congregation of faithful Jews and Gentiles as 'one in Christ'. It is the combination of this idea, grown from Paul's experiences in Antioch and the congregations he himself raised subsequently, and his eschatological view of God's ultimate intervention in history having begun in the Christ event, that ultimately made Paul into what he was.

CHAPTER ONE

JEWISH PROPAGANDA
AND THE SPREAD OF JUDAISM

In the Graeco-Roman period a considerable part of the area surrounding the Mediterranean Sea had Jewish inhabitants. The *Sibylline Oracles*, in a *vaticinium ex eventu*, mention the fact that as a result of the Assyrian exile Jews would spread over the entire earth: 'the whole earth will be filled with you and every sea.'[1] This fact of Jews spreading far afield is confirmed by Josephus, *Ant.* xiv,115, who cites Strabo's description of the Jewish inhabitants of Cyrene at the time Sulla made war on Mithridates: 'There were four classes in the state of Cyrene; the first consisted of citizens, the second of farmers, the third of resident aliens, and the fourth of Jews. This people has already made its way into every city, and it is not easy to find any place in the habitable world which has not received this nation and in which it has not made its power felt.'[2] It follows from this description that Jews were not only present in many towns, but also that they could not be ignored wherever they settled: they formed the 'fourth class' in Cyrene.

The passages cited are but two examples of the ample evidence for the spread of Jewish communities throughout the Roman Empire (and further to the east). Philo of Alexandria, for instance, confirms the state of affairs depicted by Strabo: 'For no single country can contain the Jews because of their multitude, and for this reason they inhabit the most extensive and wealthiest districts in Europe and Asia both on islands and on mainlands, and while they regard the Holy City as their mother-city, in which is founded and consecrated the temple of the most high God, yet they severally hold that land as their fatherland which they have obtained by inheritance from fathers and grandfathers and great-grandfathers and still more remote ancestors for their portion to dwell in, in which they were

---

[1] *Sib. Or.* III,271: πᾶσα δὲ γαῖα σέθεη πλήρης καὶ πᾶσα θάλασσα.
[2] Αὕτη δ'εἰς πᾶσαν πόλιν ἤδη παρελήλυθε, καὶ τόπον οὐκ ἐστι ῥαδίως εὑρεῖν τῆς οἰκουμένης ὃς οὐ παραδέδεκται τοῦτο τὸ φῦλον, μηδ'ἐπικρατεῖται ὑπ'αὐτοῦ. Text and translation by R. Marcus, LCL. Other references by Josephus to the great number of Jews living in the Mediterranean area are e.g. *c. Ap.* II,282; *BJ* II,398; VII,43.

born and reared' (*In Flacc.* VII,45-46).[3] This literary evidence for the spread of Jews throughout the Mediterranean is underpinned by archaeological, papyrological, and epigraphic evidence. In his still valuable survey of Jewish communities in the Roman Empire, J. Juster had to use twenty-nine pages in order to mention them all, together with the literary and epigraphic evidence known at the time.[4]

In the course of the 20th century several attempts have been made to prove that Jews throughout the Roman Empire often lived in an integrated manner as full-blooded Greeks who happened to adhere to the Jewish religion. E.R. Goodenough's majestic work on Jewish symbols in the Hellenistic age is indeed an attempt to show the degree of assimilation that occurred within Jewish communities.[5] Works like this point out that Diaspora Judaism cannot be treated as a unity, or as a group with a clearly defined centre and obvious margin. Judaism within the Diaspora appears to have consisted of a wide variety of Jews who varied from very strict observers of the law to more integrated or even syncretistic Jews. In this respect it probably differed little from Judaism within Palestine.[6]

---

[3] Ἰουδαίους γὰρ χώρα μία διὰ πολυανθρωπίαν οὐ χωρεῖ. Text and translation taken from H. Box, *Philonis Alexandrini In Flaccum* (London, New York, Toronto: Oxford University Press, 1939), pp. 16-17. See also *Leg. ad Gaium* XXXVI,281-283, where Philo gives a survey of the regions where Jews live: Judea, Egypt, Phoenicia, Syria, Pamphylia, Cilicia, Asia, Thessaly, Boeotia, Macedonia, Aetolia, Attica, Argos, Corinth, the Peleponnese, Euboea, Cyprus, Crete, and also 'beyond the Euphrates' there are Jewish inhabitants.

[4] J. Juster, *Les Juifs dans l'empire romain. Leur condition juridique, économique et sociale* vol. 1 (Paris: Geuthner, 1914), pp. 180-209. Although since Juster's day a number of important findings have been made (for instance: the synagogue at Dura Europos), the survey he gives is still extremely valuable. Papyrological evidence on the Jews in Egypt is presented by V.A. Tcherikover, A. Fuks, *Corpus Papyrorum Iudaicarum*, 2 vols. (Cambridge, Mass.: Harvard University Press, 1957 and 1960).

[5] E.R. Goodenough, *Jewish Symbols in the Graeco-Roman Period* 13 vols. (BS 37; Princeton: Princeton University Press, 1953-1968), now edited and abridged by J. Neusner, Princeton, 1988.

[6] M. Hengel, *Judentum und Hellenismus. Studien zu ihrer Begegnung unter besonderer Berücksichtigung Palästinas bis zur Mitte des 2. Jahrhunderts vor Christus* (WUNT 10; Tübingen: Mohr, 1969, 2nd ed. 1973), clearly pointed out that it is wrong to distinguish between Palestinian Judaism and Hellenistic Judaism as two separate kinds of Judaism in which the former would have been rather strict in observing the law, whereas the latter would have consisted to a high degree of assimilated Jews. Cf. p. 93: 'Das gesammte Judentum ab etwa der Mitte des 3. Jhs v.Chr. müßte im strengen Sinne als "hellenistisches Judentum" bezeichnet werden, und man sollte besser zwischen dem griechischsprechenden Judentum der westlichen Diaspora und dem aramäisch/hebräischsprechenden Judentum Palästinas bzw. Babyloniens unterscheiden. Aber auch diese Distinktion ist einseitig.' Hengel continues with the statement that since the Ptolemaic period people in Jerusalem had spoken Greek more and more. See also Hengel, 'The Interpenetration

The discussion of the topic is burdened by one notoriously difficult matter: the question whether there ever existed a more or less fixed group of pagans who did not become full proselytes, but remained 'friends of the Jewish religion' commonly known as 'God-fearers'. Did such a group exist *as a group* in the first century CE or not? In the course of the last century or so, an extensive debate has developed among scholars. Recently, however, this debate has been given a new impulse by an inscription found in Aphrodisias and published in 1987.[7] This inscription should be counted as evidence for the existence of such a separate group at least in Aphrodisias in the third century CE. Unfortunately, however, it remains unclear whether this group was merely a local phenomenon or not and whether this phenomenon already existed in the first century CE. Since a full-scale discussion of the topic would exceed the boundaries set for this volume, it is best to start here with a tentatively formulated observation: There were indeed Gentiles, attracted to the Jewish customs and traditions, who lived in close harmony with Jewish communities in the first century CE. Whether or not these Gentiles formed a more or less organised group is basically irrelevant to the present subject. What is important is that these Gentiles were there, close to the Jewish communities.

Not only is the existence of the God-fearers as a well defined group in the first century CE hotly debated, it also remains a matter of dispute whether any such thing as a 'Jewish proselytising mission' existed. It is evident that there were proselytes, but did Jewish communities actively seek them for or not? In the Introduction above it has been stated that in the last decade of the 20th century a number of scholars have argued against the existence of a Jewish proselytising mission in the period under discussion.[8] Others hold different opinions. L.H. Feldman, for instance,

---

of Judaism and Hellenism in the pre-Maccabean Period', in: W.D. Davis, L. Finkelstein (eds.), *The Cambridge History of Judaism* vol. 2: *The Hellenistic Age* (Cambridge [etc.]: Cambridge University Press, 1989), pp. 167-228.

[7] J. Reynolds, R. Tannenbaum, *Jews and God-fearers at Aphrodisias* (Cambridge: The Cambridge Philological Society, 1987). See the careful discussion of the problem by I. Levinskaya, *The Book of Acts in its Diaspora Setting* (BAFCS 5; Grand Rapids: Eerdmans; Carlisle: Paternoster, 1996), pp. 51-126. Levinskaya's position is summarised on p. 51: 'While all the findings before the Aphrodisias inscription became known were inconclusive and open to different interpretations, the latter tipped the balance and proved both the existence of a category of friendly Gentiles and the application to this category of the term *theosebes* which was known from other inscriptions.'

[8] See especially Goodman, *Mission and Conversion*, and McKnight, *Light among Gentiles*. For a discussion, see above pp. 4-6.

has more or less renewed Harnack's arguments in favour of a Jewish mission.[9] Feldman mentions four arguments:[10] 1) the enormous growth of the Jewish population in the Roman Empire between the sixth century BCE and the middle of the first century CE; 2) evidence from Greek Jewish literature; 3) evidence from pagan literature showing resentment against Jewish proselytism; 4) expulsions of Jews as evidence of missionary activity. Unfortunately, all four of Feldman's arguments fail to convince. The problem with all arguments in favour of active Jewish proselytising is that the evidence is not conclusive. Let us take a closer look.

1. The growth of the Jewish population may indeed have been as large as Feldman assumes.[11] Pagan proselytes may have caused part of this growth. But this does not *ipso facto* indicate that the Jewish population of the Roman Empire actively sought for proselytes. The growth of the Jewish population in the area around the Mediterranean Sea is no proof of proselytising activities. Philo mentions overpopulation in Palestine as a reason for the Jewish Diaspora, and Tacitus speaks of the fact that the Jews did not practice abortion and infanticide (cf. below, p. 41).[12]

2. Whereas the growth of the Jewish population should be disregarded in relation to the question of whether active and planned proselytising existed, the case for Jewish literature in Greek is somewhat different. Its sheer existence has often been regarded as proof of Jewish proselytising: for what other reason would Jews have written in Greek than to convince pagans that the Jewish religion was the proper one? This approach, however, is wrong. In an important article of 1956 V. Tcherikover pointed out that Jews wrote in Greek to reach Greek-speaking Jews.[13] His judgement is plain, but effective: 'Jewish Alexandrian literature was directed inwards and not outwards.'[14] As plain and simple as this thesis may seem, it is a very important observation. Tcherikover did not intend to say that there was no contact at all between Jewish apologetic literature and pagan audiences. 'Single copies would of course be given by the author directly to Greeks, and there were also books, which were sent to the authorities in

---

[9] Harnack, *Mission und Ausbreitung*, vol. 1, pp. 1-16; cf. the discussion of Harnack's reconstruction, above, pp. 2-3.

[10] Feldman, *Jew and Gentile*, pp. 293-304.

[11] Feldman bases his observation on S.W. Baron, 'Population', *Encyclopaedia Judaica* vol. 13 (Jerusalem: Keter, 1971), cols. 866-903.

[12] Philo, *Vit. Mos.* II,232; Tacitus, *Hist.* V,5; both texts are also mentioned by Goodman, *Mission and Conversion*, p. 84.

[13] V.A. Tcherikover, 'Jewish Apologetic Literature Reconsidered', *Eos* 48.3 (1956), pp. 169-193.

[14] Tcherikover, 'Jewish Apologetic Literature', p. 182.

the form of memoranda (...). We may also assume that some Jewish book might occasionally have found its way to a bookshop. But it is not single cases and exceptions that the scholars have in mind when they speak about Jewish propaganda among Greeks.'[15]

3. In his argument Tcherikover rightly draws attention to the fact that pagan authors, time and again, give a completely distorted impression of Judaism and its origins. The foundation for this distorted impression should foremostly be attributed to a lack of understanding and knowledge of Judaism.[16] It is also for this reason that Jewish authors had to deal with the problem of their relation to paganism. Propagandistic features in Greek Jewish literature should therefore be interpreted as aimed at informing rather than proselytising.[17]

4. Feldman's fourth argument is as unconvincing as the other three. There have indeed been a number of expulsions of Jews from Rome as well as great problems in Alexandria. Since the problems in Alexandria were evidently caused by other factors than proselytising, they need not be considered here.[18] As to the expulsions from Rome, it is unclear from the reports whether they originated in active proselytising, in the growth of the Jewish community due to its attracting pagans or in other factors. In any case they do not form solid evidence for the existence of a proselytising attitude of Jews in antiquity.

Because of the importance of the subject for a reconstruction of Paul's ministry within his early Christian and contemporary Jewish context, more discussion is needed of the categories of evidence that Feldman mentions in favour of the theory of active Jewish proselytising. These categories are: evidence from Jewish literature composed in Greek, evidence from pagan authors referring to the Jewish religion, and evidence

---

[15] Tcherikover, 'Jewish Apologetic Literature', p. 173.

[16] See for instance Juvenal, *Saturae* XIV, 96-106 (below, p. 40), and Tacitus, *Hist.* V,4-5 (below, p. 41). On the prejudices against Judaism, see Feldman, *Jew and Gentile*, pp. 107-176; also: J.N. Sevenster, *The Roots of Pagan Anti-Semitism in the Ancient World* (SNT 41; Leiden: Brill, 1975), and J.L. Daniel, 'Anti-Semitism in the Hellenistic-Roman Period', *JBL* 98 (1979), pp. 45-65.

[17] See Goodman, *Mission and Conversion*, p. 4. Goodman describes 'apologetic mission' as an activity in which 'some missionaries requested recognition by others of the power of a particular divinity without expecting their audience to devote themselves to his or her worship.' This kind of mission aimed at informing in a specific sense: the information conveyed on Judaism was intended to gain acceptation of the Jewish religion by non-Jews as an honourable religion. The intention was not to convert pagans to Judaism, but to have Judaism accepted by pagans as a religion in its own right.

[18] For a thorough discussion and presentation of the evidence, see Tcherikover, Fuks, *Corpus Papyrorum Iudaicarum*, vol. 1, pp. 48-93, and vol. 2, pp. 25-107.

on expulsions of Jews. Finally, some attention will be paid to the *locus classicus* from the New Testament that is often mentioned as evidence *par excellence* of the existence of a Jewish mission, Matt 23,15, as well as to Paul's introduction to his letter to the Romans.

Demographic evidence will not be considered here because of two problems. The first is that it is extremely difficult to obtain exact figures. S.W. Baron's article 'population' in the *Encyclopaedia Judaica* is a careful attempt at evaluating the data, but still the outcome remains uncertain.[19] The second reason is that even if the outcome of Baron's calculation could be reckoned trustworthy, the data in itself is meaningless. Even if the Jewish population of the Roman Empire increased as much as Baron suggests in the last centuries before the Common Era, this is not *per se* evidence of active Jewish proselytising. This evidence should be found in the fields to be discussed now.

1. Jewish Literature in Greek

In the course of the 20th century a number of writings have been mentioned as evidence of active Jewish proselytising. Josephus and other Jewish historiographers writing in Greek, the *Letter of Aristeas*, the Septuagint itself, *Joseph and Aseneth*, the writings of Philo, and the Jewish sections of the *Sibylline Oracles* have been used as such. In the above the false assumption that all Jewish literature in Greek would have been aimed at Greek readers has already been rejected. But if we have to view this corpus of literature as primarily aimed at Greek-speaking Jews, what information can we obtain on the attitude of these Jews towards pagans?

The first piece of evidence that should be considered is a remark by Josephus in which he explicitly denies the active search for proselytes. In *Contra Apionem* (II,259-261) Josephus compares Jewish customs with those of the Lacedaemonians:

> The Lacedaemonians made a practice of expelling foreigners and would not allow their own citizens to travel abroad, in both cases apprehensive of their laws being corrupted. They might perhaps be justly reproached for discourtesy, because they accorded to no one the rights either of citizenship or of residence among them. We, on the contrary, while we have no desire to emulate the customs of others, yet gladly welcome any who wish to share our own. That, I think, may be taken as a proof both of humanity and magnanimity.[20]

---

[19] Baron, 'Population'; cf. above, note 11.
[20] Translation H.St.J. Thackeray, LCL.

It is clear that Josephus is defending Judaism against Apion's attacks,[21] and therefore does not aim at giving an impartial perspective on the state of affairs. Nevertheless, Josephus clearly states that the Jewish attitude towards pagans was not one of active proselytising, but of welcoming those who felt attracted towards Judaism: ἡμεῖς δὲ τὰ μὲν τῶν ἄλλων ζηλοῦν οὐκ ἀξιοῦμεν, τοὺς μέντοι μετέχειν τῶν ἡμετέρων βουλομένους ἡδέως δεχόμεθα. Often overlooked by scholars dealing with the subject of Jewish proselytising, this remark is an important argument against the existence of a Jewish 'mission'. The readiness to accept proselytes, as indicated by Josephus, is part of the explanation for the great attraction that the Jewish religion obviously had for pagans. But Josephus could not have stated the absence of the urge to change other people's customs in this explicit way if Jewish communities had actively encouraged proselytism.

Josephus' statement underlines the approach by Goodman and McKnight. Evidence is ambiguous in that there is no clear indication of the existence of active Jewish proselytising. If, however, this evidence is seen from the perspective of Josephus' remark, the ambiguity disappears. The absence of active proselytising should therefore be taken as our starting-point. This does not mean, however, that there were no proselytes in the Graeco-Roman period or that there was no Jewish propaganda at all.

The fact that conversion to Judaism did occur on the basis of incidental contacts is further illustrated by an event often mentioned as an argument in favour of active Jewish proselytising: the conversion of the house of Adiabene. Josephus gives a report of this event in *Ant.* xx,2-4. According to Josephus' account, prince Izates of Adiabene converted to Judaism together with his mother, Queen Helena. The story commences with the wives of king Monobazus, who was Izates' father and half-brother. His wives convert to Judaism because a Jewish merchant Ananias taught them to worship God after the manner of the Jewish tradition (ἐδίδασκεν αὐτὰς τὸν θεὸν σέβειν, ὡς Ἰουδαίοις πάτριον ἦν; xx,34). At the same time Izates' mother Helena independently converts to Judaism thanks to

---

[21] Josephus' *Contra Apionem* was evidently not primarily aimed at Greek Jews, but at Apion himself. The writing is best characterised as 'a polemical and apologetic tract' – H.W. Attridge, 'Josephus and his Works', in: M.E. Stone (ed.), *Jewish Writings of the Second Temple Period* (CRINT 2,2; Assen: Van Gorcum; Philadelphia: Fortress Press, 1984), pp. 185-232, quotation from p. 227. Apion's accusations are summed up by Attridge in four categories (p. 229): Apion's account of the Exodus (II,8-32), accusations against the Jews of Alexandria (II,33-78), stories about the temple worship (II,79-111), and various miscellaneous accusations (II,112-142).

her contact with another Jew. Finally, a third Jewish merchant, named Eleazar, convinces Izates that he should be circumcised. The mention of the merchants in Josephus' narrative has been reason to assume that Jewish merchants often acted as missionaries.[22] If the mention of Ananias is trustworthy,[23] it may indeed have been the way he depicted Judaism that made the king's wives convert to Judaism. The same thing apparently happened to his mother Helena. Finally, the king's wives, together with Ananias, attempted to convert Izates, and eventually they succeeded in that (κἀκεῖνον ὁμοίως συνανέπεισεν xx,34).

This story is a test case for our approach of the subject. Josephus writes about the influence that Ananias had on the wives of Monobazus, and subsequently mentions the fact that Ananias was brought to the attention of Izates as a result of the wives' actions. It is clear that the process leading up to Izates' conversion starts with the Jewish merchants. But does the story thereby irrevocably point at Jewish proselytising activities? Josephus does not suggest that Ananias purposely went out on a mission to convert the Adiabene royals. The same observation is valid for Eleazar the traveller who, according to Josephus, convinced Izates to have himself circumcised (*Ant.* xx,43-46). The whole episode is most likely to be evidence of a close contact between the Jewish religion and the surrounding peoples. Furthermore, as J. Neusner has argued, it is not unlikely that the Adiabenians also had a political motive for the conversions of Helena and Izates to Judaism.[24]

A remarkable detail in the story is the fact that Ananias does not wish to circumcise the king, and even explicitly advises him against it (xx, 38-42). Eleazar's advice, however, contradicts that of Ananias and points out that there were other options for pagan sympathisers to Judaism. Thus, the conclusion to be drawn from this narrative is, that there were close contacts between Jews and non-Jews in religious matters, and that these

---

[22] See for instance G. Klein, *Der älteste christliche Katechismus und die jüdische Propaganda-Literatur* (Berlin: Reimer, 1909), pp. 137: 'Daß der jüdische Handelsstand sich nicht damit begnügte, seine Ware an den Mann zu bringen, sondern bei Gelegenheit auch an die Seele seiner Käufer dachte, wissen wir schon aus Josephus.'

[23] See L.H. Schiffman, 'The Conversion of the Royal House of Adiabene in Josephus and Rabbinic Sources', in: L.H. Feldman, G. Hata (eds.), *Josephus, Judaism, and Christianity* (Detroit: Wayne State University Press, 1987), 293-312.

[24] See J. Neusner, *A History of the Jews in Babylonia. Vol. 1: the Parthian Period* (SPB 9; Leiden: Brill, 1965), pp. 58-64; cf. p. 64: 'At this time, it was common for the royal families of Near Eastern principalities to lay great emphasis on religious rites. (...) The Adiabenians acted no differently therefore in cultivating the religion of a powerful minority in the Mesopotamian valley. They thus enhanced their possibilities of winning the alliance of other Jewish dynasties in the Near East and Asia Minor, and of the Palestinian Jews to the West.'

close contacts could occasionally lead the non-Jews into becoming full proselytes. But once again, the literary evidence is inconclusive with regard to the question whether or not Jews actively sought for this 'full conversion'.

Jewish literature in the Greek language shows that there must have been a great variety of assimilated forms of Judaism in the Graeco-Roman world. Jewish authors adopted Greek forms and also Greek thoughts. *Joseph and Aseneth* was probably modelled on the Hellenistic novel and for this reason shares a number of characteristics with, for instance, *Daphnis and Chloe*. The so-called *Letter of Aristeas* purports that the Septuagint was created at the request of king Ptolemy II Philadelphus (285-247 BCE). Various Jewish authors write as Greek historians (Demetrius, Eupolemus, Ps.-Eupolemus, Cleodemus Malchus, Josephus), a Greek tragedian (Ezechiel Tragicus), Greek poets (Ps.-Phocylides, Theodotus, Philo the Poet) or Greek philosophers (Aristobulus, Philo Alexandrinus). Furthermore, the literature of Hellenistic Judaism also incorporated a collection of Jewish Sibylline Oracles.

Already in this first survey it is evident that the various forms of literature that have been preserved – which is still only a minor part of what must have been written in the Graeco-Roman period – can by no means all be categorised as 'propagandistic literature'. The wide variety of literary forms and influences of which they are evidence is in itself an indication of the wide variety of views within Judaism.

It is not necessary for the present subject to discuss all features of this Greek literature in detail. The assumption that all these writings would be missionary in character, either because of the Greek language used or because of the 'Greek' thoughts which they comprise, has already been rejected. But there is still enough to be learned from this literature for a reconstruction of Paul's position within his contemporary context.

The prime observation to be made on the basis of this Jewish literature in Greek is that it shows how 'assimilated' Jewish authors could be.[25] Many authors apparently felt so much at ease with their Greek surroundings that they even argued that the origin of Greek philosophy and

---

[25] P. Borgen, 'Philo of Alexandria', in: Stone, *Jewish Writings of the Second Temple Period*, pp. 233-282; cf. p. 279: 'The translation of the Bible into Greek is not only an indication of the numerical strength of Alexandrian Jewry early in the Hellenistic period, but also of its integration into the Greek-speaking world. Along with the Septuagint, Alexandrian Jews produced their own Greek literature, of which the historian Demetrius and the tragedian Ezekiel, both from the 3rd century B.C.E., are the earliest representatives.'

culture laid within Judaism. Aristobulus, in a fragment preserved in Eusebius' *Praeparatio Evangelica*, remarks that Plato and Pythagoras originally drew from Moses' laws. Eusebius introduces the fragment with a reference to this theory:

> That also Aristobulus, who lived before us and was of the Hebrew people, the peripatetic (philosopher), agreed that the Greeks begin from the philosophy of the Hebrews; from the (books) of Aristobulus dedicated to King Ptolemy:
> 'It is evident that Plato imitated our legislation and that he had investigated thoroughly each of the elements in it. For it had been translated by others before Demetrius Phalereus, before the conquests of Alexander and the Persians. (...) So it is very clear that the philosopher mentioned above took many things (from it). For he was very learned, as was Pythagoras, who transferred many of our doctrines and integrated them into his own system of beliefs...'[26]

In another fragment Aristobulus describes how Pythagoras, Socrates, and Plato were dependent on Jewish law and that also Orpheus imitated Moses.[27] The same wish to 'Judaize' Greek history and culture is discernible in another fragment preserved in Eusebius' *Praeparatio Evangelica*. Eusebius cites Alexander Polyhistor, who in turn quotes Eupolemus:

> And Eupolemus says that Moses was the first wise man, that he first taught the alphabet to the Jews, and the Phoenicians received it from the Jews, and the Greeks received it from the Phoenicians, and that Moses first wrote laws for the Jews.[28]

It is interesting to see that occasionally a mixture evolved of Jewish historiography and Greek mythology. Again the prime source is Eusebius citing Alexander Polyhistor, who this time quotes Cleodemus Malchus:

> Cleodemus states that Keturah bore Abraham mighty sons. Cleodemus gives their names, calling three of them Afera, Surim, Iafra. Assyria was named after Surim; the city of Afra and the region Africa were named after Afera and Iafra, for Afera and Iafra fought with Heracles in his campaign in Libya against Antaios. Heracles married the daughter of Afera and had by her a son, Diodorus.[29]

---

[26] Aristobulus, fr. 3, Eusebius, *Praep. Ev.* XIII,12,1; translation by A. Yarbro Collins, *OTPseud* vol. 2, p. 839.
[27] Aristobulus, fr. 4, Eusebius, *Praep. Ev.* XIII,13,3-8.
[28] Translation by F. Fallon, *OTPseud* vol. 2, p. 865.
[29] Translation by R. Doran, *OTPseud* vol. 2, p. 887.

Thus, Heracles becomes related to Abraham. Apparently the author felt the need to bring Greek past into contact with Jewish tradition.

The book of *Joseph and Aseneth* reflects another form of contact between Greek and Jewish traditions. The form of the Greek Hellenistic novel is used by an author who must have been living in the Jewish community in Egypt, probably somewhere between the early second century BCE and the Bar-Kochba revolt.[30] The first part of the writing discusses the conversion of Aseneth. This daughter of the priest Pentephres at first despises and scorns Joseph, but later comes to regret her arrogance, bids farewell to the gods of her parents, and prostrates herself before the God of Joseph. He sends his messenger, 'the chief of the house of the Lord and commander of the whole host of the Most High' (15,8).[31] Aseneth's repentance (μετανοία) is accepted and she is renamed 'City of Refuge' (πόλις καταφυγῆς). Although the exact meaning of her new name escapes us, it is clear that the intention was that Aseneth should be a model and example for all who convert to Judaism: 'your name shall be City of Refuge, because in you many nations will take refuge with the Lord our God, the Most High, and under your wings many peoples trusting in the Lord God will be sheltered, and behind your walls will be guarded those who attach themselves to the Most High God in the name of repentance' (15,7).

Since *Joseph and Aseneth* requires a rather thorough acquaintance with Jewish customs, it would be wrong to interpret this writing as a missionary tract. The intended readers were probably Jews and proselytes.[32] C. Burchard's interpretation of the writing confirms the observation made on the basis of Josephus' remark in *c. Ap.* II, 261: 'Judaism is not depicted as mission-minded in Joseph and Aseneth. Proselytes are welcomed, not sought, and conversion certainly is not an easy affair. Moreover, Joseph and Aseneth is not a beginner's book. The reader is supposed to know Genesis, at least the Joseph story, and to understand allusions to other scriptural passages. (...) As a specimen of Introducing Judaism, Joseph and Aseneth is remarkably ill-suited.'[33]

Seen from this perspective, it is important to note that *Joseph and Aseneth* is very outspoken on the relation of the traditional Egyptian gods

---

[30] For this date, see C. Burchard, *Joseph und Aseneth* (JSHRZ; Gütersloh: Mohn, 1983), pp. 613-614.

[31] Translation by C. Burchard, *OTPseud*, vol. 2.

[32] Cf. Burchard, *OTPseud*, vol. 2, pp. 194-195.

[33] Burchard, *OTPseud*, vol. 2, p. 195.

to the God of Joseph. Aseneth first casts out all idols, and feeds the meat sacrificed to them to strange dogs: 'by no means must my dogs eat from my dinner and from the sacrifice of the idols' (10,12-13). In her two soliloquies Aseneth shows her remorse for having served the Egyptian gods (11,3-14.16-18), even to such an extent that she is afraid to address the Most High. Then, when she has found the courage to address God himself, Aseneth again speaks of her past:

> My mouth is defiled from the sacrifices of the idols
> and from the tables of the gods of the Egyptians.
> I have sinned, Lord,
> before you I have sinned much in ignorance,
> and have worshiped dead and dumb idols.
> And now I am not worthy to open my mouth to you, Lord. (12,5)[34]

In the eyes of the author of *Jos. Asen.* entry into Judaism meant a great change. It implied a complete rupture with the past in that idols had to be cast away.

The same polemic against idolatry can be discerned in the Jewish sections of the *Sibylline Oracles*. This writing is another example of a Greek literary form used by Jewish authors. From the fourth century BCE onward many Sibyls are mentioned in Greek literature. Often authors refer to a list of ten Sibyls, and sometimes the Hebrew Sibyl figures as the eleventh.[35] Sibylline oracles enjoyed a high status.[36] Even though already in ancient times there were those who had their doubts because of the vagueness of the oracles,[37] the Roman senate consulted them in situations of great political distress. The fact that Jewish authors used this specific form indicates that they were thoroughly familiar with the usual form and contents of *Sibylline Oracles* and therefore also with Greek culture in general. This familiarity, however, is no indication of missionary zeal underlying the oracles. In J.J. Collins' view, book 3 of the *Sibylline Ora-*

---

[34] Translation by C. Burchard, *OTPseud*, vol. 2.
[35] Varro mentions the Persian, Libyan, Delphic, Cimmerian, Erythrean, Samian, Cumean, Hellespontian, Phrygian, and Tiburtine sibyls – Lactantius, *Div. Inst.* I,6; cf. J.J. Collins, *The Sibylline Oracles of Egyptian Judaism* (SBLDS 13; Missoula: SBL, 1972), pp. 1-2.
[36] Collins, *Sibylline Oracles*, pp. 1-19.
[37] Collins, *Sibylline Oracles*, p. 4, mentions Cicero, *De Div.* II,54,110-111 as an example of this scepsis: 'For it was clever in the author to take care that whatever happened should appear foretold, because all reference to persons or time had been omitted. He also employed a maze of obscurity so that the same verses might be adapted to different situations at different times.'
[38] Collins, *Sibylline Oracles*, p. 113.

cles was originally intended to present Judaism to Greeks 'in a familiar dress' in order to 'attract Gentiles to Judaism'.[38] It would seem that Collins' conclusion is in need of further specification. We have to distinguish carefully between apologetic, propagandistic, and proselytising purposes here. As a result, we should regard a Jewish writing as apologetic if it primarily aims at a Jewish public. A piece is propagandistic if it aims at informing Greeks about Judaism. Proselytising is the active approach towards pagans in order to turn them into Jews. There is no indication that this last intention underlies book 3 or any other section of the *Sibylline Oracles*. The fact that these oracles were put in so traditional a Greek form does imply that the writing was aimed at a Greek public. Since these oracles nowhere explicitly state the need for pagans to become proselytes, the initial intention underlying the earliest parts of the *Sibylline Oracles* has rather been propagandistic than proselytising. Furthermore, *Sibylline Oracles* contains passages that are clearly aimed at Jewish readers. That they were addressed in so traditional a Greek form implies that these readers, too, were familiar with that form. It is therefore most likely that at least the main corpus of book 3 of *Sibylline Oracles* was written for Greek Jews and non-Jewish Greeks alike. The authors may indeed have looked to 'establish common ground',[39] but this effort aimed at informing Greeks and exhorting Jews. There is no indication its intended effect was to proselytise.

The fact that these oracles have not been written for Greeks alone appears from e.g. *Sib. Or.* III,268-277, a passage that clearly addresses Jewish readers:

> You will be led to the Assyrians and you will see
> innocent children and wives in slavery
> to hostile men. All means of livelihood and wealth will perish.
> The whole earth will be filled with you and every sea.
> Everyone will be offended at your customs.
> Your whole land will be desolate; your fortified altar
> and temple of the great God and long walls
> will all fall to the ground, because you did not obey in your heart
> the holy law of the immortal God, but in error
> you worshiped unseemly idols...[40]

The addressees of this passage must have been Jews. It is remarkable that this passage mentions idolatry as the reason for their exile under the

---

[39] Collins, *Sibylline Oracles*, p. 113.
[40] Translation by Collins, *OTPseud*, vol. 2.

Assyrians. This same negative approach towards idolatry can be found in
III,586-590:

> They (= the Jews) do not honor with empty deceits works of men,
> either gold or bronze, or silver or ivory,
> or wooden, stone, or clay idols of dead gods,
> red-painted likenesses of beasts,
> such as mortals honor with empty-minded counsel.[41]

Polemics against idolatry thus formed an important element within the
apologetics and propaganda of the *Sibylline Oracles*. In another oracle,
this time on the final judgement of the earth, the idolaters will repent and
confess their sins, saying: 'With mindless spirit we revered things made
by hand, idols and statues of dead men' (III,722-723). The same feature is
found in *Sib. Or.* v,403-405, where abstinence from idolatry is mentioned
as a characteristic of the 'holy people' who built the second temple in
Jerusalem.

The polemic against idolatry can be found in numerous other Jewish
writings from the Graeco-Roman period as well. Idolatry is in fact a standard feature in the portrayal of pagans and often it is described as the
worst sin. This polemic has ancient roots. Already in the Old Testament
idolatry is seen as a terrible vice. It is mentioned in the Decalogue as the
first and second commandments (Exod 20,3-5). Often in the Old Testament it figures as a terrible offence against God.[42] This same abhorrence
of idolatry is found in Jewish literature from period under discussion here.
The first seven chapters of the *Apocalypse of Abraham* are fully dedicated
to the problem of idolatry. The general Jewish attitude in this matter is
reflected by the words of Abraham in *Apoc. Abr.* 4,4: 'They (= the idols)
did not help themselves; how then can they help you or me?' Idols are
considered as dumb and silent, and to worship them is regarded as just
as foolish as adultery (cf. *2 Enoch* 34,1-2). Often idolatry is even presented
as the root of all sins (*2 Apoc. Bar.* 62,1-4; *3 Apoc. Bar.* 13,4; *1 Enoch*
99,7; *2 Enoch* 10,6; *Jub.* 11,4; *LAB* 6; 25,9-13; 34; 36,3; 38; 44,1-6). In
T. Job 2,1-5,3 Job is depicted as a very pious man who shows his piety

---

[41] Translation by Collins, *OTPseud*, vol. 2.
[42] See among many other passages: Lev 19,4; Deut 4,28; 28,36.64; 29,16-17; 1 Kgs
21,26; 2 Kgs 19,18; 1 Chron 16,26 (= Ps 96,5); Ps 97,7; 106,36.38; 115,4; 135,15;
Isa 2,8.20; 31,7; 37,19; Ezek 8,10; 14,3-4; 20,32.

by destroying the temple of an idol. To be forced to worship idols is a terrible punishment (*As. Mos.* 2,8-9), and those who are stupid enough to do so willingly, deserve to die (*Vit. Proph.* 21,11).

It is telling that the description of pagans as worshippers of idols is sometimes put in words that reflect a genuine abhorrence of pagans themselves (*Jub.* 22,16-18):

> Separate yourself from the Gentiles,
> and do not eat with them,
> and do not perform deeds like theirs.
> And do not become associates of theirs.
> Because their deeds are defiled,
> and all of their ways are contaminated,
> and despicable, and abominable.
> They slaughter their sacrifices to the dead,
> and to the demons they bow down.
> And they eat in tombs.
> And all their deeds are worthless and vain.
> And they have no heart to perceive,
> and they have no eyes to see what their deeds are,
> and where they wander astray,
> saying to the tree 'you are my god',
> and to a stone 'you are my lord, and you are my savior';
> and they have no heart.[43]

It is clear from the evidence discussed that in Jewish literature of the Graeco-Roman age the rejection of pagan worship of idols functioned as a literary *topos*. This does not mean, however, that those who used the *topos* were not genuinely disgusted by pagan worship. This abhorrence had deep roots in the writings of the Jewish Bible. Time and again pagans are depicted as the worshippers of dumb statues. But does this polemic against idolatry prove any missionary zeal? Is it a symptom of proselytising activity? The answer should be negative. The clear rejection of idol worship in Jewish literature of the period under discussion is primarily aimed at Jewish readers. Therefore, it is an attempt to encourage Jews to refrain from participating in pagan cults rather than to persuade Greeks to stop worshipping their deities. While Graeco-Roman authors warned their countrymen against the atheism and misanthropy of the Jews (cf. below, pp. 38-43), Jewish authors exhorted their fellow Jews not to join in pagan idolatry. Furthermore, they intended to inform their non-Jewish readers on the true nature of Judaism.

---

[43] Translation by O.S. Wintermute, *OTPseud*, vol. 2.

The above interpretation of the polemics against idolatry as primarily a feature of internal apologetics, and not as an attempt to persuade Greeks to give up their ways, is sustained by a sociological observation. Notwithstanding the great number of Jewish residents in the Roman Empire, they were still a minority. Remarks on pagan idolatry made in Jewish literature aiming at Jewish readers should therefore not be interpreted as proselytising in character. These authors were in no position to prescribe to the pagan majority what they should and should not do. It is far more likely that they wrote on behalf of the Jewish minority and exhorted their fellow-Jews not to give in to the appeal of pagan cults. The polemics against idolatry found throughout Jewish literature of the period under discussion should be interpreted as paraenetic and apologetic, not as primarily propagandistic or even proselytising remarks.

The above observation does not mean, however, that Jewish authors of the period had no propagandistic aims whatsoever. In his presentation of Jewish history in *Antiquitates* Josephus clearly aims at a pagan public, and it is evident that one of his aims is to present the Jewish people as ancient and respectable and their religion as one with high moral standards.[44] Other Jewish historiographers also seem to have had this aim. In his introduction to the edition of fragments of Hellenistic Jewish authors, C.R. Holladay correctly pointed out the position of these authors:

> The mere fact that they have chosen what at the time must have been novel genres in which to reflect and write about their Jewish heritage is itself significant, for it shows that they had entered a new literary arena, and were expecting their efforts to be judged in a much broader setting. It also reflects a confident position vis-à-vis the culture in which they lived. That they were doing so on behalf of their faith is almost unexceptionally true, and in this sense they are engaged in religious propaganda.[45]

But this religious propaganda was aimed at informing, not at converting.

The same goal of presenting Judaism as an ancient religion with high standards influenced the so-called *Epistle of Aristeas*. Although this tract,

---

[44] Schürer *et al.*, *History*, vol. 3, p. 545: 'Its trend is apologetic. With his whole representation Josephus wishes not only to instruct his Gentile readers, for whom the book was intended in the first place, in the history of his people, but also to inspire in them an esteem for the Jewish people by showing that they had a very ancient history and a great number of outstanding men both in war and peace, and that in regard to their laws and institutions they compared favourably with other peoples (…).'

[45] C.R. Holladay, *Fragments from Hellenistic Jewish Authors. Vol. 1: Historians* (TTPS 20; Chico: Scholars Press, 1983), p. 3.

too, was probably written for Jewish readers rather than Greeks, the long section on the conversation of king Ptolemy with the seventy translators (*Ep. Aris.* 187-294) obviously wishes to present these translators as exemplary wise and pious men, who display the high standards of Judaism. Time and again the king puts the translators to the test, and time and again they give him an adequate pious reply in which God is presented as the source of prosperity and goodness and contempt for God's ways is mentioned as the source of evil. In *Ep. Aris.* 295-296 the author points out that this presentation of the translators as true wise and pious men is one of his aims: 'I admired these men tremendously, the way in which they gave immediate answers which needed a long time (to ponder), and while the questioner had thought out details in each case, those answering gave their replies immediately one after another'.

According to the *Epistle of Aristeas*, it is these translators who were responsible for the creation of the Septuagint. The way in which they respond to the request of Demetrius Phalereus, who is supported by king Ptolemy II, very likely reveals the purpose of *Ep. Aris.* Their behaviour is presented as an example of how to behave in matters where Jews and Greeks had to interact.[46] 'The implied warning is twofold: The danger with some of the Jews was that they might become excessively exclusive in their attitude to others, and the danger with the Greeks, or the Hellenists, was that their attitude might be too syncretistic.'[47]

The Septuagint is also mentioned by Philo as an important element in the attraction of the Jewish religion. In his *De vita Mosis* II,17-44 Philo describes the great impact that the Jewish Law had within the Graeco-Roman world:

> There is something surely still more wonderful – even this: not only Jews but almost every other people, particularly those which take more account of virtue, have so far grown in holiness as to value and honour our laws. In this they have received a special distinction which belongs to no other code. Here is the proof. Throughout the world of Greeks and barbarians, there is practically no state which honours the

---

[46] Feldman's interpretation of the evidence appears somewhat biased by his remark on *Ep. Aris.* 227 (*Jew and Gentile*, p. 294): 'That the Jews take the initiative in evangelizing (sic!; LP) is clear.' Feldman bases this view on the passage where one of the translators of the Septuagint declares that 'we must show liberal charity to our opponents so that in this manner we may lead them to change to what is proper and fitting for them.' Nothing suggests that a conversion to Judaism is intended.

[47] R.J.H. Shutt, *OTPseud* vol. 2, pp. 9-10.

institutions of any other. (...) It is not so with ours. They attract and win the attention of all (πάντας γὰρ ἐπάγεται καὶ συνεπιστρέφει), of barbarians, of Greeks, of dwellers on the mainland and islands, of nations of the east and the west, of Europe and Asia, of the whole inhabited world from end to end.[48]

Philo evidently describes a situation in which the Jewish laws drew the attention of many non-Jews and even met with great sympathy. He continues with a rather idealised description of the origin of the Septuagint. In this description Philo pictures the spread of the Jewish religion as caused not by active propagation, but by its own outstanding appeal:

> In ancient times the laws were written in the Chaldean tongue, and remained in that form for many years, without any change of language, so long as they had not yet revealed their beauty to the rest of mankind. But, in the course of time, the daily, unbroken regularity of practice exercised by those who observed them brought them to the knowledge of others, and their fame began to spread on every side.[49]

Philo continues with the remark that 'some people, thinking it was a shame that the laws should be found in one half only of the human race, the barbarians, and denied altogether to the Greeks, took steps to have them translated.' In his description of the process of translation, Philo points out that the initiative came from king Ptolemy Philadelphus. 'This great man, having conceived an ardent affection for our laws, determined to have the Chaldean translated into Greek (...)' (§31).

Philo subsequently describes how Chaldean translators created the Septuagint and how they, inspired by God himself, all individually made the exact same translation of the Chaldean/Hebrew bible. By their work as translators, they acted as ἱεροφάνται καὶ προφῆται, i.e. they made the sacred mysteries available for Greek readers.[50] They did this, according to Philo's account, on the island of Pharos. Philo then continues with a description of the feast held annually on the island to commemorate the creation of the Septuagint. On this occasion 'not only Jews but multitudes of others cross the water, both to do honour to the place in which the light of that version first shone out, and also to thank God for the good gifts so old yet ever so young' (§31). It is Philo's clear conviction that if the nation of Israel prospered, the attraction of its laws would be

---

[48] *Vit. Mos.* II,17-20; text and translation taken from F.H. Colson, LCL.
[49] *Vit. Mos.* II,26-27.
[50] S. Jellicoe, 'Aristeas, Philo and the Septuagint *Vorlage*', *JThS* ns 12 (1961), pp. 261-271, refers to this passage and argues that ἱεροφάντης has the meaning given by LSJ ('one who teaches the rites of sacrifice and worship') – cf. Jellicoe, 'Aristeas', p. 270, n. 4.

even greater: 'I believe that each nation would abandon its peculiar ways, and, throwing overboard their ancestral customs, turn to honouring our laws alone.'

This last phrase could be interpreted as evidence that Philo propagated a Jewish proselytising mission. Yet this would be a misinterpretation of his words. First of all, his words on the abandoning of each nation's peculiar ways form a rhetorical climax put in a hypothetical form. Philo expresses his view that the Jewish laws are so good that a prospering Jewish nation would enlarge their popularity even further. Secondly, Philo's intention throughout the passage under discussion is to point out how very great was the appeal of Jewish laws in the pagan world.

The passage discussed is but one fragment from the entire philonic corpus. Others have already dealt with the propagandistic aspects of Philo's work and therefore it is not necessary to dwell on the subject at great length.[51] Our conclusion from the short extract from Philo may be extended to Philo as a whole: Philo depicts the Jewish laws as being so important that they attract Gentiles simply because of their splendour. In his way of formulating this view, Philo may be considered propagandistic. But all the same, he may not have been far from the truth in his picture: it was because of the strong appeal of the Jewish religion that pagans felt attracted.

The brief survey of a number of Hellenistic Jewish writings given in this section is of course far from exhaustive. Yet it does point out that it is too simple to generally assume a proselytising aim for Hellenistic Jewish writings in Greek. Rather than to convert, the aim of many Jewish authors writing in Greek was to exhort their Jewish readers and to inform the Greeks. Within the various forms of contact between the Jewish religion and Greek culture, idolatry was a crucial issue for Jewish authors. Often Greeks are reproached for worshipping dumb idols made of clay or even silver and gold. Over against the multitude of idols and gods, Jewish authors present the one God of Israel, the Most High, as the true God. Yet the fact that they do so does not mean that these authors intended to convert Greeks.

---

[51] See for instance McKnight, *Light among Gentiles*, pp. 69-70.92-96. A pointed, but good summary of Philo's position is given in Schürer *et al.*, *History*, vol. 3, pp. 587-588. See also S. Sandmel, *Philo's Place in Judaism. A Study of Conceptions of Abraham in Jewish Literature* (New York: KTAV, 1956; augmented edition, 1971), p. 211: '(…) Philonic Judaism is the result of a hellenization which transcends mere language; it is as complete a hellenization as was possible for a group which retained throughout its loyalty to the Torah, and the separateness of the group.'

2. Pagan Authors on Judaism

In the above it appeared that Jewish authors were often vehemently engaged in a polemic against pagan idolatry. Furthermore, a good deal of Jewish literature intended for a Greek audience aimed at correcting their views by informing the Greek readers. The need for such a correction of pagan views on Jews and Judaism becomes evident as soon as we take a look at these views as displayed throughout pagan sources of the period.

Graeco-Roman authors sometimes spoke of Jews with great regard but more often with enormous disdain.[52] The regard for Judaism was usually restricted to its high moral standards. Hermippus of Smyrna, for instance, who wrote about 200 BCE, makes a simular point as Cleodemus Malchus (cf. above, p. 28), viz. that Pythagoras took his philosophy from the Jews. Such is the claim of Origen:

> It is said that also Hermippus, in his first book on legislators, related that Pythagoras brought his own philosophy from the Jews to the Greeks.[53]

Hecataeus of Abdera (c. 300 BCE) held Moses in high esteem. In his description of Moses, he pictured him as 'outstanding both for his wisdom and for his courage' (φρονήσει τε καὶ ἀνδρείᾳ πολὺ διαφέρων).[54] This esteem for Judaism and its lawgiver, however, comprises only a small part of the references to Judaism in pagan literature. The greater number of these references is far less positive.

Josephus, in his response to Apion, defends Judaism against the attacks of pagan authors who apparently gave a distorted picture of the Jewish religion and people. Throughout the writing Josephus refers to the picture Apion gave of Judaism. And time and again Josephus corrects him:

> In the argument to which I now proceed Apion's extraordinary sagacity is most astonishing. A clear proof, according to him, that our laws are unjust and our religious ceremonies erroneous is that we are not masters of an empire, but rather the slaves, first of one nation, then of another, and that calamity has more than once befallen our city.[55]

---

[52] On this subject, see M. Stern, 'The Jews in Greek and Latin Literature', in: S. Safrai, M. Stern, et al (eds.), The Jewish People in the First Century, vol. 2: Historical Geography, Political History, Social, Cultural and Religious Life and Institutions (CRINT 1,2; Assen, Amsterdam: Van Gorcum, 1976), pp. 1101-1159.

[53] GLAJJ, nr. 26; Origen, c. Cels. I,15,334.

[54] GLAJJ, nr. 11; Diodorus Siculus, Bib. Hist. XL,3,3.

[55] Josephus, c. Ap. II,125; GLAJJ, nr. 174, translation by H.St.J. Thackeray, LCL.

Yet Apion is not the first to give such a distorted picture of Jewish customs. It is evident that he was one in a series of authors who had a rather negative view of Judaism. Josephus makes this clear:

> I am no less amazed at the proceedings of the authors who supplied him with his materials, I mean Posidonius and Apollonius Molon. On the one hand they charge us with not worshipping the same gods as other people; on the other, they tell lies and invent absurd calumnies about our temple, without showing any consciousness of impiety.[56]

Josephus even mentions the reason for this distorted description of Jewish customs in pagan literature when he comes to speak of Apollonius Molon:

> Seeing, however, that Apollonius Molon, Lysimachus, and others, partly from ignorance, mainly from ill will, have made reflections, which are neither just nor true, upon our lawgiver Moses and his code, maligning the one as charlatan and impostor, and asserting that from the other we receive lessons in vice and none in virtue, I desire to give, to the best of my ability, a brief account of our constitution as a whole and of its details...[57]

Of course Josephus' account is polemic and can not be read as an impartial description of the reason why pagan authors gave a distorted picture of Jewish customs. But it is likely that the two factors he mentions would both have been valid reasons: indeed some pagan remarks against Jewish customs would have been the result of ignorance and others of ill will.

On the way in which Apollonius and Apion wrote against the Jews Josephus makes an illustrative remark in *c. Ap.* II,148:

> ...Apollonius, unlike Apion, has not grouped his accusations together, but scattered them here and there all over his work, reviling us in one place as atheists and misanthropes, in another reproaching us as cowards, whereas elsewhere, on the contrary, he accuses us of temerity and reckless madness. He adds that we are the most witless of all barbarians, and are consequently the only people who have contributed no useful invention to civilization.[58]

If we had only Josephus at our disposal, it would be appealing to think that the apologetic rhetoric had brought him to accuse the pagan authors he mentions of giving a distorted picture of Judaism. A number of passages from pagan authors themselves, however, do support Josephus' view. The philosopher Seneca, for instance, mentions the fact that non-Jews adopt

---

[56] Josephus, *c.Ap.* II,79; *GLAJJ*, nr. 48, translation by H.St.J. Thackeray, LCL.
[57] Josephus, *c. Ap.* II,145; *GLAJJ*, nr. 49, translation by H.St.J. Thackeray, LCL.
[58] *GLAJJ*, nr. 49, translation by H.St.J. Thackeray, LCL.

Jewish customs as an example of how 'the vanquished' prescribe 'their laws' for 'the victors'. Augustine gives the evidence:

> Along with other superstitions of the civil theology Seneca also censures the sacred institutions of the Jews, especially the sabbath. He declares that their practice is inexpedient, because by introducing one day of rest in every seven they lose in idleness almost a seventh of their life, and by failing to act in times of urgency they often suffer loss... But when speaking of the Jews he says: 'Meanwhile the customs of this accursed race have gained such influence that they are now received throughout all the world. The vanquished have given laws to their victors.' (victi victoribus leges dederunt).[59]

Juvenal mocks the same habit of pagans adopting Jewish customs in his famous satire on the bad influence of the vices of parents on their children:

> Some who have had a father who reveres the Sabbath, worship nothing but the clouds, and the divinity of the heavens, and see no difference between eating swine's flesh, from which their father abstained, and that of man; and in time they take to circumcision. Having been wont to flout the laws of Rome, they learn and practice and revere the Jewish law, and all that Moses handed down in his secret tome, forbidding to point out the way to any not worshipping the same rites, and conducting none but the circumcised to the desired fountain. For all which the father was to blame, who gave up every seventh day to idleness, keeping it apart from all the concerns of life.[60]

In this picture of the Jewish rites Juvenal mentions the fact that these rites were incomprehensible to outsiders. He speaks of Moses' 'secret tome',[61] and mentions the fact that Moses forbade the giving of an explanation of these rites to outsiders. Here we have a strong example of what also appears from the other passages mentioned so far: the Jewish custom of revering their own laws, both dietary and other, was little understood by pagans. The worship of a god without statues, circumscribed with terms such as 'heavens', must have seemed very strange in the eyes of those loyal to traditional Graeco-Roman cults. Indeed, the two reproaches made most often against Jews are those of misanthropy and atheism (cf. Jos., c. Ap. II,148; above).[62] The former

---

[59] Seneca, De Superstitione; in: Augustin, De Civ. Dei VI,11; GLAJJ, nr. 186, translation by W.M. Green, LCL.

[60] Juvenal, Sat. XIV,96-106; GLAJJ, nr. 301, translation by G.C. Ramsay, LCL.

[61] tradidit arcano quodcumque volumine Moyses...

[62] On the accusation of atheism, see Julian, c. Gal. 43B = GLAJJ, nr. 481a; cf. GLAJJ, vol. 2, p. 545, where a number of passages are mentioned in which the same reproach of atheism is directed at Christians.

must have resulted from the Jewish fear of joining pagans at their meals, whereas the latter was clearly a result of worshipping but one, invisible God.

The accusation of misanthropy was wide spread. Diodorus, for instance, speaks of the Jews as a people with 'misanthropic and lawless customs'.[63] According to Josephus, Apion described the Jews as a people who would 'show no good-will to a single alien, above all to Greeks'.[64] Especially revealing is the account given by Tacitus in his description of the Jewish people. In *Hist.* v,1-13 he describes the origins and practices of the Jews in a manner that betrays both lack of real adequate knowledge and grave contempt. In his picture of Moses, for instance, Tacitus reveals the latter:

> To establish his influence over this people for all time, Moses introduced new religious practices, quite opposed to those of all other religions. The Jews regard as profane all that we hold sacred; on the other hand, they permit all that we abhor.[65]

In a passage following the above, Tacitus further dwells upon the 'despicable character' of the Jews:

> ... the other customs of the Jews are base and abominable, and owe their persistence to their depravity: for the worst rascals among other peoples, renouncing their ancestral religions, always kept sending tribute and contributing to Jerusalem, thereby increasing the wealth of the Jews; again, the Jews are extremely loyal toward one another, and always ready to show compassion, but toward every other people they feel only hate and enmity (*misericordia in promptu, sed adversus omnes alios hostile odium*). They sit apart at meals and they sleep apart, and although as a race, they are prone to lust, they abstain from intercourse with foreign women; yet among themselves nothing is unlawful. They adopted circumcision to distinguish themselves from other peoples by this difference. Those who are converted to their ways follow the same practice, and the earliest lesson they receive is to despise the gods, to disown their country, and to regard their parents, children, and brothers as of little account. However, they take thought to increase their numbers; for they regard it as a crime to kill any late-born child, and they believe that the souls of those who are killed in battle or by the executioner are immortal:

---

[63] Diodorus Siculus, *Bib. Hist.* XXXV,1,3 mentions Moses as the one who had ordained τὰ μισάνθρωπα καὶ παράνομα ἔθη τοῖς Ἰουδαίοις; cf. *GLAJJ*, nr. 63.

[64] Josephus, *c. Ap.* II,121; cf. *GLAJJ*, nr. 173.

[65] Tacitus, *Hist.* v,4,1; *GLAJJ*, nr. 281.

[66] Tacitus, *Hist.* v,5,1-3; *GLAJJ*, nr. 281.

> hence comes their passion for begetting children, and their scorn of
> death.[66]

Apart from showing his own scorn for the Jewish people, Tacitus also
mentions one of the reasons for what appears to have been an enormous
increase in the Jewish population within the Roman empire (cf. above,
p. 22): the Jews did not practice infanticide and considered children a
blessing.[67]

Contempt for the Jewish disregard of the traditional Graeco-Roman
deities and the custom of refusing to have a common meal together with
pagans is found in the writings of other authors as well. Philostratus, for
instance, mentions the Jews as 'a race that has made its own a life apart
and irreconcilable, that cannot share with the rest of mankind in the
pleasures of the table nor join in their libations or prayers or sacrifices'.[68]
The fact that contempt for the Jews did not weaken with the passing of
time is illustrated by Synesius, a Greek author from the fourth century CE.
A letter he wrote in his pre-Christian period contains a reference to the
captain and half of the crew of the ship with which he sailed. Synesius
describes their hateful character and blames it to their being Jewish. The
reference is put in extreme terms since Synesius speaks of the Jews as 'a
graceless race and fully convinced of the piety of sending to Hades as
many Greeks as possible'.[69]

A passage often mentioned in favour of Jewish proselytising is Horace,
Serm. I,4,142-143. In this passage Horace rhetorically compares the fact
that one who disagrees with him could be forced to agree just as the Jews
urged converts to Judaism:

> This is one of the lesser frailties I spoke of, and if you should make no
> allowance for it, then would a big band of poets come to my aid – for
> we are the big majority – and we, like the Jews, will compel you to
> make one of our throng.[70]

The final words are usually interpreted as evidence of 'strong Jewish
missionary activity in Rome'.[71] Yet as the text-external evidence for such

---

[67] See also Hecataeus of Abdera, in Diodorus Siculus, *Bib. Hist.* XL,3,8 (= *GLAJJ*, nr. 11,
see esp. Stern's comment, vol. 1, pp. 33-34).

[68] *Vit. Ap.* V,33; *GLAJJ*, nr. 403.

[69] γένος ἔκσπονδον καὶ εὐσεβεῖν ἀναπεπεισμένον ἦν ὅτι πλείστους ἄνδρας Ἕλλη-
νας ἀποθανεῖν αἴτιοι γένωνται – Synesius, *Ep.* V; Cf. *GLAJJ*, nr. 569. Translation
by A. Fitzgerald.

[70] *GLAJJ*, nr. 127; translation by H. Rushton Fairclough, *LCL*.

[71] *GLAJJ*, nr. 127, vol. 1, p. 323.

missionary activity is to be rejected, the 'missionary activity' should appear from the words Horace used. At first sight they may seem to indicate such activity: *te ... cogemus ... concedere* is a very strong expression by which a forced entry into the group is described. At a closer look, however, it becomes less obvious that a proselytising mission is described here. Is it likely that the phrase describes a situation in which Jews *force* pagans to enter Judaism? If there was any such thing as a proselytising mission, it can hardly have functioned by forcing someone to enter Judaism against his will. Of course, Horace may have used the word *cogemus* as a poetic hyperbole, but since the compulsion of pagans by Jews is clearly used as a reference in a comparison, this is not very likely. Horace refers to a well-known Jewish practice in which pagans are forced to join the group. We do know of one such practice: the obligation for the proselyte to keep the entire Law, including circumcision. The verb used by Horace – *cogere* – therefore probably points to this obligation for proselytes. In this interpretation Horace mentions the way in which full proselytes were received into the Jewish community as a point in the comparison: they were forced to take on their responsibility and keep the entire Law. What can be concluded on the basis of this evidence is not the existence of a Jewish proselytising mission, but rather the fact that the obligation taken on by a full proselyte was well known in Horace's day.

The evidence of pagan authors writing on Jewish customs and Judaism in general shows that Jewish religion was not exactly treated favourably in Graeco-Roman literature. The concern for keeping the Mosaic law, visible in for instance circumcision, the dietary segregation, and the strict reverence of the one, invisible God, these habits were barely understood by pagan authors. It is probably because of this lack of understanding in certain Graeco-Roman circles that a number of propagandistic Jewish writings of the period aimed at informing their pagan readers. From the pagan's point of view, Jewish customs could be characterised as atheism and misanthropy. From the Jew's point of view, the traditional Graeco-Roman cults practised immoral forms of idolatry. And yet these pictures were the extremes. The Jewish religion was apparently very attractive to many pagans, precisely because of its high moral standards, its monotheistic cult, and its ancient provenance. It is not surprising that the attraction of the Jewish religion should sometimes lead to conflicts of which two expulsions of Jews from Rome are the most significant examples.

3. Expulsions of Jews from Rome

A number of references in pagan literature point at two expulsions of
Jews from Rome.[72] The first is to be dated in 139 BCE, and the second in
19 CE. Evidence for the former event is given by Valerius Maximus,
whereas Tacitus, Suetonius, Josephus, and Dio Cassius mention the latter. Let us consider the evidence for both these events.

Valerius Maximus wrote on the first expulsion of Jews from Rome at
the beginning of the first century CE. Unfortunately, his remark has not
been preserved in an original work but only in that of two epitomists
from presumably the fourth or fifth century CE.[73] These two epitomists
give rather different accounts of the event. In both versions the first sentence describes the expulsion of astrologers (Chaldeans) from Rome. The
second sentence speaks of the expulsion of Jews from Rome but the two
versions give different reasons for the event:[74]

> A) The same Hispalus banished the Jews from Rome, because they
> attempted to transmit their sacred rites to the Romans, and he cast
> down their private altars from public places.
> B) The same praetor compelled the Jews, who attempted to infect
> the Roman customs with the cult of Jupiter Sabazius, to return to
> their homes.

The fact that these reports differ as much as they do, prevents any firm
conclusion as to the reason for the expulsion. The first version explicitly
speaks of an attempt by the Jews to 'transmit their sacred rites to the
Romans' (*Romanis tradere sacra sua*), whereas the second mentions the
spread of the cult of Jupiter Sabazius as the reason (*Sabazi Iovis cultu
Romanos inficere mores*). Furthermore, the result of the praetor's decision
is also depicted rather differently: Nepotianus speaks of the casting down
of 'their private altars from public places', and Paris of the fact that
the Jews should 'return to their homes'. On the basis of this evidence
E.N. Lane has argued that the praetor – whose real name was Cn. Cor-

---

[72] On the relation of the Roman Empire and its Jewish residents, see K.L. Noethlichs, *Das
Judentum und der römische Staat. Minderheitenpolitik im antiken Rom* (Darmstadt:
Wissenschaftliche Buchgesellschaft, 1996). A description of the evidence on the incidents at Elephantine and Alexandria, see P. Schäfer, *Judeophobia. Attitudes towards
the Jews in the Ancient World* (London, Cambridge: Harvard University Press, 1997),
pp. 121-160. On pp. 106-118 Schäfer discusses the pagan reactions to Jewish proselytism.
[73] Cf. *GLAJJ*, nrs. 147a and 147b.
[74] A) *Iudaeos quoque, qui Romanis tradere sacra sua conati erant, idem Hispalus urbe
exterminavit arasque privatas e publicis locis abiecit* – Januarius Nepotianus; Stern,
GLAJJ, nr. 147a; B) *Idem Iudaeos, qui Sabazi Iovis cultu Romanos inficere mores
conati erant, repetere domos suas coegit* – Julius Paris; Stern, *GLAJJ*, nr 147b.

nelius Scipio Hispanus[75] – acted against three different groups, viz. the Chaldeans, the Sabazius-worshippers, and the Jews.[76] The true reason for acting against the Jews can hardly have been their erecting of altars throughout Rome. The most likely interpretation of the passage is offered by Goodman:[77] 'What was at issue here, then, if the account is not totally confused (...), was something rather less than the conversion of proselytes to Judaism. I suggest that the Jews were accused not of teaching Romans to despise their native cults, which would be the most obvious and objectionable effect of conversion, but simply of bringing in a new cult into public places without authority, a practice which the Romans traditionally deprecated, as they had shown recently in their opposition to the spread of the cult of Dionysus.'

This interpretation of the evidence attributed to Valerius Maximus does not, therefore, refer to active proselytising by Jews. It either points out the effect of the introduction of the Jewish cult in Rome, or it refers to the illegitimate character of that introduction.

On the second expulsion of Jews from Rome, in 19 CE, there is more evidence. The event is reported by Tacitus, Suetonius, Dio Cassius, and probably also by Josephus. Their reports indicate that Tiberius had Jews expelled from Rome, presumably in 19 CE, but they differ in regard to the reasons for this expulsion and in their account of its judicial impact.

Tacitus reports in his *Annales* (II,85,4) that Tiberius expelled part of the Jewish population from Rome, and dates this event in the year 19 CE:

> Another debate dealt with the proscription of the Egyptian and Jewish rites, and a senatorial edict directed that four thousand descendants of enfranchised slaves, tainted with that superstition and suitable in point of age, were to be shipped to Sardinia and there employed in suppressing brigandage: 'if they succumbed to the pestilential climate, it was a cheap loss'. The rest had orders to leave Italy, unless they had renounced their impious ceremonial by a given date.[78]

Tacitus' report has some important implications. Firstly, it focuses on the 'descendants of enfranchised slaves' (*libertini generis*), i.e. not on all Jewish residents of Rome. Unless Tacitus regarded all Jewish inhabitants of Rome as belonging to this category, it is probable that his report describes how a large section, but not all of the Jewish population, was

---

[75] Levinskaya, *Diaspora Setting*, p. 29.

[76] E.N. Lane, 'Sabazius and the Jews in Valerius Maximus: a Re-examination', *JRS* 69 (1979), p. 37; cf. Levinskaya, *Diaspora Setting*, p. 29.

[77] Goodman, *Mission and Conversion*, pp. 82-83.

[78] Translation by J. Jackson, *LCL*; *GLAJJ*, nr. 284.

banned from Rome. Secondly, Tacitus mentions the Jewish rites in combination with Egyptian rites. It is evident that in this period of Roman history oriental cults very much appealed to the Romans (see below, pp. 56-64). Therefore, it is most likely that the origin of the event described by Tacitus lies not in active proselytising, but in the enormous attraction of the Jewish and Egyptian cults. In this interpretation, Tacitus points to the great influence the Jewish religion had in Rome in 19 CE, but not necessarily to active proselytising.[79]

Suetonius reports the same expulsion from Rome. In his *Tiberius* 36 he gives the following description of the event:

> He abolished foreign cults, especially the Egyptian and the Jewish rites, compelling all who were addicted to such superstitions to burn their religious vestments and all their paraphernalia. Those of the Jews who were of military age he assigned to provinces of less healthy climate, ostensibly to serve in the army; the others of the same race or of similar beliefs he banished from the city, on pain of slavery for life if they did not obey.[80]

It has already been noted by others that the words used by Suetonius to describe the Jewish cult (*ea superstitione*) are the same as those used by Tacitus. This observation can be explained by the assumption of a common source, either the genuine *senatus consultum* or some intermediate historian.[81] Suetonius' report differs from that of Tacitus in some respects. For instance, Suetonius appears to focus on the Egyptian cults in his description of the religious vestments, and notes a division in the punishment of the Jews in that the young men were sent to serve in the army whereas 'all others' (*reliquos gentis eiusdem*) were banned with the severe threat of everlasting slavery. An important point of agreement with the report by Tacitus, however, is the fact that the Jewish cult is described as being obviously strong, but not explicitly as proselytising.

The only report in which this is the case is that of a later author, Dio Cassius. Dio briefly reports on this incident and mentions proselytising as the origin of the event:

---

[79] For this interpretation, see Levinskaya, *Diaspora Setting*, pp. 31-32.
[80] Text and translation by J.C. Rolfe, *LCL*; *GLAJJ*, nr. 306.
[81] *GLAJJ*, vol. 2, p. 113: 'Both Tacitus and Suetonius apparently derived the expression "superstitione ea" from some common source, either the *senatus consultum* itself or some intermediate work. Suetonius' *in provincias gravioris caeli* may also be compared with Tacitus' *ob gravitatem caeli*, a resemblance that also suggests a common ultimate source.'

As the Jews flocked to Rome in great numbers and were converting many of the natives to their ways, he (= Tiberius) banished most of them.[82]

At first sight, this is an important indication in favour of the existence of active proselytising by the Jewish community in Rome at the beginning of the first century CE.[83] Nevertheless, the fact is that the only witness to testify that their active proselytising caused the expulsion of Jews from Rome is also the youngest witness: Dio lived *c.* 160 CE – 230 CE, and wrote more than a century after Tacitus and Suetonius. I. Levinskaya correctly notes that Dio Cassius' report was probably coloured by the circumstances of the period in which he wrote, the end of the second and beginning of the third century CE: 'That was a period when Christian mission was fully in operation and had changed the religious atmosphere dramatically. This consideration makes it necessary to regard Dio's explanation of the cause of the expulsion as unreliable, given especially that it is not supported by earlier historians and is preserved only in quotation.'[84]

Another witness to an expulsion of Jews from Rome is Flavius Josephus. In *Ant.* XVIII,81-84 he reports on the banishing of Jews from Rome as a result of the fact that a high-placed Roman lady, Fulvia, had converted to Judaism and had sent money to the temple in Jerusalem. Four Jewish impostors had taken the money and used it for their own purposes, and as a result the Jews were banned from Rome.

This expulsion may be the same as the one reported by Tacitus, Suetonius, and Dio Cassius. Yet its reason, as given by Josephus, is very different in that neither the lady Fulvia nor the impostors are mentioned by any of the other authors. Also the date of the event, as reported by Josephus, differs from that of Tacitus: Josephus describes the whole event as having taken place during Pilate's reign of Judea. It may therefore be asked whether the event mentioned by Josephus is indeed the same event as that reported by Tacitus, Suetonius, and Dio Cassius. Even if it were, it only reveals that there was extensive contact between the Jewish community of Rome and Romans who were drawn towards Judaism.

In our discussion of the data on the expulsions from Rome, it has become clear that these two events are indeed evidence of the great attraction that the Jewish religion had for Romans, but not necessarily of active

---

[82] Dio Cassius, *Hist. Rom.* LVII,18,5a; text and translation by E. Cary, *LCL*; *GLAJJ*, nr. 419. [83] See for instance Feldman, *Jew and Gentile*, p. 32.

[84] Levinskaya, *Diaspora Setting*, p. 30. The quotation mentioned by Levinskaya refers to the fact that these words of Dio are kept only in a fragment preserved by a seventh-century Christian writer, John of Antioch.

proselytising. The Roman authorities were obviously afraid of the alien influences of Egyptian and Jewish cults and banned them, just as they had done with the cult of Bacchus/Dionysus some time earlier.[85]

Another expulsion from Rome known to us is mentioned in the New Testament (Claudius' ban that probably struck Prisca and Aquila; Acts 18,2; 1 Cor 16,19; Rom 16,3-5), and again by Suetonius (*Claudius* 25,4).[86] This expulsion has clearly resulted from a disturbance of order in the Jewish community of Rome. According to Suetonius a certain Chrestus caused the unrest. Either this name refers to an otherwise unknown Jew from Rome or it is a misspelling of the name *Christos*, Christ. If the latter is indeed the case, as many scholars assume, the disturbances in the Jewish community in Rome were caused by the proclamation of the Christian gospel. If not, the reason for the upheaval remains unknown to us. Either way, however, the event cannot be used as proof for the existence of Jewish proselytising in Rome.

To conclude this section: the expulsions of Jews from Rome cannot be used as an argument in favour of the existence of Jewish proselytising, since they were *ad hoc* events, prompted by different situations.[87] Although they are evidence of the prominent position taken by Jews in Rome in the period under discussion, they do not indicate a 'missionary zeal' by these Jewish residents of Rome.

4. Christian Evidence on Jewish Proselytising: Matthew 23,15 and Romans 2,17-24

A text that is often mentioned as evidence in favour of the existence of Jewish proselytising is Matt 23,15: 'Woe to you, scribes and Pharisees,

---

[85] Dionysiac worship was banned from Rome in 186 BCE. The *senatus consultum de Bacchanalibus* has been preserved as CIL[2] 581 – cf. Livy, *Ab urbe condita* XXXIX,8ff.; M. Nilsson, *Dionysiac Mysteries* (Lund: Gleerup, 1957), pp. 12-21; and M. Nilsson, *Geschichte der griechischen Religion*. vol. 2: *Die Hellenistische und Römische Zeit* (HAW 5.2; München: Beck, 2nd ed., 1961), pp. 246-247.

[86] *Iudaeos impulsore Chresto assidue tumultuantis Roma expulit* ('Since the Jews constantly made disturbances at the instigation of Chrestus, he [= Claudius] expelled them from Rome'). Text and translation by J.C. Rolfe, *LCL*; *GLAJJ*, nr. 307; for literature on this famous passage, see *GLAJJ*, vol. 2, p. 114.

[87] See L.V. Rutgers, 'Roman policy toward the Jews: Expulsions from the city of Rome during the first century C.E.', in: K.P. Donfried, P. Richardson (eds.), *Judaism and Christianity in first-century Rome*. (Grand Rapids [etc.]: Eerdmans, 1998), pp. 93-116, who concludes: 'The *senatus consulta* of the late first century B.C.E. and the expulsions of Jews from Rome a few decades later are examples of a policy that responded to situations' (p. 114).

hypocrites! For you cross sea and land to make a single convert, and you make the new convert twice as much a child of hell as yourselves'.[88] This verse belongs to the Matthean *Sondergut*, and mentions the proselytising zeal of the scribes and Pharisees whom Jesus addresses. Goodman dismisses this evidence as wanting by interpreting the phrase 'you cross sea and land to make a single convert' as being aimed at the Pharisees who tried everything to persuade a person to adopt their views. In the eyes of Goodman, the 'convert' is, therefore, not a pagan who becomes a Jew, but a Jew who starts to live his life according to the rules of the Pharisees.[89] To prove his point, Goodman argues that the term *proselytos* 'in the first century had both a technical and non-technical sense'.[90] Goodman points at LXX Lev 19,10 where *proselytos* is used for 'a resident alien', and finds this meaning extended in Exod 22,20.[91] In that verse the Israelites in Egypt are described as *proselytoi*. According to Goodman, the case of *proselytos* should be compared to that of the 'God-fearers' in that the expression σεβεῖν τὸν θεόν can not only point at pagans who live according to Jewish customs, but also at pious Jews.

Goodman's case for the two possible meanings of προσήλυτος is a strong one. As a result, it is by no means certain that Matt 23,15 speaks of pagan converts to Judaism; the verse would then refer to Jews being converted to Pharisaism.[92] An important precondition for this interpretation, however, is that the words ποιῆσαι ἕνα προσήλυτον belong to the same traditional stratum as the introduction to the verse (οὐαὶ ὑμῖν,

---

[88] See for instance Feldman, *Jew and Gentile*, pp. 298-299. Also E. Lohmeyer, W. Schmauch, *Das Evangelium des Matthäus* (KEK; Göttingen: Vandenhoeck & Ruprecht, 1956), pp. 343-344; D. Hill, *The Gospel of Matthew* (NCB; London: Oliphants, 1972), p. 312 (who points at Jos., *Ant.* xx,38-48 which 'illustrates the lengths to which this excessive zeal [sic!; LP] would go in attempting to convert those who had already become adherents of the Jewish faith under the influence of the more liberal propaganda of Hellenistic Judaism'); E. Schweizer, *Das Evangelium nach Matthäus* (NTD; Göttingen: Vandenhoeck&Ruprecht, 1973), p. 287; J. Gnilka, *Das Matthäusevangelium*, vol. 2 (HThK; Freiburg [etc.]: Herder, 1988), p. 286; U. Luck *Das Evangelium nach Matthäus* (ZB; Zürich: Theologischer Verlag, 1993), pp. 250-251.

[89] Goodman, *Mission and Conversion*, pp. 69-74.
[90] Goodman, *Mission and Conversion*, p. 73.
[91] Goodman, *Mission and Conversion*, p. 73.
[92] K.G. Kuhn, *ThWNT* vol. 6, p. 742, argues that Pharisees within Palestinian Judaism took a different stand over against proselytes from hellenistic Jews: the latter accepted the existence of the σεβόμενοι τὸν θεόν as the correct form of conversion, whereas Pharisees in Palestine insisted upon full conversion including circumcision. Thus, according to Kuhn, the Pharisees sought for pagans to become 'their kind of Jews'.

γραμματεῖς καὶ Φαρισαῖοι ὑποκριταί, ὅτι). Since this introduction is evidently a redactional feature of the speech of Matthew 23 as a whole (cf. vv. 1-3.13.23.25.27.29), which was composed from Markan, Matthean, and Q-materials, Matt 23,15 would therefore have to be regarded as a redactional verse. This is indeed likely. It has been argued by students of the passage that the words are heavily coloured by Matthean redaction: περιάγω, ποιέω, εἷς, and γεέννα should be considered favourite Matthean words.[93] With these words the whole of 23,15 should characterised as redactional.

Given this redactional character of Matt 23,15 Goodman's interpretation is not only likely but very plausible: the whole of the speech in Matthew 23 is directed at the 'scribes and Pharisees', which is more or less a stock phrase for Pharisees. Since the gospel of Matthew should be dated well after the fall of the temple in 70 CE, it is pertinent to ask whether the bitter reproach may reflect the situation in which the gospel itself came into existence. The answer should probably be affirmative. It may be inferred from various sources that the Pharisees were more or less the sole survivors of the great catastrophe that had struck Judaism. The Essenes and the Sadducees had apparently been wiped out. It is probably for this reason also that, in the gospel of John, the Pharisees often form a *pars pro toto* of Judaism as a whole. In this context the reproach of 23,15 is very understandable: the author/redactor of Matthew points at the regrouping of Judaism by the Pharisees who must have actively promoted their views among their fellow Jews. The expression 'to cross sea and land' in this verse should be interpreted as a metaphor pointing at the Pharisees' eagerness to gain followers for their type of Judaism, not as an accurate description of missionary journeys undertaken by Jews in general.[94]

---

[93] See U. Luz, *Das Evangelium nach Matthäus*, vol. 3 (EKK; Zürich [etc.]: Benziger; Neukirchen-Vluyn: Neukirchener Verlag, 1997), pp. 323-325, who refers to R.H. Gundry, *Mark. A Commentary on his Apology for the Cross* (Grand Rapids: Eerdmans, 1993), pp. 460-461. Luz refuses, however, to go beyond a 'Matthean colouring' of the words for which he presupposes an origin in Q or a Matthean version of Q.

[94] The order of the words ('sea and land') may be singular as well as the use of ξήρα in stead of γῇ, but the combination 'land and sea' is often used as a metaphor. See for instance *Pss. Sol.* 2,29 where the Dragon (2,25; = Pompey) states his haughtiness by proclaiming his future as 'Lord of the earth and the sea' (ἐγὼ κύριος γῆς καὶ θαλάσσης ἔσομαι). Note the irony given by the contrast between this statement and the description by the poet who states that the Dragon will be despised by the smallest creature on earth and in the sea (2,26)! The same combination of earth and sea is found in *Vit. Ad.* 29,11; *Sib. Or.* III,85.223.271.323. Especially *Sib. Or.* III,271 is important in this respect (see the discussion above, p. 31).

This interpretation of Matt 23,15, however, means that this text can no longer be used as a *locus probans* for the case of Jewish proselytising mission. It may give us an insight into the development of Judaism after 70 CE, but it does not indicate that Jews actively sought the conversion of pagans.

A second possible reference to a missionary attitude by Jews is Rom 2,17-24. Here Paul reproaches 'the Jew' for failing to recognise God's revelation in Christ, while at the same time 'the Jew' considers himself as a teacher of the uneducated. Paul mentions four characteristics that point out the Jew's moral and religious superiority: to rely on the Law, to live in a supreme relation to God, to know God's will, and to be able to judge what really matters (2,17-18). Based on this description Paul mentions four ways to describe the relation of Jews to non-Jews. The implied Jew Paul addresses is a guide to the blind, a light to those who are in darkness, a corrector of the foolish, and a teacher of children (2,19-20). The Jew knows the outline of knowledge and truth by the Law (2,21a), and yet does not keep the Law (2,21b) but despises God by breaking it (2,22-23).

In Paul's description of the special status of Jews the Law is their means for knowing the will of God. Yet by not keeping the Law, Jews are a disgrace to God. Paul's argument ends in a new definition of Judaism: 'a person is a Jew who is one inwardly, and real circumcision is a matter of the heart' (2,29). This position enables Paul to contrast his 'new' Judaism with the 'old'.

The terminology Paul uses in his description apparently reflects a missionary attitude: 'guide to the blind', 'light to those who are in darkness', 'corrector of the foolish', and 'teacher of children'. The problem is, however, that none of these characterisations describe any intended action by the 'blind', by 'those who are in darkness', the 'foolish', or the 'children'. The characterisations no doubt intend to describe the moral and religious superiority of the Jews to pagans. Comparable terms are used for instance in *T. Job* 53,3, where Job's death is lamented and Job is described as 'the strength of the helpless', the 'light of the blind', the 'father of the orphans', the 'host of strangers' and the 'clothing of widows' (τὸ φῶς τῶν τυφλῶν, ὁ πατὴρ τῶν ὀρφανῶν, ὁ τῶν ξένων ξενόδος, ἡ ἔνδυσις τῶν χηρῶν). These descriptions clearly focus on the character of Job as a righteous and pious person. The only match with Paul's description of 'the Jew' in Romans 2 is the metaphor of 'light for the blind' in which apparently two of Paul's characterisations are combined: 'guide for the blind' and 'light for those who are in darkness'. These two designations use similar metaphors found in Isa 42,6-7. The idea of Jews being the guides for the nations of the earth is also present in *1 Enoch*

105,1 and *Sib. Or.* III,195. Yet in Romans 2 as elsewhere this terminology rather expresses the superiority of the Jewish religion to those of the pagans than a missionary appeal by the Jews.

In summa: Paul's description of the Jewish attitude in Rom 2,17-24 does not point at a proselytising attitude among the Jews. Rather, it is evidence of the moral and religious superiority claimed by 'the Jew' Paul addresses.

Conclusion

Although the survey of evidence given in this chapter is scanty compared to the abundance of material from the period, some conclusions can be drawn. Evidence on the contact between the Jews and their Gentile surroundings is clear: there was a certain amount of religious exchange as well as a reciprocal animosity. Nevertheless, the Jewish religion did attract a great number of Gentiles. Its power of attraction probably lay in its antiquity, in its high moral standards, the prominent position of Moses,[95] and in the monotheistic view that suited the inclination of Graeco-Roman philosophy and culture in general.

It is obvious that many Gentiles became Jews or sympathisers with the Jewish religion in the first century CE.[96] But in the evidence on Jewish religious propaganda surveyed here, no conclusive proof has been found on the existence of active Jewish proselytising in the period up to the first century CE.[97] Jewish literature in Greek testifies to the polemics between Jews and Gentiles. Gentile adherents to Graeco-Roman cults were obviously regarded as idolaters by strict Law-observing Jews who considered themselves as moral and religious examples. Yet those same

---

[95] See Feldman, *Jew and Gentile*, pp. 177-287, who treats exactly these three subjects as important 'attractions of the Jews'. With regard to Moses, see esp. J.G. Gager, *Moses in Greco-Roman Paganism* (Nashville, New York: Abingdon, 1972).

[96] For a good discussion of this phenomenon, see S.J.D. Cohen, *The Beginnings of Jewishness. Boundaries, Varieties, Uncertainties* (Berkeley [etc.]: University of California Press, 1999), esp. pp. 109-197. Cohen's reconstruction of the interaction between Jews and their Greek surroundings is very careful: 'The Jewish communities of these Greek cities allowed outsiders to join as members (to become proselytes) or to affiliate loosely (to become "God-venerators").' (p. 172). This is not exactly a proselytising mission to the Gentiles.

[97] On proselytising mission in the rabbinic era, see R. Goldenberg, *The Nations that Know Thee Not. Ancient Jewish Attitudes towards Other Religions* (BibS 52; Sheffield: Academic Press, 1997), pp. 90-94. Goldenberg concludes (p. 94): 'There may have been Jewish missionaries in the period of the Talmud, but they were not rabbis, and the rabbis paid no attention to their activities.'

strict Law-observing Jews were regarded as atheists and misanthropes by traditional Graeco-Roman authors describing Jewish customs from the point of view of their traditional religious beliefs.

The fact that Graeco-Roman literature often deals with Jewish customs in such a negative way testifies to the lack of knowledge of its authors. It is no doubt for this reason that Jewish authors did sometimes try to inform a pagan audience as Josephus does in his *Life*, *Against Apion*, the *Jewish War* and his *Jewish Antiquities*. These activities point at the wish to gain acceptance. This is something different, though, from a wish to convert. Evidence for an actively proselytising Jewish mission in the period up to the first century CE is inconclusive.[98] The most probable reason for this is that a Jewish proselytising mission was itself non-existent in the first century CE.

---

[98] *Pace* a.o. Paul W. Barnett, who gives a careful evaluation of the evidence in his 'Jewish mission in the era of the New Testament and the apostle Paul', in: P. Bolt, M. Thompson (eds.), *The Gospel to the Nations. Perspectives on Paul's Mission* (Leicester: Apollos; Downers Grove: Intervarsity, 2000), pp. 263-283, but nevertheless does conclude to 'the missionising by Jews of Gentiles' as a 'fascinating backdrop to the conversion and ministry of Paul' (p. 280).

CHAPTER TWO

THE SPREAD OF PAGAN CULTS
AND PHILOSOPHIES

Having seen that the existence of a Jewish proselytising mission in the
Graeco-Roman period cannot be proven, we should now turn to the pagan
context of early Christianity. Was there any such thing as a proselytising
mission among the Greeks and the Romans?

Anyone dealing with the phenomenon of religious propaganda of
Graeco-Roman cults has first to admit that the propaganda and spread of
these cults essentially differ from that of Judaism since the latter was a
more or less clearly defined phenomenon: notwithstanding the many varieties of Judaisms, its monotheistic tradition formed so strong a religious
core that one must speak of a single religion. Paganism, however, did not
exist as such a single phenomenon.[1] There was a multiplicity of cults,
and most of these cults were connected to specific sites or sanctuaries
with the *polis* as the centre of religious activities.

The spread of Hellenism had great impact upon this traditional Greek
polis-religion,[2] as it also had its influence upon the traditional religions
of the non-Greek areas that were conquered by Alexander. This is probably best witnessed by the growth of the Hellenistic cult of Sarapis as the
interpretatio graeca of the Egyptian gods Osiris and Apis. But apart from
the growing influence of Greek interpretations of traditional deities, the
most important observation on Graeco-Roman religions after Alexander
is that they form a multitude of autonomous cults, not one system. It is
true that this multitude of cults and sanctuaries may be considered as one
polytheistic family of religions, but at the core was the idea of multiplicity. An inhabitant of Ephesus would probably worship Artemis just
as the inhabitants of Delphi would worship Apollo. And yet for both of
them it would be self-evident that the worship of the one god did not

---

[1] Cf. Goodman, *Mission and Conversion*, p. 20: '...paganism was never a single articulate
system of thought; it was defined negatively by the early Church as the religion of all
those inhabitants of their society who were neither Jews nor Christians.'

[2] M.P. Nilsson, *Geschichte der griechischen Religion*.Vol. 2: *Die hellenistische und
römische Zeit* (HAW 5.2; München: Beck, 2nd ed., 1961, ¹1950), p. 30-31.

exclude that of the other. Clea, the person for whom Plutarch wrote his tract on Isis and Osiris, was both a servant of Apollo and an initiate of the cult of Dionysus.[3]

Judaism was different. The God of Judaism demanded sole worship and left no room for other gods. The exclusiveness of the Jewish religion was one of the elements that attracted some pagans and severely shook others. The universal character of the one Jewish God implied that he could make his power felt to each and every human being. It is this monotheistic universalism of the Jewish religion that had great implications for its relationship to pagan cults. Whereas the Jewish God could not accept the reverence of another deity, this exclusive character is absent in the cults of pagan gods.

As was argued in the previous chapter, Judaism did not actively seek proselytes. It did promote the view that its God was the only one, and that others did not matter at all. But this did not imply that pagans were addressed in order to convert them to Judaism. Religious propaganda of the Jews aimed at acceptance by pagans rather than at their conversion.

This chapter will deal with religious propaganda of pagan cults and philosophies. Do we have evidence to label this propaganda as proselytising mission? In looking for an answer to this question one should acknowledge that the material to be considered far outweighs the scope of this book. It is, therefore, not the intention of the present chapter to reconstruct the phenomenon of religious propaganda of pagan cults in great detail. Such treatment of the subject would require a more elaborate presentation of the evidence. What is presented in this chapter is an overall impression based on a number of literary and epigraphic sources.

1. New Cults from the East

The Graeco-Roman period witnessed a great spread of cults from the East. Isis and Sarapis, Meter and Attis, Sabazios, the Most High God, and Mithras gained enormous popularity.[4] Isis especially stood on the brink of becoming the one universally honoured deity of the first and second centuries CE.[5] It is the spread of these new cults that will provide

---

[3] See Plutarch, *De Iside et Osiride* 35 (*Moralia* 364E-F); cf. below, p. 60.
[4] See Nilsson, *Geschichte*, vol. 2, pp. 622-679.
[5] On the cult of Isis see especially F. Dunand, *Le culte d'Isis dans le bassin oriental de la Méditerranée*, 3 vols (EPROER 26; Leiden [etc.]: Brill, 1973).

us with examples of pagan religious propaganda. Later will come the treatment of the more traditional and political cults, and the propaganda by philosophic teachers.

In spite of the fact that these new cults may form the best evidence of pagan religious propaganda, few scholars have explicitly studied the way in which such cults spread. Many students of the subject take a certain missionary character for granted. But the question should be put as to whether this is justified. The spread of the cult of Mithras, for instance, was greatly enhanced by soldiers who had enlisted in the Roman army.[6] This observation often leads to the conclusion that soldiers acted as missionaries on behalf of the cult of Mithras. Yet it is far more likely that its spread was caused by their physical mobility. Soldiers often moved from one part of the empire to another, taking their cult with them. There is thus a direct relation between the spread of a cult and the group of adherents responsible for it. If a cult found its adherents among travellers, we are likely to have located the origin of its spread.[7]

A second element to be considered is the fact already recorded above, that apparently none of these cults was exclusive in its claims. As far as Isis was concerned, it was of great importance that people should revere her, but she was still not considered as the only deity. The effect of this polytheistic context in which the cults of Isis and other deities were propagated is that none of these cults presented itself as the *only* means for salvation. The terminology of 'being saved' and 'salvation' is to be found among the evidence of Graeco-Roman cults, but it lacks the universal, exclusive character it has in early Christian sources.[8] It is for this reason

---

[6] According to M. Clauss, *Cultores Mithrae. Die Anhängerschaft des Mithras-Kultes* (HABES 10; Stuttgart: Steiner, 1992), pp. 267-269, soldiers were largely responsible for the spread of the cult. Yet after they had taken Mithras with them into a new area, the local citizens would soon participate in the cult eventually forming the majority of its adherents. Clauss estimates the percentage of soldiers among the Mithraeans as being 10.6%, but due to their mobility it is this relatively small group of adherents that was largely responsible for the spread of the cult. Cf. p. 254: 'Der Mithras-Kult ist folglich von Italien aus sowohl an den Rhein wie an die Donau gelangt. Es waren in Italien rekrutierte Soldaten, Angehörige des Personals italischer Zollpächter oder sonstige römische Bürger aus dem Mutterland, die den neuen Kult in die Provinzen trugen.'

[7] This view is in accordance with, for instance, La Piana's old theory that groups of immigrants in Rome at first practised their native religion among themselves, only to see their cult naturally extended outside their own group; cf. G. La Piana, 'Foreign Groups in Rome during the First Centuries of the Empire', *HTR* 20 (1927), pp. 183-403, par. IV, pp. 282-320.

[8] It is used for instance for Zeus who was worshipped as Ζεὺς σωτήρ in harbours like Piraeus (cf. Strabo, *Geogr.* IX,1,15). Apollo was sometimes mentioned with the epithet ὁ σῳζῶν; cf. W.H. Buckler, W.M. Calder, C.W.M. Cox, 'Monuments from Iconium, Lycaonia and Isauria', *JRS* 14 (1924), pp. 24-84, esp. p. 28; W.M. Ramsay, 'Lycaonian

that A.D. Nock came to speak of *adherents* of a cult rather than converts.[9]

In what follows the cult of Isis will function as the most important example of the spread of a new cult in the Graeco-Roman period and the conclusions will be extrapolated to a certain degree to other cults.

Isis was originally an Egyptian goddess who was worshipped in the valley of the Nile as the sister and wife of Osiris.[10] The myth recounts in its various versions that the latter was murdered by the anti-god Seth: he dismembered Osiris and spread his parts over the entire country of Egypt. Mourning over her brother and husband, Isis sought for the remnants of his body and collected all but one of them. His penis could not be found and for that reason she made one of clay. Isis then rebuilt and revived Osiris and subsequently gave birth to their son Horus who would eventually kill Seth.

After his conquest of Egypt, Alexander the Great sacrificed to the gods, and Arrian's *Anabasis* states that it was especially Apis that Alexander was interested in.[11] Later, at the founding of Alexandria, Alexander himself conceives the plan of the city and the sanctuaries which were to be erected. These sanctuaries would be dedicated to Greek gods and to Isis: 'he himself marked out where the city's marketplace was to be built, how many temples there were to be and the gods, some Greek, and Isis the Egyptian, for whom they were to be erected, and where the wall was to be built around it' (III,1).[12] Arrian's remark probably indicates that at the time Alexander founded his city on the Nile, Isis was the prime goddess in Egypt.[13] Travelling soldiers and merchants subsequently introduced the cult of Isis in the Graeco-Roman world.[14]

---

and Phrygian Notes', *CIR* 19 (1905), pp. 367-370, states on p. 368 that the use of this epithet for Apollo was 'common in Pisidia and Phrygia'.

[9] A.D. Nock, *Conversion. The Old and the New in Religion from Alexander the Great to Augustine of Hippo* (Oxford: Clarendon, 1933), p. 15: 'Nevertheless, although there was no basis for conversion in these worships, men did adhere to forms other than those which they had known from childhood, and did so as a result of deliberate choice.' – cf. Goodman, *Mission and Conversion*, p. 27.

[10] For a good collection of evidence on Isis, see R. Merkelbach, *Isis Regina – Zeus Sarapis. Die griechisch-ägyptische Religion nach den Quellen dargestellt* (Stuttgard, Leipzig: Teubner, 1995).

[11] Ἐκεῖθεν δὲ διαβὰς τὸν πόρον ἧκεν ἐς Μέμφιν· καὶ θύει ἐκεῖ τοῖς τε ἄλλοις θεοῖς καὶ τῷ Ἄπιδι – '(He) went to Memphis, where he sacrificed to the gods, especially Apis' (*Anabasis* III,1,4; text and translation P.A. Brunt, LCL).

[12] Καὶ αὐτὸς τὰ σημεῖα τῇ πόλει ἔθηκεν, ἵνα τε ἀγορὰν ἐν αὐτῇ δείμασθαι ἔδει καὶ ἱερὰ ὅσα καὶ θεῶν ὧντινων, τῶν μὲν Ἑλληνικῶν, Ἴσιδος δὲ Αἰγυπτίας, καὶ τὸ τεῖχος ᾗ περιβεβλῆσθαι – text and translation P.A. Brunt, LCL.

[13] Had these words reflected the circumstances of Arrian's day rather than those of Alexander's, the reference to Apis would presumably have been to Sarapis – the cult of Sarapis originated in a moulding together of those of Apis and Osiris. In Arrian's day it was Sarapis who was revered, rather than Apis.

[14] See Merkelbach, *Isis-Regina*, pp. 122-130.

Fortunately enough we have some extensive descriptions of the myth and cult of Isis in Plutarch's *De Iside et Osiride*, and in Apuleius' *Metamorphoses* (also known as *The Golden Ass*). Neither of these writings provides us with detailed information on the way in which the cult spread, but they do give some clues. Apparently, processions were an important part of the cult of Isis, as they were of that of Osiris/Sarapis and numerous other gods. In his at times hilarious description of the adventures of his hero Lucius, Apuleius changes to a more serious tone in book 11. There, he pictures Lucius' transformation from being an ass back to his human shape. This transformation coincides with Lucius' initiation into the cult of Isis, which appears to have taken place in three stages. As an upbeat for Lucius' final initiation, Apuleius describes the procession of worshippers of Isis during the spring festival. The procession 'had the air of a costume parade',[15] but was in fact a serious religious act.[16] Processions as these were no doubt intended to show the power of the deity, and as such they had a propagandistic purpose. In showing the living presence of the deity they worshipped, the followers of Isis proclaimed her great might.

It is telling to see how Apuleius refers to Isis in his description of the procession: 'While these amusing delights of the people were appearing all over the place, the procession proper of the Saviour Goddess was on its way.'[17] It is not by accident that Apuleius mentions Isis as *dea sospitatrix*, a goddess who brings salvation. Of course this is exactly what she is about to do for Lucius, and soon he receives his human shape again. The high priest of Isis then welcomes Lucius to his new cult, and states that by joining the worship of Isis people are saved from fate: 'Let her (= blind Fortune; LP) quit now and rage in her wildest frenzy and seek another object for her cruelty. For hostile fate has no power over those whose lives have been claimed by the majesty of our goddess. (...) Now you have been received into the protection of a Fortune who is not blind, but sees, and who illumines the other gods too with the radiance of her light.'[18]

---

[15] E. Ferguson, *Backgrounds of Early Christianity* (Grand Rapids: Eerdmans, 2nd ed., 1993), p. 254.

[16] See the analysis by R. Merkelbach, *Isisfeste in griechisch-römischer Zeit. Daten und Riten* (BKP 5; Meisenheim: Hain, 1963), pp. 39-41.

[17] *Inter has oblectationes ludicras popularium, quae passim vagabantur, iam sospitatricis deae peculiaris pompa moliebatur* – *Metamorphoses* XI,9; text and translation taken from J. Gwyn Griffiths, *Apuleius of Madauros, the Isis-Book (Metamorphoses, Book XI)* (EPROER 29; Leiden: Brill, 1975). On the use of *sospitatrix* as a neologism in stead of *sospita*, see Gwyn Griffiths, *Isis-Book*, p. 59.

[18] *Metamorphoses* XI,15; translation Gwyn Griffiths; *eat nunc* (sc. fortuna; LP) *et summo furore saeviat, et crudelitati suae materiem quaerat aliam: nam in eos quorum sibi vitas*

Evidently her followers considered Isis as the goddess who could reverse fate. Life was thought to be ruled by fate, but those who sought the protection of Isis could escape its power. This has no doubt been an important element in the spread of the cult, as it may have been in that of many others. People lived in great fear of fate. Amulets, magic spells, sacrifices – anything was helpful as long as it could protect man against the power of *fortuna* or *fatum*. The promise that the goddess would give exactly this protection must have greatly attracted possible adherents.

A strong example of this element within the cult of Isis is found in the aretalogy from Kyme: ἐγὼ τὸ ἱμαρμένον νικῶ, ἐμοῦ τὸ εἱμαρμένον ἀκούει ('I overcome Fate, Fate harkens to me').[19] The prime element in the worship of Isis was therefore the belief that she saved people from all kinds of dangers. In fact, Isis was even worshipped as the *pansoteira*.[20] Her followers thus regarded her as a safeguard against fate.[21]

That Isis was proclaimed as a saviour goddess, at least at public festivals, is not a single, exclusive phenomenon: Isis was not the only deity who attracted her worshippers by processions and promises of salvation. Public ceremonies formed an important element in many popular cults.[22] Plutarch gives us a description of a procession as proof of his claim that Osiris/Sarapis is the same deity as Dionysus/Bacchus:

> 'That Osiris is identical with Dionysus who could more fittingly know than yourself, Clea? For you are at the head of the inspired maidens of Delphi, and have been consecrated by your father and mother in the holy rites of Osiris. If, however, for the benefit of others it is needful to adduce proof of this identity, let us leave undisturbed what may not be told, but the public ceremonies which the priests perform in the burial of Apis, when they convey his body on an improvised bier, do not in any way come short of a Bacchic procession; for they fasten skins of fawns about themselves, and carry Bacchic wands and indulge in

---

in servitium deae nostrae maiestas vindicavit, non habet locum casus infestus. (...)
In tutetelam iam receptus es Fortunae, sed videntis, quae suae lucis splendore ceteros etiam deos illuminat.

[19] Quoted in H.S. Versnel, *Inconsistencies in Greek and Roman Religion I: Ter Unus. Isis, Dionysos, Hermes, Three Studies in Henotheism* (SGRR 6; Leiden, New York, København, Köln: Brill, 1990), pp. 44-45. For the text of the aretalogy of Kyme, see A. Salac, 'Inscriptions de Kymé d'Eolide', *BCH* 51 (1927), 378-383, and the editions mentioned by Versnel, p. 41, n. 6, and p. 44, n. 14.

[20] Versnel, *Ter Unus*, p. 45; see also Merkelbach, *Isis Regina* §117, pp. 66-67, and §170, p. 98.

[21] Merkelbach, *Isis Regina* §499, pp. 281-282.

[22] For a survey of public ceremonies in pagan religions, see H.H. Scullard, *Festivals and Ceremonies of the Roman Republic* (London: Thames & Hudson, 1981).

shoutings and movements exactly as do those who are under the spell of the Dionysiac ecstasies.'[23]

The fact that the processions of Osiris are highly comparable to those of Dionysus proves for Plutarch that the two deities are identical. Plutarch had already identified Osiris/Sarapis as Pluto/Hades (*De Iside et Osiride* 28 = *Moralia* 361F-362B), and it is difficult to escape the impression that the comparison he makes between the various gods reflects his own philosophical point of view rather than the popular beliefs in these deities.

Be this as it may, Plutarch and Apuleius provide us with the evidence that the cults of Isis and Osiris/Sarapis manifested themselves in public ceremonies and, for instance, processions. It is on these occasions that the power of the deity was proclaimed for all to hear. This is a clear form of religious, i.e. cultic propaganda, but quite different from the way in which Paul propagated his Christian message.[24] To put the differences in very general terms: as far as we can discern, Paul did not aim at large public meetings as manifestations of the power of the deity. Also his proclamation did not focus on the liberation from fate, but rather on salvation at the ultimate intervention of the one God who – Paul thought – was about to judge the entire earth. Furthermore, a choice in favour of Isis or any other deity within the polytheistic framework did not entail a negation of all other gods, as Paul demanded from his believers.[25]

It is a matter for further study whether the worship of Isis and Osiris/Sarapis spread through active propaganda of one kind or another, or through a 'natural' progression. It has been stated that Isis worship was actively promoted by missionising priests,[26] but the nature of this

---

[23] Ὅτι μὲν οὖν ὁ αὐτός ἐστι Διονύσῳ τίνα μᾶλλον ἢ σε γινώσκειν, ὦ Κλέα, δὴ προσῆκόν ἐστιν, ἀρχηίδα μεν οὖσαν ἐν Δελφοῖς τῶν Θυιάδων, τοῖς δ᾽ Ὀσιριακοῖς καθωσιωμένην ἱεροῖς ἀπὸ πατρὸς καὶ μητρός· εἰ δὲ τῶν ἄλλων ἕνεκα δεῖ μαρτύρια παραθέσθαι, τὰ μὲν ἀπόρρητα κατὰ χώραν ἐῶμεν, ἃ δ᾽ ἐμφανῶς δρῶσι θάπτοντες τὸν Ἆπιν οἱ ἱερεῖς, ὅταν παρακομίζωσιν ἐπὶ σχεδίας τὸ σῶμα, βακχείας οὐδὲν ἀποδεῖ. καὶ γὰρ νεβρίδας περικαθάπτονται καὶ θύρσους φοροῦσι, καὶ βοαῖς χρῶνται καὶ κινήσεσιν ὥσπερ οἱ κάτοχοι τοῖς περὶ τὸν Διόνυσον ὀργιασμοῖς – *De Iside et Osiride* 35 (*Moralia* 364 E-F); translation by F.C. Babbitt, LCL.

[24] See e.g. F. Dunand, *Isis. Mère des Dieux* (Paris: Errance, 2000), pp. 65-79. According to Dunand there definitely was a more or less organised form of cultic propaganda, but it did not aim at 'conversion'.

[25] Dunand, *Mère des Dieux*, p. 65: '(...) il ne s'agit en aucune manière de "convertir", c'est-à-dire de faire prévaloir, par la persuasion ou par la force, ses dieux sur les dieux de l'autre.'

[26] See E.R. Witt, *Isis in the Ancient World* (London: Thames & Hudson; 1997), p. 20 [= *Isis in the Graeco-Roman World* (Ithaca: Cornell University Press, 1971)]: 'Her priests

alleged mission remains in darkness. In the case of Osiris/Sarapis it is argued that the cult actively sought converts and as evidence for this view, reference is made to the founding of a Sarapis temple at the island of Delos in the early third century BCE by the Egyptian priest Apollonios.[27] The founding story, however, is so clearly legendary in character – the command to build a new temple was given by the god in a dream – that the true way in which the cult spread is not discernible from the inscriptions. In reconstruction probably the safest interpretation is that the adherents to the cult moved to Delos and there, due to its growth, found the need to organise their cult on new ground.[28]

Here we probably have one of the most important elements in the spread of various new cults in the Graeco-Roman period. Adherents to a cult moved from one place to another, bringing their cult with them. The conquest of the Mediterranean area by Alexander had a great impact on politics and economic matters, mainly because the unification of this large empire under one rule opened up the existing boundaries for travellers and tradesmen. The wide spread use of the Greek language throughout Alexander's empire, which continued after his death, formed an important *conditio sine qua non* for the intensification of contacts between tradesmen of the various parts of the area now united by one *lingua franca*. Thus, the Hellenistic age provided a fine infrastructure for the intense exchange of goods and ideas, which was later even improved on by the Roman conquest of the East. It is only a slight exaggeration to say that the military movement towards the East (and South) resulted in an economic movement towards the West. In this economic movement of tradesmen and politicians, religion came along as an important mark of identity. This process was even enforced in the beginning of the imperial age.

What seem to have been an important element in the spread of the cults of Isis and Osiris/Sarapis and also an active force in the spread of

were dedicated missionaries like soldiers crusading on hallowed service.' Apparently Witt bases his metaphor on Apuleius, *Metamorphoses* XI,15 ('*da nomen sanctae huic militiae*'). The use of military terminology, however, does not prove any missionary zeal. For this, see J. Gwyn Griffiths, *Isis-Book*, pp. 254-255, who points at Mithraism (*miles* as the third grade of initiate) and Christianity (2 Tim 2,3) as other examples of religious, metaphoric use of military terminology. Versnel, *Ter Unus*, p. 40, speaks of the 'missionary zeal of her priests'.

[27] See Nock, *Conversion*, pp. 51-54.

[28] Nock, *Conversion*, p. 52: 'Here we have a small cultus in an alien land, brought by an individual who at first conducts worship in hired quarters. Then the cult grows sufficiently to need an independent temple.'

other mystery cults were votive offerings.[29] This custom enhanced the popularity of deities who took care of their adherents. According to W. Burkert, the votive character of the worship of, for instance, Meter, Isis, and Mithras is telling: 'All these gods are worshiped in a search for "salvation", which takes many forms.'[30] Even if Isis is most important as the giver of life and a healer, her cult may, according to Burkert, still be compared to votive religion, since the hopes and wishes expressed are comparable.[31] Votive offerings, as tokens of gratitude towards a deity, helped enhance its popularity since they pointed out how good a god was to his adherents. Furthermore, they would be seen by non-adherents to the cult who were thus informed on the character of the god or goddess. It is therefore safe to assume a certain propagandistic function for these votive offerings.

From the above survey, fragmentary as it may be, the conclusion should be drawn that there were two important elements in the spread of religious cults. Firstly, the attraction of their promised liberation from fate witnessed as true by, for instance, votive offerings, and secondly, the fact that travellers took these cults along on their journeys through the Mediterranean region. Most likely priests did indeed propagate their cult at public festivals and other occasions. But nevertheless there is no evidence that this activity resulted from the view that only the adherents of their own cult would be saved. These conclusions may, *mutatis mutandis*, be extrapolated for the cults of the Most High God and other oriental deities. It is important to note that the element of exclusiveness is lacking. The healing character of, for instance, Isis does not prevent her worshippers from adhering to Asclepius as well.

This last observation brings to mind another remark by Burkert, viz. that entry into the cult of Isis did not mean a radical break with the former way of life in that the new life is a substitute for the old: it is rather a 'prolongation'.[32] One could adhere to a cult as a 'useful supplement'.[33] A careful study of the subject shows that most worshippers of Isis did

---

[29] W. Burkert, *Ancient Mystery Cults* (Cambridge Mass., London: Harvard University Press; 1987), p. 15: 'the spreading of the so-called Oriental mystery religions occurred primarily in the form of votive religion' (see also Versnel, *Ter Unus*, p. 45).

[30] Burkert, *Ancient Mystery Cults*, p. 15.

[31] 'Salvation of this kind, as guaranteed by the mysteries of Isis, is more radical and, it is hoped, more permanent than other experiences of *soteria*, but it still stays on the same level as the hopes expressed in votive religion.' – cf. Burkert, *Ancient Mystery Cults*, p. 18.

[32] Burkert, *Ancient Mystery Cults*, p. 18.

[33] Nock, *Conversion*, p. 7; Burkert, *Ancient Mystery Cults*, p. 14.

indeed also worship, for instance, Sarapis, Anubis, Harpocrates or yet another deity.[34] This situation radically differs from that of the first Christians. Paul is very explicit in his letter to the Thessalonians in stating that they had 'turned away from the idols' (1 Thess 1,10). For Paul the worship of Jesus Christ did imply a radical break with all other cults, and in this respect his stance is fully in line with the Jewish view that only the one God may be worshipped.

2. Asclepius

The more traditional Greek and Roman cults were considerably less in need of religious propaganda. Their centres of worship were located in old sanctuaries and the reputation of many of these was firmly established. Much of what was said in the previous section could be repeated here. The polytheistic context of these cults entailed people worshipping a number of gods either simultaneously or in turn.

Notwithstanding the strong relation of the traditional cults of Apollo, Athena, Zeus, and many others of the Homeric and Hesiodic pantheon, to the sanctuaries where these gods were traditionally worshipped, there were certain cults that spread over a wide region. A striking example of this kind is provided by the worship of Asclepius. This cult spread rapidly from its various sanctuaries at Epidauros, on the island of Kos, Pergamum, and Athens, Corinth and other cities. Apparently the priests of Epidauros had already founded related cult-centres in other places in the fifth century BCE, and the popularity of this deity increased to such an extent that at the beginning of the Common Era there were hundreds of sanctuaries of Asclepius.[35] This great number is interpreted by H. Koester as evidence of the propagandistic zeal of the cult. According to him, the multitude of sanctuaries is 'striking proof for the successful propaganda of Epidauros, Kos, and other leading Asklepieia. The expansion of this cult was the result of methodical propaganda aided, no doubt, by favorable circumstances rooted in the general religious mood of the time.'[36]

---

[34] Cf. F. Mora, *Prosopografia isiaca. Vol. 2: Prosopografia storica e statistica del culto isiaco* (EPROER 113; Leiden, København, Köln: Brill, 1990), pp. 30-32.

[35] H. Koester, *Introduction to the New Testament, volume 1: History, Culture, and Religion of the Hellenistic Age* (New York, Berlin: W. de Gruyter, 1995), p. 165, speaks of 300 sanctuaries; E. Thrämer mentions 186 centres in Pauly-Wissowa, II, cols. 1662-1677, and speaks of a number of 410 in ERE, VI, p. 550.

[36] Koester, *Introduction*, p. 165.

The great ease with which methodical propaganda of Epidauros is assumed by Koester is striking. There are numerous votaries dedicated to Asclepius that describe a cure received from this deity. These votaries may have been an important element in the spread of the cult. But methodical propaganda in order to spread the cult? It is safer to regard the attractiveness of the cult of Asclepius as the main reason for its dissemination. People worshipped Asclepius as the healing deity. Therefore, it is reasonable to assume that the wish of so many people to be cured of their illness caused a certain readiness to worship the healing god. Since the Asklepieion at Epidauros was a luxurious site with 160 rooms for guests, it attracted great crowds in the ancient days.[37] After their visit to the sanctuary they took its fame home along with them. Especially if someone had indeed been cured the news would spread rapidly.

Koester's view on the propaganda of the Asclepius cult is not new. It is also found in, for instance, M. Nilsson's classic volumes on Greek religion. In fact, Nilsson describes the spread of the cult as follows:

> 'Epidauros hat aber nicht nur Propaganda, sondern auch Mission getrieben und eine Reihe von Filialen gegründet. Das fing früh, schon im fünften Jahrhundert, an; die Wunderberichte, welche den Höhepunkt dieses Treibens bezeichnen, gehören jedoch dem Anfang der hellenistischen Zeit an. Wenn Mission und Propaganda immer als für die orientalischen Kulte eigentümlich hingestellt werden, so ist demgegenüber zo betonen, daß sie schon früh in einem Kulte erscheinen, in dem keine Spuren von orientalischem Einfluß vorhanden sind.'[38]

For the present enquiry it is of great importance to be very careful in our terminology. It is true that the cult of Asclepius expanded from Epidauros to other sanctuaries. And it may even be true, that this was initiated by the priests from Epidauros. But this does not mean that such a phenomenon may be regarded as an example of 'mission'. There is no evidence that Asclepius priests either urged people to change their ways to conform to the code of the adherents of Asclepius, or to regard their entry into the group of the faithful as a break with their former life.

If the spread of Asclepius may not be seen as being caused by missionary activities, and perhaps not even by any 'methodical propaganda', how should this spread then be interpreted? Most likely we should speak of a gradual expansion of the cult from its centre at Epidauros to a large

---

[37] See Koester, *Introduction*, p. 167.
[38] Nilsson, *Geschichte*, vol. 2, p. 225; cf. vol. 1, 2nd ed., p. 806.

number of sanctuaries throughout the Graeco-Roman world. In their presentation and interpretation of the evidence on Asclepius, E.J. and L. Edelstein point to two important moments in the process of the cult's spread, viz. Asclepius' introduction in Athens (6th cent. BCE), and that in Rome (ca. 291 BCE).[39] Especially the latter event is important, since Asclepius was apparently one of the first non-Roman deities to be accepted in Rome.[40] The wish to worship a healing deity must have been great and thus the circumstances for the spread of the cult were favourable. But this does not answer the question: by what means did the cult spread?

In one of his descriptions of the cult of Asclepius, Pausanias gives what is probably the solution to the problem. First, he writes that Epidauros did indeed form the original sanctuary where 'the most famous sanctuaries of Asclepius had their origins'.[41] Then he continues with an account of how other sanctuaries were founded from Epidauros, giving the example of the Asklepieion at Pergamum:

> 'Again, when Archias, son of Aristaechmus, was healed in Epidauria after spraining himself while hunting about Pindasus, he brought the god to Pergamum.'[42]

The person described here, Archias, had apparently travelled to Epidauros hoping to be cured. After this had indeed happened, he went back to his hometown Pergamum and took Asclepius along with him. This kind of travelling was of course only for the wealthy. But it is exactly these rich visitors to Epidauros, travelling a long way to be cured, who were capable of founding a new sanctuary in response to their being healed. It thus appears that the spread of Asclepius is indeed to be understood from this perspective rather than from the idea of a methodical propaganda, or even mission. A visitor healed at an Asklepieion would of course honour the god who had cured him and would proclaim the power of this god. Next to that, the cult centres were evidently ready to proclaim their importance. But this type of propaganda can certainly not be labelled as

---

[39] E.J. Edelstein, L. Edelstein, *Asclepius, A Collection and Interpretation of the Testimonies* (TD 2; Baltimore: John Hopkins Press, 1945 = repr. 1998), 2 vols. For the description of the Epidaurean origin of the cult, and its spread, see vol. 2, pp. 238-255.

[40] The erection of two Asclepius temples in Rome is described by Ovid, *Fasti* I, 290-294 – cf. Edelstein, *Asclepius*, vol. 1, T. 855.

[41] Pausanias, *Graeciae Descriptio* II,26,8: τὰ γὰρ Ἀσκληπιεῖα εὑρίσκω τὰ ἐπιφανέστατα γεγονότα ἐξ Ἐπιδαύρου; cf. Edelstein, *Asclepius*, vol. 1, T. 709.

[42] Τοῦτο δὲ Ἀρχίας ὁ Ἀρισταίχμου τὸ συμβὰν σπάσμα θηρεύοντί οἱ περὶ τὸν πίνδασον ἰαθεὶς ἐν Ἐπιδαυρίᾳ, τὸν θεὸν ἐπηγάγετο ἐς Πέργαμον; cf. Edelstein, *Asclepius*, vol. 1, T. 709.

'missionary zeal'. It would be better, in the case of Asclepius, to speak of *cultic propaganda* instead of confusing this action with proselytising mission.

3. The Imperial Cult

According to Goodman the only pagan cult that was more or less proselytising by nature was the imperial cult.[43] Evidence shows that after the formal establishment of the state cult in Rome by Augustus in April of the year 28 BCE,[44] its worship spread rapidly throughout the empire. It was accomplished almost immediately in the East, and from August 1, 12 BCE onward also in the West.[45] Although it is evident that the reasons for promoting this cult were in part of a political nature,[46] the religious element in its worship should not be underestimated. The fact that Augustus had decreed that the *genius* of the emperor should be worshipped at the *lararium* of each family shows how the state cult effectively entered the houses of Roman citizens.[47]

In his study of the imperial cult in Asia Minor, S.R.F. Price has argued that it is the relationship between the organised communities in which a cult was rooted and Rome that made the difference concerning local cults.[48] In a careful consideration of the position of the imperial cult, Price concludes that this cult 'was the outgrowth of a complex, urban culture, and was constantly sustained by a variety of local forces (...). The cult became one of the major contexts in which the competitive spirit of the

---

[43] Goodman, *Mission and Conversion*, pp. 30-32. For literature on the emperor cult, see P. Herz, 'Bibliografie zum römischen Kaiserkult (1955-1975)', in: W. Haase (ed.), *ANRW 2 Prinzipat*, 16/2, pp. 833-910.

[44] Cf. Ovid, *Fasti* IV,949-954; see also *Fasti* III,421-422; L. Ross Taylor, *The Divinity of the Roman Emperor* (Middletown, Connecticut: American Philological Association, 1931), p. 184.

[45] On that date the state altar was dedicated by Drusus in Lugdunum; cf. D. Fishwick, 'The Development of Provincial Ruler Worship in the Western Roman Empire', in: W. Haase (ed.), *ANRW 2 Prinzipat* 16/2, pp. 1201-1253, esp. p. 1204.

[46] See Ross Taylor, *Divinity*, p. 205. The emperor cult was not exactly the only cult with political dimensions. Since the reform of Augustus, for instance, 'the official cult of the Capitoline triad, Jupiter, Juno, and Minerva, more and more assumed a highly political significance.' – La Piana, 'Foreign Groups', p. 282.

[47] See B. Gladigow, 'Roman Religion', in: *ABD* vol. 5, pp. 809-816, p. 811: 'The consistent separation of household and public cult was blurred by an innovation of Augustus, which ordained that the genius of the emperor be venerated between the two *lares* in the *compita larum*.'

[48] S.R.F. Price, *Rituals and Power. The Roman Imperial Cult in Asia Minor* (Cambridge, London [etc.]: Cambridge University Press, 1984), ch. 4, esp. p. 98.

local elites was worked out; it formed one of a range of civic provisions by which the prestige of the city was measured; it shared in the dominance of Greek culture as a whole. The hegemonial role of this culture over local culture was a product of the power of the cities. Access to this culture was the crucial path for advancement both for individuals and for communities.'[49] Price gives a balanced view of the social and religious position of the imperial cult within the context of Graeco-Roman Asia Minor. He pictures the cult within its social and political contexts, but unfortunately hardly mentions the manner of its spread at all.

Regarding the dissemination of the imperial cult there are probably two decisive elements. Firstly, there is the main cult centre, which is also an object of veneration: Rome. It is obvious that the imperial cult grew from a mixture of politics and religion. The dissemination of the imperial power partially coincided with the spread of the cult. Secondly, there is the ambition of the cities that sought the favour of Rome. By venerating the emperor and the city of Rome, the *dea Roma*, a city – or rather: the elite of a city – showed its loyalty to the emperor. In return for this loyalty favours might be expected. An important element within the spread of the imperial cult, therefore, is a tangible attitude of *do ut des*.[50]

In an important article of 1973 E. Bickerman has argued that there was in fact not one universal imperial cult, but a multitude of cults.[51] In his view all the various cults of the emperor or the *dea Roma* were coloured by their local settings. Hence, they should be regarded primarily as local phenomena. The important difference between the Roman veneration of the emperor and that outside Rome was, according to Bickerman, that within Roman religion the emperor became recognised as a deity only after his death,[52] whereas outside Rome he was already venerated as a god during his lifetime. Although Bickerman's view is not shared by all, it is important. It underlines the fact that the imperial cult was based on a kind of reciprocity: the Roman authorities propagated the cult as a means of imperial propaganda, but local populations responded to that by establishing their own specific forms of this cult.

---

[49] Price, *Rituals and Power*, p. 100.

[50] See also L.J. Lietaert Peerbolte, 'To Worship the Beast. The Revelation of John and the Imperial Cult in Asia Minor', in: M. Labahn, J. Zangenberg (eds.), *Zwischen den Reichen. Neues Testament und Römische Herrschaft* (TANZ 36; Tübingen, Basel: Francke, 2002), pp. 239-259.

[51] E. Bickerman, 'Consecratio', in W. den Boer (ed.), *Le culte des souverains dans l'empire romain* (EAC 19; Geneva: Fondation Hardt, 1973), pp. 3-25; cf. p. 9: 'Thus, a universal cult of the ruler did not exist in the Roman Empire.'

[52] Bickerman, 'Consecratio', pp. 9-10.

If the imperial cult is to be regarded from the perspective of comprising a variety of different cults, the lack of universal organisation corresponds to that of the Isis cults (cf. above, pp. 57-64). The same observation is valid for this multiplicity of imperial cults as was made above for the worship of Isis: the polytheistic framework within which the cult functioned prevented the adherents of the cult from proclaiming this specific deity as the one universal god. Even though the power of the Roman emperor was enormous, he was not, as was the God of Judaism, proclaimed as the one universal god. Furthermore, the spread of the emperor cult should be interpreted as an attempt by Rome to establish its power, and, by cities outside Rome, to gain imperial favours.[53] The Roman emperor was venerated because he brought peace, stability, and prosperity, and probably most of all because he could help Roman citizens in climbing the professional ladder. But unlike, for instance, Isis the emperor could not reverse fate. Furthermore, Roman religion was a matter of paying honours and doing what one was obliged to do, rather than of personal devotion.[54] This means that the imperial cult does not provide us with a clear example for the spread of the early Christian movement either. We will have to turn elsewhere in order to find a type of propaganda that may have influenced the early Christians in general and Paul in particular.

4. Apollonius of Tyana

In book 39 of his *Ab urbe condita*, Livy describes the Bacchanalian uproar in Rome in 136 BCE. The rapid spread of the worship of Dionysus in Rome was apparently ushered in by the teaching of a single follower of Greek descent. Livy pictures the man as a charlatan and compares him to philosophers who apparently taught the people by publicly proclaiming their views. Livy evidently had a negative regard for such philosophers, but considers the nameless Greek Bacchant as being even worse:

---

[53] La Piana, 'Foreign Groups', pp. 283-284: 'Detailed analysis of the historical evidence, especially of the abundant epigraphic material, has revealed that in the western provinces of the empire, the cult of Rome and of the emperors was practised mainly by the provincial aristocracy, by officials of the administration and army, and by the municipal bourgeoisie, all persons who in general possessed Roman citizenship and were eager to fill public office and acquire titles of honor and social distinction.'

[54] Bickerman, 'Consecratio', pp. 11-14; cf. p. 11: 'What we call religion is *religio animi*, as Augustinus says.' See also A.D. Nock, 'Religious Developments from the Close of the Republic to the Reign of Nero', ch. 15 in: *The Cambridge Ancient History* vol. X (Cambridge: University Press, 1934), pp. 465-511, who stresses the fact that Roman religion was a matter of civic duties rather than of personal devotion (p. 465).

'A nameless Greek came first to Etruria, possessed of none of those many arts which the Greek people, supreme as it is in learning, brought to us in numbers for the cultivation of mind and body, but a dabbler in sacrifices and a fortune-teller; nor was he one who, by frankly disclosing his creed and publicly proclaiming both his profession and his system, filled minds with error, but a priest of secret rites performed at night.'[55]

It is clear that Livy is well acquainted with travelling philosophers who brought their teachings to market-squares or other public places. Livy's example is important for our subject, because it shows two things. Firstly, he shows us that the worship of Bacchus was introduced by a single Greek who had probably brought his own religion along with him when coming to Rome, and subsequently found success in seeking fellow-worshippers. Secondly, Livy is a witness to the phenomenon of travelling philosophers proclaiming their views. It is this second point that is of great interest here.

A striking example of a travelling philosopher who made a great impact on his followers is Apollonius of Tyana.[56] Apparently Apollonius was a Pythagorean philosopher who wandered from Europe to India and back during the first century CE, absorbing the wisdom he encountered as well as teaching his views to those he met. The parallel with Jesus has already been noted in ancient times.[57] Indeed the account Flavius Philostratus gives of his life describes a number of miraculous events, including the resurrection of a girl who had died at the hour of her marriage (*Vit.Ap.* IV,45), and the prediction of the way in which the emperor Titus would die (VI, 32). Also Apollonius' birth and death are said to have been surrounded by miraculous events (cf. I,4-5; VIII,30-31).

Even though Philostratus' narrative dates to the third century and is therefore historically anything but reliable, his description of Apollonius does give us a view of the world Paul lived in. Apollonius' way of

---

[55] Livy, *Ab urbe condita* XXXIX, 8, 3-4: *Graecus ignobilis in Etruriam primum venit nulla cum arte earum, quas multas ad animorum corporumque cultum nobis eruditissima omnium gens invexit, sacrificulus et vates; nec is qui aperta religione, propalam et quaestum et disciplinam profitendo, animos errore imbueret, sed occultorum et nocturnorum antistes sacrorum.* Text and translation E.T. Sage, in LCL.

[56] F.C. Baur noted the remarkable similarities between Apollonius and Jesus: see his *Apollonius von Tyana und Christus. Ein Beitrag zur Religionsgeschichte der ersten Jahrhunderte nach Christus* (Hildesheim: Olms, 1966 = Leipzig 1876). For more recent discussions of Apollonius, see G. Petzke, *Die Traditionen über Apollonius von Tyana und das Neue Testament* (SCHNT 1; Leiden [etc.]: Brill, 1970), and M. Dzielska, *Apollonius of Tyana in Legend and History* (PRSA 10; Roma: Bretschneider, 1986).

[57] The parallel has apparently been used by Hierocles to argue that Jesus was no special man; cf. *The Treatise of Eusebius* in the LCL edition of Philostratus, *Vita Apollonii*, vol. 2, pp. 484-605.

teaching, for instance, shows some remarkable similarities to Paul's. Apollonius was educated in Tarsus, Paul's place of birth, and became devoted to the teaching of Pythagoras. Just like Paul, Apollonius had a clear message: he taught a strict abstinence from all luxury and from the eating of animal flesh, that the soul was immortal, and insisted on the cessation of animal sacrifices in the sanctuaries he visited. Just like Paul, Apollonius met with considerable opposition to his views; he was arrested and jailed a number of times but, according to Philostratus' account, always came out a winner. Finally, just like Paul, Apollonius visited a town, stayed for some time and then moved on.[58] In the period after Apollonius' death a number of sanctuaries were kept as centres of worship in Apollonius' fashion. He even appears to have founded a philosophical school at Ephesus and several letters have been preserved bearing his name.[59] All this forms an important parallel to the ministry of Paul. Apparently a philosopher could stroll through the country bringing his message to the various towns he visited. The example given by Apollonius points out that Paul's approach was not entirely unique. Even though Philostratus' account is coloured by events and developments dating to the period after Apollonius' death, it is important to note the similarities between Paul and this third-century perception of another first-century preacher.

5. Alexander of Abonouteichos

The pupil of a pupil of Apollonius, Alexander of Abonouteichos, gives a quite different example of religious propaganda. Alexander founded a sanctuary of Asclepius in the town of Abonouteichos and sent out messengers to attract the crowds. The account given by Lucian in his *Alexander* is bitingly sarcastic and utterly crushes Alexander's credibility. Nevertheless epigraphic material and coins prove that his story was not made up.[60]

---

[58] The places Apollonius apparently visited are too many to sum up here. He starts (Book I) with a visit to Pamphylia and Cilicia (I,15), and Antioch in Syria (I,16), and makes a journey to India during which he visits Nineveh (I,19), Ctesiphon (I,21), and Babylon (I,21). In Books II and III his journey to and subsequent stay in India are described, as well as his return to Ionia. After that, Apollonius continues to visit numerous towns. Among them are for instance Athens (IV,17), Alexandria (V,24), and Rome (IV,39).

[59] See R.J. Penella, *The Letters of Apollonius of Tyana. A Critical Text with Prolegomena, Translation and Commentary* (MS 56; Leiden [etc.]: Brill, 1979).

[60] See U. Victor, *Lukian von Samosata: Alexandros oder der Lügenprophet* (RGRW 132; Leiden, New York, Köln: Brill, 1997), pp. 1-26. See especially the pictures 1-5 of a statue, an amulet, and coins that depict Glycon/Asclepius in a manner confirming Lucian's description.

The sarcasm of Lucian's account diminishes its credibility, but still the treatise does give some interesting information on the methods of propaganda by which the cult's fame spread. In Lucian's version Alexander had set up the oracle of Glycon, grandson of Zeus and newborn Asclepius, for the sake of material gain. According to Lucian, Alexander deceived simple-minded believers by his sanctuary:

> 'For some days he remained at home, expecting what actually happened – that as the news spread, crowds of Paphlagonians would come running in. When the city had become over-full of people, all of them already bereft of their brains and sense, and not in the least like bread-eating humans, but different from beasts of the field only in their looks, he seated himself on a couch in a certain chamber, clothed in apparel well suited to a god, and took into his bosom his Asclepius from Pella, who, as I have said, was of uncommon size and beauty. Coiling him about his neck, and letting the tail, which was long, stream over his lap and drag part of its length on the floor, he concealed only the head by holding it under his arm – the creature would submit to anything – and showed the linen head at one side of his own beard, as if it certainly belonged to the creature that was in view.'[61]

In this fake oracular setting Alexander gave the deity's advice to those who paid for it, and he did this in such a shrewd way that he convinced many people. Lucian was obviously not one of them:

> 'A price had been fixed for each oracle, a drachma and two obols. Do not think that it was low, my friend, or that the revenue from this source was scanty! He gleaned as much as seventy or eighty thousand a year, since men were so greedy as to send in ten and fifteen questions each.'[62]

Thus Alexander's oracles became big business:

> 'What he received he did not use for himself alone nor treasure up to make himself rich, but since he had many men about him by this time as assistants, servants, collectors of information, writers of oracles, custodians of oracles, clerks, sealers, and expounders, he divided with all, giving each one what was proportionate to his worth.'[63]

Whereas the sanctuary of Glycon had at first attracted people of its own accord,[64] Alexander now sent his envoys abroad 'to create rumours in the

---

[61] Translation LCL, *Alexander*, 15.
[62] Translation LCL, *Alexander*, 23.
[63] Ibid.
[64] *Alexander* 18: 'Little by little, Bithynia, Galatia, and Thrace came pouring in, for everyone who carried the news very likely said that he not only had seen the god born but had subsequently touched him, after he had grown very great in a short time and had a face that looked like a man's.'

different nations in regard to the oracle and to say that he made predictions, discovered fugitive slaves, detected thieves and robbers, caused treasures to be dug up, healed the sick, and in some cases had actually raised the dead.'[65]

The example of Alexander of Abonouteichos provides us with evidence for two kinds of religious propaganda, viz. the spread of the cult's fame through rumours, and the sending of envoys who were to promote the cult abroad. Although it is not explicitly stated that these envoys were paid to proclaim their message, the implication is evident. In any case they were sent out to spread lies on behalf of Alexander's cult. In Lucian's description it appears that the first form of propaganda was more or less natural: a new sanctuary emerges, and its fame spreads over the entire surrounding region. This type of propaganda can be compared to what happens when the Holy Virgin Mary appears in the refrigerator of a small-town supermarket: as soon as people hear about it, they want to visit this new holy place.[66]

Lucian, however, apparently considered the second type of propaganda, less normal. The emphatic ἤδη with which he introduces the mention of the envoys who went abroad to present the cult to new believers, betrays Lucian's indignation. Since this indignation is obviously directed at the fact that these envoys purposely went out to proclaim a false cult, and not at the fact of their being sent out as such, we cannot draw any firm conclusion as to whether this sending of envoys was a customary habit. It is, however, tempting to think of it as an exception, since Lucian does not mention the fact that they were paid. For him, his rather dry description of the event is already example enough of the low character of Alexander.

6. The Philosophers

The two examples discussed in the previous sections, those of Apollonius and Alexander, show us two opposing religious attitudes. Alexander on

---

[65] *Alexander* 24.

[66] A report of such an event was given by the *Chicago Daily Herald* on May 29, 1998: 'People are flocking to a supermarket in Jersey City, N.J., after a vision of the Virgin Mary appeared on a freezer door. The image is saidette of a woman in a hooded garment. Witnesses said it appeared for about four days and then faded. Hundreds of religious pilgrims have left candles, notes and flowers in honor of the vision.' See also the *Orange County Register* of May 19, 1998. These articles were brought to the author's attention by the kind co-operation of mr. J.W.E. Metselaar.

the one hand reflects the 'cultic attitude', in that he establishes a sanctuary at a certain place from where its fame subsequently spreads. The movement is towards the cult centre – believers have to visit the sanctuary themselves. Apollonius, on the other hand, is more an example of the 'instructive attitude': his aim is to teach people, and he moves around doing so. Here the movement is the reverse. The teacher visits his pupils and instructs them.

Already in 1912 P. Wendland has argued that philosophical propaganda had great impact on the way in which Christian preachers brought their message.[67] Yet in Wendland's view the influence of philosophical propaganda can be discerned only at the second stage of Christian teaching. The prime influences from which it originated, in Wendland's view, are teachings in the synagogue and prophetic enthusiasm.[68] Philosophical propaganda would have become influential only after the growth of Christian mission. Today, Wendland's reconstruction appears somewhat dated in that it is too schematic. A recent, and refined, restatement of his view however is given by A.J. Malherbe, first in a number of articles, and then in a summary and expansion of these articles in 1987: *Paul and the Thessalonians*. In this monograph Malherbe pictures Paul as being influenced to a high degree by the tradition of Cynic philosophy: 'We have seen that in many respects Paul's methods had their counterparts in those of the philosophers.'[69]

If we look for similarities between Paul and (Cynic) philosophers with regard to Paul's views, there are many interesting parallels. Epictetus, for instance, speaks of the authority of the philosopher as a divine messenger who has been sent by God to instruct people concerning good and evil (*Diss.* III,22,23).[70] This view of the philosopher's task more or less resembles Paul's view of himself as an envoy sent by God to proclaim the gospel (cf. below, pp. 206-208). Many other parallels can be found.[71] Yet with regard to the present subject, it is of interest to search for the spe-

---

[67] P. Wendland, *Die Hellenistisch-Römische Kultur in ihren Beziehungen zum Judentum und Christentum* (HNT 2; Tübingen: Mohr, 1912, 4th. ed. 1972), pp. 92-93: 'Wirksamkeit, Lebensart, Auftreten der freien christlichen Prediger der alten Kirche, die von Gemeinde zu Gemeinde wanderten, glich äußerlich dem Treiben der heidnische Volksprediger, und es war natürlich, daß die Formen und Gewohnheiten der heidnischen Propaganda in den Dienst der christlichen Mission gestellt wurden und ihr zugute kamen.'

[68] Wendland, *Hellenistisch-Römische Kultur*, p. 92.

[69] A.J. Malherbe, *Paul and the Thessalonians. The Philosophic Tradition of Pastoral Care* (Philadelphia: Fortress, 1987), p. 108.

[70] Epictetus, *Diss.* III,22,23: εἰδέναι δεῖ, ὅτι ἄγγελος ἀπὸ τοῦ Διὸς ἀπέσταλται καὶ πρὸς τοὺς ἀνθρώπους περὶ ἀγαθῶν καὶ κακῶν ὑποδείξων αὐτοῖς …

[71] For this, see F.G. Downing, *Christ and the Cynics* (JSOTM 4; Sheffield: JSOT Press, 1988), pp. 187-191.

cific forms of philosophical propaganda. Here, too, Malherbe mentions an important element:

> '... itinerant philosophers frequently made their converts from persons of the artisan class, who then abandoned their trades or were at least accused of doing so, in order themselves to become itinerant preachers.'[72]

In literature of the Graeco-Roman period there are many examples of philosophical propaganda. Cynic philosophers especially were in the habit of teaching people at public places. The many legendary stories about Diogenes of Sinope all have in common that Diogenes teaches men to be free from human conventions. According to the Cynic, a life of true freedom, self-supportiveness, and a disdain of luxury corresponds to the natural state of human life. In order to show his own freedom from conventions, Diogenes apparently lived at the edge of society and taught anyone he met with complete disregard for status. Legend has it that even Alexander the Great was treated by Diogenes as any ordinary man (cf. Cicero, *Tusc.* v,92; cf. Dio Chrystostom, *Oratio IV de Regno*, esp. §15). In Lucian's satires Cynics are often depicted as annoying each and everyone present. In *Convivium* it is the Cynic Alcidamas who eventually turns a dinner-party into a great fight. Feared by all present, Alcidamas is the first to become drunk, and almost starts a fight only to be stopped by a huge cake being brought in. Alcidamas stuffs himself with the cake. A little later, fighting is indeed started by the Cynic, and eventually the entire party ends in total chaos:

> 'At last Alcidamas knocked over the lamp-stand and brought on profound darkness, and as you can imagine, the situation became far worse, for it was not easy for them to provide more light, while on the other hand many dire deeds were done in the darkness. When some one finally came in with a lamp, Alcidamas was caught stripping the flute-girl and trying to ravish her ...'[73]

The picture of Alcidamas is pure satire, of course. But the way in which Lucian exaggerates Alcidamas' contempt for conventions did apparently have a basis in the actual behaviour of Cynics. They obviously preferred to demonstrate their freedom from conventions in shocking bystanders by their attitude.

A striking example of this attitude of the Cynics is given in one of the pseudepigraphic letters ascribed to Diogenes. In letter 38 'Diogenes'

---

[72] Malherbe, *Paul and the Thessalonians*, p. 19. Malherbe bases this conclusion on Lucian, *The Runaways* 12 and *The Double Indictment* 6.

[73] Lucian, *The Carousal* 46.

describes how he once entered a house fully adorned with inscriptions and gold. At a certain moment Diogenes felt the need to spit. After having sought for a place fit to do so, Diogenes spat onto the owner of the house. His defence of this act is yet another example of the manner in which Cynics protested against luxury and human conventions: '.. do you blame me for what happened and not yourself? It was you who decorated the walls and pavement of the banquet hall, leaving only yourself unadorned, as a place fit to spit onto.'[74] Perhaps even more striking than Diogenes' attitude is that of the young man he spat onto. According to 'Diogenes' the man distributed his entire property to his relatives, 'took up the wallet, doubled his coarse cloak, and followed me'.

The Cynics thus appear to have proclaimed a life free from conventions. The desires of luxury enslave a man, whereas the Cynic attitude is one of freedom: by turning down the demands of luxury as well as by refusing to live according to human conventions, the Cynic lives in accordance with nature. In a pseudepigraphon ascribed to Crates, the Cynic freedom is described like this: 'But as for us, we observe complete peace since we have been freed from every evil by Diogenes of Sinope' (παντὸς κακοῦ ἐλεύθεροι γενόμενοι ὑπὸ Σινωπέως Διογένους).[75] The Cynics even regarded themselves as sent by the gods. The Cynic attributes like the cloak and the wallet can even be mentioned as 'the weapons of the gods' (τὰ θεῶν ὅπλα).[76]

The parallels between Paul and the Cynics are important. To mention but one: just like the Cynics Paul laid great emphasis on his freedom – he did not allow the Corinthians to pay him for his work as an apostle (1 Cor 9,1.6.19). Apparently, Paul refused to become dependent upon the group to whom he was preaching the gospel. It is exactly for this reason that Cynic philosophers lived on the margin of society. According to R. F. Hock, Paul's artisanship should be viewed from the perspective of the philosopher working for his own livelihood.[77] And there are more similarities with Paul to be found among the descriptions of Cynic philosophers. Paul also travelled from one city to another, often compelled by expulsion or another form of opposition. He subsequently stayed in contact with the congregations he had founded by means of letters.

---

[74] Translation by B. Fiore in A.J. Malherbe (ed.), *The Cynic Epistles. A Study Edition* (SBLSBS 12; Atlanta: Scholars Press, 1977), p. 163.

[75] Ps. Crates, *Ep.* 7, in Malherbe, *Cynic Epistles*, p. 58-59.

[76] Ps. Crates, *Ep.* 16, in Malherbe, *Cynic Epistles*, p. 66-67.

[77] R.F. Hock, *The Social Context of Paul's Ministry. Tentmaking and Apostleship* (Philadelphia: Fortress, 1980); cf. the discussion below, pp. 221-228.

Paul saw his preaching of the gospel as a task laid upon him by God. In spite of the opposition he had to face time and again, Paul spoke with great frankness (παρρησία; 2 Cor 3,12; 7,4; Phil 1,20; 1 Thess 2,2). He was obviously not the only one:[78] Diogenes Laertius reports that the great Cynic, Diogenes of Sinope, travelled around and lived at Sinope, Athens, Megara, Samothrace, Olympia, Aegina, and Corinth.[79] The Cynic can embody true freedom by not having a home, and by travelling with a rod and a knapsack, although the latter in itself is not sufficient to be truly free.[80] The Cynic is depicted in literature of the period as the personification of shamelessness, and as such always acts with boldness and frankness (cf. Epictetus, *Diss.* III,22). It is often because of his shamelessness that the Cynic runs into trouble: severe opposition often led to expulsion (cf. Epictetus, *Diss.* III 22,22). Finally, like Paul, Cynic and other philosophers used letters to convey their views in their own physical absence.[81]

It thus appears that the way in which philosophers, especially Cynics, proclaimed their views may have influenced Paul. After all, if we accept Paul's provenance as Tarsus (cf. below, p. 157), he was born and at least partly raised in one of the most important centres of Cynic-Stoic philosophy of the first century CE. Evidence shows that Paul was thoroughly familiar with the way in which these philosophers addressed their audiences. The frequent use of the *diatribe*-form by Paul proves this, but also the similarities, for instance, between Paul's view on liberty and that of the Cynic philosophers points in this direction.[82]

The similarities between Paul's and the philosophers' attitude cannot, however, veil the great differences. Paul did not teach people to educate them but to save them. His monotheistic Jewish paradigm was a precondition belonging to the core of his message: he considered the ultimate intervention of the one God of Israel imminent, and this eschatological

---

[78] I am much obliged to dr. J. Tromp, University of Leiden, who first drew my attention to this material.

[79] Diogenes Laertius, *Vit. Phil.*: VI,20 (Sinope), VI,21 (Athens), VI,41 (Megara), VI,59 (Samothrace), VI,60 (Olympia), VI,74 (Aegina), and VI,74 (Corinth).

[80] Cf. Epictetus, *Diss.* III,22,9-10.47; Philo, *De vita contemplativa* 14.

[81] A good example is found in the collection of epistles edited by Malherbe, *Cynic Epistles*.

[82] On Paul's understanding of 'freedom' as rooted in the socratic tradition see F.S. Jones, *'Freiheit' in den Briefen des Apostels Paulus. Eine historische, exegetische und religionsgeschichtliche Studie* (GTA 34; Göttingen: Vandenhoeck & Ruprecht, 1987), pp. 44-69. According to Jones Cynic ideas on freedom had influenced the Corinthians rather than Paul. T. Engberg-Pedersen has even argued for a new model of interpreting Paul through the Stoic paradigm: see Engberg-Pedersen, *Paul and the Stoics*.

expectation defined the enormous impact of the Christ event. Further-more, the Pauline school, as far as it can be discerned, was something quite different from philosophical and rhetorical training schools.[83] For these reasons it would be too much to present Paul as a Cynic philosopher; he most certainly was not. It will appear below that Paul saw his own task as more like that of a prophet. But to some degree, he was influenced by philosophical propaganda and rhetoric.

Conclusion

This short survey of pagan religious propaganda, fragmentary as it may be, is revealing in that it shows the similarities and differences between Paul and the surrounding culture. Religious propaganda of pagan cults and philoso-phies was different from the propaganda of the early Christian movement in a number of respects. The prime difference is the fact that the Christian movement originated in Jewish monotheism. This excluded the polytheis-tic framework that appears to have been highly influential in pagan cults.[84]

With regard to the ways in which a cult could spread its fame, there were several possibilities. One option was cultic propaganda, in which believers were invited to visit the cult centre in order to pay their respect to the deity revered. Public manifestations of a deity formed another option to attract believers, just as votive offerings functioned as a factor in the spread of, for instance, the cult of Asclepius. Individual propa-ganda as used by Paul finds its closest parallel in the teaching of philoso-phers, Cynics in particular. A comparison shows that Paul shares a num-ber of characteristics with them. He shares their instruments (for instance: the *diatribe*), he is influenced by their views, he travels as they do and, finally, he meets with the same kind of opposition as they do. As we shall see, however, there were also great distinctions: Paul was a Jewish apoc-alyptic preacher who considered himself to be one of the prophets.

There are important parallels between Hellenistic cults and Paul's proclamation of the gospel. Apparently, salvation (σωτηρία) was an important element in Hellenistic cults. The adherents of Isis worshipped the goddess as the ruler of fate and fortune. Similarly, the worshippers of Asclepius hoped to be freed from disease or illness. The Cynics pro-claimed exactly such a life in freedom (ἐλευθερία), to be realised by

---

[83] For this, see W.A. Meeks, *The First Urban Christians. The Social World of the Apostle Paul* (New Haven, London: Yale University Press, 1983), pp. 81-84.

[84] See Goodman, *Mission and Conversion*, p. 27.

fully becoming free from social conventions, speaking frankly (with παρρησία). Paul's gospel also promised 'salvation' and 'freedom'.[85] Furthermore, Paul obviously proclaimed it in the same frank manner that characterised the Cynic and Stoic philosophers. But Paul's pagan context did not provide him with a matrix for proselytising mission.

---

[85] Paul speaks of σωτηρία in Rom 1,16; 10,1.10; 11,11; 13,11; 2 Cor 1,6; 6,2; 7,10; Phil 1,19.28; 2,12; 1 Thess 5,8.9; cf. especially this last verse: ὅτι οὐκ ἔθετο ἡμᾶς ὁ θεὸς εἰς ὀργὴν ἀλλὰ εἰς περιποίησιν σωτηρίας διὰ τοῦ κυρίου ἡμῶν Ἰησοῦ Χριστοῦ. He also mentions the effect of the Christ event as 'freedom': Rom 8,21; (1 Cor 10,29: on Paul's own freedom); 2 Cor 3,17; Gal 2,4; 5,1.13. Paul mentions the origin of this freedom as 'the Spirit of the Lord' (οὗ δὲ τὸ πνεῦμα κυρίου, ἐλευθερία – 2 Cor 3,17) or Christ himself (τῇ ἐλευθερίᾳ ἡμᾶς Χριστὸς ἠλευθέρωσεν – Gal 5,1).

CHAPTER THREE

THE PRE-PAULINE MOVEMENT

It is evident that Paul did not initiate the spread of the Christian move-ment. On several occasions in his letters he refers to other 'missionaries' who spread the gospel. Apollos for instance is mentioned several times in the Corinthian correspondence as one who was active in that congre-gation.[1] Also Peter apparently travelled around,[2] and we have evidence that other preachers went out to proclaim the gospel too: in the synoptic gospels we find a double tradition on a commissioning of disciples by Jesus. This tradition no doubt points back to an early stratum of mis-sionary activities. After the synoptic material has been treated, we will turn to a discussion of pre-literary formulae in Paul's letters. Thus a rough sketch is made of the pre-Pauline Christian movement. It will be argued that this movement focused on the Christ event, that it did so in direct continuity with Jesus' own preaching activities during his ministry, and that already before Paul became active, there was a new mixed Jesus-community of Jews and Gentiles together.

The Book of Acts confirms this picture. Although the author wishes to depict Paul as the one whose activity gave the greatest impulse to the spread of the Christian movement, several indications are given in Acts of the form and content of the pre-Pauline movement. For instance, the initial spread of Jesus movement from Jerusalem is described as being the result of the persecution of the 'Hellenists', Greek-speaking Jewish Chris-tians (8,1-3). These Hellenists would have been critical on the temple and its cult and would have focused on a more lenient form of Judaism in stead. Subsequently Acts 8 mentions the activities of Philip, and the chap-ters 10-11 describe in detail how the Gentile Cornelius became a convert as a result of his meeting with Peter, and how the conversion of Gentiles to the movement was accepted by the apostles in Jerusalem. Notwith-standing the theological and literary character of the description in Acts,

---

[1] Paul mentions him in 1 Cor 1,12; 3,4.5.6.22; 4,6; 16,12; cf. Acts 18,24; 19,1; Tit 3,13.

[2] At least to Antioch: Gal 2,11. On the Petrine emissaries in Corinth, see M.D. Goulder, *Paul and the Competing Mission in Corinth* (LPS; Peabody: Hendrickson, 2001), pp. 16-46.

some details will prove to be of importance to the present subject. The discussion of Acts is preceded by an excursus on the historical value of the book.

Finally, the missionary commandment in Matt 28,16-20 is treated. This pericope seems to reflect a universal missionary strategy, in which proselytising is central to the understanding of Christianity. A similar thought is found in an earlier stratum of tradition, viz. Mark 13,10. These passages mark the end of a development that must have started early in the Jesus movement. After the stage has thus been set, the next chapters will discuss Paul's part in the play.

1. Jesus' Commissioning of his Disciples in the Synoptics

Mark 6,7-13 contains an account of Jesus' commissioning the twelve disciples to go out in pairs. This account originates in a pre-Markan tradition that has its parallel in a passage in Q which can be reconstructed from Luke 10,1-12/Matt 10,1-17.[3] The description Matthew gives of the commissioning results from a combination of the two traditions (Mark and Q) with other traditional materials into one narrative. Luke contains both traditions but not together, the Markan narrative being reworked into Luke 9,1-6, whereas the material from Q has been included in 10,1-12. The first commissioning describes the sending out of the twelve disciples, whereas the second refers to seventy-two envoys.[4]

With regard to the historical value of the commissioning of disciples by Jesus, scholarly opinions are profoundly divided. Whereas J. Wellhausen for instance was utterly negative,[5] T.W. Manson was sure that

---

[3] For the text, see J.M. Robinson, P. Hoffmann, J.S. Kloppenborg, *The Critical Edition of Q. Synopsis including the Gospels of Matthew and Luke, Mark and Thomas with English, German, and French Translations of Q and Thomas* (Leuven: Peeters, 2000), pp. 158-181.

[4] The textual evidence in Luke 10,1 on the number of the disciples is difficult to weigh. Nevertheless, K. Aland was probably right in his comment in B.M. Metzger (ed.), *A Textual Commentary on the Greek New Testament* (Stuttgart: Deutsche Bibelgesellschaft, United Bible Societies, 2nd ed., 1994, [1]1974), p. 127, that the number of seventy-two is clearly *lectio difficilior*: 'A reading that in the Gospels has in its support P[75] B D, the Old Syriac, the Old Latin, etc., etc. is ordinarily regarded at once as the original reading. If in addition the opposing reading lies under the suspicion of ecclesiastical "normalizing," the testimony becomes irrefutable.'

[5] J. Wellhausen, *Das Evangelium Marci* (Berlin: Reimer, 1903), pp. 45-46, argues that Mark 6,6b-13 'enthält keine historische Tradition. Der Apostolat wird hier schon durch Jesus gegründet, ohne jedoch nun auch wirklich in Erscheinung zu treten; die Zwölf (…) machen nur ein Experiment und sind hinter her genau so unselbständig und passiv

this event was 'one of the best attested facts in the life of Jesus'.[6] More recently John Dominic Crossan argued that 'what lies behind' this evidence 'is a standard procedure in the early Jesus movement'.[7]

The most important issue in this debate is the question of whether or not the Markan material should be judged as being independent from the Q evidence. Only if we face two independent traditions here, we have a double attestation of a commissioning of followers of Jesus. The starting point here has to be the independent attestation of this tradition in both Mark and Q. If the pre-Markan tradition depended on (an early version of) Q, this would have to be established by compelling evidence showing the redaction of Q in the Markan tradition. This can only be done by comparing the reconstructed pre-Markan tradition with the reconstructed content of Q. Although this way of arguing in which many hypotheses are built on one another is dangerous, it may still lead to a result. It will, however, have to go beyond the similarities in structure and the few words that we find comparing Mark 6,6b-13 with the reconstructed passage from Q 10,2-11.[8] Since the Markan tradition differs from that of

---

wie zuvor, obwohl das Experiment gelingt. In Wahrheit hat Jesus keine Übungsreisen mit einem Seminar veranstaltet.'

[6] T.W. Manson, *The Sayings of Jesus* (London: SCM Press, 1949 [= 1937]), p. 73.

[7] J.D. Crossan, *The Historical Jesus. The Life of a Mediterranean Jewish Peasant* (San Francisco: Harper, 1991), p. 336.

[8] Against H. Schürmann, 'Mt 10,5b-6 und die Vorgeschichte des synoptischen Aussendungsberichtes', in: J. Blinzer, O. Kuss, F. Mußner, *Neutestamentliche Aufsätze* (FS J. Schmid; Regensburg: Pustet, 1963), pp. 270-282. According to Schürmann, Mark 6 should be interpreted as an excerpt from the commissioning tradition in Q: 'dieser ist von Markus – vielleichte in einem früheren Überlieferungsstadium – in Mk 6,6b-13 exzerpiert und so (...) auch von Lk 9,1-6 wiedergegeben.' (p. 270). On the relation of Mark to Q, see also D. Lührmann, *Die Redaktion der Logienquelle. Anhang: Zur weiteren Überlieferung der Logienquelle* (WMANT 33; Neukirchen: Neukirchener Verlag, 1969), p. 20; M. Devisch, 'La relation entre l'évangile de Marc et le document Q', in: M. Sabbe (ed.), *L'évangile selon Marc. Tradition et rédaction* (BETL 34; Leuven: Peeters/University Press, 1988), pp. 59-91. Lührmann opts for two parallel traditions, whereas Devisch seriously wants to reckon with the possibility that Mark depends on an early form of Q. Literary independence of Mark and Q has been convincingly argued by R. Laufen, *Die Doppelüberlieferungen der Logienquelle und des Markusevangeliums* (BBB 54; Königstein/Bonn: Hanstein, 1980), who concludes that 'Die Untersuchung hat bestätigt, daß weder der Q-Bearbeiter das Markusevangelium noch umgekehrt Markus die Logienquelle als direkte literarische Vorlage benutzt hat. Beide Möglichkeiten sind durch die Tatsache ausgeschlossen, daß teilweise Q, teilweise Markus die ältere und ursprünglichere Fassung eines Logions bietet' (p. 385). See also A.D. Jacobson, 'The Literary Unity of Q. Lc 10,2-16 and Parallels as a Test Case', in: J. Delobel (ed.), *Logia. Les paroles de Jésus/The Sayings of Jesus. Mémorial Joseph Coppens* (BETL 59; Leuven: Peeters/University Press, 1982), pp. 419-423. For the text of this Q passage, see Robinson, Hoffmann, Kloppenborg, *Critical Edition*, pp. 160-179.

Q with regard to the instruction of those who are commissioned,[9] we do indeed face two independent traditions in Q and Mark.

If we consider the commissioning of the disciples in Mark and in Q as two independent versions of a tradition on Jesus' sending out of envoys, the observation that also the special material (the *Sondergut*) in Matt 10,5-6 contains independent evidence, leads to the conclusion that there is ample proof – by means of multiple attestation – for an early tradition on the instruction of disciples by Jesus.[10] Furthermore, two logia in the *Gospel of Thomas* (6,1 and 14,1-3) add to the multiplicity of the attestation.

As said in the introduction to this section, the Matthean redaction has shaped the material from Mark and Q into a new discourse, to which at several points elements from Matthew's own special material were added. One such element is no doubt 10,5b-6.[11] In this *logion* Jesus instructs his disciples not to go preaching to the Gentiles or the Samaritans, but just to the 'lost sheep of the house of Israel'. Since the construction εἰς ὁδόν is used only here in Matthew, just as the Samaritans are never mentioned in Matthew except in this verse, the words must come from Matthean tradition, not redaction.[12] The origin of such a tradition is difficult to envisage in a context in which the Christian gospel was being proclaimed to pagans – as was already the case early in the development of the Christian movement. Therefore, it is very likely that the *logion* under discussion originated in Palestine at a very early stage. The *Sitz im Leben* it demands is that of the instruction of the coming Kingdom to a group of heralds who in their proclamation were to aim at Israel's eschatological

---

[9] In Mark 6,8-9 the disciples are instructed to take along a staff, a pair of sandals, and a cloak. The instruction in Q 10,4 describes more or less the opposite.

[10] Manson, *Sayings*, pp. 73-74, is very optimistic in regard to the historicity of the material. He ascribes the Matthean material that does not come from either Mark or Q automatically to Matthew's special source, without discussing the possibility that this material is redactional in origin. The evidence that Luke's special source contained a tradition derived from the commissioning material, is taken from 22,35. That verse contains a saying corresponding to 10,8. Both sayings contain the noun βαλλάντιον, which occurs only four times in the NT – all in Luke: 10,4; 12,33; 22,35.36. Yet this evidence may also point at the redactional origin of the verses discussed. The main argument why 10,1 and 17-20 may be an elaboration of a tradition from the special source is the fact that Luke mentions the number of seventy(-two) envoys.

[11] See U. Luz, *Das Evangelium nach Matthäus*, vol. 2 (EKK; Zürich, Braunschweig: Benziger; Neukirchen-Vluyn: Neukirchener Verlag, 1990), p. 88. Also W. Trilling, *Das wahre Israel. Studien zur Theologie des Matthäus-Evangeliums* (SANT 10; München: Kösel, 1964), pp. 99-103. *Pace* Kasting, *Anfänge*, p. 113.

[12] See W.D. Davies, D.C. Allison jr., *The Gospel according to Saint Matthew*, vol. 2 (ICC; Edinburgh: Clark, 1991), pp. 165-166.

repentance. It may thus find its origin in the period shortly after, or perhaps even before Jesus' death, reflecting the proclamation of the coming Kingdom as limited to Israel.[13]

For the present subject it is important to answer two questions: Firstly, what is the earliest traditional content of the message with which those commissioned were sent out? And secondly, does this early tradition reflect the Christian proclamation of the gospel after Jesus' death or does it bear witness to a special role played by the disciples during Jesus' life?

The answer to the first question is that the earliest traditional material describes followers of Jesus as partaking in his ministry and proclamation. The evidence from Mark and Q shows a tradition on how Jesus sent out his envoys to proclaim the nearness of the Kingdom of God. He apparently instructed them to partake in his own ministry by proclaiming the same message he did and performing the same deeds he performed.[14] Let us take a closer look at the evidence by first considering Mark and then the evidence from Q.

The Markan account of the commissioning consists of six elements:

1. Jesus called for the twelve (v. 7a);
2. he started to send them out in pairs (v. 7b);
3. he gave the disciples authority over unclean spirits (v. 7c);
4. he instructed them in regard to what they should take along: only a staff, a pair of sandals, and a cloak (v. 8-9);
5. he instructed them as to their attitude in case of a negative reception: shake off the dust under your feet (v. 10-11);
6. they went out to preach, cast out many demons, and cured many of the diseased (v. 12).

A reconstruction of the exact form of the pre-Markan tradition is not our objective. Therefore, the analysis of this passage focuses on the identity of the commissioned and the character of their activities.

The group that are sent out consist of 'the twelve' (v. 7a). It is important to recall that the first introduction of the twelve in Mark 3,14 contains a reference to the narrative of this commissioning in Mark 6 (cf. 3,14:

---

[13] According to the criterion of dissimilarity, the fact that a *logion* does not fit into the situation of the communities who passed it on, is an argument in favour of its ancient character.

[14] Cf. J. Gnilka, *Das Evangelium nach Markus*, vol. 1 (EKK; Zürich [etc.]: Benziger; Neukirchen-Vluyn: Neukirchener Verlag, 1978), p. 241: 'Welche Intentionen Jesus mit der Aussendung verband, ist schwer zu sagen (...). Auf jeden Fall galt es für Jesus, die eigene Tätigkeit zu unterstützen.'

δώδεκα ἵνα ὦσιν μετ᾽ αὐτοῦ καὶ ἵνα ἀποστέλλῃ αὐτοὺς κηρύσσειν καὶ ἔχειν ἐξουσίαν ἐκβάλλειν τὰ δαιμόνια).[15] Jesus' close followers are often referred to in Mark as 'the twelve',[16] and the vocabulary used in the introduction in 6,6b-7 is clearly redactional.[17] The combination of the words used in 6,6b-7, and the reference to the commissioning narrative in 3,14 indicates that the introduction of the narrative should be interpreted as Markan redaction. In consequence, the description of the group that are being commissioned in this narrative, consisting of the close circle around Jesus ('the Twelve'), was not an element in pre-Markan tradition. Therefore, from pre-Markan tradition we know nothing concerning the identity of the group that Jesus sent out, except that we may infer that they were followers of Jesus.

Unfortunately, the same problem occurs in Q: the introduction of the narrative in Luke 10,1 belongs to the redactional stratum of Luke,[18] and therefore the mention of the seventy-two is probably also an element from the redaction of Luke.[19] The Matthean discourse is directed at 'the Twelve' (Matt 10,5), and no doubt depends on the characterisation in Mark 6. This means that the group that according to Q were sent out by Jesus are not described here either. The argument made in the previous paragraph may, however, be repeated: that Jesus sends out this group must imply that its members were already among his followers. We can therefore repeat Crossan's conclusion: those commissioned 'can only be identified in very general terms as followers or disciples of Jesus.'[20] This brings us to the question: what were these followers sent out to do?

In the Markan version, there are two elements in the account that point to what Jesus intended his disciples to do: they were to cast out demons (δαιμόνια ἐκβάλλειν; 6,7.13), and call for conversion (κηρύσσειν ἵνα

---

[15] The words οὓς καὶ ἀποστόλους ὠνόμασεν are probably an interpolation of later date.

[16] Together with 6,7 there are nine passages in which the terminology of οἱ δώδεκα is found: 3,16; 9,35; 10,32; 11,11; 14,10.17.20.43.

[17] Cf. Gnilka, *Markus*, vol. 1, p. 237, according to whom προσκαλέομαι, δώδεκα, and ἄρχω with infinitive are redactional.

[18] See for instance the use of ὁ κύριος in the narrative for Jesus, a feature found only in Luke: 7,19; 10,41; 11,39; 12,42; 13,15; 17,6; 18,6; 19,8; (19,34); 20,13.15; 22,61; 24,34.

[19] See J.A. Fitzmyer, *The Gospel according to Luke*, vol. 2 (AB; Garden City: Doubleday, 1985), p. 843. Fitzmyer argues on the basis of Jesus' remark in 22,35, and notes that 'that question (…) refers not to 9,3, addressed to the Twelve, but to 10,4, addressed to the "others"'. The number of 70 is probably a reference to the 70 elders mentioned in Exod 24,1.9; Num 11,16.24 – cf. H. Schürmann, *Das Lukasevangelium*, vol. 2.1 (HThK; Freiburg [etc.]: Herder, 1993), p. 54.

[20] Crossan, *Historical Jesus*, p. 334.

μετανοῶσιν; 6,12). Again, this information appears to be redactional: the same two elements had already been mentioned in 3,14, and verses 6,6.12-13 are redactional. But as with the case of the identity of the group commissioned, the redactional description of their activities does give us some information as to what they may have done. The two characteristics of the activities of the Twelve as described in 6,7-13 (and 3,14) are very similar to the characteristics of Jesus' public appearance: Jesus calls for repentance (cf. 1,15), and his first public act is to cast out a demon (1,23-28). The same combination of words – κηρύσσειν and δαιμόνια ἐκβάλλειν – is used for the description of Jesus' activities in 1,39. This means that the author of Mark presents the commissioning of the disciples as the sending out of his followers by Jesus in order that they might proclaim his message and perform his deeds. They were dispatched to do what Jesus did.

It should be acknowledged that, redactional as the rendering of the activities of the Twelve may be in Mark 6, it is very likely that already in the pre-Markan tradition the followers of Jesus, who were sent out, were commissioned to support his ministry by acting and preaching as he did.

The Q-material proves to be more conclusive in this respect. Luke 10,9/Matt 10,7-8 mentions two characteristics of Jesus' envoys, viz. the healing of the sick, and the announcement of the coming Kingdom of God:[21] as in Mark 6 the envoys perform a combination of act and proclamation. Both elements were probably taken from an older tradition in which the proclamation of the Kingdom was combined with acts of healing – as it was, apparently, in the ministry of Jesus. The fact that the phrase ἤγγικεν ἡ βασιλεῖα τοῦ θεοῦ is retained in Luke 10,8.11 is remarkable, because in 4,14-15 in his reworking of Mark 1,15 Luke had left these words out. In 10,8 the phrase is put in a different perspective by simply adding the words ἐφ᾽ ὑμᾶς, probably indicating that the Kingdom has already partly come because the healing and proclamation referred to it.[22]

The observation that in Q Jesus sends his envoys to proclaim the nearness of the Kingdom is important for the present subject. It was argued above that the Markan redaction depicts the envoys as supporting Jesus' work. The fact that Q mentions the envoys as proclaiming the Kingdom

---

[21] As elsewhere in his use of Q Matthew rather than Luke has reversed the order of the words – thus is the judgement of, e.g., Bultmann, Bussmann, Hahn, Hoffmann, Jacobson, Kloppenborg, Polag, Schenk, Schmid, Schulz, and Schürmann; cf. J.S. Kloppenborg, *Q-Parallels. Synopsis, Critical Notes & Concordance* (Sonoma: Polebridge, 1988), p. 72.

[22] Schürman, *Lukasevangelium*, vol. 2.1, p. 74.

means that an old tradition confirms the redactional interpretation in Mark of the pre-Markan tradition on the commissioning of the disciples.[23] Hence, the first question asked above can be answered now. It appears that in early synoptic tradition Jesus commissions a group of his followers to act as he himself did.

This brings us to the next question: does this state of affairs reflect the situation in the Christian community after Jesus' death or does it date back to Jesus' lifetime?

As always, the question concerning the historical origin of the material studied is difficult to answer. There are two indications, however. Firstly, in his analysis of Q, S. Schulz considers the passage Q 10,1-12 as belonging not to the oldest, but to the second layer of Q.[24] His main argument is, that Jesus is not presented as the risen and present Lord, but in his earthly ministry. J.S. Kloppenborg has argued against Schulz that the section Q 10,2-16 was not 'a unitary speech from the beginning'. In stead, Kloppenborg reconstructs various layers in the evidence, and concludes that only 10,2 may have originated in a setting that pre-dated the Gentile mission. Different as Kloppenborg's analysis may be from that of Schulz, he too argues for a date well after Easter.[25]

There is also a second indication that the material under discussion should be dated to a post-Easter date. If Jesus' proclamation of the coming Kingdom had indeed been supported by a group of followers who not only shared his ideas, but also actively proclaimed them, it is difficult to understand that apparently only Jesus was eventually crucified. Other examples from the first century show how the Romans usually not only executed the leader of a popular movement, but also a large number of its adherents. R.A. Horsley correctly notes a difference between 'popular prophetic movements' and 'oracular prophets', and refers to

---

[23] Cf. J.P. Meyer, *A Marginal Jew. Rethinking the Historical Jesus* Vol. 2: *Mentor, Message, and Miracles* (ABRL; New York [etc.]: Doubleday, 1994), p. 432: 'On the whole, therefore, it is likely that the core proclamation "the kingdom of God has drawn near" existed in Q as well as in Mark.'

[24] S. Schulz, *Q. Die Spruchquelle der Evangelisten* (Zürich: Theologischer Verlag, 1972), p. 409.

[25] J.S. Kloppenborg, *The Formation of Q. Trajectories in Ancient Wisdom Collections* (SAC; Philadelphia: Fortress, 1987), pp. 192-197. See also Kloppenborg's verdict on p. 202: 'Beginning as a cluster of instruction specifically for missionaries, the composition was augmented by framing sayings (10,3.16) and by the addition of 10,2 and 10,7b. Both of these sets of additions signal a shift in *Sitz im Leben* from missionary instruction to instruction for a church engaged in the sending and support of missionaries.'

Josephus, who describes how the Romans usually not only had the leaders of popular movements executed, but also a certain amount of their followers.[26] This would indicate that Jesus more or less acted on his own as a kind of oracular prophet.

The two indications mentioned point at a post-Easter date for the traditions under survey here. And indeed there is a good explanation why this material would have been formed in the early Christian community. The tradition on the commissioning of disciples by Jesus probably emerged out of the need for early Christian preachers to clearly distinguish themselves from their Cynic 'colleagues': the attributes mentioned in the gospel traditions are frequently found in descriptions of Cynics. In many descriptions of Cynic philosophers the attributes mentioned in the commissioning narrative play an important part. Often they speak of the 'double, coarse cloak', a 'wallet' and a 'staff'. To mention but one example, Pseudo-Diogenes writes in *Epistle* 7: 'Do not be upset, father, that I am called a dog and put on a double, coarse cloak, carry a wallet over my shoulders, and have a staff in my hand.'[27]

The synoptic instruction not to carry a double cloak, nor a staff or a wallet should be understood as an attempt to point out the difference between Christian preachers and Cynics. Just as the Cynics, Christian preachers were 'heimatlos vagabondierende Propagandisten ohne Erwerb und Wohnsitz.'[28] Therefore, the similarities between the two groups may have prevented outsiders from seeing the differences.

The only indication that Jesus indeed instructed his followers to proclaim the coming Kingdom throughout Israel is found in Matt 10,5b-6. This *logion* indicates that Jesus probably indeed instructed his followers to herald the Kingdom.

In summa: the synoptic evidence on the instruction and commissioning of disciples by Jesus as preserved in at least Mark 6 and Q 10 originated largely in early post-Easter instructions of Christian preachers. They

---

[26] R.A. Horsley, J.S. Hanson, *Bandits, Prophets and Messiahs. Popular Movements in the Time of Jesus* (Harrisburg: Trinity Press, 1999 = 1985), pp. 160-187. See e.g. Josephus' descriptions of the Egyptian prophet (*Ant.* xx,169-171; *BJ* ii,261-263), Theudas (*Ant.* xx,97-98), and the Samaritan prophet (*Ant.* xviii,85-87).

[27] See also Ps. Crates, *Ep.* 16.23.33; Ps. Diog. *Ep.* 15.19.26.30.34.38.46 – A.J. Marlherbe, *The Cynic Epistles* (SBLSBS 12; Atlanta: Scholars Press, 1986 = 1977).

[28] G. Theissen, 'Legitimation und Lebensunterhalt. Ein Beitrag zur Soziologie urchristlicher Missionäre', in: idem, *Studien zur Soziologie des Urchristentums* (WUNT 19; Tübingen: Mohr Siebeck, 1979), pp. 201-230 [previously published in *NTS* 21 (1975), pp. 192-221]. Quotation from p. 202.

intended to distinguish themselves from wandering Cynics. Their appearance differed from that of these Cynics, and they thought of their own proclamation as a direct continuation of Jesus' ministry. Because of this direct continuation, the proclamation of the Kingdom of God and the miraculous healings Jesus performed were named as characteristics of his followers as well. This post-Easter tradition described a situation within Jesus' life in order to legitimise and characterise the activities of Christian preachers who proclaimed the gospel. The direct continuity with Jesus should therefore be sought in the eschatological content of the proclamation of the Kingdom as is indicated by Matt 10,5b-6. This may indicate that Jesus did indeed send out followers to proclaim his message, but the traditions describing that aspect of Jesus' ministry were formed in a post-Easter context.

2. Pre-literary Formulae in the Letters of Paul

In our search for pre-Pauline Christianity, our next task is to scrutinise those formulae and expressions in the Pauline epistles that may predate Paul, or at least the writing of the epistle. If we can trace any pre-Pauline traditions, we can subsequently relate Paul's ministry to these traditions and evaluate Paul's role.

A methodological remark must be made first. How can we be sure that a certain formula or expression predates the activities of Paul? Unfortunately, we cannot. We can only establish with a reasonable amount of probability that certain expressions predate the letter in which we find them.[29] In his *Geschichte der urchristlichen Literatur*, Ph. Vielhauer mentions a number of criteria that may indicate that a formula or expression has been taken from an older tradition.[30] In most cases the probability is

---

[29] The most thorough exposition of this material is given by K. Wengst, *Christologische Formeln und Lieder des Urchristentums* (SNT 7; Gütersloh: Mohn, 1972). See also Ph. Vielhauer, *Geschichte der urchristlichen Literatur* (Berlin, New York: De Gruyter, 1975), §2 'Vorliterarische Formen', pp. 9-57.

[30] Vielhauer, *Geschichte*, p. 12, mentions the following criteria for reconstructing pre-literary material: 1. Quotation-formulae introducing traditional material; 2. great stylistic differences between a pericope and its context; 3. the use of terminology that differs from the author's usual terminology; 4. theological thoughts that differ from the author's usual theological position; 5. the repetition of comparable terminology in a formulaic manner in writings of different authors; 6. thoughts that exceed the context in which they are found, and are characterised by a very strict formulation; 7. grammatical incorrectness and stylistic breaks. Cf. also Wengst, *Christologische Formeln*, pp. 11-26.

that the material found does indeed pre-date Paul's ministry. But then again, Paul did write his letters some fourteen years or more after his call. Within this period there was an important development in the forms and content of worship as well as confessions. For this reason the safest approach is to regard pre-literary formulae found in the epistles of Paul as reflecting the views of the earliest Christian movement. Strictly spoken they may not pre-date the Christian period in Paul's life, and this means we will not be able to distinguish sharply between pre-Pauline and para-Pauline materials. Nevertheless, this evidence forms an important testimony on the focus of the early Christian movement, and may thus provide evidence on the themes that were crucial to its expansion.

The most important thing to note in studying these pre-literary formulae is that the content consistently focuses on christology.[31] A clear example of this is found in what are classified among the πίστις-formulae, the surrender- and dying-formula. The 'surrender-formula' is found in Rom 8,32; Gal 1,4; 2,20 and outside Paul's letters in Mark 10,45 par.; Eph 5,2.25; 1 Tim 2,6; Tit 2,14.[32] The several variations of the words 'give for us' all go back to an early interpretation of Jesus' death as a saving event.[33] Only once is Christ the object of the action, and then Paul mentions that Christ 'is given' by God for us (Rom 8,32). In all other occurrences of the formula the act of surrendering is described in a reflexive way: Christ has given himself for us. Closely related to this surrender-formula is the dying-formula: χριστὸς ἀπέθανεν ὑπέρ. Paul uses this formula in Rom 5,6.8; 14,15; 1 Cor 8,11 (with διά instead of ὑπέρ); 15,3; 2 Cor 5,14-15; 1 Thess 5,10.[34] The martyrological background of both these formulae defines this interpretation as one in which the death of the one brings about atonement for the many on whose behalf he has died.[35] For the latter formula a clear example of the martyrological

---

[31] The above discussion of the pre-literary formulae in Paul does not intend to offer a full reconstruction of all formulae preserved in Paul's letters.

[32] For a discussion of the surrender-formula see Wengst, *Christologische Formeln*, pp. 55-77.

[33] M. de Jonge has shown that there were three models by means of which the death of Christ was interpreted: that of the Envoy of God rejected by Israel, that of the Suffering Righteous Servant, and that of the Man Who Died for Others. It is remarkable that in the first model Jesus' vindication plays no part at all – cf. M. de Jonge, *God's Final Envoy. Early Christology and Jesus' Own View of His Mission* (Grand Rapids, Cambridge: Eerdmans, 1998), pp. 12-33.

[34] For a discussion of the dying-formula see Wengst, *Christologische Formeln*, pp. 78-86.

[35] Wengst, *Christologische Formeln*, pp. 67-70. Cf. especially pp. 68-69: 'Diese Sinngebung des gewaltsamen Todes hervorragender Männer hat das hellenistische Judentum vom Griechentum übernommen. Sie wurde weiter "ausgebaut" durch ihre Verbindung

meaning of the expression is found in John 11,50-51. There, the high priest Caiaphas argues that Jesus should die, because his death would prevent the people from being killed: συμφέρει ὑμῖν ἵνα εἷς ἄνθρωπος ἀποθάνῃ ὑπὲρ τοῦ λαοῦ καὶ μὴ ὅλον τὸ ἔθνος ἀπόληται.

Closely related to these phrases, used to describe the death of Christ, are the formulae that include his resurrection. According to K. Wengst these resurrection-formulae should be classified among the earliest ones originating in the Aramaic-speaking Christian movement.[36]

It is noteworthy that both the dying- and resurrection-formula are used in a passage in which Paul explicitly states that he has drawn on an older tradition: 1 Cor 15,3-5(7?). In this pericope Paul gives what appears to be a traditional summary of the gospel as it had come to him.[37] He does so in order to underline his own position within the early Christian tradition: παρέδωκα γὰρ ὑμῖν ἐν πρώτοις ὃ καὶ παρέλαβον κτλ. It is not clear whether the vv. 6-7 originally belonged to the pre-Pauline tradition or not. But be that as it may, the content of the gospel, as depicted here, is that Christ died, was buried, was raised on the third day, and appeared to his followers. In the case of his dying and his being raised, it is added that this happened κατὰ τὰς γράφας. Since this short summary of the gospel is probably genuinely pre-Pauline, i.e. really predates the Christian Paul, it is of the greatest importance for any reconstruction of the early Christian movement. It clearly affirms that the earliest Christian proclamation was strictly christocentric. It is the death and resurrection of Christ that forms the core of the proclamation. Christ's burial is little more than the consequence of his death, and the appearance illustrates his resurrection. It is probably for this reason that the phrase κατὰ τὰς γράφας is only added at the mention of the death and resurrection of Christ.

The death and resurrection of Christ are mentioned on numerous occasions throughout Paul's letters.[38] The short summary of the gospel as

---

mit dem alttestamentlich-jüdischen Sühnegedanken, daß der vor Gott sündige Mensch einer Sühne bedarf; aber dieser "Ausbau", diese Verbindung brachte etwas Neues hervor, das weder der alttestamentlichen Tradition geläufig noch in der griechischen Tradition da war: die Vorstellung vom stellvertretenden Sühnetod einzelner für andere.' Wengst subsequently mentions 2 Macc 7,37f.; 4 Macc 6,27-29; 7,37; 17,21f. as examples of this thought. Cf. also W. Popkes, *Christus Traditus. Eine Untersuchung zum Begriff der Dahingabe im Neuen Testament* (ATANT 49; Zürich: Zwingli Verlag, 1967), esp. pp. 82-99 and pp. 131-270.

[36] Wengst, *Christologische Formeln*, pp. 27-47.
[37] Cf. below, pp. 163-166.
[38] Cf. e.g. Rom 4,24-25; 5,6.8.15; 6, 4.8-9; 8, 11.34; 10,9; 14,9.15; 1 Cor 1,23; 2,2; 6,14; 8,11; 15 passim; 2 Cor 4,14; 5,15; 13,4; Gal 1,1; 3,1; 2,21; 6,14.

given in 1 Cor 15,3-5 proves, however, that Paul found this theme in the tradition which preceded his Christian existence.

Perhaps an even earlier tradition, and at least as important, can be reconstructed from the description of Christ as 'Jesus Christ' or 'Christ Jesus'. Paul uses these words as a name, although sometimes the titular function of χριστός appears to shine through the words.[39] This name can only have been formed as a result of the confession that Ἰησοῦς (ἔστιν) ὁ χριστός. This confession must reach far back in the earliest Christian movement. It appears to have had a parallel in the confession that κύριος Ἰησοῦς. V. Neufeld regarded this confession as one of the earliest and most prominent within the early movement.[40] At a second stage in the development both confession-formulae were joined into the phrase 'Lord is Jesus Christ'.[41] Paul in 1 Cor 8,5-6 prominently expresses the exclusive character of this claim.

It can hardly be by accident that the confession of Jesus as Lord forms the climax of the undoubtedly pre-literary hymn on Christ contained in Phil 2,6-11. Much has been written on this hymn, and there is no need to discuss it in great detail here.[42] Its importance for the present chapter is that it contains a poetic description of the meaning of Christ, culminating

---

[39] The most evident example is Rom 9,5; cf. M. de Jonge, *Christology in Context. The Earliest Christian Response to Jesus* (Philadelphia: Westminster, 1988), p. 114: 'Jesus Christ, in Paul, becomes a double name, as, for example, the very frequent use of the expression "Jesus Christ the Lord" shows.'

[40] V.H. Neufeld, *The Earliest Christian Confessions* (NTTS 5; Leiden: Brill, 1963), p. 68: 'In the life and worship of the Christian community, *kyrios Jesus* was an acclamation uttered during worship (Phil 2,11); it probably was a confession made in connection with baptism (?Rom 10,9); it formed the heart of the *kerygma* (Rom 10,8-10; 2 Cor 4,5); and it lay at the basis of the *didache* (Col 2,6-7). In the relationship of the church to the non-Christian world, *kyrios Jesus* was the open acknowledgement of loyalty before pagan or Jewish opponents (1 Cor 12,3); it was the polemical declaration against Hellenistic polytheism and the Caesar-cult (1 Cor 8,5-6); and it was an *apologia* for the Christian faith in the face of Jewish opposition (1 Cor 12,3; 15,3-5; cf. 1,23).'

[41] From Paul's use of these words – Jesus Christ, (our) Lord – it appears that for him the combination 'Jesus Christ' had indeed become a name, which was combined with the title 'Lord'. Nevertheless, this is only possible if the first stage of the development was that χριστός was used as a title so frequently that it came to be recognised as a name. On this development, see F. Hahn, *Christologische Hoheitstitel: ihre Geschichte im frühen Christentum* (UTB 1873; Göttingen: Vandenhoeck & Ruprecht, 5th rev. and enl. ed. 1995, ¹1963).

[42] See among the various books and articles on this hymn especially R. Deichgräber, *Gotteshymnus und Christushymnus. Untersuchungen zu Form, Sprache und Stil der frühchristlichen Hymnen* (SUNT 5; Göttingen: Vandenhoeck & Ruprecht, 1967), pp. 118-133; and R.P. Martin, *Carmen Christi. Philippians ii,5-11 in Recent Interpretation and in the Setting of Early Christian Worship* (SNTSMS 4; Cambridge: University Press, 1967) [now also as: *A Hymn of Christ. Philippians 2:5-11 in Recent Interpretation and in the Setting of Early Christian Worship* (Downers Grove: Intervarsity, 1997)].

in the confession that Jesus Christ is Lord. The hymn probably originates from a liturgical setting, and therefore proves that this confession-formula was also used in the worship of the early Christian movement.[43]

Yet we should go one step beyond this observation. The two final verses of the hymn state that God has exalted Christ 'in order that in the name of Jesus every knee will bend of those who are in the heavens, on the earth, and under the earth, and every tongue will confess that Jesus Christ is Lord to the glory of God the father.' In this phrase the words of LXX Isa 45,23 are adapted to a new, Christian context.[44] In Isaiah, God's claim for worship aims at the 'those who are saved from the Gentiles' (Isa 45,20). In Phil 2,11 this claim is adapted to the worship of Christ. In their context in Isaiah the description probably refers to those of the people of Israel who had escaped from the nations. Yet in Phil 2,11 the meaning of the last phrase is undoubtedly universalistic: 'every tongue should confess that Jesus Christ is Lord'. Especially the addition ἐπουρανίων καὶ ἐπιγείων καὶ καταχθονίων after πᾶν γόνυ points out that the importance of Christ exceeds the boundaries of man, let alone Judaism.[45] This is an important observation, for it implies that already at an early stage of the development of Christianity the Christ event was interpreted as having a universal, cosmological impact. Although the words of this hymn have the character of a doxological, poetic hyperbole, their cosmological intention does bear witness to a very early conviction of Christians that what had happened in Christ had meaning for the entire universe. Since this hymn should be dated to the period preceding Paul's literary activities, and was probably not composed by Paul himself, we have evidence here of a cosmological interpretation of the coming of Christ by Christians somewhere probably in the thirties or early forties of the first century. For them, the purport of the Christ event extended to the entire world.[46]

---

[43] *Pace* Martin, *Carmen Christi*, p. 282: '(Christ's lordship) is set in a framework which has little connection with the Church's worship; rather the primary application of the lordship is to the cosmic spirit-powers which admit their subservience to the enthroned Christ.'

[44] LXX Isa 45,23: κατ᾽ ἐμαυτοῦ ὀμνύω, εἰ μὴ ἐξελεύσεται ἐκ τοῦ στόματός μου δικαιοσύνη, οἱ λόγοι μου οὐκ ἀποστραφήσονται, ὅτι ἐμοὶ κάμψει πᾶν γόνυ, καὶ ὀμεῖται πᾶσα γλῶσσα τὸν θεόν, κτλ.

[45] Martin, *Carmen Christi*, p. 269: 'The humiliated and exalted Christ is proclaimed and acclaimed as Lord of all the spiritual forces throughout the universe.'

[46] See e.g. De Jonge, *Christology in Context*, p. 185: 'The exalted Jesus, the Lord, is worthy of the same adoration as Yahweh, the God of Israel himself, although he remains subordinate to God the Father ("to the glory of God the Father," Phil. 2:11). As in 1

Having established this, we should now proceed to 1 Thess 1,9-10. These verses are often interpreted as an early example of Paul's preaching of the gospel, sometimes even as a summary of 'Antiochene theology'.[47] Vielhauer rightly remarks that these two verses are formulated by Paul, but reflect the main themes within the early preaching of the gospel.[48] Early in his letter to the Thessalonians Paul refers to the way in which they had come to faith. This conversion of the Thessalonians is described as a double movement. Firstly, they had turned away from the idols to the one, true God. And secondly, they had come to expect Christ 'from the heavens', in order to save them from the coming wrath of God. The soteriological impact of Christ, as described here, is eschatological in character: Jesus will save his followers from the retribution by God. Yet the importance of these verses for the present subject lays not so much in its soteriology, as in its description of the conversion of pagans to the worship of the one God. The terminology in which the singularity of the one true God is depicted over against the εἴδωλα originates in Jewish monotheistic polemics against polytheism.[49] The combination of this monotheistic criticism of pagan religion and the soteriological function of Christ points out that also in the pre-Pauline circles in which this proclamation originated the impact of the Christ event was thought of as universal. In this respect the theological context of 1 Thess 1,9-10 is closely related to that of Phil 2,6-11.

That 1 Thess 1,9-10 offers a trustworthy summary of the early proclamation of the gospel, not only by his predecessors but also by Paul himself, may be inferred from several other passages in which he dwells upon the same subject. In Gal 4,8-9, for instance, Paul mentions the conversion of the Galatians in more or less the same terms: before they had come to know God they had worshipped 'beings that by nature are not gods'. The

---

Cor. 8:5-6, it is clear that his Lordship is not restricted to the Christian community, but extends over the entire creation.' K. Berger, *Theologiegeschichte des Urchristentums. Theologie des Neuen Testaments* (UTB; Tübingen, Basel: Franke, 2nd rev. ed., 1995), p. 238, regards Phil 2,9-11 as a legitimisation of universal mission.

[47] M. Dibelius, *An die Thessalonicher I, II* (HNT; Tübingen: Mohr, 3rd ed., 1937), p. 6; cf. a.o. also Becker, *Paulus*, pp. 110-113; Riesner, *Frühzeit*, pp. 357-358.

[48] Vielhauer, *Geschichte*, p. 28: 'Freilich handelt es sich bei dem Text nicht um das Zitat einer geprägten Formel, sondern um Aufzählung der Topoi des gemein-christlichen Missionskerygmas, deren Reihenfolge im obigen Text (= 1 Thess 1,9-10; LP) auf Paulus zurückgeht (...)'.

[49] See W. Bousset, H. Gressmann, *Die Religion des Judentums im späthellenistischen Zeitalter* (HNT 21; Tübingen: Mohr, 1926, 4th ed., 1966), pp. 302-320; for the polemic against idolatry, see especially the passages mentioned on p. 305. For a brief description of these polemics, see Lietaert Peerbolte, 'To Worship the Beast', pp. 249-251.

same polemic against other gods also underlies the remark by Paul in 1 Cor 8,5-6: 'Indeed, even though there may be so-called gods in heaven or on earth – as in fact there are many gods and many lords – yet for us there is one God, the Father, from whom are all things and for whom we exist, and one Lord, Jesus Christ, through whom are all things and through whom we exist.' Obviously the monotheistic view that there are indeed many gods, but that just one god is the true one, formed an important part in the proclamation of the gospel by Paul. As in 1 Thess 1,10, however, the monotheistic remark in Gal 4,8-9 is followed by a reference to Christ. This means that the message to the Gentiles probably contained exactly these two elements: the one, true God, and his envoy Jesus Christ through whom 'we will be saved'.

Another reference by Paul to a confession-formula is found in Rom 10,9: 'if you confess with your lips that Jesus is Lord and believe in your heart that God raised him from the dead, you will be saved'. The focus of this formula is on the status of Jesus as κύριος, which is linked to his resurrection and future salvation. The resurrection of Christ is clearly presented here as the '*articulus stantis et cadentis ecclesiae*',[50] and its saving effect is evidently regarded as a future event. It is thus clear that the earliest Christian community in which Paul became active already understood itself as an eschatological community formed by its faith in Christ by whom they would eventually be saved.

This view of the Christian congregation is also apparent from the eucharistic formula Paul refers to in 1 Cor 11,23-26. These words are taken from liturgical tradition, and therefore may be assumed to reflect the understanding of the community in which they were used. The first part, concerning the bread, implies the interpretation of Jesus' death as an event resulting in salvation for his followers: τοῦτό μού ἐστιν τὸ σῶμα τὸ ὑπὲρ ὑμῶν. The use of ὑπέρ is probably influenced by the dying-formula discussed above. Hence the effect of the death of Christ is interpreted as salvific. The ὑμεῖς presupposed here are of course those addressed by Jesus at the time he supposedly spoke these words, i.e. his followers. The narrative context of this tradition presented in the gospels is that of the Last Supper. In this context Jesus addresses his disciples, and there is no good reason to assume a different context for these words in the tradition that Paul refers to. This means that the understanding of

[50] C.E.B. Cranfield, *The Epistle to the Romans*, vol. 2 (ICC; Edinburgh: Clark, 1979/1989), p. 530.

the community in which this eucharistic formula was used focuses on salvation through Christ.[51]

The death and resurrection of Christ, together with the fact that he will bring about eschatological salvation at the final intervention of God in history, thus appear to have formed the core of the earliest Christian gospel. In regard to the Gentiles this core was combined with the monotheistic proclamation of the one, true God. It is because of the great importance of the Christ event that Paul can refer to its proclamation as being fundamental to his instruction to the Thessalonians (cf. 1 Thess 4,14) and the Corinthians (1 Cor 15,3-5, see above). In what should probably be interpreted as a later elaboration of the earliest Christian kerygma by Paul himself, he establishes the fact that Christ died and was resurrected in order to rule over all, both the living and the dead (Rom 14,9). Also, the great stress Paul lays on the fact that Christ had been crucified – 1 Cor 1,23; 2,2 and Gal 3,1 – puts him in line with the earliest Christian traditions on the death and resurrection of Christ as an event which will bring salvation.

After this survey of the relevant pre-literary traditions contained in the letters of Paul, a first conclusion should be drawn as to Paul's relationship to the Christian movement of which he became such a prominent member.

It is of great importance that the central figure within all the passages mentioned in this section is Christ. *The earliest retrievable Christian formulae focus on christology and on the soteriological consequences of the Christ event.* It had apparently been the eschatological message of Jesus, followed by the tremendous impact of his life and death, and the experience of his resurrection by his followers that formed the core of the gospel at this very early stage of Christianity. Thus, the death and resurrection of Christ naturally became prominent within the early Christian community. Yet judging from the material contained in Paul, the Christ event remained embedded in the expectation of the imminent, ultimate intervention of God in history. The salvation Christ would bring about is defined as a future event: he will save his followers from the coming wrath of God. This expectation cannot be understood apart from Jewish apocalypticism. Within apocalyptic literature a universalistic tendency is

---

[51] The Lord's Supper was celebrated as a commemoration of the past, and in anticipation of the future. During the meal, in the presence of the Lord, the Christian congregation proleptically experiences the salvation that has been promised. See J. Jeremias, *Die Abendmahlsworte Jesu* (Göttingen: Vandenhoeck & Ruprecht, 4th ed. 1967, [1]1935), e.g. p. 252: 'Die Tischgemeinschaft mit Jesus ist Vorweggabe der Vollerfüllung.' See also G.D. Fee, *The first Epistle to the Corinthians* (NIC; Grand Rapids: Eerdmans, 1987), p. 551.

present: the intervention of God in history will not just aim at restoring Israel, but will entail a judgement of the entire world.[52]

The same universalistic tendency appears to be present in the pre-epistolary, or at any rate early, hymn Paul takes up in Phil 2,6-11. Assuming that Paul did not compose this hymn, the conclusion should be drawn that, at the latest, already in the early stage of Paul's activities the implications of the Christ event were extended *beyond the realm of Israel*. It may be inferred that at this very same stage the point was reached where it was thought necessary for pagans, in order to be saved at the coming retribution, to turn to the one, true God and his envoy Jesus Christ (1 Thess 1,9-10; Gal 4,8-9; cf. the influence of Isa 45, 20-23 in Phil 2,6-11). We should thus conclude that the proclamation of the one true God by the early Christian movement coincided with the proclamation of the Christ event. The coming of Christ together with his eschatological significance was considered to be of universal importance. Nevertheless, a necessary pre-condition to recognising this universal impact is faith in the one God who had sent him. This means that for pagans the acceptance of the Christ event could not be complete without the recognition of the monotheistic framework in which this event gained its importance.

For a reconstruction of Paul's position within the early Christian missionary movement the latter observation is of great importance. It means that, already in the thirties or early forties, the saving effect of the Christ event was considered to extend beyond the range of Judaism. The theological foundation we found in the pre-epistolary traditions contained in Paul's letters, points to an apocalyptic interpretation of salvation brought about by Christ: since God's ultimate intervention in history affects the entire world, salvation can be obtained by anyone who confesses Christ as well as worshipping the one, true God.[53] This view can only be situated in a context in which Jews and Gentiles together formed the Jesus movement. *Thus, Christianity as an open movement formed by Jews and Gentiles alike preceded Paul.*

When compared to the proclamation of the coming Kingdom that formed the core of Jesus' message, two elements have changed significantly. In the first place, the object of proclamation is no longer the Kingdom of God expected to come soon. Instead of proclaiming the imminent intervention of God in history, the post-Easter Jesus movement proclaimed

---

[52] See Bousset, Gressmann, *Religion*, pp. 257-286.
[53] See for instance 1 Cor 8,5-6; Gal 4,4-11; 1 Thess 4,15-18.

that God's intervention had already begun in Jesus Christ. Salvation was bound to come for his followers – all who confessed Christ as Lord were reckoned among the eschatological elect. In the second place the universal character of this salvation was considered to extend to Gentiles as well as Jews.

The observation that Paul apparently entered the scene when the Jesus movement already entailed a mission to Gentiles, is of crucial importance for our quest. Throughout his letters Paul defends the community of Jews and Gentiles in Christ. But obviously Paul did not invent the inclusion of Gentiles within the Christian movement; he was merely its greatest defender. The Book of Acts will show us, however, that there were others who preceded Paul's activities as an apostle to the Gentiles.

EXCURSUS: The Historical Value of the Book of Acts

At first sight the Book of Acts contains an abundance of evidence on the earliest expansion of the Jesus movement after Easter as well as on its development towards becoming an independent religion separated from Judaism. Unfortunately, the evidence is not unproblematic.

The Book of Acts has long been held as the principal source for the history of early Christianity. Both the description of the congregation in Jerusalem and its picture of Paul are still very influential.[54] But the nineteenth century brought about an enormous change. The rise of historical criticism profoundly altered the evaluation of Acts' historical reliability. Provoked by the theories of the *Tübinger Schule* scholars of the Book of Acts had to acknowledge the apologetic character of the book.[55] It was now widely agreed upon that the book primarily serves theological purposes. This turned the scholarly opinion on the Book of Acts to a more careful approach of its value as a historical source.

Any analysis of the development of the early Christian movement must take a clear stand with regard to the question to what degree the Book of Acts is historically reliable.[56] No general answer can be given here. It is

---

[54] On Acts' portrait of Paul, see I.H. Marshall, 'Luke's Portrait of the Pauline Mission', in: P. Bolt, M. Thompson (eds.), *The Gospel to the Nations. Perspectives on Paul's Mission* (Leicester: Apollos; Downers Grove: Intervarsity, 2000), pp. 99-113.

[55] F.C. Baur, K. Schrader, A. Schwegler, E. Zeller, followed by a number of others – cf. A.C. McGiffert, 'The Historical Criticism of Acts in Germany', in: *Beginnings*, vol. 2, pp. 363-395, esp. pp. 367-376.

[56] See for instance W.W. Gasque, 'The Historical Value of the Book of Acts. An Essay in the History of New Testament Criticism', *EvQ* 41 (1969), pp. 68-88; A.J. Matill,

evident that the author had certain theological and propagandistic or apologetic intentions in writing the book the way he did. Hence it is safe to say that at the level of redaction the Book of Acts is primarily a theological writing.[57] It is also clear that the author created a *book* by using the literary techniques and instruments he had at his disposal, so that Acts' portrayal of Paul is primarily literary in character.[58] Yet at the same time it does depict the history of the early Christian community, albeit in a theological way. Can pieces of that history still be recovered?

M. Hengel has argued that the Book of Acts should be judged against the criteria of the first century CE, not our own.[59] According to him historiography as a more or less objective description of the past is an invention of the modern era. The author of Acts was committed to the history he described in such a way as to render it in a trustworthy version.[60] Paul's companion Luke, whom Hengel holds to be the author, described the history of the developing Christian community as a reliable historiographer.[61] This does not mean that his work has not been coloured by his theological and apologetic purposes: the author wishes, among other things, to describe the history of the early Christian community in such a way as to present it as a sympathetic movement which was inaugurated,

---

'The Value of Acts as a Source for the Study of Paul', *PRS* 5 (1978), pp. 76-98. The most careful approach is the one by G. Lüdemann, 'Acts of the Apostles as a Historical Source', in: J. Neusner, P. Borgen, E.S. Frerichs, R. Horsley (eds.), *The Social World of Formative Christianity and Judaism. Essays in Tribute to Howard Clark Kee* (Philadelphia: Fortress Press, 1988), pp. 109-125. Lüdeman argues that the traditions that have been reworked in Acts contain historically reliable information on early Christianity. See also his *Das frühe Christentum nach den Traditionen der Apostelgeschichte* (Göttingen: Vandenhoeck&Ruprecht, 1987), pp. 9-29.

[57] J. Panagopoulos, 'Zur Theologie der Apostelgeschichte', *NT* 14 (1972), pp. 137-159; cf. esp. p. 140: 'Die Eigentümlichkeit des Lukas besteht eben darin (…), daß er seine Zeit und die sie bewegenden Fragen mit der ihm bekannten theologischen Tradition zu interpretieren weiß.'

[58] This is evident from e.g. the picture Acts gives of Paul in cc. 27-28; for an analysis, see M. Labahn, 'Paulus – ein *homo honestus et iustus*. Das lukanische Paulusportrait von Act 27-28 im Lichte ausgewählter antiker Parallellen', in: F. W. Horn (ed.), *Das Ende des Paulus. Historische, theologische und literaturgeschichtliche Aspekte* (BZNW 106; Berlin, New York: De Gruyter, 2001), pp. 74-106.

[59] See e.g. M. Dibelius, 'Die Apostelgeschichte als Geschichtsquelle', in: Dibelius, *Aufsätze zur Apostelgeschichte* hrsg. von H. Greeven (FRLANT nf 42; Göttingen: Vandenhoeck&Ruprecht; 1951), pp. 91-95; F.F. Bruce, *The Acts of the Apostles. The Greek Text with Introduction and Commentary* (Grand Rapids: Eerdmans, 1951, repr. 1986), pp. 15-18, cf. p. 15: 'Of all the Evangelists, it is Luke who approaches most nearly the standards of the classical historians.'

[60] M. Hengel, *Zur urchristlichen Geschichtsschreibung* (CP; Stuttgart: Calwer, 1979), see esp. pp. 11-61 ('Antike und urchristliche Geschichtsschreibung').

[61] Hengel, *Geschichtsschreibung*, pp. 60-61.

formed, and directed by God himself.[62] Yet, for Hengel, this does not diminish its historical trustworthiness. A glimpse at for instance Flavius Josephus or Suetonius is enough to see that other Graeco-Roman historiographers could also allow their rendering of history to be influenced by the aim of their work. In this respect the Book of Acts does not really differ from contemporary historiography.

It seems that Hengel pursues the argument at least one step too far. Indeed, the fact that the author of Acts writes from a certain theological and apologetic point of view does not necessarily imply that his rendering of historical developments and events is totally unreliable. But Hengel's position seems to undervalue the theological impetus of the Book of Acts. The author of this work was primarily concerned with the divine origin, spread, and identity of the Church. He therefore described the way in which it spread in its early history in a favourable manner. The method the author used for collecting and presenting his material is indeed comparable to that of (other) ancient historiographers.[63] He obviously collected as much material as he could on the subjects he wrote about. The final narrative is the result of his combining the different traditions and maybe even some written sources that he had gathered.[64] Nevertheless, the Book of Acts focuses not primarily on a historically reliable picture of the growth of the church, but on the divine origin of the Christian movement and its spread.

Two themes are decisive for the structure and narrative of Acts: its theological and geographical programme (1,8), and the wise advice of Gamaliel given in 5,37-38. The programmatic verse 1,8 has been identified as the geographical framework of the writing as a whole.[65] The action

---

[62] See Bruce, *Acts*, pp. 29-34.

[63] See H. Steichele, *Vergleich der Apostelgeschichte mit der antiken Geschichtsschreibung. Eine Studie zur Erzählkunst in der Apostelgeschichte* (München, diss. 1971). According to Steichele, the Book of Acts is very much comparable to ancient historiography, but: 'Wer von den echten Paulusbriefen herkommend die Apg betrachtet, wird weiterhin, wie einst K. Schrader, beteuern müssen: "Kaum eine Spur von dem echten Paulus"' (p. 105).

[64] C.K. Barrett, *A Critical and Exegetical Commentary on the Acts of the Apostles*, vol. 1 (ICC; Edinburgh: Clark, 1994), pp. 49-56, argues that for the first part of Acts (cc. 1-14) the author had four main sources of supply: 1. traditions that came to him by Philip the Evangelist (cf. 21,8); 2. traditions from Caesarea (21,8 and 8,40); 3. specific Antiochene traditions; 4. information from Pauline sources. For the second part of the writing similar sources (oral or literary) must have been available.

[65] Panagopoulos, 'Theologie', p. 140, speaks of a double meaning of 1,8: 1,8a contains a 'theocratic principle', whereas 1,8b geographic. According to W.C. van Unnik, 'Der Ausdruck ἕως ἐσχάτου τῆς γῆς (Apostelgeschichte 1:8) und sein alttestamentlichen

starts in Jerusalem and ends in Rome. The entire narrative in between is a theological reconstruction of how the Spirit drove the apostles, and Paul, to the fulfilment of the missionary programme of 1,8. What has been noted less often is that Gamaliel's advice forms the clue for interpreting the way in which the Christian movement spread.[66] After each attempt at suppressing it, the movement spread further. Thus, the divine origin of Christianity is shown time and time again.

For the present day historian, who aims at reconstructing the rise of Christianity in its first days, the above approach to the Book of Acts may still make it possible to evaluate carefully the data it contains. Assuming that the chronological and geographical development of the narrative was largely formed by the author's hand, the smaller units may be isolated and regarded as the result of an elaboration of earlier traditions.[67] This approach can safely be applied to the first part of Acts, i.e. to cc. 1-12. With regard to cc. 13-28, however, matters are different. M. Dibelius' theory of an *itinerarium* that would have formed the basis for 13,4-21,16 offers a quite acceptable explanation for a number of inconsistencies.[68] It furthermore explains why certain places are mentioned that play no part at all in the narrative. It is uncertain, however, whether any more sources can be identified, such as the alleged source for the process against Paul.[69] The use of the first person plural in the so-called 'we-passages', often used as an argument for ascribing these passages to an autonomous source, can be explained as a literary device used by the author to create the impression of authenticity. It is certainly possible that the description of the sea travel in 27,1-28,1 was indeed based upon a

Hintergrund', in: *Studia Biblica et Semitica Theodoro Christiano Vriezen Dedicata* (Wageningen: Veenman, 1966), pp. 335-349, 1,8 does not aim at a spread of the Christian movement to Rome. T.C.G. Thornton, 'To the end of the earth: Acts 8,1', *ExpTim* 89 (1978), pp. 374-375, argues that in the first century CE Ethiopia was regarded as the 'end of the world', and therefore the description of ch. 8 fulfills the programme of 1,8.

[66] R. Pesch, *Die Apostelgeschichte* (EKK; Zürich: Benziger Verlag; Neukirchen-Vluyn: Neukirchener Verlag, 1986), vol. 1, p. 220, points at 2,23 and 4,28 to indicate that according to Peter the Jesus movement was indeed ἐκ θεοῦ. This implies that the Jewish opposition to the gospel as depicted in Acts, for the author at least, was a form of θεομάχειν. It resulted not in the disappearance of the movement, but in its spread (cf. e.g. 13,48-52).

[67] For this method, see Lüdemann, *Das frühe Christentum*, passim.

[68] For a survey of authors defending and rejecting the hypothesis of an itinerary, see J. Jervell, *Die Apostelgeschichte* (KEK; Göttingen: Vandenhoeck & Ruprecht, 1998), p. 64, n. 71.

[69] See Jervell, *Apostelgeschichte*, pp. 61-72, for a discussion of the matter and a survey of literature. Jervell's position is, however, difficult to maintain: his assumption that Luke-Acts were written by Paul's travelling companion Luke is highly problematic.

travel journal that originally had nothing to do with Paul.[70] And it is probable that certain episodes in the final part of Acts also go back to earlier traditions or even written material. But it is extremely difficult to substantiate any such theory.

For the present purpose it is enough to state that the various episodes in the Book of Acts were probably created by the author moulding the data he had at his disposal in the form of earlier, oral or literary, data. These data must, at least in part, have come from local traditions concerning either Peter, Philip, Paul or the congregations at Jerusalem and Antioch. Careful comparison of these data and other early Christian sources, primarily the Pauline epistles, may shed some light on the history described in Acts. In other words: the Book of Acts may contain historically reliable descriptions of events, but these can only be reconstructed by comparing the individual data with the theology and purpose of Acts on the one hand, and other early Christian writings on the other. In spite of Hengel's polemic against those interpreters of Acts who are suspicious of its historical value, Acts cannot be trusted at face value.[71]

Two examples of this verdict may be given in the accounts of Paul's circumcision of Timothy and his Nazirite vow. The circumcision of Timothy is a difficult matter: Paul, who in his letters clearly speaks of the Jewish Law as belonging to the past, would have applied this law to Timothy. There appears to be a contradiction between the Paul of the letters and the picture in Acts. For this apparent contradiction three possible solutions are usually mentioned: (1) either the author of Acts has invented the whole episode, or (2) it comes from a false tradition on Paul, or (3) it reflects an event that actually took place.

---

[70] Thus Ph. Vielhauer, *Geschichte*, p. 393.

[71] M. Hengel, A.M. Schwemer, *Paul between Damascus and Antioch. The Unknown Years* (London: SCM, 1997), p. 6: 'We know too little to be able to reject in advance what sources say, in a hypercritical attitude which is at the same time hostile to history, without examining them carefully. (…) The real danger in the interpretation of Acts (and the Gospels) is no longer an uncritical apologetic but the hypercritical ignorance and arrogance which – often combined with unbridled fantasy – has lost any understanding of living historical reality.' In the present author's opinion, quite the reverse is true: we know too little to be able to *accept* in advance what the sources say. The two clearest examples of how the author of Luke-Acts confuses his data are the chronology in Luke 2,1-2, and the fact that Gamaliel in Acts 5,36 refers to the activities of Theudas as preceding those of Judas the Galilean, whereas they should be dated after Gamaliel's day. On the first example, see Schürer *et al.*, *History*, vol. 1, pp. 399-427; on the second, E. Haenchen, *Die Apostelgeschichte* (KEK; Göttingen: Vandenhoeck & Ruprecht, 5th ed., 1965, ¹1956), pp. 211-212 ('Nicht eine ältere Quelle, die den Ereignissen noch näher stand, sondern Lukas selber, von späteren Nachrichten unvollkommen unterrichtet, kommt hier zu Wort' – p. 212).

For the Tübingen school of the 19th century the first solution was the obvious one. F.C. Baur, for example, took it for granted that it was the author of Acts who made up Timothy's circumcision.[72] Present interpreters of Acts are usually more careful. It is argued mostly that the passage has been derived from tradition. The question that divides the students of Acts, however, is whether this tradition is historically reliable.[73] Since we have no means to verify or falsify this we have to work with degrees of probability. Most interpreters either mention 1 Cor 9,20 in their attempt to make it plausible that Paul did indeed circumcise Timothy or refer to Gal 5,11 to show that Paul could certainly not have done so. The solution that many choose is the following: Paul did not reject the Jewish Law as such, but only as the means to obtain salvation. According to Acts Timothy was not circumcised in order to find salvation within the Jewish Law but to improve their chances on missionary success, and therefore it is considered quite plausible that Paul did indeed do such a thing.[74] According to F.F. Bruce, for instance, circumcision was so completely irrelevant to Paul that he may even have practiced it in order to improve the prospects of his own missionary task.[75]

If Bruce and others following his line of argument are correct, the question remains why Paul could become so agitated in regard to exactly this point, circumcision, in his letter to the Galatians. It is therefore best to think of the author of Acts as a 'victim of unreliable tradition'.[76] This

---

[72] 'Dass derselbe Paulus, welcher in Jerusalem mit aller Macht sich weigerte, den Titus aus Rücksicht auf die Juden und Judenchristen beschneiden zu lassen, nicht lange nachher aus derselben Rücksicht den Timotheus selbst soll beschnitten haben (...) gehört gleichfalls zum schlechthin Unglaublichen der Apostelgeschichte' – F.C. Baur, *Paulus, der Apostel Jesu Christi. Sein Leben und Wirken, seine Briefe und seine Lehre*, vol. 1 (Leipzig: Fues, 2nd ed., 1866), p. 147, n. 1.

[73] To mention but some of the interpreters who dealt with the issue: A. Weiser, *Die Apostelgeschichte*, 2 vols. (OTKNT; Gütersloh: Mohn, 1981.1985), p. 400, considers the report to rely on an untrustworthy tradition; Barrett, *Acts*, vol. 2, p. 762, shares this verdict. Pesch, *Apostelgeschichte*, vol. 2, p. 97, considers the event historically reliable; so does Jervell, *Apostelgeschichte*, p. 412. G. Schneider, *Apostelgeschichte*, vol. 2 (HThK; Herder: Freiburg [etc.]: Herder, 1982), pp. 200-201 leaves the matter undecided.

[74] See for instance W. Schmithals, *Die Apostelgeschichte des Lukas* (ZB; Zürich: Theologischer Verlag, 1982), pp. 145-146, who in regard of Timothy's circumcision judges: 'Damit beschränkte Paulus weder seine gesetzesfreie Mission unter den Heiden noch bejahte er für die Juden das Gesetz als *Heilsweg* (ital. Schmithals).' Cf. also Pesch, *Apostelgeschichte*, pp. 98-99.

[75] F.F. Bruce, *The Book of Acts* (Grand Rapids: Eerdmans, 1954, rev. ed., 1988), p. 304, argues this while referring to Gal 5,6; 6,15 and 1 Cor 9,23.

[76] Haenchen, *Apostelgeschichte*, pp. 463-465: 'Opfer einer unzuverlässigen Überlieferung'. Haenchen regards the passage as resulting from anti-Pauline tradition of his opponents in the Galatian congregations who apparently spread the message on Paul that he 'still preached circumcision' (Gal 5,11). See also H. Conzelmann, *Die Apostelgeschichte* (HNT; Tübingen: Mohr, 2nd ed., 1972), p. 97.

means, however, that the report on Timothy's circumcision in Acts 16, 1-5 has no value for the reconstruction of Paul's method.[77]

Unfortunately the same conclusion is valid for Paul as a Nazirite. In Acts 18,18 it is said of Paul that he had his head shaved at Cenchrae because 'he was under a vow'.[78] This remark creates a problem. Apparently Paul had made the vow of a Nazirite, but in Num 6,18 it is stated that the Nazirite should shave his head, not before the vow, but after its release in the temple. It has been argued that the author of Acts misinterpreted the custom, and placed the shaving of the head before the period of the vow, instead of at its end.[79] Nevertheless, in 21,23-26 Paul goes to the temple in Jerusalem because of the Nazirite vow of the four men mentioned in v. 23. Here, the custom is described in the proper manner, and the shaving of the head is mentioned as the sign of the vow's remittal. Recently a proposal was made to interpret the 18,18 not as a description of a Nazirite vow but as reflecting a Graeco-Roman custom: Juvenal describes a similar vow in *Sat.* 12,81-82 that has nothing to do with Nazirite vows.[80] This observation should lead to some caution: in 18,18 Luke probably depends on tradition, since the vow mentioned has no specific meaning at the redactional level of Acts. It may well be that this tradition contained some relevant information, but it is difficult to decide whether what we have here reflects a Greek custom or a misinterpreted Nazirite vow.

It thus appears in two test cases that the Book of Acts does at first sight appear to add important information to what is known from Paul himself. At a closer look, however, this information cannot be trusted that easily.

3. Pre-Pauline Mission in Acts

Based on the approach described above, we will be able to look for some information on pre-Pauline mission in the data contained in the Book of Acts. The description in Acts presents us with four sections containing traditions on Paul's early Christian context. It describes the group of the

---

[77] See also Barrett, *Acts*, vol. 2, pp. 761-762. Jervell, *Apostelgeschichte*, pp. 412-413 argues in favour of historicity of the circumcision of Timothy.

[78] The words κειράμενος ἐν Κεγχρεαῖς τὴν κεφαλήν, εἶχεν γὰρ εὐχήν no doubt refer to Paul and not to Aquila who is mentioned immediately before these words.

[79] *Beginnings of Christianity*, vol. 4, p. 230.

[80] Cf. G.H.R. Horsley (ed.), *New Documents Illustrating Early Christianity*, (North Ryde: The Ancient History Documentary Research Centre, 1981-), vol. 4, vol. 4, pp. 114-115; Barrett, *Acts*, vol. 2, p. 878.

'Hellenists', the ministry of Philip the evangelist, the conversion of Cornelius, and the formation of the Antiochene community as the first 'Christians'.

a. The Hellenists

The Book of Acts depicts the activities of the 'Hellenists', i.e. Greek-speaking Jews who had become part of the early Christian movement, as crucial for the spread of Christianity from Jerusalem throughout Judea and Samaria. After the book's portrayal of the life of the first Christian congregation in Jerusalem in cc. 1-5, it continues with the description of a conflict between the 'Hellenists' and the 'Hebrews' (6,1).[81] The situation portrayed is that of two Christian groups of which the latter spoke Aramaic and the former Greek.[82] The focus of the conflict is on the widows among the Hellenists: they were apparently being neglected whilst in the care of the Hebrews.[83] To solve this problem, the apostles appointed seven leaders among the Hellenists: Stephen, Philip, Prochoros, Nikanor, Timon, Parmenas, and Nikolaos.[84] The last one is mentioned as a proselyte from Antioch, the first two are depicted in cc. 7-8 as the first Christian martyr and the first Christian preacher to win a non-Jew for the Christian faith.

The importance of the Hellenists for the present subject is that the Book of Acts presents them as a bridge between the Aramaic-speaking congregation in Jerusalem and the Church in Antioch (8,1; 11,19-20).[85]

---

[81] For a survey of literature on the Hellenists, see Pesch, *Die Apostelgeschichte*, vol. 1, pp. 224-225; Jervell, *Apostelgeschichte*, pp. 214-215; cf. also H. Räisänen, 'Die "Hellenisten" der Urgemeinde', in: W. Haase, *ANRW II Principat* 26/2 (1995), pp. 1468-1514.

[82] For this interpretation of 'Hellenists' as Greek-speaking Jews and 'Hebrews' as Aramaic speaking Jews, see M. Hengel, 'Zwischen Jesus und Paulus'; R. Pesch, E. Gerhart, F. Schilling, '"Hellenisten" und "Hebräer". Zu Apg. 9,29 und 6,1', *BZ* 23 (1979), pp. 87-92.

[83] The point is probably that the category mentioned, the widows of Greek-speaking Jews, were neglected in the support of the poor – cf. A. Strobel, 'Armenpfleger "um des Friedens willen"', *ZNW* 63 (1972), pp. 271-276.

[84] Although the passage 6,1-7 is highly coloured by the redaction of Acts, vv. 1.5-6 probably reflect a tradition on the installation of seven leaders – J.T. Lienhard, 'Acts 6,1-6: A Redactional View', *CBQ* 37 (1975), pp. 228-236.

[85] Cf. the discussion by Hengel, *Between Jesus and Paul*, pp. 1-29; also E. Lohse, 'Die urchristliche Mission', in: R. Kottje, B. Moeller (eds.), *Ökumenische Kirchengeschichte. Vol. 1: Alte Kirche und Ostkirche* (Mainz: Grünewald; Munchen: Kaiser, 1970), pp. 37-41. A critical treatment of the subject is given by H. Räisänen, 'The "Hellenists": a Bridge between Jesus and Paul?', in: idem, *Jesus, Paul and Torah. Collected Essays* (JSNTSS 43; Sheffield: Sheffield Academic Press, 1992), pp. 149-202. According to

From 6,1 it appears that the language of this group was Greek, and 6,2 identifies them as a Christian group. This means that according to the Book of Acts there already existed, at a very early stage, two groups of Christians in Jerusalem: Greek-speaking Jewish Christians, and Aramaic-speaking Jewish Christians.

The report in 6,1-7 on the tension between these two groups and on the way in which it was resolved probably reflects a genuine problem within the early movement. It is very unlikely that the installation of the seven leaders by 'the Twelve' is merely a literary attempt by the author of Acts to depict a troubled relationship between the two groups in a harmonious way. The author of Acts would not have invented seven fictional persons here to have played such a key-role in the congregation of Jerusalem. Any Christian who had participated in the history of this congregation would have been able to correct him. Therefore, the picture of two factions within the early Christian movement is probably basically correct.[86]

In Acts 7 it appears that the group of Greek-speaking Jewish Christians met with fierce opposition from the Aramaic-speaking non-Christian Jews: they stoned Stephen to death in what appears to have been an unorganised lynching party.[87] Acts mentions Stephen's theological stance as the reason for his lynching. The accusation in 6,14 contains two elements that are often considered typical of the Hellenists: a reference to Jesus' criticism of the temple and a criticism of the Law. The former element derives directly from Mark: in Mark 14,58 false witnesses accuse Jesus of an attack against the temple. This element from Mark is taken up by Matthew,[88] but left out by Luke in his version of the trial of Jesus. In stead, Luke used the whole scene of false witnesses who wrongly accuse Jesus of having threatened to destroy the temple in his description of Stephen's 'trial'. Acts 6,14 is thus modelled after Mark 14,58. Next, the author of Acts adds Stephen's loose attitude towards the Law. Many interpreters conclude therefore that these two elements were the main characteristics of the Hellenists' theological position, and as such led to the death of Stephen. Their position apparently triggered some existing tension, which resulted in the stoning of Stephen.

Räisänen the Hellenists did form an important bridge between Palestine and Asia, but not so much between Jesus and Paul.

[86] Cf. Lienhard, 'Acts 6,1-6'.

[87] Pesch, *Apostelgeschichte*, vol. 1, p. 267, notes that 'erst Lukas für die Übermalung einer ursprünglichen Lynchjustiz der hellenistischen Synagoge durch die Züge einer offiziellen Synedrialverhandlung verantwortlich ist.'

[88] Matt 26,61; 27,40.

It is not very likely though that the two elements mentioned in 6,14 are enough to account for the death of Stephen. Criticism of the temple is also accorded to Jesus himself,[89] and was therefore not strictly limited to Graeco-Jewish Christians. Indeed, the purely Palestinian congregation of Qumran abhorred the temple-cult in Jerusalem, and heavily criticised it.[90] The criticism of a strict interpretation of the Mosaic Law was not restricted to the Hellenistic Christian movement. It was a characteristic of many Greek-speaking Jewish communities and could easily be perceived alongside Jesus' eschatological restriction of the value of the Law.[91]

If criticism of the temple and a loose attitude to the Law were not restricted to the Hellenists, what other reason could there have been for the stoning of Stephen? At this point we can only assume that it was the combination of the Greek language, criticism of the temple, a loose attitude to the Law, and, on top of all that, the confession of Jesus as the Anointed One sent by God as his final envoy. This combination of views must have been too much for at least some strict, law-abiding, Aramaic speaking, Palestinian Jews.

In its present form, Stephen's speech is probably an adaptation of an earlier composition that has been inserted by the author into the narrative of Acts.[92] It is evident that this speech is not a trustworthy account of Stephen's final words: an angry mob, ready to lynch its victim, would not have had the patience to sit back and endure Stephen's sermon. The speech is therefore an example of literary apologetics employed by the author of Acts. The historical core of his description would have been the fact that fierce opposition from Palestinian Jews led to the death of Stephen. Within its redactional context the speech serves an apologetic

---

[89] See E.P. Sanders, *Jesus and Judaism* (London: SCM, 1985), pp. 61-76.

[90] For a comparison of the themes of Acts 7 with 1QS, cf. A.F.J. Klijn, 'Stephen's Speech – Acts VII.2-53', *NTS* 4 (1957/1958), pp. 25-31. See, however, H. Braun, *Qumran und das Neue Testament*, vol. 2 (Tübingen: Mohr, 1966), pp. 157-158.

[91] Several lines of synoptic tradition report, e.g., that Jesus himself was critical of the strict observation of the sabbath rules; cf. e.g. Mark 2,27-28parr.; Luke 14,2-6. Nevertheless, it is to be doubted whether Jesus was actually critical of the Mosaic Law itself – cf. Sanders, *Jesus and Judaism*, pp. 245-269. According to Sanders, Jesus 'did not think that it (= the Law; LP) could be freely transgressed, but rather that it was not final' (p. 267).

[92] F.J. Foakes Jackson, 'Stephen's Speech in Acts', *JBL* 49 (1930), pp. 283-286; U. Wilckens, *Die Missionsreden der Apostelgeschichte. Form- und traditionsgeschichtliche Untersuchungen* (WMANT 5; Neukirchen-Vluyn: Neukirchener Verlag, 3rd ed., 1974, ¹1961), pp. 208-224.

goal.[93] For the present purpose, we may disregard this apologetic speech, and focus on the effect of the event as depicted in Acts.

The sequel to Stephen's death is the persecution of the entire congregation in Jerusalem, described in 8,1-3. According to Acts this persecution leads to a further spread of the gospel. This development is fully in line with the two main themes of the work: the spread of the movement towards the outer limits of the earth, and the fact that persecution would result not in the disappearance of the Christian movement, but in its spread – thereby proving its divine origin (cf. p. 102). Together with the language used in the passage, this slant in the book implies that 8,1-3 forms a redactional transition to the account of the activities of Philip given in 8,4-40.[94] Given the scantiness of information on Christianity outside Jerusalem, the historian should not focus too much on the spread of the movement as described in 8,1-3. It is implausible that there were only Christians in Jerusalem – the *auctor ad Theophilum* completely leaves out Jesus' Galilean followers and Judean Christianity outside Jerusalem.[95]

In his commentary on Acts, E. Haenchen has argued that the account of the persecution of the church in Jerusalem is in fact a narrative rendering of the persecution of the 'Hellenists'. According to Haenchen, it was not the entire congregation that was cast out of town, but just those who were Greek-speaking.[96] Haenchen, and later Hengel, argued that this expulsion of the 'Hellenists' was the origin of Christian mission.[97] The author of Acts, however, according to Haenchen, focused on Paul as the great missionary to the Gentiles, and was not really interested in the genuine development that formed the first stage of the spread of Christianity into the Greek world:

---

[93] See for instance already W. Mundle, 'Die Stephanusrede Apg 7: eine Märtyrerapologie', *ZNW* 20 (1921), pp. 133-147. 'Die Rede, die Stephanus an das Synhedrium richtet, ist in Wirklichkeit eine apologetische Ansprache, in der sich der Verfasser der Apostelgeschichte an die Gegner des Christentums seiner Zeit richtet (...)' (p. 139).

[94] Althought the verbs συγκομίζειν, κοπετός, and λυμαίνειν are *hapax legomena*, the whole of 8,1-3 is clearly redactional – cf. Barrett, *Acts*, vol. 1, pp. 388-393.

[95] The latter is attested by e.g. Gal 1,22, the former implied by Mark 16,6 and Matt 28, 16-20.

[96] Haenchen, *Apostelgeschichte*, p. 248: 'Wir haben bereits (...) gesehen, daß Lukas irrtümlich annimmt, die ganze Gemeinde Jerusalems (außer den Aposteln) sei vertrieben worden. Da er sich nicht vorstellen konnte, daß sie in zwei sehr unterschiedliche Gruppen zerfiel, mußte er mit einer Zerstreuung der Gesamtgemeinde rechnen. Andererseits sagte die Überlieferung nichts von einer Verfolgung der Apostel – also hatten diese ausgeharrt und damit die Kontinuität der Urgemeinde gewahrt! Daß diese Konstruktion am Widerspruch von 9,31 und 11,19 scheitert, ist Lukas nicht bewußt geworden.'

[97] Ibid.; and Hengel, *Between Jesus and Paul*, pp. 1-29.

In Wirklichkeit ist der paulinischen Mission zunächst ein 'anonymes' Stadium der christlichen Mission vorangegangen, das sich nicht an bestimmte und berühmte Namen knüpft, und diese für uns namenlose Mission ist auch neben der paulinischen hergegangen: der Beginn christlicher Gemeinden in Damaskus, Antiochia, Ephesus und Rom ist in Wirklichkeit nicht von Paulus ausgegangen.[98]

Haenchen's analysis gives a solution to the problem of why the Twelve could remain in Jerusalem. They apparently function as a symbol for the Palestinian Christian congregation. It is the Greek speaking part of the Jesus movement that was expelled from Jerusalem. If this is correct, it was indeed this group of Hellenists that initiated the further spread of the church in the anonymous manner described by Haenchen.

For the present purpose the following observations should be made in regard to the Hellenists. Firstly, it can be taken for granted that a group of Greek-speaking Jewish Christians existed as a more or less separate group. Secondly, this group would have had leaders, among them Philip and Stephen. Thirdly, that the gospel spread to Antioch and other cities by means of Greek-speaking followers of Jesus is highly plausible. Fourthly, we cannot with any degree of certainty say how this happened, i.e. as a result of persecution or by natural spread. Finally, though the lenient attitude towards the Mosaic Law and criticism of the temple were not restricted to the Greek-speaking Jewish Christians, this theological position did create a good foundation for this group of Jewish Christians to attract Gentiles.

b. Philip

The Book of Acts presents Paul as the great missionary who went to the Gentiles in order to spread the gospel to the four corners of the earth. Yet before his story is told, Philip and Peter are described as having initiated this mission. This is an important observation that calls for evaluation.

In ch. 8 Philip and Peter are the main characters. The structure of the chapter is as follows. After the persecution of the congregation in Jerusalem, the movement was scattered and this caused a further spread of the gospel (8,4). Then, the preaching of Philip in Samaria is described (8,5-8). The conversion of Simon Magus is presented as resulting from this (8,9-13). Philip's work is subsequently finished and perfected by Peter and John who, sent out by the apostles in Jerusalem, come to bring

---

[98] Haenchen, *Apostelgeschichte*, p. 250.

the spirit to the newly converted Samaritans (8,14-25). They thus come
to Simon Magus and rebuke him for his impiety. Then, they return to
Jerusalem, having preached the gospel in many villages and towns in
Samaria. The final part of ch. 8 contains the enigmatic description of the
meeting of Philip and the ἀνὴρ αἰθίοψ (8,26-40). This chapter thus contains three separate sections that may be important to a study on pre-
Pauline mission, especially since they may rest on divergent traditions:
a) Philip in Samaria; b) Peter and John in Samaria; c) the conversion of
the Ethiopic eunuch.

1. Philip in Samaria (8,4-13)

The author of Acts introduces Philip as a wandering charismatic
preacher.[99] Apparently, the author had some traditional information at his
disposal concerning the activities of Philip.[100] He is mentioned as one of
the seven leaders of the Hellenists in 6,5, the first after Stephen. Also in
21,8 his position as 'one of the seven' plays a part, and in that verse
Philip is introduced as ὁ εὐαγγελιστής. This reference to 'Philip the
evangelist' is no doubt traditional: Luke/Acts uses the rare word εὐαγγελιστής only on this occasion. In the Book of Acts evangelists are not
mentioned as a separate group of Christian missionaries, whereas they
are in Eph 4,11.[101] There, they are presented as a distinct category,
together with apostles, prophets, shepherds, and teachers. The term
εὐαγγελίστης probably reflects a relatively late tradition.[102] It must have
been applied to Philip at a relatively late stage because it was thought to
describe his activities adequately without turning him into an apostle.

Of course, the previous observation does not imply that this relatively
late tradition on Philip may not contain some early information. But this
information has to be extracted from the report in Acts. A significant

---

[99] Pesch, *Apostelgeschichte*, vol. 1, p. 272: 'Wie Stephanus hat die Tradition auch Philippus als Pneumatiker gezeichnet (vgl. 6,3; 8,29.39; 21,8f.).'

[100] Many students of Acts take into account the possibility that the author had direct
contact with Philip's home environment. Cf. Barrett, *Acts*, vol. 1, p. 51: 'Whatever we
make of the historical value of 21,8, the verse claims, on the author's part, some contact with Philip the Evangelist.' See already H. Waitz, 'Die Quelle der Philippus-
Geschichten in der Apostelgeschichte 8,5-40', *ZNW* 7 (1906), pp. 340-355; Pesch,
Apostelgeschichte, vol. 1, pp. 270-271.

[101] See also 2 Tim 4,5.

[102] H. Merklein, *Das kirchliche Amt nach dem Epheserbrief* (SANT 33; München: Kösel,
1973), p. 347: 'Die Herkunft des Begriffes εὐαγγελιστής ist also in dogmatischen
Überlegungen der nachapostolischen Zeit zu suchen.'

phrase in this report is the statement in 8,5, that Philip 'proclaimed the Christ to them' (ἐκήρυσσεν αὐτοῖς τὸν χριστόν). The expression is also used in 9,20 (τὸν Ἰησοῦν) and in 19,13 (Ἰησοῦν). The verb κηρύσσειν with Jesus or Christ as its object is used by Paul in 1 Cor 1,23; 15,12; 2 Cor 1,19; 4,5; 11,4 and Phil 1,15.[103] Synoptic tradition uses it for John the Baptist (Mark 1,4 parr; cf. Acts 10,37) as well as for Jesus,[104] and for the activities of the apostles sent out by him.[105] It was obviously a standard expression to describe the Christian proclamation (cf. the Lukan summary of the gospel in Acts 10,42). Other elements in the description of Philip in Samaria clearly reflect the redaction of Acts: ὁμοθυμαδόν, for instance, is a favourite Lukan word.[106] And the reaction of the crowd is described by the verb προσέχειν, just as in Acts 16,14. The performance of signs is traditionally characteristic of a prophet,[107] and Luke uses this theme in order to depict Philip as a counterpart to Simon Magus. The account of Philip's healing powers draws a parallel to the healings performed by Jesus (cf. Luke 4,33; 6,18; cf. Mark 5,7 parr.).

Probably the only historical information contained in these verses is the fact that Philip went to Samaria to preach the gospel and baptise there.[108] An important element in this respect is formed by the remark that Philip preached in the city of 'Samaria'. This city should be identified as either Sebaste or Sichem.[109] Philip is therefore clearly presented here as the first to preach the gospel to those on the margin of Judaism.[110]

This observation probably accounts for the fact that the description of the conversion of Simon Magus continues with the coming of Peter and John from Jerusalem. It is not immediately clear how the two traditions on Simon Magus – i.e. the encounter with Philip and the conflict with

---

[103] In an absolute sense or with another object: Rom 2,21; 10,8.14.15; 1 Cor 9,27; 15,11; Gal 2,2; 5,11; 1 Thess 2,9; cf. the use in deutero-Pauline letters: Col 1,23; 1 Tim 3,16; 2 Tim 4,2.

[104] Matt 4,17.23; 9,35; Mark 1,7.14.38-39.45; 5,20; Luke 4,18-19.44; 8,1.39.

[105] Matt 10,7.27; 11,1; 24,14; 26,13; Mark 3,14; 6,12; 7,36; 13,10; 14,9; (16,15.20); Luke 9,2; 12,3; 24,47.

[106] Used ten times in Acts, and outside Acts only once – Rom 15,6.

[107] See e.g. W.A. Meeks, *The Prophet-King. Moses Traditions and the Johannine Christology* (SNT 14; Leiden: Brill, 1967), pp. 47-55.

[108] Lüdemann, *Das frühe Christentum*, p. 103.

[109] Haenchen, *Apostelgeschichte*, p. 252.

[110] Barrett, *Acts*, vol. 1, p. 399, correctly argues that 'Luke must have got Philip's Samaritan mission from tradition because it does not correspond to his own idea of an *apostolic* mission carried out by the Twelve.' For the Samaritans, see Jervell, *Apostelgeschichte*, p. 266; Haenchen, *Apostelgeschichte*, p. 297.

Peter – are related.[111] C.K. Barrett for instance argues that vv. 5-13 reflect a Hellenistic mission in Samaria, whereas vv. 14-25 are evidence of an early conflict within the Christian congregation as to whether or not a mission to Samaria was allowed (cf. the conflicting attitudes in Matt 10,5 and John 4,39-42).[112] Whatever the exact relation between the two sections may be, the most important thing is that 8,5-13 is evidence of early Hellenistic missionary activity in Samaria. For the subject of this study it is of great importance to scrutinise the description of these activities in detail.

Philip's activities are described by means of the following words: κηρύσσειν (v. 5), σημεῖα ποιεῖν (v. 6), εὐαγγελίζεσθαι (v. 12), and βαπτίζεσθαι (vv. 12.13). As argued above, the verb κηρύσσειν and its cognates are standard Christian vocabulary for preaching. The use of this word throughout early Christian literature leads to the conclusion that κηρύσσειν is an early characterisation of the activities of Christian preachers. It has already been argued that the earliest Christian preachers must have functioned as heralds of God's triumph in Christ. The use of κηρύσσειν is therefore very fitting in the historical context.

The second element in the description of Philip is the performance of signs (σημεῖα ποιεῖν). This expression is absent from synoptic tradition, but is used frequently in John as a description of Jesus' miracles.[113] Although the synoptics do contain numerous accounts of healings and wonders, these events are not interpreted *expressis verbis* as 'signs' in synoptic tradition. Hence it is all the more remarkable that Peter in Acts 2,22 speaks of Jesus as of one through whom 'God performed miracles and wonders and signs'.[114] Further on in the Book of Acts, the author takes this theme of performing signs to underline the divine authorisation of the characters he describes. Thus it is the case with Stephen (6,8), Moses (7,36), and Paul and Barnabas (15,2). The presentation of Philip as one who performs signs is therefore totally in line with the way in which the *auctor ad Theophilum* presents divinely inspired persons. There-

---

[111] The chapter as a whole is clearly the result of Lukan redaction, into which several traditional elements have been incorporated – Pesch, *Apostelgeschichte*, vol. 1, pp. 271-272. There is great difference of opinion concerning the content of these traditional elements. Pesch, for instance, argues that the fact that Simon is not presented as a pagan sorcerer, but as a Christian, implies his conversion. Therefore, the account of that event is probably based on tradition. Jervell, *Apostelgeschichte*, p. 268, on the other hand, is very certain in his statement: 'Von einer christlichen Bekehrung des Simon darf man kaum reden.'

[112] Barrett, *Acts*, vol. 1, pp. 395-400.

[113] John 2,11.18.23; 3,2; 4,54; 6,2.14.30; 7,31; 9,16; 10,41; 11,47; 12,18.37; 20.30.

[114] See Meeks, *Prophet-King*, pp. 47-55.

fore, this element in the description of Philip is not very likely to be traditional. To describe Philip as one who performs signs is a literary device of the author to present him as divinely inspired.[115]

The third expression used to depict Philip's activities is εὐαγγελίζεσθαι. Apart from one passage in Q (Luke 7,22/Matt 11,5) and a few occurrences in Ephesians, Hebrews, 1 Peter, and the book of Revelation, the verb is used only by Paul and Luke.[116] In Luke it is used to describe the activity of the angel announcing the birth of John the Baptist (1,19), and of the angels proclaiming the birth of Jesus (2,10). The teaching of the Baptist is described by means of this verb (3,18), and after the quotation of Isa 61,1-2 in 4,18, it functions as the description of the teaching of Jesus or his followers (4,43; 8,1; 9,6; 16,16; 20,1). In the Book of Acts εὐαγγελίζεσθαι is a stock-phrase for the spread of the gospel.[117] It would be tempting to think of this expression as a typically Lukan word, reflecting merely the redaction of Luke-Acts,[118] were it not for Paul. We are certain of the fact that this expression was used early in the Christian tradition, since Paul frequently uses it to describe his own activities.[119] Notwithstanding the fact that the expression εὐαγγελίζεσθαι περί (Acts 8,12) is a *hapax legomenon*, it does not point at a traditional background of this verse.[120]

The fourth and final word with which Philip's activities are described is βαπτίζεσθαι. There are several passages in the gospels in which this verb is used for the activity of John the Baptist, and once even for Jesus

---

[115] See F.S. Spencer, *The Portrait of Philip in Acts. A Study of Roles and Relations* (JSNTSS 67; Sheffield: Sheffield Academic Press, 1992), pp. 44-48 – 'Luke consistently regards signs and wonders as convincing demonstrations of authentic ministry' (p. 48).

[116] In Q 7,22 εὐαγγελίζεσθαι is used in a non-Christian way, probably reflecting an early stage of its use. In the later passages the term is used for the proclamation of either the kingdom of God/heavens or Christ himself, just as in the case of κηρύσσειν. The non-Lukan and non-Pauline passages in which the word occurs, are: Eph 3,8; Heb 4,2.6; 1 Pet 1,12.25; 4,6; Rev 10,7; 14,6.

[117] Cf. Acts 5,42; 8,4; 8,12.25.35.40; 10,36; 11,20; 13,32; 14,7.15.21; 15,35; 16,10; 17,18.

[118] Thus, for instance, Spencer, *Portrait of Philip*, pp. 36-44, who correctly observes that the 'two verbs, κηρύσσω and εὐαγγελίζω, comprise part of a rich Lukan vocabulary designating that central component of Christian ministry, the act of preaching' (p. 37). Nonetheless, Spencer overlooks the traditional character of the rare expression εὐαγγελίζεσθαι περί.

[119] Rom 1,15; (10,15;) 15,20; 1 Cor 1,17; 9,16; 15,1-2; 2 Cor 10,16; 11,7; Gal 1,8-9,11.16.23; 4,13; 1 Thess 3,6 (Timothy) – see G. Friedrich, εὐαγγελίζομαι, *ThWNT*, vol. 2, pp. 705-718.

[120] See also Lüdemann, *Das frühe Christentum*, p. 100.

himself (John 3,22.26). But in the Book of Acts it usually refers to the Christian baptism, the cleansing ritual that functioned as a sign of repentance and thus formed the initiation into the Christian movement. That baptism was practised as the *rite de passage* for new Christians, and constituted the basis of the community, is evident from Paul.[121] In the Book of Acts baptism is practised by the apostles in Jerusalem (2,41), by Philip (8,12-13.36.38), Ananias (9,18), Peter (10,47-48; 11,16), and Paul (16,15.33; 18,8; 19,3-5; 22,16). The episode 8,14-25 points out that at least for the author of Acts there was a difference between baptism and the giving of the spirit.

Since this is not the place for a reconstruction of the different forms of Christian baptism,[122] the observation must suffice that baptising was obviously a fixed element in the activities of the earliest Christian preachers. The closest non-Christian parallel known to us is the baptism of John who baptised people in response to his call for μετάνοια (cf. Mark 1,4 and Jos., *Ant.* xviii,117).[123] This element in the preaching of John comes very close to the summary of the teaching of Jesus as given in e.g. Mark 1,14-15. The necessity of conversion before the coming of God's ultimate intervention must have formed the basis for Christian baptism as it did for that of John. The distinctive difference was that in the case of Christian baptism the ultimate intervention of God was thought of as having already begun in the coming of Jesus.[124]

There is more to the problem of baptism, however. For Paul baptism marks the entry into the union with Christ. His discussion of the meaning of baptism in Rom 6,1-11 points out that for him, baptism was a sign of entering a new life. It marked the beginning of the believer's life 'in Christ', since Paul equals the act of baptism as a participation in Christ's death which results in 'the newness of life' (6,4). Elsewhere, Paul speaks about the union with Christ in the metaphor of putting on a garment (Gal 3,27). Another metaphor he uses is that of being baptised 'into one body' (1 Cor 12,13).

---

[121] Cf. Rom 6,3; 1 Cor 1,13-17; 10,2; 12,13; 15,29; Gal 3,27.

[122] For this subject, see G. Barth, *Die Taufe in frühchristlicher Zeit* (BtS 4; Neukirchen-Vluyn: Neukirchener Verlag, 1981), passim; also: L. Hartman, s.v. 'Baptism', *ABD* vol. I, pp. 583-594. Hartman: '... John's baptism is the point of departure of Christian baptismal practice' (p. 585). For an extensive discussion of the origin of Christian baptism, see A.J.M Wedderburn, *Baptism and Resurrection* (WUNT 44; Tübingen: Mohr Siebeck, 1983).

[123] For the baptism of John as the origin of Christian baptism, see Barth, *Taufe*, pp. 37-43.

[124] Barth, *Taufe*, pp. 44-72, points out that Christian baptism focused on christology, and on the fact that the person baptised received the Spirit as an eschatological gift.

The controversy among the Corinthians to which Paul responds in the first chapters of 1 Corinthians apparently focused on baptism, at least in part. Acts 18 describes how Apollos baptised people in 'John's baptism' not knowing the correct way to act within the Christian community. Paul's argument in 1 Corinthians clearly reveals that the Corinthians' misinterpretation of baptism was somehow connected to Apollos' activities (1,17): Apollos and the Corinthians obviously did not share Paul's ideas on baptism. Judging from Acts 8 a comparable problem occurred in the case of Philip. Therefore it is safe to conclude that within earliest Christianity there were at least two different views of baptism: either it was regarded as an individual act of cultic cleansing (cf. Apollos, Philip) or it was understood as an entry into the mystical union with Christ through the gift of the spirit (Paul). Judging from Matt 28,16-20 Paul's view of baptism ultimately lasted longer within Christian tradition than the view of those who regarded baptism as merely an act of cleansing.[125]

Verses 9-13 of Acts 8 give a description of the meeting between Philip and Simon Magus. This meeting has clearly been coloured to a high degree by the redaction of Acts. Referring to K. Beyschlag, G. Lüdemann shows how Philip and Simon mirror each other's actions:[126]

Philip	Simon
1. enters town (v. 5)	1. is already in town (v. 9)
2. preaches Christ (and the kingdom of God, v. 5+12)	2. designates himself as a powerful man (v. 9)
3. performs great signs (or 'great powers' v. 6-7+13)	3. performs magic in public and apparently has great power (v. 9-11)
4. the entire people hears him, sees his acts, and 'has regard to him' (v. 6+12)	4. the entire people 'gives heed' and 'has regard to him' (v. 9+11)

---

[125] Barth, *Taufe*, pp. 37-45, describes the character of Christian baptism, which shares a number of characteristics with the Johannine baptism: 1. it is performed by a baptiser, and cannot be performed by the one being baptised; 2. it is a unique event, not to be compared with repeated washings; 3. it is performed by submerging in the water (of the Jordan e.g.); 4. it is connected with the call for repentance and μετάνοια; and 5. it promises forgiveness of sins to those baptised.

[126] Lüdemann, *Das frühe Christentum*, p. 101.

5. great joy among the people,
faith and the baptism of all
(v. 8+12).

5. Simon sees the great signs
by Philip and becomes exalted
(v. 13).

The comparison points out that this pericope has been formed by the redaction of Acts. Is there any need then to conclude to the existence of a tradition on Simon and Philip? If such a tradition formed the background to the pericope, it probably did not contain much more than information on a conflict between Christians and the followers of Simon.[127] In its present form the meeting of Philip and Simon has been devised by the author of Acts in order to anticipate the story of Peter and Simon in the account of Philip's mission in Samaria. Simon's Christian identity is assumed in vv. 18-24, but this does not necessarily imply that Simon had been baptised by Philip.[128]

In regard to the description of Philip in Acts 8,5-13 the following conclusion should be drawn. Three of the four elements in this description – κηρύσσειν, εὐαγγελίζεσθαι, βαπτίζειν – are standard elements in descriptions of the activities of early Christian preachers. They are also found in Paul and other early Christian literature. The fourth element – σημεῖα ποιεῖν – was probably added by Luke for a special reason, viz. to accentuate the prophetic character of Philip's appearance, and thus to depict him as the counterpart of Simon Magus. Hence, the picture of Philip in Acts 8,5-13 is largely redactional. At the same time it cannot have been pure fiction. It does not say anything explicitly on the exact nature of Philip's activities in Samaria, but does indicate that the proclamation of the Christ event crossed the boundary between Judean and Samaritan Judaism. Notwithstanding the fact that Samaritan Judaism may still be regarded as a specific form of Judaism, the boundary in the strictest sense had been crossed. In R.J. Coggins' words: 'Being neither Jew nor Gentile, they thus defy the attempts of those, both in the ancient and in the modern world, who wish to classify them neatly.'[129] Nevertheless, the gospel was still proclaimed within the boundaries of circumcision.

---

[127] Lüdemann, *Das frühe Christentum*, p. 104.
[128] *Pace* Pesch, *Apostelgeschichte*, vol. 1, p. 271.
[129] R.J. Coggins, 'The Samaritans and Acts', *NTS* 28 (1982), pp. 423-434, quotation from p. 433.

2. Peter and John in Samaria (8,14-25)

The episode of 8,14-25 strangely interrupts the description of Philip's activities. The pericope does not mention Philip at all, and reflects an independent tradition that has been linked by the author to that on Philip's mission in Samaria. The section on John and Peter describes two separate activities: firstly, the giving of the Spirit as the 'finishing touch' to Philip's activities, and secondly, the conflict with Simon Magus.

The laying on of hands by Peter and John in Samaria is a redactional passage, whereas the conflict of Peter with Simon contains traces of earlier tradition. The vocabulary of the passages points this out: the words used in vv. 14-17 are typically Lukan.[130] Yet, in vv. 18-24 the vocabulary is distinctively different: some expressions used are *hapax legomena*, others are rarely used in Acts or early Christian literature in general.[131] If this evidence is taken into account, the conclusion should be that vv. 14-17 are a redactional passage created by the author of Acts in order to put John and Peter on the scene. Subsequently, the episode in vv. 18-24 is taken up from a traditional account. These scenes are framed by two sections that are obviously stated in a certain parallelism: vv. 4-13 and vv. 14-25. In ch. 8 as a whole, therefore, two older traditions have been combined and intertwined, viz. that on Philip's evangelising activities in Samaria, and that on Peter's conflict with Simon Magus.

Now why would the author of Acts depict John and Peter as having to lay their hands on the Samaritans in order to give the Spirit? What is the relationship of the baptism performed by Philip and the laying on of hands by Peter and John? According to 6,3 the seven leaders of the Hellenists were 'full of the Spirit and of wisdom'. In 6,5 Stephen is depicted as 'a man full of faith and the Holy Spirit'. There is thus no reason to think that for the author of Acts only the Twelve in Jerusalem were able to pass on the Spirit. Philip is one of the seven leaders mentioned in 6,3, and

---

[130] For instance: δέχομαι τὸν λόγον (τοῦ θεοῦ), cf. 11,1; 17,1; ἀποστέλλω: 5,21; 7,14.34.35; 8,14; 9,38; 10,8.17; 11,11.13.30; 13,15; 15,27.33; 16,35.36; 19,22; καταβαίνω as a description of travel: 7,15 (.34); 8,15.26.38; 10,20.21; 14,25; 16,8; 18,22; 22,10; 23,10; 24,10.22; 25,6.7; πνεῦμα ἅγιον λαμβάνειν: 1,8; 2,33.38; 8,15.17.19; 10,47; 19,2; ἐπιπίπτειν used of the Holy Spirit: 8,16; 10,44; 11,15; and ἐπιτίθεσθαι τὰς χεῖρας: 6,6; 8,17.19; 9,12.17; 13,3; 19,6. See further: Lüdemann, *Das frühe Christentum*, pp. 101-102.

[131] For instance: ἐπίθεσις τῶν χειρῶν τῶν ἀποστόλων: *hapax*; εὐθύς used metaphorically for the straightness of the heart: *hapax*; ἔναντι τοῦ θεοῦ: Luke 1,8 (*ante*) and Acts 8,21 (*coram*); ἐπίνοια: *hapax*; χολή: Matt 27,34; Acts 8,23; πικρία: Acts 8,23; Rom 3,14; Eph 4,31; Heb 12,15; σύνδεσμος: Acts 8,23; Eph 4,3; Col 2,19; 3,14.

Stephen's status receives emphasis in 6,5 because of his martyrdom, not because he had a special gift of the Spirit in which the others did not share. Furthermore, the seven leaders of the Hellenists were bestowed with the Spirit by the Twelve (6,6). Philip had received the Spirit as one of the seven leaders of the Hellenists, and therefore he should be considered capable of passing it on too. The traditional episode on Peter and Simon no doubt contained a discussion of the giving of the Spirit. Thus, the author had to introduce Peter as the one who passed on the Spirit in Samaria immediately after he had described Philip's missionary activities in the same area. The best solution was to present Philip's activities as somehow wanting. If Peter came to Samaria in order to finish the job begun by Philip, the author had a perfect legitimisation for Peter's introduction. The fact that he does not introduce Peter on his own, but as accompanied by John, is in accordance with the prominent position of these two as mentioned in 3,1.3.4.11; 4,13.19. Furthermore, the earliest Christian preachers often acted in pairs.[132] Seen against this background it is surprising that Philip apparently acted alone.

The tradition behind the meeting of Peter and Simon Magus most likely did not contain much more information than what is described above. Since the entire passage of vv. 18-24 does not describe any missionary activity by Peter, it does not contribute to a reconstruction of pre- and para-Pauline mission. The message of v. 25 (πολλάς τε κώμας τῶν Σαμαριτῶν εὐηγγελίζοντο) is the redactional transition to the next pericope and cannot be counted as relevant evidence of the preaching activities of Peter and John in Samaria.[133] The only element that should be kept in mind is the fact that Peter apparently acted in Samaria.[134]

3. Philip and the Ethiopian eunuch (8,26-40)

The description of Philip's activities continues in 8,26-40. This passage has been much discussed and it is not necessary to go into great detail

---

[132] Cf. above, pp. 82-90.

[133] The vocabulary of v. 25 is thoroughly redactional: διαμαρτύρομαι cf. Acts 2,40; 10,42; 18,5; 20,21.23.24; 23,11; 28,23; λαλεῖν τὸν λόγον τοῦ θεοῦ is used only in Acts (cf. 4,29; 16,32); ὑποστρέφειν is a favourite word for Luke-Acts (out of a total of 35 times in the NT, it is used 32 times in Luke-Acts).

[134] On the historicity and character of Peter's journey, Jervell is again quite brief: 'Für die Visitationsreise des Petrus und den Zusammenstoß mit Simon aber haben wir keine historische Belege' – Apostelgeschichte, p. 268.

here.[135] It is important, however, to note that the status of the Ethiopian may be compared to that of the Samaritans. Samaritans were often considered as non-Jews, but they did respect the Torah and practiced circumcision. In a way, the proclamation of the gospel to the Samaritans was still an inner-Jewish activity. It is very likely that Luke regarded it as such, since the real transition beyond the border of Judaism is depicted in cc. 10-11.

It has been noted that the ministry of Philip, as described in ch. 8, more or less fulfils the command of 1,8: the Christian movement is scattered throughout Judea, and Philip subsequently preaches the gospel in Samaria and to someone coming from the ends of the earth, the kingdom of Meroe.[136] Thus, at the redactional level of Acts, ch. 8 sets the stage for the Gentile mission to be initiated by the call of Paul (ch. 9), the conversion of Cornelius (ch. 10), and the description of the Christian congregation of Antioch (ch. 11). In regard to the reconstruction of pre- and para-Pauline mission, the following observations on ch. 8 should be made.

1. It is important to acknowledge that the pericope is a Lukan adaptation of an older tradition on Philip. The tradition no doubt dealt with the encounter of Philip with the Ethiopian eunuch, but whether the local details were originally part of this tradition is difficult to establish, since the present form of the narrative has been fashioned to a high degree by Luke: the form of the pericope vv. 26-40 is chiastic,[137] and the number of words is also a strong indication of the great care with which this passage has been constructed.[138] The mention of the road from Jerusalem to Gaza is probably traditional. Gaza does not play any part in the narrative of Acts and the mention of Jerusalem is not very logical here, since Philip is situated in Samaria.[139] But whether it is a reliable description of the place where this encounter happened remains uncertain. The tradition on the encounter may have consisted of the introduction of the Ethiopian, the finding of the water, the baptism and the parting of the ways.[140] In this respect it is important to note the prominent position of the Ethiopian.

---

[135] For a thorough and recent discussion, see Spencer, *Portrait of Philip*, pp. 128-187.

[136] B.R. Gaventa, 'Ethiopian Eunuch', *ABD*, vol. 2, p. 667.

[137] See Spencer, *Portrait of Philip*, p. 132. On Ethiopia as 'the end of the earth' from a Graeco-Roman perspective, see J.S. Romm, *The Edges of the Earth in Ancient Thought: Geography, Exploration, and Fiction* (Princeton NJ: Princeton University Press, 1992), pp. 45-60.

[138] Vv. 26-32a comprise 120 words, the quotation from Isaiah in vv. 32b-33 40 words, and the final section (vv. 24-40) 119. This is evidence of a careful composition.

[139] See Jervell, *Apostelgeschichte*, p. 270.

[140] Lüdemann, *Das frühe Christentum*, p. 110.

He was not just an accidental passer-by, but the minister of finance of the kingdom of Ethiopia.[141] This high status of the Ethiopian makes it all the more probable that the tradition on his conversion basically describes a historical event: this is the kind of event that is long remembered. This means that the passage as a whole should be interpreted as reflecting an early conversion by Philip.

2. The religious status of the Ethiopian eunuch is kept obscure. Since eunuchs could probably not be admitted as proselytes to Judaism,[142] the pre-Lukan tradition probably described the Ethiopian as a Gentile. Still, the author of Acts presents the conversion of Cornelius as the moment at which the first non-Jews entered the Christian movement, and he consciously or unconsciously downplayed the Gentile identity of the Ethiopian. By mentioning the man's visit to (the temple in) Jerusalem Luke creates a problem: either the man was accepted as a Jew (a proselyte and thus no eunuch), or he was a Gentile (who could not become Jewish, since he was a eunuch). Either way, the account contradicts itself, for in the first case the man is explicitly introduced as a eunuch when he is not, and in the second case the eunuch is introduced as having visited Jerusalem and reading an Isaiah-scroll. All options have been defended here.[143] Whatever the solution to the problem may be, it is important to note that the Ethiopian is depicted as being at least a sympathiser with Judaism. He came to Jerusalem in order to worship, not to pay his respects on behalf of the Ethiopian government (ἐληλύθει προσκυνήσων εἰς Ἰερουσαλήμ; v. 27). This fact is further stressed by the element of his reading of Isaiah 53, which is no doubt a narrative elaboration of the fact that the Ethiopian must have had some theological discussion with Philip.

---

[141] See e.g. Jervell, *Apostelgeschichte*, p. 271.

[142] See Deut 23,1-2; Josephus, *Ant.* IV,290-291.

[143] S.G. Wilson, *The Gentiles and the Gentile Mission in Luke-Acts* (Cambridge: University Press, 1973), pp. 171-172, argues that 'it is (...) very likely that Luke did not realise that the eunuch was a Gentile.' Cf. E. Dinkler, 'Philippus und der ANHP ΑΙΘΙΟΨ', in: E.E. Ellis, E. Gräßer, *Jesus und Paulus* (FS Kümmel; Göttingen: Vandenhoeck & Ruprecht, 1975), pp. 85-95, comes to a similar conclusion ('Ungewollt läßt Lukas den schwarzhäutigen Heiden vor dem Römer eine Bekehrung und Taufe erfahren, Afrika vor Europa die Botschaft von Jesus Christus hören' – p. 95). According to Jervell, *Apostelgeschichte*, p. 271, the Ethiopian was a proselyte, and εὐνοῦχος is merely an indication of his function. See also Pesch, *Apostelgeschichte*, vol. 1, p. 289. Haenchen defends the opposite view, viz. that the Ethiopian was a eunuch and a Gentile, and that Luke consciously downplayed this fact – Haenchen, *Apostelgeschichte*, p. 265: 'es war die erste Heidenbekehrung (...) und der erste Heidenbekehrer hieß nicht Petrus, sondern Philippus!'.

3. The encounter between Philip and the Ethiopian is presented as being evoked by God. Philip is warned by an angel of God that he should go to the road from Jerusalem to Gaza (8,26), there he finds the Ethiopian reading Isaiah, then there is the water in the middle of the desert (8,36; cf. 8,26 ὅ ἐστὶν ἔρημος), and finally Philip is taken away by the spirit (8,39). Far from being the miracle-worker he was presented as in the first pericope of ch. 8, Philip is now depicted as the instrument by means of which God himself directs the action.

4. It appears that the crucial element in this encounter of Philip with the Ethiopian is not so much the latter's conversion as his baptism. The fact that the Ethiopian returns to his own country after his baptism is indicative of the character of this event as it was understood by the community that transmitted the tradition. The meaning of this baptism is not so much that the Ethiopian becomes a member of the Christian movement. Had this been so, the fact that the Ethiopian could not join any Christian congregation in his homeland would have become problematic. Yet the author appears to have no difficulties at all at this point. For him the baptism of the Ethiopian does not primarily signify his entry into the Christian movement as it does in e.g. Rom 6,1-11 and Matt 28,16-20 (cf. pp. 132-135). It rather marks his individual conversion completed by a ritual cleansing. Since this is presumably the earliest meaning of Christian baptism, out of which its function as a ritual initiation evolved, the fact that the baptism of the Ethiopian is presented as an individual baptism is an indication of the early character of the tradition underlying this narrative: the Ethiopian is not baptised in order to enter the Christian congregation of Meroe – such a congregation did not exist.

5. It is to be noted that neither in v. 26 nor in vv. 39-40 any indication is given of the moment at which Philip's meeting with the Ethiopian took place. Therefore the moment in the Book of Acts is set by the narrative framework and cannot be traced in history. We thus have no certainty as to whether this meeting of Philip and the Ethiopian took place before or after Paul's conversion. There are, however, two indications that the meeting took place at an early stage. Firstly there is the early character of the baptism described. Secondly the fact that Philip's activities are described before the conversion of Cornelius could indicate its early date: the redactional interest in Jerusalem as the centre for the spread of Christianity demands the earliest possible date for the conversion of Cornelius. Because Philip's activities are described first they seemingly interfere with the redactional intention, and this may indicate the early date of the tradition the author used here.

For a reconstruction of pre- and para-Pauline mission the following conclusions should be drawn from the material discussed.

It is apparent from the description of Philip in ch. 8 and his mention in 21,8 as 'the evangelist' that he actively preached the gospel. Since this activity would not have been limited to him, we may assume that the earliest Christians actively proclaimed Jesus as God's envoy. This proclamation was embedded in the eschatological message brought by Jesus concerning the necessity of conversion in the face of God's ultimate intervention in history, which was considered to be near at hand. The combination of the necessity to convert and the proclamation of Jesus as God's final messenger somehow resulted in the birth of Christian baptism. This baptism should be regarded as an individual cleansing ritual that later developed into a rite for entrance into the Christian community.

In the evaluation of the traditional data underlying Acts 8 two elements should be made clear. Firstly, Philip and the two envoys from Jerusalem, Peter and John, apparently did not aim at converting people to membership of the Christian community. What they did was proclaim the gospel. Their activity is thus fully in line with the analysis made above of the earliest Christian movement. Secondly, Philip obviously proclaimed his gospel to people on the margin of Judaism. Within the composition of Acts the boundaries of Judaism are crossed in ch. 10. This is a narrative order, though, not a chronologically correct rendering of the process. Therefore the evidence we can distribute from the material discussed is only that the gospel was apparently preached to people related to Judaism at an early stage of its spread.

c. The Conversion of Cornelius and Its Reception (10,1-11,18)

The section 10,1-11,18 marks an important turning point within the narrative of Acts. It describes how God himself through the meeting of Peter and Cornelius has inaugurated the Gentile mission.[144] Since this topic, the Gentile mission, is one of the central themes of the Book of Acts as a whole, the meeting of Cornelius and Peter must be considered a crucial chapter. Because this chapter is so important for the literary goals of Acts, it should be treated with great suspicion in regard to the traditional elements it may contain.

Dibelius has shown that the account of the conversion of Cornelius is coloured to a high degree by the redaction of Acts.[145] Yet the extent of

---

[144] There is an abundance of literature on this section. For a survey, see Jervell, *Apostelgeschichte*, p. 302.

[145] M. Dibelius, 'Die Bekehrung des Cornelius' (1947), in: idem, *Aufsätze zur Apostelgeschichte* (ed. by H. Greeven; FRLANT nf 60; Berlin: Evangelische Verlagsanstalt, 1951), pp. 96-107.

this colouring and the reconstruction of the tradition behind the account of Acts can, some decades after Dibelius' famous essay, be judged in a different manner. It is remarkable to see how easily Dibelius identified the prime elements that in his eyes were contributed by the redaction of Acts: 10,9-16.27-29.34-43 and 11,1-18.[146] By stripping at least these elements Dibelius hoped to identify the tradition behind the narrative in Acts.

Lüdemann offers an analysis of the same pericope in which he starts at the other end.[147] The entire passage is redactional: both its structure and its terminology show this.[148] Yet within this redactional passage older tradition is preserved that contains some relevant historical elements. This tradition reached the author of Acts, according to Lüdemann, by means of a literary source.[149] In pre-Lukan tradition the story of Cornelius would have had the following content: it would have been the account of the conversion of a Gentile named Cornelius, by Peter, in Caesarea. Cornelius, warned by an angel, would have sent for Peter to meet him in Caesarea. Instructed by the Spirit, Peter would have gone to Caesarea, preached before Cornelius and his house and have baptised them all. Subsequently, Cornelius would have received the Holy Spirit.

For the present subject it would go too far to analyse the passage in the greatest possible detail. It should suffice here to focus on the two questions that are directly relevant to our enquiry: What does the account of the conversion of Cornelius state on the way in which the early Christian movement spread? And what is the status of Cornelius, who is introduced as φοβούμενος τὸν θεόν?

The answers to these two questions will lead us one important step further in our search for pre- and para-Pauline missionary activities. Let us begin with the first question.

The present structure of the narrative is clearly redactional. After the introduction of Cornelius and the description of his vision (vv. 1-8), the focus shifts to Peter (vv. 9-16). The contact between Peter and Cornelius is made through the visions: God himself draws Cornelius' attention to Peter, and it is the who prepares Peter for the meeting with Cornelius.[150]

---

[146] Dibelius, 'Bekehrung', pp. 96-100.
[147] Lüdemann, *Frühe Christentum*, pp. 130-139.
[148] See e.g. p. 136: 'So, wie die Geschichte dasteht, kann sie Vers für Vers luk. Erzählstil und Theologie zugeordnet werden.'
[149] Lüdemann, *Das frühe Christentum*, p. 136: '...eine bereits von Lukas bearbeitete Vorlage'.
[150] For the use of the technique of *double visions*, see also Acts 9.

Then, servants of Cornelius approach Peter and ask him to accompany them to their master (vv. 17-23a). This takes place and the next day they both meet in Caesarea (vv. 23b-33). On this occasion Peter gives a sermon summarising the entire gospel (vv. 34-43), and subsequently the Spirit is bestowed on Cornelius and his house (vv. 44-48). The beginning of the narrative closely resembles the story of the centurion in Luke 7: the Roman sends for Jesus through his servants and, as in the case of Cornelius and Peter, Jesus comes to him.[151] Both Roman soldiers are described as sympathetic to Judaism and function as a literary model for the readers of Luke-Acts.

It is important to note that in the account of Peter and Cornelius the action starts with God. It is God who inspires Cornelius to send for Peter. As in the case of Philip and the Ethiopian eunuch it is neither missionary zeal by Peter that leads to the conversion of Cornelius nor any undefined attraction to the Roman that draws him near. Here we are no doubt confronted by the redactional message: God himself initiated the mission outside Israel.[152] This is the Lukan interpretation of the pre-Lukan tradition on Cornelius, which makes it difficult to reconstruct the original tradition. Yet there is one important clue: the narrative as a whole starts with Cornelius and the focus of the chapter is primarily on him.[153] Here we do not have a story about Peter, but one about Cornelius and the way in which he was drawn to Christianity. This is indeed an important observation.

A second clue for a reconstruction of the tradition behind the narrative is Peter's unwillingness to eat any unclean food. It is very unlikely that a story about Peter's active missionising of a Roman officer would have turned into a narrative on the way in which his resistance to the conversion of pagans had been overcome. It is far more likely that a story on the conversion of a Roman officer, who happened to have been drawn to the gospel, received this slant during the process of being transmitted or written down.

It is an important observation that the narrative on Cornelius does not contain any evidence of active proselytising by Peter. Here we have the answer to the first question posed above. Since there is no reason to

---

[151] Lüdemann, *Das frühe Christentum*, pp. 131-132.

[152] Wilson, *Gentile Mission*, p. 177, stresses the fact that the episode in ch. 10 is treated at great length, and referred to repeatedly: 'It is for Luke the test-case *par excellence* for the admission of the Gentiles into the Church. God has made it clear that the Gentiles need no circumcision before entering the Church, since he has poured out his Spirit on them freely, as at Pentecost (Acts 10:44, 11:15f.).'

[153] Lüdemann, *Das frühe Christentum*, p. 137; *pace* Pesch, *Apostelgeschichte* vol. 1, pp. 330.333.

assume that this element of active proselytising had been present in the tradition preceding the present form of the story, we should conclude that the proclamation of the gospel reached Cornelius through his socio-religious network. At this point the second question becomes relevant: what was the status of Cornelius?

The question of the status of Cornelius is in fact part of a much broader issue, viz. what is the meaning of his introduction as φοβούμενος τὸν θεόν? In order to find an answer we should take a closer look at the picture of Cornelius. Then we should search for parallels in the Book of Acts itself and finally compare this evidence to that outside the Book of Acts.

In chapter 10 the following statements introduce Cornelius:

  – ἑκατοντάρχης ἐκ σπείρης τῆς καλουμένης Ἰταλικῆς (v. 1)
  – εὐσεβής (v. 2)
  – φοβούμενος τὸν θεὸν σὺν παντὶ τῷ οἴκῳ αὐτοῦ (v. 2)
  – ποιῶν ἐλεημοσύνας πολλὰς τῷ λαῷ (v. 2)
  – δεόμενος τοῦ θεοῦ διὰ παντός (v. 2)
  – ἑκατοντάρχης (v. 22)
  – ἀνὴρ δίκαιος (v. 22)
  – φοβούμενος τὸν θεόν (v. 22)
  – μαρτυρούμενος ὑπὸ ὅλου τοῦ ἔθνους τῶν Ἰουδαίων (v. 22).

The characterisations given in v. 22 should be considered redactional: they are put into the mouth of the servants who come to fetch Peter, and form a recapitulation of the introduction of Cornelius in vv. 1-2. The words ἑκατοντάρχης and φοβούμενος τὸν θεόν are repetitions of v. 2, and ἀνὴρ δίκαιος and μαρτυρούμενος κτλ. are a redactional accentuation of the picture of Cornelius as a righteous and prominent person. This is likely, since similar descriptions are used in Luke 2,25 (Simeon: ἄνθρωπος δίκαιος) and 23,50 (Joseph: ἀνὴρ ἀγαθὸς καὶ δίκαιος), and μαρτυρούμενος ('of good reputation') in Acts 6,3 and 22,12. Any information on Cornelius that might come from tradition should therefore be sought in vv. 1-2.

The introduction of Cornelius as a centurion of the Italian regiment obviously raises a difficulty. There is no hint of evidence for the presence of this regiment in Palestine during the thirties and forties of the first century. It is attested to have been present in Coele-Syria in 69 CE,[154] but this only aggravates the problem.[155] To put it in Hengel's words: 'The old

---

[154] See Levinskaya, *Diaspora Setting*, p. 121, n. 11.
[155] According to Tacitus, *Hist.* I,59 the Italian Legion would have been situated in Gaul during the year of the three emperors. Dio Cassius, *Hist. Rom.* LV,24 mentions that this legion was installed by Nero, which would make it impossible for Cornelius to have been enlisted in it two or three decades earlier.

dispute over the "historicity" of this information is pointless. It may be an anachronism but need not necessarily be so.'[156] It may certainly be that Luke made a chronological error, such as he also made for instance concerning the date of the birth of Christ in Luke 2.[157] It is therefore conceivable that Cornelius was indeed a prominent Roman soldier, a centurion, not of the *cohors italica*, but of another regiment. Yet it may also be that the *cohors italica* was indeed stationed in Palestine in the thirties or forties of the first century, but left no evidence.

The two characterisations by which Cornelius is first introduced are εὐσεβής and φοβούμενος τὸν θεὸν σὺν παντὶ τῷ οἴκῳ αὐτοῦ. The first of these can only be found in 2 Pet 2,9 and on this occasion. Although it is the common Greek word for 'pious', it is not used in any other NT writing. More important, however, is the fact that the author of Acts only uses it here. This may indicate that the word was part of the tradition the author of Acts used for his description of Cornelius.[158]

The same point should be made for the phrase φοβούμενος τὸν θεὸν σὺν παντὶ τῷ οἴκῳ αὐτοῦ.[159] Apart from the account of the conversion of Cornelius φοβεῖσθαι τὸν θεόν is found only in 13,16.26, where Paul addresses the people in the synagogue of Pisidian Antioch. It is well worth the effort to take a look at Paul's words in these verses before evaluating the status of Cornelius. In 13,16 Paul commences his sermon with the words ἄνδρες Ἰσραηλῖται καὶ οἱ φοβούμενοι τὸν θεόν. Since he finds himself in the synagogue, and the first two words clearly indicate those born as Jews, the meaning of the latter designation is clear: those present in the synagogue, therefore drawn to Judaism, who themselves do not belong to the people of Israel. This interpretation is proved to be correct by 13,26 where the 'men of Israel' are mentioned as 'sons of the stock of Abraham' and the fearers of God clearly denote the rest. But is this 'rest' to be defined as pagan sympathisers with the synagogue whereas all the others, Jews and proselytes alike, are subsumed under the one heading ἄνδρες Ἰσραηλῖται? It appears that the category of proselytes plays no part at all in this episode as only the reaction of 'the Jews'

[156] Hengel, *Between Jesus and Paul*, p. 203, n. 111. See there for a further exposition of the evidence.
[157] For Luke's famous chronological error concerning the date of the census, see Schürer *et al.*, *History*, vol. 1, pp. 399-427.
[158] For εὐσεβής see W. Foerster in: *ThWNT*, vol. 7, pp. 175-184.
[159] A discussion of the evidence on God-Fearers is offered by Levinskaya, *Diaspora Setting*, pp. 51-126. For an older treatment, see K. Lake, 'Proselytes and God-Fearers', *Beginnings* vol. 5, pp. 74-77.

(οἱ Ἰουδαῖοι, v. 45) and 'the Gentiles' (τὰ ἔθνη, v. 48) to the appearance of Paul and Barnabas is given. Thus the designation God-fearers in Acts indeed points to pagan sympathisers with the synagogue, not just to any random group of Gentiles.

In the case of the story of Cornelius a similar point can be made. Whatever the status of Cornelius as a φοβούμενος τὸν θεόν, the meaning of his conversion is summarised in 11,1: καὶ τὰ ἔθνη ἐδέξαντο τὸν λόγον τοῦ θεοῦ. Thus, notwithstanding Cornelius' piety, his position within the narrative is clearly that of a non-Jew. Sympathetic as Cornelius may have been to the Jewish religion, he did not belong to the Jewish people.[160]

In chapter one (cf. above, p. 21) it has been stated that there was indeed a group of Gentile sympathisers who lived in close contact with the Jewish congregations. Whether or not this group was more or less fixed in character, stuck to certain rules and regulations, and was known as φοβουμένοι τὸν θεόν or σεβόμενοι τὸν θεόν cannot be decided on the basis of Acts only. The problem is that the existence of the 'God-fearers' as a fixed group has not been attested for the first century. Because of the ambiguity of the evidence in this matter, the safest approach is to leave the matter undecided as we did above. For our reconstruction of the spread of the early Christian movement the issue is not of the utmost importance: obviously the proclamation of the gospel at some point crossed the borders of the Jewish religion. Whether it did so through a fixed group of 'God-fearers' or through a loose group of sympathisers does not really make too much of a difference.

How should the account of Cornelius' conversion be evaluated then? It ought to be taken as an illustration of the way in which the proclamation of the gospel crossed over the boundary of the Jewish religion exactly at the point where this boundary was fluid. Seen from this perspective the short summary of the meaning of Cornelius' conversion in 11,1 becomes all the more remarkable. In these few redactional words the author of Acts stresses his interpretation of the event. However fluid the boundary between those within Judaism and its sympathisers may have been, the author of Acts regards it as real. He presents the story of Cornelius as a paradigmatic event in which this border was crossed, and does so in such a way as to point out that it was God himself who crossed it.

In real life the boundary cannot have been crossed by one single event. An indication of the problems that were caused by the acceptance of the

---

[160] There is no reason to assume that in the pre-Lukan tradition Cornelius may have counted as a proselyte. At best, he was a sympathiser.

gospel by non-Jews is given in 11,18. There, Peter offers an extensive defence for the admission of Gentiles to the gospel. This literary defence no doubt betrays the actual discussion that made such a literary apologetic necessary. This discussion still took place at the time in which Acts was written: the entire writing forms an apologetic presentation of the way in which the Church grew from Jerusalem to Rome containing also a defence of the Christian community as formed out of Jews and pagans alike.

d. The First 'Christians' in Antioch

Acts 11,19-26 describes in just a few words the actual birth of Christianity as a separate movement. The development depicted in this passage is as follows: Greek-speaking Jewish Christians who had fled from Jerusalem due to the persecution after Stephen's violent death went to Phoenicia, Cyprus, and Antioch; a group of Cyprians and Cyrenaeans preached the gospel to pagan Greeks many of whom converted; the congregation in Jerusalem heard of this and immediately sent Barnabas to check the situation in Antioch.

As in many other passages in Acts it is very difficult to distinguish between tradition and redaction here. The terminology is redactional to a high degree.[161] For the present purpose, three elements in this passage should be evaluated. Firstly, there is the preaching of the gospel by the men from Cyprus and Cyrene (τινες ... ἄνδρες Κύπριοι καὶ Κυρηναῖοι) in Antioch to the Greeks. Secondly, there is the fact that Barnabas was sent by the community in Jerusalem in response to this new development in Antioch. And thirdly, 11,26 mentions the followers of Jesus for the first time as χριστιανοί. Let us begin with the first point.

The process described here is that of the preaching of the gospel by Greek-speaking Jewish Jesus people from Cyprus and Cyrene to the non-Jewish Greek residents of Antioch.[162] This event marked the point at which the boundaries of Judaism were apparently definitively and consciously crossed. The chronology of events is again redactional: the report of the first non-Jewish Christian mission is given immediately after the description of the conversion of Cornelius. It illustrates the conclusion of that episode, as given in 11,18. Again, this redactional order does not mean that the historical chronology of events was the same. The rendering of

---

[161] Lüdemann, *Das frühe Christentum*, pp. 139-141.
[162] According to 6,9 there was a separate synagogue of freedmen and men from Cyrene and Alexandria, as there was such a synagogue for men from Cilicia and Asia.

Acts is determined by the wish to identify a single point within the development of the Christian movement at which the boundary between Jews and pagans was consciously crossed. The fact, however, that Antioch is identified as the place where this happened is significant. We can doubt whether there was such a fixed moment in history at which the gospel was first consciously proclaimed to pagans. But given Paul's description of the incident at Antioch in Galatians 2, it is as good as certain that the congregation of Antioch did indeed play a very important role in this process.[163]

The detail that the first preachers who brought the gospel to non-Jews were men from Cyprus and Cyrene cannot be explained from the function of these regions in the Book of Acts. Men from Cyprus and Cyrene are mentioned several times in the Book of Acts. For instance, Barnabas is introduced in 4,36 as being 'of the country of Cyprus', and in 13,1 Barnabas and Saul/Paul are mentioned side by side with Lucius the Cyrenaean. In 21,16 Mnason of Cyprus is mentioned as an old disciple. And in 6,9 the synagogue of the Cyrenaeans is mentioned as one of the sources of turmoil in the reaction to Stephen. The safest conclusion is that these communities did indeed play a certain part in the development of the early Christian movement. Since there is no redactional reason why these first 'missionaries' should have come from these communities, it is very probable that Luke depends on tradition here.

If the conversion of Greeks was indeed the result of the preaching of the gospel it is important to take a closer look at the terminology used for this activity. The expression used is εὐαγγελίζεσθαι τὸν κύριον Ἰησοῦν (v. 20). Jesus as the object of preaching also occurs in 5,42; 8,12 (together with the Kingdom of God); 8,35; and 17,18 (together with the resurrection). The verb εὐαγγελίζεσθαι is used frequently by Paul to describe the act of preaching. It appears that its use in Acts reflects early Christian vocabulary, also present in Paul, in which the preaching of the gospel coincided with the proclamation of Jesus as the Anointed One. Therefore, the conclusion must be that the author of Acts portrays the activity of the Greek-speaking Jewish Christians in Antioch as that of proclaiming Jesus as the Anointed One. Although this is a redactional

---

[163] Cf. B. Lifshitz, 'L'origin du nom des chrétiens', VigChr 16 (1962), pp. 65-70: 'Per la suite de la mission de Paul et Barnabé à Antioche les convertus juifs et surtout les gentils devinrent nombreux et la jeune communauté ne voulait ni ne pouvait plus être regardée comme une secte juive.' Lifshitz argues that the name χριστιανοί was taken by the congregation of Antioch to distinguish itself from the existing Jewish community that expected the political restauration of Israel. Instead, Lifshitz argues that the Christians proclaimed universal salvation for the entire world.

feature, it can hardly be far from historical reality. The proclamation to the first non-Jewish Christians in Antioch would indeed have focused on Jesus as God's final, eschatological envoy.

The very fact that there were followers of Jesus who crossed the boundaries of Judaism in their proclamation of the gospel is significant. This can only be explained in one of two ways: either for these Jews boundaries between them and non-Jews had hardly existed before they became Christians, or the coming of Christ had, for them, removed such boundaries. The evidence of Gal 2,12 does give some further information: Paul states that the Christians in Antioch were eating together with the Gentiles before James sent his envoys. Unfortunately, Paul does not mention the reason for this commensality: was this already a habit before the congregation of Antioch became involved in the Jesus movement or was it started by their confession of Jesus? Although we don't know the answer for certain, there is no indication that this commensality of Jews and Gentiles started within the Jesus movement. It may have antedated the Christian community.

The second feature from Acts 11,19-26 that is of interest for our analysis is the sending of Barnabas as an envoy from Jerusalem. This feature is remarkably similar to the sending of Peter and John described in 8,14-25 as well as to the sending of James' envoys mentioned in Gal 2,12. It was argued above that Acts 8,14-25 originates in a pre-Lukan tradition. In that case the sending of envoys from Jerusalem must be regarded as a genuine feature within the development of the earliest Christian movement, for in the present passage the same feature occurs: Barnabas is sent as an envoy to check the new congregation and to encourage them to cling to the confession.

On the redactional level the purpose of 11,19-26 is probably twofold: firstly, it describes how the boundary between Jews and non-Jews was crossed in Antioch immediately after the episode with Cornelius; secondly, it shows how the congregation in Jerusalem felt responsible for the development in Antioch by sending Barnabas as an envoy. As regards the tradition behind the passage things are less clear. The chronology of events is so obviously redactional that it is impossible to reconstruct the moment at which this mixed Antiochene community came into existence. In the narrative of Acts it does not precede Paul's call, only his own preaching activities. Yet the formation of this mixed Antiochene community should obviously be dated to the early years of the Christian movement. Judging from Paul's description in Gal 2,11-14 the habit of commensality of Jews and Gentiles within this community must have preceded Paul's Christian years. When Paul started his career as an envoy from Antioch, together with Barnabas, he obviously became involved in a group that was already open to Gentiles and confessed Jesus Christ.

The third element to be considered here is the fact that the new congregation is addressed for the first time with the name χριστιανοί. H.J. Cadbury has argued that this adjective[164] is formed 'by adding – *ianus*, – ιανός to a personal name as in Ἡρωδιανοί Mark III.6 XII.13.'[165] He points out the fact that this word indicates that χριστός was understood as a personal name and that the termination is probably Latin. The mention of this new name for the congregation of Antioch probably indicates that this congregation formed a new mixture of Jews and pagans. Again, we must admit that the chronology is Lukan redaction, and that the moment at which the name χριστιανοί first appeared cannot be traced.[166]

For the present purpose it is important to observe that the congregation in Antioch consisted of a mixed community of Jews and Gentiles, and that the formation of this community took place at a very early stage within the development of the Christian movement. It was this congregation that formed the basis for Paul's activities, and thus we must conclude that the open community that focused on Jesus Christ as its identity marker instead of the law formed the starting point for Paul. Paul didn't create Antioch – Antioch created Paul.

4. The Need for a Worldwide Proclamation of the Gospel: *docete omnes gentes*

So far, this chapter focused on evidence of the pre-Pauline Christian movement. At the end of the first century CE this movement was well on its way of becoming an independent religion characterised by great missionary zeal.

---

[164] Cf. P.J. Searle, 'Christian – Noun or Adjective?', *ExpTim* 87 (1975/76), 307-308.

[165] H.J. Cadbury, 'Names for Christians and Christianity in Acts', *Beginnings* vol. 5, pp. 375-392; quotation on p. 384.

[166] H.B. Mattingly, 'The Origin of the Name "Christians"', *JThS* 9 (1958), pp. 26-37, has made an interesting but unconvincing attempt to date the name to the reign of Nero. It was during his reign that a group of adherents formed together under the name *Augustiani*. 'This paramilitary corps of handsom, tough youths devoted themselves to rythmic praise of the emperor's person and his divine voice. Their whole life became an act of worship.' (p. 29) By referring to this group in the description of the followers of Christ, the Antiochene citizens could mock both the followers of Nero and the Christians: 'Were they not ludicrously like Nero's *Augustiani*? Christ had *his* claque at Antioch! The name *Christiani* would adroitly ridicule both groups at once.' Provoking as his theory may be, Mattingly unfortunately overlooks the fact that a grammatical agreement does not automatically point to an historical proximity.

The idea of a worldwide mission to proclaim Christ is found only in a relatively late stratum of the writings of the New Testament, its most explicit formulation being the closing section of Matthew.[167] In Matt 28, 16-20 the risen Lord Jesus instructs his disciples on what they should do. This instruction (vv. 18-20) indeed appears to include such a worldwide missionary programme. Jesus presents himself as having received all power in heaven and on earth, and because of his universal significance he instructs his disciples to 'instruct all nations'. Their instruction of the nations was to consist of two elements: the disciples were to baptise the people 'in the name of the Father and of the Son and of the Holy Spirit', and they were to teach them to observe all that Jesus had told his followers.[168]

The fact that these words form the end of the gospel of Matthew implies that they are fully redactional.[169] Moreover, the triadic formula that was to be used for baptising points to a late moment in the development of these traditions.[170] Evidence shows that during the late first and early second century, baptism was indeed practiced using this formula.[171] The exact same words are found in *Did.* 7,1-3.[172] Traces of an older formula, preceding the one under discussion, are found in 1 Cor 1,13;

---

[167] On this pericope and the concept of mission in Matthew see J. LaGrand, *The Earliest Christian Mission to 'All Nations' in the Light of Matthew's Gospel* (Grand Rapids: Eerdmans, 1999 = University of South Florida: Scholars Press 1995), esp. pp. 235-247.

[168] The finite verb μαθητεύσατε should be interpreted 'not as the first in a series but as a general imperative which is filled out (...) by what follows: baptism and instruction in obedience belong to discipleship.' – W.D. Davies, D.C. Allison jr., *The Gospel according to Saint Matthew*, vol. 3 (ICC; Edinburgh: Clark, 1997), p. 686.

[169] See e.g. Davies, Allison, *Matthew*, vol. 3, pp. 687-688 – '28,16-20 (...) is, from the literary point of view, perfect, in the sense that it satisfyingly completes the Gospel' (p. 687). See also O.S. Brooks, 'Matthew 28,16-20 and the Design of the First Gospel', *JSNT* 10 (1981), pp. 2-18. According to Brooks the passage is the redactional ending to the gospel as a whole. This ending focuses on exactly the two themes central to the gospel, viz. 'authority and teaching' (p. 15). Cf. R.H. Smith, 'Matthew 28,16-20, Anti-climax or Key to the Gospel?', *SBL Seminar Papers* (Atlanta: Scholars Press, 1993), pp. 589-602. Pace J. Schaberg, *The Father, the Son and the Holy Spirit. The Triadic Phrase in Matthew 28:19b* (SBLDS 61; Chico: Scholars Press, 1982), esp. pp. 335-340, who concludes that Matt 28,16-20 is based on a traditional midrash.

[170] Cf. Schaberg, *Triadic Phrase*, p. 5: 'Material is considered "triadic" if, regardless of titles used, the three figures of Jesus, God and Spirit appear in a fashion that indicates their coordination in the mind of the author and/or the tradition being used'. Schaberg uses the terms 'Trinity' and 'Trinitarian' 'for the stage of formal doctrine at which God is clearly perceived as tri-personal, coequal.' (p. 9).

[171] Cf. L. Abramowski, 'Die Entstehung der dreigliedrichen Taufformel – ein Versuch', *ZTK* 81 (1984), pp. 417-446.

[172] Barth, *Taufe*, pp. 13-17 – 'Eine solche triadische Formel war offenbar gegen Ende des 1. Jahrhunderts im syrischen Raum bereits in Gebrauch' (p. 17).

Gal 3,27; Acts 8,16; 19,5; *Did.* 9,5; and Herm., *Vis.* III,7.[173] This older form of the baptismal formula must have been something like 'baptising in the name of (the Lord) Jesus' (βαπτίζειν εἰς τὸ ὄνομα [τοῦ κυρίου] Ἰησοῦ).[174] The formula used in Matt 28,19 therefore reflects a well developed and theologically defined practice of baptism. The combination of this triadic formula and the instruction to keep all the teachings of Jesus (with the use of the verbs βαπτίζειν and τήρειν; cf. 28,20) closely resembles the paraenetic exhortation to 'cling to the baptism' found in *2 Clem.* 6,9 (τήρειν τὸ βάπτισμα).[175] As is no doubt the case with that passage, the words used in Matt 28,18-20 are rooted in the vocabulary used in the instruction of new members of the Christian congregation. Consequently, the words of Jesus under discussion call for an expansion of the Christian movement, the Church, rather than for a profound change in behaviour and attitude related to the coming Kingdom of God.

The final words of Matthew are universalistic in two respects. The instruction comes from Jesus, who has received 'all power' in heaven and on earth, and 'all nations' should hear his gospel and be baptised. Although baptism was a sign of personal conversion, the demand for baptism in combination with the triadic formula as the first element of the instruction by the disciples is revealing. The central issue here is not conversion (μετάνοια) and obeisance as a reaction to the coming intervention of God in history, but entry into the social group that is formed by the confession of Jesus, i.e. the church. The significance of Jesus is indicated by his claim to universal authority. This universal claim is made by the risen Lord, who during his life was already characterised as acting with God's authority (cf. 9,6 and 11,27).[176]

The prominence of the church as displayed in the closing section of Matthew is the direct effect of an interpretation of the gospel as a message of universal importance. In 24,14 Matthew gives a more explicit version of Mark 13,10, in which 'all nations' are mentioned in a comparable manner.[177] Mark 13,10 proves that the thought of universal procla-

---

[173] See K. Wengst, *Didache (Apostellehre), Barnabasbrief, Zweiter Klemensbrief, Schrift an Diognet* (Darmstadt: Wissenschaftliche Buchgesellschaft, 1984), p. 77, n. 56.

[174] See Barth, *Taufe*, pp. 44-59.

[175] *2 Clem.* 6,9:... ἡμεῖς ἐὰν μὴ **τηρήσωμεν** τὸ **βάπτισμα** ἁγνὸν καὶ ἐμίαντον, ποίᾳ πεποιθήσει εἰσελευσόμεθα εἰς τὸ βασίλειον τοῦ θεοῦ.

[176] The terminology ἐδόθη μοι κτλ. is an allusion to LXX Dan 7,13-14; see Davies, Allison, *Matthew*, vol. 3, pp. 682-683.

[177] Matt 24,14: καὶ κηρυχθήσεται τοῦτο τὸ εὐαγγέλιον τῆς βασιλείας ἐν ὅλῃ τῇ οἰκουμένῃ εἰς μαρτύριον πᾶσιν τοῖς ἔθνεσιν, καὶ τότε ἥξει τὸ τέλος. Mark 13,10:

mation of the gospel already existed around 70 CE. Such a universal proclamation of the gospel is mentioned in Mark 14,9 as well, this time not as an imperative, but as an indicative: the words referred to indicate that the gospel is being proclaimed 'everywhere in the world'.[178] The additions to Mark 13,10 in Matt 24,14 point out that in this perception the coming of 'the end' is related to the preaching of the gospel. Obviously, this is a further development of the eschatological character of the gospel as it was understood also in the earliest stage of the Christian movement.

The closing section of Matthew thus indicates the close of a development in which the proclamation of the gospel is interpreted as an event of universal impact that should reach the entire world.[179] Apparently, however, Matthew 28 has a different scope in that it focuses on entry into the Christian community as the central point of attention. To put it sharply: what had started with Jesus as the proclamation of God's intervention in history, after Jesus' death became the universal proclamation of the Christ event, ultimately to develop into the universal proclamation of the Christian community.

Conclusion

The above survey of passages that may contain evidence for a pre-Pauline missionary movement results in the following conclusion.

There is abundant evidence that Jesus proclaimed the coming Kingdom of God, and that at some early post-Easter date his followers described their ministry as commissioned by Jesus himself. After Jesus' death his followers did not stop proclaiming God's intervention in history. In stead, the Jesus movement now gradually turned into the early Christian movement, who regarded the coming of Jesus Christ, including his death and resurrection, as the beginning of God's final intervention. This is indicated by pre-epistolary formulae contained in the letters of Paul. They focus on

καὶ εἰς πάντα τὰ ἔθνη πρῶτον δεῖ κηρυχθῆναι τὸ εὐαγγέλιον. For a discussion of these passages, see Hahn, *Mission*, pp. 103-111.

[178] Cf. the slightly more explicit version in Matt 26,13.

[179] Hahn, *Mission*, pp. 110-111: 'Wie der irdische Jesus, der selbst zu Israel gesandt war, den Auftrag gegeben hat, unter dem alten Gottesvolk zu wirken, so hat der Auferstandene und Erhöhte als der Herr über die ganze Welt den Befehl zur Mission unter allen Völkern gegeben.' Hahn relates 28,16-20 to 24,14 and 26,13. See also B.J. Hubbard, *The Matthean Redaction of a Primitive Apostolic Commissioning: An Exegesis of Matthew 28:16-20* (SBLDS 19; Missoula: SBL, 1974), pp. 84-87.

christology and the soteriological function of Christ and in both cases the accent is eschatological: salvation has already been brought about, but its final form is still to be awaited. Christ's death and vindication were fully central to the early Christian movement. The Christ event was thus inter-preted as leading the followers of Jesus into salvation at the final inter-vention of God in history.

This focus on the Christ event is also present in the terminology used later in Acts to describe the activities of Philip and the Greek Jewish Christians in Antioch. They preach 'the good news' concerning Jesus Christ: 8,5.12.35; 11,19. The similarity in content between the descrip-tion of the preaching activities of Philip and the preachers from Antioch and the pre-epistolary formulae in Paul, makes it probable that the Book of Acts provides us with an adequate picture of the content of the procla-mation by the Greek-speaking Jewish Christians, the Hellenists. This observation does not imply, however, that the christocentric gospel was restricted to the Hellenists. It was rather *the* feature of all early Christian preaching, including that of the Aramaic-speaking community. This inevitably leads to the conclusion that the earliest Christian movement focused on the Christ event as part of the proclamation of the coming intervention of God in history. This proclamation had started with Jesus himself and was carried on after his death and resurrection, only now with Jesus as an integral part of it.

If this was the content of the earliest preaching activities, which audi-ence was it directed towards and what was the hoped for effect?

The Book of Acts provides us with a description that reflects a grad-ual development. At first the Christ event was proclaimed within Judaism itself. Subsequently – intentionally or not – people on the margin of Judaism were reached by this proclamation. At a certain moment in this development the line was finally crossed and not only pagan sympathis-ers with Judaism were addressed, but also pagan Greeks who did not explicitly sympathise. Within this process it was apparently the transition of the gospel from the Aramaic-speaking community to the Hellenists that formed the catalyst. It is highly plausible that this description is more or less accurate, but at the same time it should be noted that the author of Acts has created the chronology of events. The gradual character of the development is a redactional feature of Acts – the actual spread no doubt went faster than is implied by Acts.

Assuming that this 'oil-stain' model is a correct rendering of the early spread of the gospel, the question of the intended purpose of the preach-ing of the gospel becomes relevant. In the introduction it was decided that we should speak of 'mission' in the sense of 'proselytising' if the intended effect is the alteration of the views of the convert, together with adherence to the new social group.[180] The earliest Christian preaching of the gospel can clearly not be identified as such a proselytising mission for although the intended effect of the preaching of the gospel was no doubt acceptance by the convert of Jesus as God's final eschatological envoy, the formation of the social group formed around the confession of Jesus had only just begun. The best illustration of the fact that the Christian movement as a social group was not automatically central to the understanding of baptism in the early days of Christianity is the story of the conversion of the Ethiopian eunuch. The fact that the eunuch went on to his homeland means that what was at stake was not the adherence to a group of Christians, but his personal salvation through the confession of Christ, i.e. his acceptance of Jesus as God's final messenger.

The eschatological enthusiasm that held the early Christians in its grasp must be identified as the prime origin of Christian missionary activities. Both in the letters of Paul and in the Book of Acts we find evidence of the spiritual and prophetic utterances that resulted from this eschatological enthusiasm. Within the context of Jewish apocalypticism, in which the final intervention of God in history was thought of as an event with universal impact, it is clear that preaching about Jesus as God's final envoy by whom man could be saved from the wrath to come, soon found its way across the borders of Judaism. But this theological development had to be triggered by a sociological pre-condition: the existence of a Jewish community in Antioch, open to Gentiles and open to the proclamation of the Jesus movement. Within this specific social context, the cosmological implications of the Christ event appeared to extend beyond the realm of Judaism.

It thus appears that we have found a number of elements in the analysis of the pre-Pauline movement that explain part of the phenomenon: the focus on Christ as God's final envoy, the universal understanding of God's expected intervention in history, and the sociological context of an open Jewish community in Antioch. One matter, however, is not made clear by this explanation: why didn't these early Christians sit back and wait for their salvation? The explanation is to be found in the continuity of Jesus' preaching during his ministry and that of his followers after his death and their experience of his resurrection. Jesus had travelled through

---

[180] Cf. p. 5.

Galilee and Judea to instruct people regarding the coming intervention of God. As appeared above, he himself had instructed his disciples on this eventuality, and probably had them sustain his proclamation by doing the same thing. After Jesus' death his followers interpreted this event as the death of a righteous martyr and considered him to be resurrected in heaven.[181] As a result, the entire ministry of Jesus was regarded as being vindicated by God. Not only the message had been proved correct, but also the messenger himself had been designated as God's final envoy.[182] This was the kind of news that could not be kept silent, and since Jesus' followers had already lived a life of active proclamation of the Kingdom before his death, they became doubly motivated to bring their new message after they experienced his resurrection.

The change in context brought about a change in content: the proclamation of the gospel after Jesus' death and resurrection focused on the Christ event as the criterion for salvation. This message stood in direct continuity with the preaching of Jesus himself and claimed vindication for the messenger as well as the message. When in Antioch this specific message became embodied in an open community of Jews and Gentiles alike the stage was set for Paul to enter the play.

---

[181] J. Holleman, *Resurrection and Parousia. A Traditio-Historical Study of Paul's Eschatology in 1 Corinthians 15* (SNT 84; Leiden [etc.]: Brill, 1996), pp. 139-157.

[182] M. de Jonge, *Final Envoy*, p. 114: 'Jesus' followers, after his death, realized that his personal vindication and the complete breakthrough of the kingdom were two separate events, though directly and intrinsically connected. (...) The conviction that God had indeed vindicated Jesus, and thereby his message about the inaugurated kingdom, led them to envisage and to experience the period of the "not yet" before the parousia as the time in which the community of the faithful already participated to some extent in the blessings of the kingdom.'

CHAPTER FOUR

THE PHARISEE CALLED BY GOD

The next task in our attempt to situate Paul and his mission is to reconstruct the prehistory to Paul's ministry. What can be recovered in regard
to his pharisaic past? And what can be said on his conversion? In this
chapter the evidence will be surveyed that is given by both Paul's letters
and the book of Acts. As was argued above, the book of Acts is primarily a theological narrative with apologetical purposes, but it may still contain some relevant data. Nevertheless, it is obvious that the letters are the
prime source of information for our purpose.[1]

1. Pharisee and Faithful to the Law

It appears that Paul was not greatly interested in reminding his readers of
his pre-Christian life. Only on a few occasions does he refer to this period,
each time in a more or less polemic or apologetic context. Paul explicitly discusses his life before Christ in but a few passages: Phil 3,4-6;
Gal 1,13-14; 2 Cor 11,22; and Rom 11,1.[2]

a. Philippians 3,4-6

'(4) If anyone else has reason to be confident in the flesh, I have more:
(5) circumcised on the eighth day, a member of the people of Israel, of
the tribe of Benjamin, a Hebrew born of Hebrews; as to the Law, a Pharisee; as to zeal, a persecutor of the church; as to righteousness under the
Law, blameless.'

In this passage Paul defends himself against preachers who wanted to
cling to the Jewish customs he had apparently left behind. Paul's defence

---

[1] The letters Paul wrote are generally regarded as 'substitutes for his personal presence'
– cf. e.g. Vielhauer, *Geschichte*, p. 63. On their occasional character and its consequences
for their interpretation, see Beker, *Paul the Apostle*, pp. 23-36.
[2] Paul's apology in 2 Cor 2-7 is left out of consideration here, because it reveals nothing
in particular on Paul's past.

is put in the genre of a so-called *synkrisis*:[3] Paul describes his past and his main achievements. He starts with a mention of his own circumcision as the first element of his Jewish existence. The stock of Israel and the tribe of Benjamin subsequently mentioned by Paul form a description of his provenance.[4] Paul thus describes himself as an authentic Israelite. He points out that he was born into a Hebrew family and was hence circumcised after his first week, in accordance with what the Mosaic Law requires.[5] The term 'Hebrew' is usually interpreted as an honorary title. 'He who, as a Jew in the Diaspora, is called a "Hebrew", is pointed out as one who has remained faithful to the national and ethnic customs.'[6] This meaning of the word is closely related to the fact that 'Hebrew' primarily expresses the language spoken. Various passages in the New Testament use the word in this way.[7]

The three remarks Paul makes on the Law, his zeal, and righteousness are brief but revealing. Paul characterises himself as a Pharisee κατὰ νόμον.[8] This means that his attitude towards the Law was that of a Pharisee. A.J. Saldarini's study of the Pharisees pictures them as a group seeking social, political, and religious change from a strict Law-abiding perspective.[9] And the picture of the Pharisees in Josephus confirms the

---

[3] U.B. Müller, *Der Brief des Paulus an die Philipper* (ThHK; Leipzig: Evangelische Verlagsanstalt, 1993), p. 147; J. Zmijewski, *Der Stil der paulinischen "Narrenrede". Analyse der Sprachgestaltung in 2 Kor 11,1-12,10 als Beitrag zur Methodik von Stiluntersuchungen neutestamentlicher Texte* (BBB 52; Köln, Bonn: Peter Hanstein, 1978), p. 322. See also the extensive argumentation in B.J. Malina, J.H. Neyrey, *Portraits of Paul. An Archeology of Ancient Personality* (Louisville: Westminster John Knox Press, 1996), pp. 19-63 on Encomium; on the passage under discussion here, cf. pp. 52-53.

[4] G.D. Fee, *Paul's Letter to the Philippians* (NIC; Grand Rapids: Eerdmans, 1995), p. 307: 'It is not difficult to hear a ring of pride in this little reminder.'

[5] Cf. Gen 17,12; 21,4; Lev 12,3. See a.o. G. Barth, *Der Brief an die Philipper* (ZB; Zürich: Theologischer Verlag, 1979), pp. 58-59; R.P. Martin. *Philippians* (NCB; London: Marshall, Morgan & Scott; Grand Rapids: Eerdmans, 1976), pp. 127-129.

[6] J. Gnilka, *Der Philipperbrief* (HThK; Freiburg etc: Herder, 1968), p. 190; cf. also Barth, *Philipper*, p. 58.

[7] See John 5,2; 19,13.17.20; Acts 6,1; 21,40; 22,2; 26,14; cf. M.R. Vincent, *A Critical and Exegetical Commentary on the Epistles to the Philippians and to Philemon* (ICC; Edinburgh: Clark, 1897), p. 96: 'Aramaic vernacular'. Nevertheless, M. Carrez, *La deuxième épitre de Saint Paul aux Corinthiens* (CNT; Geneva: Labor et Fides, 1986), in his comment on 2 Cor 11,22 denies this specific meaning: 'Dans le monde hellénistique, hébreu signifierait simplement juif et non pas comme en Ac 6,1 celui qui parle la lange hébraïque par opposition à l'helléniste qui est un juif parlant grec.'

[8] These words should be translated 'in regard to the Law'; cf. Fee, *Philippians*, p. 308.

[9] A.J. Saldarini, *Pharisees, Scribes and Sadducees in Palestinian Society. A Sociological Approach* (Wilmington: Glazier, 1988), esp. pp. 281-282: 'The Pharisees probably sought a new, communal commitment to a strict Jewish way of life based on adherence to the covenant.'

fact that they were a group that was primarily concerned with ἀκριβεία regarding the Mosaic Law and the oral tradition following it.[10] Hence, Paul belonged to a group 'whose reputation for careful and earnest observance of the Mosaic Law and its tradition was the distinguishing feature (Josephus, *Life*, 9f.) of their life.'[11]

Paul's second remark is somewhat less clear. 'Concerning (his) zeal' Paul was a persecutor of the church. As was already stated above, the word 'zeal' is often used for describing those righteous Jews who wanted to defend Judaism against non-Jewish influences.[12] Paul places himself in line with those righteous faithful who strove to uphold the Law. His remark on his persecution of the church is therefore made from the perspective of those 'zealous' righteous who wished to adhere to the Mosaic Law in a very strict way. Many interpreters believe that Paul directed his persecution of the church against Hellenistic Jewish Christians[13] because they criticised the Law.[14] Yet A.J. Hultgren has convincingly argued that this is unlikely.[15] As will be argued below, Paul persecuted the earliest church because it confessed the *crucified* Jesus as the Anointed One, a confession that according to Gal 3,13 was totally incompatible with the Mosaic Law.

Finally, Paul mentions the fact that he was ἄμεμπτος concerning righteousness. The adjective used here expresses the notion that Paul maintained a righteous attitude towards the Law and God. This is not a moral

---

[10] S. Mason, *Flavius Josephus on the Pharisees* (SPB 39; Leiden etc: Brill, 1991), esp. pp. 372-375, argues that Josephus himself was fully responsible for the picture of the Pharisees in his works. Mason's concern is not so much to reconstruct Pharisaism, but to deal with Josephus' vision of the Pharisees. Nevertheless, the fact that Josephus pictures the Pharisees as a religious movement (in Josephus' terms: a 'philosophical school' – αἵρεσις), that was primarily concerned with ἀκριβεία in the Laws, provides some important information on the nature of Pharisaism.

[11] Martin, *Philippians*, p. 128.

[12] See below, pp. 145-146, for the discussion of ζηλωτής.

[13] See e.g. M. Hengel, *The Pre-Christian Paul* (London: SCM Press, 1991) [= 'Der vorchristliche Paulus', in M. Hengel, U. Heckel (eds.), *Paulus und das antike Judentum* (WUNT 58; Tübingen: Mohr, 1991)], pp. 63-86; also Hengel, Schwemer, *Paul between Damascus and Antioch*, pp. 35-38; J. Becker, U. Luz, *Die Briefe an die Galater, Epheser und Kolosser* (NTD; Göttingen, Vandenhoeck&Ruprecht, 18th ed., 1998), p. 17; F. Lang, *Die Briefe an die Korinther* (NTD; Göttingen: Vandenhoeck & Ruprecht, 1986), p. 214; more literature mentioned by A.J. Hultgren, 'Paul's Pre-Christian Persecutions of the Church: their Purpose, Locale, and Nature', *JBL* 95 (1976), pp. 97-111, cf. p. 97, n.1.

[14] Hengel, *Pre-Christian Paul*, p. 85: 'The proclamation of the Greek-speaking followers of the messiah Jesus of Nazareth, crucified a short time earlier, which was critical of the ritual parts of the Torah and the cult, was a provocation to the majority who were loyal to the Law.'

[15] Hultgren, 'Persecutions', pp. 97-111.

justification of Paul's life as a Pharisee,[16] but merely an observation: in his pre-Christian life Paul was a righteous Pharisee who fulfilled the commandments of the Law. Within the context this remark functions as a strong argument against Paul's opponents.[17]

b. Galatians 1,13-14

'(13) You have heard, no doubt, of my earlier life in Judaism. I was violently persecuting the church of God and was trying to destroy it. (14) I advanced in Judaism beyond many among my people of the same age, for I was far more zealous for the traditions of my ancestors.'

In his epistle to the Galatians Paul emphasises the independence of his gospel and authority from that of the apostles in Jerusalem. Paul argues that he received his call straight from God. It was a revelation that gave him the gospel he preached and the authority to do so. In 1,15-17 Paul describes his call, and the verses preceding this description (vv. 13-14) speak of his life before the great change. A short glimpse of Paul's past is necessary to enable him to describe the change his call brought about.

These verses cast a little more light on Paul's past and his own view of it than most other Pauline passages. Firstly, they present Paul speaking about his Jewish period as belonging to his past: ἡ ἐμὴ ἀναστροφή ποτε ἐν τῷ Ἰουδαϊσμῷ. The use of ποτέ implies that for Paul this ἀναστροφή is finished.[18] By explicitly characterising the way of his past as 'Judaism', Paul reveals that his view of his present state is a different one. The term Ἰουδαϊσμός is used here as a description of the Jewish, national religion.[19] At this point a remark by E. De Witt Burton in his ICC commentary is still valuable:

---

[16] Cf. Müller, *Philipper*, p. 149: 'Dieses Selbsturteil ist nicht moralisch mißzuverstehen.'
[17] See B. Mengel, *Studien zum Philipperbrief. Untersuchungen zum situativen Kontext unter besonderer Berücksichtigung der Frage nach der Ganzheit oder Einheitlichkeit eines paulinischen Briefes* (WUNT 2.8; Tübingen: Mohr, 1982), pp. 262-265.
[18] The temporal designation ποτέ 'belongs with ἀναστροφή' – H.D. Betz, *Galatians: a Commentary on Paul's Letter to the Churches in Galatia* (Hermeneia; Philadelphia: Fortress Press, 1979) p. 67, n. 106. For Paul, however, the end of this ἀναστροφή coincides with the end of his Ἰουδαϊσμός.
[19] See 2 Macc 2,21; 8,1; 14,38; 4 Macc 4,26; cf. the inscription found in the synagogue of Stobi – M. Hengel, 'Die Synagogeninschriften von Stobi', *ZNW* 57 (1966), pp. 145-183. Ignatius uses the word as the opposite of χριστιανισμός: *Phld.* 6,1; cf. also *Magn.* 8,1. Ps.-Just., *Quaestiones et responsiones ad orthodoxos*, speaks of ἰουδαϊσμός τε καὶ ἑλληνισμός (*PG*, vol. 6, col. 1252).

The very use of the term in this way is significant of the apostle's conception of the relation between his former and his present faith, indicating that he held the latter, and had presented it to the Galatians, not as a type of Judaism, but as an independent religion distinct from that of the Jews. Though the word Christianity was probably not yet in use, the fact was in existence.[20]

Indeed, Paul's remark implies that his present ἀναστροφή is no longer to be placed within Judaism. This is a very important observation for the present purpose, since it marks the point where, in Paul's view, a certain transition was made that went beyond the boundaries of his Pharisaic religion.[21]

Secondly, Paul, in his description of his past, pictures himself as a former persecutor of Christians. The words he uses are often interpreted as describing a violent persecution: he speaks of διώκω καθ' ὑπερβολήν, and πορθέω. He 'excessively persecuted' the church of God, and 'tried to destroy' it.[22] It is more likely, however, that the violence refers to the way Paul perceived his deeds retrospectively rather than to the way he acted at the time. Thus, Gal 1,13 would describe the vehemence with which Paul opposed the views of the church rather than any violence against Christians.[23]

The above interpretation is supported by the evidence: the words used – διώκω and πορθέω – do not necessarily imply the use of force. Throughout his epistles Paul uses the verb διώκω eighteen times. Four

---

[20] E. de Witt Burton, *A Critical and Exegetical Commentary on the Epistle to the Galatians* (ICC; Edinburgh: Clark, 1921) p. 44.

[21] J.D.G. Dunn, *A Commentary on the Epistle to the Galatians* (BNTC; London: Black, 1993), p. 56-57, connects the ἀναστροφή with *halakha*, 'the word which more than any other characterises the Jewish understanding of the obligations laid upon the devout', and mentions 1 Kgs 6,12; Prov 20,7; *T. Ash.* 6,3; and 2 Macc 6,23 as illuminating parallels. While referring to A.F. Segal, *Paul the Convert. The Apostolate and Apostasy of Saul the Pharisee* (New Haven, London: Yale University Press, 1990), Dunn states that the end of Paul's ἀναστροφή within Judaism resulted in his transition 'from one Jewish movement, the Pharisees, into another, the Christians' (p. 57). According to J.L. Martyn, *Galatians: a New Translation with Introduction and Commentary* (AB; New York [etc.]: Doubleday, 1998), p. 164, Paul regarded the advent of Christ as 'the end of religion'. Martyn interprets Paul's call as the intrusion of the new aeon into Paul's life – 'it is the form taken in his own case by God's calling into existence the new creation.'

[22] The verb πορθέω should be translated as a conative imperfect – 'try to destroy'; cf. BDF §326.

[23] Hultgren, 'Persecutions', rightly argues that 'contrary to prevailing practices, Gal 1:13 should be translated and interpreted in terms of a Pauline – not Lucan – understanding of the nature of persecution, i.e., that he persecuted the church with an intensity of zeal (not an intensity of violence), which was beyond compare, and tried to hinder its progress' (p. 110).

times it describes his pre-Christian activities against the church (Gal 1,13.23; Phil 3,6; and 1 Cor 15,9). In order to grasp the verb's meaning in these passages we will have to investigate Paul's use of the word in other contexts. In eight cases the meaning is evidently 'to pursue something'.[24] Contrary to the passage under discussion, this use of the verb is metaphorical. Therefore, it does not shed light on the meaning of διώκω in Gal 1,13. In Rom 12,14; 1 Cor 4,12; 2 Cor 4,9 the verb is used in catalogues of hardships. In these passages it functions as a general description of a situation of persecution in which it is not clear whether any physical threat was included in this danger. The use of διώκω in Gal 4,29; 5,11; and 6,12 does not imply the use of force either. In 4,29 Paul alludes to the persecution of the followers of Christ by Jews, and in 5,11 he adds that he himself is being persecuted because of what he preaches. Finally, in 6,12 Paul states that those who have themselves been circumcised have done so, out of fear of persecution. That Paul had to face serious opposition from Jews, which occasionally led to attempts to kill him, is evident from 2 Cor 11,24-25. But it is unlikely that Paul refers to such a specific assault in the passages mentioned. The references in 4,29; 5,11; and 6,12 are to an extreme form form of opposition. In consequence, διώκω in Gal 1,13 would have the same meaning. It most likely describes a fierce opposition against the Christians by Paul, without necessarily indicating the use of violence.[25]

The subsequent use of πορθέω – '(seek to) destroy' – does not imply any violent action by Paul either, even though some interpret the word as though it does.[26] The intended destruction of the church does not point to the use of force against its members: Paul merely speaks of an aggressive attempt to eradicate the church's views. Therefore, the conclusion should be that Paul presents himself here not as one who tried to exterminate Christians by using violence, but rather as one who fiercely opposed the church of God.[27] It is a subtle but important distinction. In

---

[24] Δικαιοσύνην: Rom 9,30-31 bis; φιλοξενίαν: Rom 12,13; τὰ τῆς εἰρήνης: Rom 14,19; ἀγαπήν: 1 Cor 14,1; τὸ ἀγαθόν: 1 Thess 5,15; absolute: Phil 3,12.14.

[25] E.P. Sanders, Paul (PM; Oxford: Oxford University Press, 1991), p. 9, considers the possibility that Paul persecuted the Christians by 'persuading synagogues to administer to those who accepted Jesus the severest punishment a synagogue could mete out – the thirty-nine lashes that he himself later suffered.'

[26] See e.g. Dunn, Galatians, p. 58.

[27] For this interpretation of Paul's persecution of the Church, see P.H. Menoud, 'Le sens du verbe ΠΟΡΘΕΙΝ (Gal 1.13,23; Act 9.21)', in: idem, Jésus-Christ et la foi. Recherches néotestamentaires (BT; Neuchatel, Paris: Dalachaux & Niestlé, 1975), pp. 40-47 [originally published in: W. Eltester, F.H. Kettler (eds.), Apophoreta. Festschrift

his life as a persecutor, Paul probably did not try to kill Christians; he tried to eradicate their views. The violence is an element of the narrative portrayal of Paul in Acts 9,1-3, and cannot be found in Paul's letters. This view of Paul's persecution of the church is supported by 1 Cor 15,9; Gal 1,23 and Phil 3,6. In Gal 1,23 Paul cites what may indeed have been a rumour in the Judean congregations. The remark he makes in that verse is important for two reasons. Firstly, it confirms Paul's statement of 1,22, viz. that Paul was unknown to the Judean congregations. Hence, Paul's actions against the church could not have been undertaken in Judea and Jerusalem, and at least this element of the picture given of Paul as persecutor of the church in Acts 7-8 is false.[28] Secondly, also in 1,23 the verb πορθέω is used for Paul's actions. This time the object is 'the faith' (ἡ πίστις). Here, too, there is no mention of physical force against the Christians, but merely of a virulent action against their views. Finally, in 1 Cor 15,9, Paul speaks of the fact that he 'persecuted the church of God' (ἐδίωξα τὴν ἐκκλησίαν τοῦ θεοῦ). These words give us no new details beyond what we already know from Gal 1,13.23. Rather, they confirm the fact that Paul acted against the church.

In v. 14 Paul describes the background of his opposition to the church. He characterises himself as one who made more progress than many others of his generation. Hence, Paul's position as a ζηλωτής ... τῶν πατρικῶν μου παραδόσεων describes the substance of Paul's progress.

In combination with the mention of the Laws of the fathers, the noun ζηλωτής refers to a religious attitude in which the Law is the centre of religious activities and all elements opposing the Law are treated as hostile. In itself, the word is neutral: Diogenes Laertius can speak of one who followed the views of the Pythagoraeans as of a ζηλωτής ... τῶν πηθαγορικῶν.[29] And Plutarch calls Phaonios a follower of Cato: ζηλωτὴς Κάτωνος.[30] Josephus, in his Life, describes how he became a follower of Bannus: ζηλωτής ἐγενόμην αὐτοῦ.[31] But as soon as it is

---

für Ernst Haenchen (BZNW 30; Berlin: De Gruyter, 1964), pp. 178-186], cf. p. 47: 'C'est aux certitudes des croyants et non à leurs personnes que s'est attaqué le pharisien brûlant de ce zèle sans discernement qu'il devait plus tard dénoncer.'

[28] Pace Hultgren, 'Persecutions', p. 107, who argues that 'in terms of the locale of Paul's persecutions of the church there is essential agreement between Acts and Galatians that he did persecute the church in Judea first.'

[29] Diogenes Laertius, Vit. Phil. IX, 37.

[30] Plutarch, Cato Minor 46,1; Pelop. 26,7; Philop. 3,1; cf. also Diod. Sic., Bib. Hist. II,1,4; XXXI, 26,5.

[31] Jos., Vita XI,6; cf. c. Ap. I,162; BJ V,104.

used in combination with the traditional Laws or customs of the fathers, it signifies the religious attitude mentioned. A good example is found in Josephus, *Ant.* XII, 270-271. There, Josephus tells the story of Mattathias' refusal to make a sacrifice to Zeus in the temple of Jerusalem. After Mattathias has killed the first Jew to obey the commands of Antiochus IV Epiphanes, he calls upon his countrymen who care for their national tradition to follow him. Mattathias' words are: εἴ τις ζηλωτής ἐστιν τῶν πατρίων ἐθῶν καὶ τῆς τοῦ θεοῦ θρησκείας, ἐπέσθω, φησίν, ἐμοί ('Whoever is zealous for our country's Laws and the worship of God, let him come with me!').[32] This kind of piety is mentioned as exemplary in 1 Macc 2,49-70, when Mattathias instructs his sons in his farewell speech. He begins his speech by telling them to 'strive for the Law' (ζηλώσατε τῷ νομῷ; 1 Macc 2,50). In the examples he subsequently gives of the pious faithful from the past, Mattathias mentions Phinehas and Elijah as the two who were most 'zealous' in their attempts to cling to the right tradition.[33] This use of the word originates in a tradition of Phinehas[34] who was 'zealous in the fear of the Lord'.[35] When Paul describes himself as a ζηλωτής τῶν πατρικῶν μου παραδόσεων he indicates the position he took within Judaism: he was a pious adherent to the Mosaic Law and the oral tradition of its interpretation.

Obviously, Paul here describes the Pharisaic view in which the Law indeed took the central position Paul assigned to it. In the Pharisaic perception the oral tradition of the fathers supplemented the Mosaic Law, and study of the Law included this oral tradition.[36] By calling himself a fervent adherent to the traditions of the fathers, Paul marks out his past as a Pharisee (as he explicitly does in Phil 3,5). To this he adds that, as a Pharisee, he had fiercely opposed the church of God. And, most importantly, Paul speaks about his life before his call in such a way as to imply that Judaism was his former religion. Indeed, Paul seems to imply that he no longer fits within Judaism.

---

[32] Translation R. Marcus, LCL, *Josephus*, vol. 7, p. 141.
[33] 1 Macc 2,54: Φινεες ὁ πατὴρ ἡμῶν ἐν τῷ ζηλῶσαι ζῆλον ἔλαβεν διαθήκην ἱερωσύνης αἰωνίας; 2,58: Ἠλίας ἐν τῷ ζηλῶσαι ζῆλον νόμου ἀνελήμφθη εἰς τὸν οὐρανόν.
[34] Num 25,1-18; Ps 106,30-31; Sir 45,23.
[35] 4 Macc 18,12; cf. also *T. Ash.* 4,5; 1QH XIV,14. – Martin, *Philippians*, p. 128.
[36] See F. Mussner, *Der Galaterbrief* (HThK; Freiburg [etc.]: Herder, 1974), p. 80. Mussner mentions a number of passages to prove that Paul refers to the Pharisaic tradition: Sir 8,9; *2 Enoch* 52,9; 2 Macc 7,2; 3 Macc 1,23; 4 Macc 16,16; Mark 7,3.5; Josephus, *Ant.* X,51; XIII,297.408; XIX,349. See also D. Lührmann, *Der Brief an die Galater* (ZB; Zürich: Theologischer Verlag, 1978), p. 31.

Finally, it is important to note that the object of Paul's opposition is described as the 'church of God'. The description ἐκκλησία τοῦ θεοῦ, which was obviously the self-designation of the earliest Christians, indicates that the pre-Pauline Christian movement characterised itself as the eschatological *kehal YHWH*, the small group of true Israelites.[37]

c. 2 Corinthians 11,22-23

'(22) Are they Hebrews? So am I. Are they Israelites? So am I. Are they descendants of Abraham? So am I. (23) Are they ministers of Christ? I am talking like a madman – I am a better one: …'

Paul directs his arguments at his opponents who apparently boasted of their Jewish background.[38] In the whole of his speech Paul argues 'as a fool'.[39] He calls his opponents οἱ ὑπερλίαν ἀπόστολοι (v. 5), and points out that they are not true servants of Christ. One of the elements that apparently played a part in the discussion is the fact that Paul's opponents had been paid for their activities, whereas Paul himself refused all support from the congregation in Corinth (11,7-12.23). Paul does admit that he had been supported by the Macedonians (the congregation of Thessolonica?), but at the same time he makes it abundantly clear that he was independent of the church in Corinth.[40]

---

[37] See, among many others, Mussner, *Galater*, p. 79; and H. Schlier, *Der Brief an die Galater* (KEK; Göttingen: Vandenhoeck & Ruprecht, 4th ed., 1965), p. 49. For a critical discussion of this theory, see K. Berger, 'Volksversammlung und Gemeinde Gottes', *ZTK* 73 (1976), pp. 167-207; H. Merklein, 'Die Ekklesia Gottes. Der Kirchenbegriff bei Paulus und in Jerusalem', *BZ* 23 (1979), pp. 48-70; J. Hainz, s.v. 'Kirche', in: M. Görg, B. Lang (eds.), *Neues Bibel-Lexikon*, vol. 2 (Zürich, Düsseldorf: Benziger, 1995), cols. 481-486.

[38] For a reconstruction of Paul's opponents in this letter, many interpreters use Georgi, *Gegner*. A discussion of this book was given above in the introduction (pp. 7-9). A good summary of characteristics of Paul's opponents is given by Lang, *Korinther*, pp. 357-359: these teachers obviously boast of their Jewish descent, they have themselves paid for being servants of Christ (11,7-10.23), and they reproach Paul for a number of failures – he is not spiritual (10,2), he has but a frail personal appearance (10,1.10), is not a skilled and trained rhetor (11,6), he does not perform the signs of an apostle (12,12), uses collection money for his own purposes (12,14-18) and finally, since he does not depend financially on the congregation he visits, he cannot be a true apostle (11,7-12). See also L. Kreitzer, *2 Corinthians* (NTG; Sheffield: Academic Press, 1996), pp. 71-82, and the literature mentioned on p. 82.

[39] Zmijewski, *Narrenrede*, esp. pp. 412-433, shows how much Paul is depending on the rhetorical styles of his day as well as creating a new form of *sermo humilis*.

[40] Paul states to have accepted an ὀψώνιον from the other churches, i.e. 'provisions' – cf. Hock, *Social Context*, p. 92; Martin, *2 Corinthians*, p. 346. Paul obviously intended to bring the gospel to the Corinthians 'free of charge'; cf. below, pp. 221-228.

148   PAUL THE MISSIONARY

In his defence, Paul 'foolishly' boasts of his Jewish identity in order to point out the fruitlessness of his opponents' claims.[41] Three times he mentions it, in different words: Paul is a 'Hebrew', an 'Israelite', and 'offspring of Abraham'. All three titles have an honorary meaning.[42] Scholarly opinions differ, though, as to the matter of whether these titles are synonyms or not. M. Carrez, for instance, regards ἑβραῖος as being equivalent to ἰουδαῖος and denies the theory that the three titles strive towards a climax.[43] J. Zmijewski, however, in accordance with Georgi, includes the fourth title (διάκονοι χριστοῦ), and divides the titles mentioned in 11,22 into two categories.[44] The first three would thus point to the Jewish origins of Paul and his opponents (in Georgi's terms: 'Herkunfts-bezeichnungen'), whereas the last title describes Paul's function within the Christian community ('Funktionsbezeichnung'). According to Zmijewski, a certain climax is presented within these first three titles. In his view 'Hebrew' is the designation for Jews by outsiders, 'Israelite' reflects the internal cohesion of the Jewish people, and 'offspring of Abraham' represents the Christian self-understanding of the group described.[45] How should these titles be regarded?

Since Paul identifies himself by the three titles referring to his Jewish descent as being the equal of his opponents (κἀγώ),[46] it is plausible that he used these three designations as synonyms in order to stress the fact that he is just as much a Jew as they are. The difference is that of his being a 'servant of Christ' (v. 23: ὑπὲρ ἐγώ!). Therefore it is very likely that the first three titles point to Paul's Jewish lineage, whereas the fourth one refers to his present state as one who has been called by Christ.[47] In

---

[41] See G. Strecker, 'Die Legitimität des paulinischen Apostolates nach 2 Korinther 10-13', *NTS* 38 (1992), pp. 566-586.
[42] See R. Bultmann, *Der zweite Brief an die Korinther* hrsg von E. Dinkler (KEK; Göttingen: VandenHoeck & Ruprecht, 1976), p. 215: 'Die drei Titel sind die Ehrentitel des palästinensischen Juden, durch die sowohl das Volk als natürliche Volksgemeinschaft wie als Volk der Heilsgeschichte mit ihren Verheißungen charakterisiert wird.' Also Lang, *Korinther*, p. 343; Carrez, *Corinthiens*, p. 221; R.P. Martin, *2 Corinthians* (WBC; Waco: Word Books, 1986), p. 373.
[43] Carrez, *Corinthiens*, p. 221; cf. H. Lietzmann, W.G. Kümmel, *An die Korinther I-II* (HNT; Tübingen: Mohr, 1949) ad loc.
[44] Zmijewski, *Narrenrede*, pp. 239-241; Georgi, *Gegner*, pp. 31-82.
[45] Zmijewski, *Narrenrede*, p. 240.
[46] Zmijewski, *Narrenrede*, pp. 241-243.
[47] In Rom 9,6-8 Paul relates the term 'offspring of Abraham' to those who confess Christ. The context, however, is quite different from that of 2 Cor 11,22-23, and for that reason Paul's conception of 'offspring of Abraham' in 2 Cor 11,22-23 cannot be explained on the basis of Rom 9,6-8.

this manner, 'offspring of Abraham' is used as an honorary title for those who cling to the true religion of Israel, as for instance in 4 Maccabees 18. That chapter includes the conclusion of the account of the martyrdom of a widow and her seven sons. In this account being a child of Abraham plays an important part: the Israelites are addressed as τῶν Ἀβραμιαίων σπερμάτων ἀπόγονοι παῖδες Ἰσραηλῖται. The widow herself is referred to as a 'daughter of Abraham' (v. 20; cf. 17, 6). By calling himself 'offspring of Abraham' in this context, Paul underlines his place within Jewish tradition. In his argument against his opponents he stresses the fact that he, too, is fully Jewish.

Paul's defence in 2 Cor 11,22-23 thus makes it clear that for Paul his Jewish identity is not just something connected with his past. Paul was born an Israelite and at the time of writing his letters he considered himself as belonging to the offspring of Abraham. At first sight, this appears to be in grave contradiction with his presentation of his 'earlier life in Judaism' of Gal 1,13. But the way in which Paul in his letter to the Romans uses the same terminology, once again to underline the continuity of his own position with the history and faith of Israel, points out that for him there was no contradiction.

d. Romans 11,1

'(1) I ask, then, has God rejected his people? By no means! I myself am an Israelite, a descendant of Abraham, a member of the tribe of Benjamin.'

The theological problem Paul faces when describing the distinction between his life before and after his call, returns in his letter to the Romans. Here, as in Galatians, Paul underlines the continuity, for in Rom 11,1 he again characterises himself as 'an Israelite, a descendant of Abraham, a member of the tribe of Benjamin'. This time, he does so in order to prove that God has not cast away his people.[48]

Again, Paul proudly presents himself as an Israelite. It is important to note that Paul mentions his Jewish roots in a passage that discusses the

---

[48] Paul's personal adherence to the Jewish people is mentioned here as proof that God did not reject Israel. Paul in person is a witness to that; cf. among others O. Michel, *Der Brief an die Römer* (KEK; Göttingen: Vandenhoeck & Ruprecht, 1966), p. 338. According to J.D.G. Dunn, *Romans 9-16* (WBC; Dallas: Word Books, 1988), p. 635, the point is, that Paul here speaks *as a Jew*: 'what is at stake is Paul's claim to express an authentically Jewish viewpoint and understanding of God's workings'. Cranfield, *Romans*, p. 544, argues that Paul wants to stress the fact that he, as an Israelite, had been appointed apostle to the Gentiles.

status of Israel. In this context Paul argues that Israel was not rejected by God. The church for Paul is by no means something new, that dissolves the relationship between God and his people. Instead, Paul considers the church to be the direct continuation of this relationship (cf. Rom 9,6-13).[49] The reference to the seven thousand Israelites who did not bow to Baal in Rom 11,4 is clear: the church is the chosen remnant of Israel.[50] All Israelites may repent their sins and become members of it, just as the Gentiles may.

For Paul's view of his own position this concept of the church as the chosen remnant of Israel into which the Gentiles are welcomed, is of great importance. The existence of the church did not imply a sharp break with Israel – instead, the church should be seen as Israel's final remnant. This view of the church implies a direct continuity before and after the coming of Christ. This continuity is also present, therefore, in Paul's own life. No matter how much things may have changed for Paul when he experienced his call, he still regarded himself as a pious member of the people of Israel.

e. Saul the Pharisee: the evidence in Acts

The book of Acts describes Paul's pre-Christian period in but a few words.[51] Paul is introduced in 7,58 as Σαῦλος, and he is mentioned by this name until 13,9. In that verse the author explicitly identifies Saul as Paul: Σαῦλος δέ, ὁ καὶ Παῦλος. This observation raises the question of why the author uses this name. In his own letters Paul never mentions the name Saul. Apparently the author of Acts was aware of a tradition in which Saul was Paul's Aramaic name. The tradition therefore either mentioned Paul as the Latin name, with Saul as the Aramaic equivalent, or Paul as a new name adopted after Saul's call.[52] The latter option is, however, rather unlikely. The author of Acts does not restrict his use of the

---

[49] Cf. Cranfield, *Romans*, p. 471, speaks of 'the inner circle of election, (...) the Israel within Israel'.
[50] Dunn, *Romans 9-16*, p. 645, stresses the fact that in the example of the 7,000 faithful – as in the prophecy of Isaiah in 9,27-29 – it is God who has retained the faith of the remnant: 'As God sustained and carried out his covenant purpose through such a minority then, so now.' See also U. Wilckens, *Der Brief an die Römer*, vol. 2: Rom 6-11 (EKK; Zürich etc: Benziger; Neukirchen-Vluyn: Neukirchener, 1980), p. 237.
[51] On the historical reliability of Acts, see the excursus above, pp. 99-105.
[52] The traditional ecclesiastic exegesis opts for the interpretation of Saul as Paul's name before his conversion. An early example is found in Jerome's description of Paul: *Paulus, qui ante Saulus* (cf. below, p. 157, n. 76).

name Saul to the period before his call, but continues using this name up to 13,9. At that point Paul and Barnabas together commence their common mission. This is probably an indication that in the pre-Lukan tradition 'Saul' was used as the Aramaic equivalent of the Latin *Paulus*, probably even indicating the fact that this was an Aramaic tradition.[53] The author of Acts substituted 'Saul' for 'Paul' at the moment in his narrative when Paul started his proclamation of the gospel to the Greeks.[54]

Since there is no plausible reason why at any given point in the development of the early Christian movement the name 'Saul' would have been made up for Paul, it is likely that he did indeed have this name. The fact that Paul also had an Aramaic or Hebrew name is all the more plausible since he characterises himself as 'a Hebrew, an Israelite' (cf. above).[55]

The description of Saul in Acts 7,58-8,3 contains a few more interesting elements. First of all Saul is mentioned as a νεανίας, who watched over the clothes of those who executed Stephen (7,58). Then, Saul is mentioned as approving of the execution (8,1). Finally, he is depicted as the one who tries to put the Christians behind bars by entering their homes and taking them away.

Paul is portrayed as a young man in 7,58. This means that, if this is correct, in the early fifties Paul must have been about fifty-five years of age.[56] As with Paul's name, it is not very likely that the author of Acts had any interest in changing Paul's age. Therefore it can be assumed safely that Paul indeed was a νεανίας at the time of Stephen's execution,

---

[53] Murphy-O'Connor, *Paul*, pp. 41-43, points out that *Saul* was probably the Semitic name for a 'Hebrew born of Hebrews', whereas *Paul* may have been his *supernomen* or *signum*. According to Murphy-O'Connor, the evidence for this latter view is found in an inscription published by C.J. Hemer, 'The Name of Paul', *TynB* 36 (1985), pp. 179-183, in which a soldier is described as 'Lucius Antionius Leo, *also called* Neon'.

[54] C. Burchard, *Der dreizehnte Zeuge. Traditions- und kompositionsgeschichtliche Untersuchungen zu Lukas' Darstellung der Frühzeit des Paulus* (FRLANT 104; Göttingen: Vandenhoeck & Ruprecht, 1970), pp. 36-37: 'Lukas wußte, daß Paulus, der sich in seinen Briefen nie anders nennt und im griechischen Sprachbereich offenbar nur unter diesem Namen gegangen ist, jüdisch Saul hieß und nennt ihn deshalb so, bis er in den Bereich eintritt, in dem sein Lebenswerk hauptsächlich geschieht.'

[55] The combination of an Hebrew and a Latin or Greek name was not uncommon; cf. e.g. G. Mussies, 'Jewish Personal Names in Some Non-Literary Sources', in: P.W. van der Horst, J.W. van Henten (eds.), *Studies in Early Jewish Epigraphy* (AGAJU 21; Leiden [etc.]: Brill, 1994), pp. 242-276. On p. 255 Mussies discusses the example of a 'freedman of Agrippina' with a Hebrew and a Greek name: Natanael/Theodotos.

[56] Murphy-O'Connor, *Paul*, pp. 1-8, argues that Paul was born in ca. 6 BCE. If the stoning of Stephen is to be dated shortly after Jesus' death, Paul would have been about 35 years old at the time.

152   PAUL THE MISSIONARY

i.e. in the early thirties. This leaves open a rather wide range of possibilities, since νεανίας can refer to the period between 24 and 40.[57] At the same time it does give us some indication as to Paul's age. It is probable that Paul was born somewhere around the beginning of the first century.

The remark in 8,1 on Saul's approving the execution of Stephen is not confirmed by Paul's own letters. The two most important words of this verse return in 22,20. Since ἀναιρεῖν is a redactional word in Luke-Acts,[58] the hapax legomenon ἀναίρεσις is likely to be redactional too. This indicates that the description of Saul's approval of Stephen's execution is a redactional element in Acts. It should be interpreted as a narrative introduction of the traditional description of the pre-Christian Paul as a persecutor of Christians. By linking Saul to the account of the death of Stephen, the author of Acts smoothly introduces Paul into his narrative. Paul is thus described as one of the opponents of the early Christian movement. This redactional introduction of Saul also accounts for the content of 7,58. It is very likely that the author depicts Saul as attending the clothes of those who executed Stephen because he wanted to link Paul to this event, but that he knew that Paul himself had not been involved in the killing.[59]

In 8,1b-2 the author makes the transition from the congregation in Jerusalem described in cc. 1-7 to Philip's activities in Judea and Samaria (8,4-40; cf. above, pp. 111-117). He does so by means of a typically redactional theme: there was a persecution of the congregation in Jerusalem, and it is exactly because of this that the Christian movement spread further afield. As was argued above, the author of Acts develops this theme throughout the book, thereby implicitly proving the divine origin of the movement. The reader or hearer remembers Gamaliel's words in 5,38-39: if the movement comes from God, there is nothing you can do against it. The redactional character of the transition may also appear from the inconsistency in 8,2b. The entire movement was spread over Judea and Samaria, and still the apostles stayed in Jerusalem.[60] This

---

[57] Cf. Bauer, Wörterbuch, s.v. νεανίας, who mentions F. Boll, 'Der Lebensalter', Neue Jahrbücher für den klassiken Altertum 31 (1913), pp. 89-91.

[58] Luke 22,2; 23,32; Acts 2,23; 5,33.36; 7,21.28; 9,23.24.29; 10,39; 12,2; 13,28; 16,27; 22,20; 23,15.21.27; 25,3; 26,10; cf. Matt 2,16; 2 Thess 2,8; Heb 10,9.

[59] A.N. Wilson, Paul. The Mind of an Apostle (London [etc.]: Sinclair-Stephenson, 1997), pp. 51-55, argues that Paul was a member of the temple-guard. As such he would have probably witnessed the death of Jesus, which would explain why 'the Crucifixion became the focus of Paul's obsessive religious attention' (p. 60). Unfortunately, this interpretation of Paul is based on a wrong evaluation of the data: Paul's picture in 7,58 and 8,1 is clearly redactional.

[60] Cf. Haenchen, Apostelgeschichte, p. 248: 'Daß diese Konstruktion am Widerspruch von 9,31 und 11,19 scheitert, ist Lukas nicht bewußt geworden.'

remark reflects the author's purpose, viz. to account for the spread of Christianity through Judea and Samaria, whilst still retaining Jerusalem as the main centre.

Having seen that the transition in 8,1-2 is redactional, one should ask how 8,3 is to be accounted for. Is the description of Saul as the one who entered the houses of Christians only to drag them off to prison histori- cally trustworthy or not? The answer should be negative. A comparison with the evidence given by Paul himself in his letters leads to the con- clusion that Acts exaggerates the information given in Paul's letters. In the previous sections it appeared that Paul portrays himself in the period before his call as one who tried to eradicate the Christian confession, thereby opposing the Christians in a fierce, but not necessarily violent way. It is this description of Paul that shines through the words of Acts 8,3. The author of Acts highlights the fact that Paul had fiercely opposed the early Christian movement by describing him in 8,3 as an officer of the law whose aim it was to put Christians behind bars.[61] The redactional character of the verse is clear from its content as well as the words used: σύρειν and παραδίδωμι εἰς φυλακήν are both redactional expressions.[62]

After his introduction in 7,58-8,3 Saul disappears from the scene in the book of Acts. Chapter 8 deals with the spread of the Christian movement through Judea and Samaria, thereby further developing the main theme of the book (cf. 1,8). In 9,1 Saul returns, however. The theme is taken up where the author had left it in 8,3: at the persecution of the Church by Paul. This time, Paul is described as the envoy of the High Priest, whose official task it was to persecute the Christians in Damascus.[63] The two

---

[61] Haenchen, *Apostelgeschichte*, p. 245, is rightly critical of this picture of Paul: the con- trast between the young guard of the clothes at the stoning of Stephen and the leader of the opposition to the Way cannot reflect the historical circumstances of Paul's opposi- tion to the church. This change in the picture of Paul may reflect the fact that the inten- stity of Paul's persecution of the Christians increases in the book of Acts: 'In 8,1 Paul is a bystander, but has some responsibility for Stephen's death; in 8,3; 9,1-2; 13-14; 21 and 22,4 his activity is more direct, putting his victims in dire straits, both men and women; in 22,4-5 and 26,11 the picture grows in intensity, revealing a man whose ferocity knew no bounds in its attempt to stamp out the Church.' – Wilson, *Gentile Mission*, p. 157 (based on the perceptions of G. Klein, *Die zwölf Apostel* [FRLANT 77; Göttingen: Vandenhoeck & Ruprecht, 1961], pp. 114-144).

[62] Σύρειν: Acts 8,3; 14,19; 17,6; cf. John 21,8; Rev 12,4. The terminology of παραδίδ- ωμι εἰς φυλακήν is typical for Luke-Acts: Luke 21,12; Acts 22,4; cf. Luke 23,25 and Acts 12,4. The only other NT passage in which it occurs is a verse from Q: Luke 12,58/Matt 5,25.

[63] In regard to the jurisdiction of the High Priest, Juster, *Les Juifs*, p. 145, n. 5, has argued that the affairs of the diaspora communities indeed came under the High Priest/ethnarch of Jerusalem. A.N. Sherwin-White, *Roman Society and Roman Law in the New Testa- ment* (Oxford: Clarendon, 1963), p. 100, is sceptical at this point, but does consider Acts 9,2 an indication in favour of Juster's position.

verses in which this is stated, 9,1-2, seemingly contain some rather important information on Paul's pre-Christian period.

Paul is described as an envoy of the High Priest whose task it was to
officially trace and persecute the followers of Jesus in Damascus. The two
verses raise a number of questions. Is it historically plausible that Paul
was sent as an envoy by the High Priest to carry out exactly this task? How
had the Christian community in Damascus come into existence? And
where does the term 'the Way' originate?

The first question is to be answered by means of circumstantial evidence. The Roman legal system was not built on the territorial principle
of law, but on the personal.[64] This meant that a Roman citizen fell under
Roman law wherever he was. In consequence, it may have been that the
High Priest in Jerusalem could extend his jurisdiction to Jews in Damascus.[65] That this practice was indeed prevalent is often argued on the basis
of a passage from 1 Maccabees: 1 Macc 15,16-21. Here, the Roman Con-
sul Lucius writes to the Egyptian king Ptolemy (probably VIII) on the
subject of Jews: 'if any scoundrels have fled to you from their country,
hand them over to the High Priest Simon, so that he may punish them
according to their law' (παράδοτε αὐτοὺς Σιμωνὶ τῷ ἀρχιερεῖ, ὅπως
ἐκδικήσῃ αὐτοὺς κατὰ τὸν νόμον αὐτῶν).[66] However, although the
assumption is that this custom was still in use in Paul's day, it is unclear
whether this is correct.[67] Many students of the book of Acts nevertheless
consider 9,1-2 as evidence that Paul was sent as a *shaliach* by the
Sanhedrin. Still, a more cautious approach is to be preferred: we simply
cannot decide with certainty on the historicity of Paul's commissioning
by the High Priest. It is a possibility, but remains far from certain. An
objection to the historicity could be Paul's own silence on the subject. The
various passages in which Paul mentions himself as a former persecutor
of the Church all emphasise the grace that Paul had received at his call.[68]

---

[64] See B. Nicholas, *An Introduction to Roman Law* (CLS 3; Oxford: Clarendon, 1962),
p. 57: 'Ancient law was in principle "personal": the law by which a man lived
depended not on where he was, but on who he was – on his nationality. Roman law
applied to Roman citizens, Athenian law to Athenian citizens.'

[65] According to Nicholas, *Introduction*, pp. 57-58, foreigners living under Roman jurisdiction fell under their own laws: 'to some extent this was done, particularly in the
field of family law and succession.'

[66] See for instance Barrett, *Acts*, vol. 1, pp. 446-447.

[67] Barrett, *Acts*, vol. 1, p. 477: 'The important historical question is that of the relation
between the High Priest and Sanhedrin and provincial synagogues. It is unfortunately
a question to which no precise answer can be given.'

[68] Cf. below, p. 168.

In this description of his past and present Paul needed to stress his ugly past in order to heighten the contrast with the present state of affairs. The effect of such a presentation would have been far greater if Paul had described himself before his call as putting Christians in jail. Especially in the passages under discussion, Paul had no reason at all to be silent on anything he had ever done wrong against the Church. Had Paul been able to mention his jailing of Christians, he would have surely have done so. From this perspective the *argumentum e silentio* is valid.

There is another reason for suspicion: the oppression of Christians by the pre-Christian Saul as depicted in Acts may be taken as a reflection of the conditions in the period before and during the writing of Acts. It is perfectly understandable that a tradition of Paul persecuting the Church and fiercely opposing the Christian confession could develop into the picture painted by Acts of Saul jailing Christians. Traditions have a tendency to grow rather than to shrink. And furthermore, Christians in the last decade of the first century were doubtlessly familiar with opposition against the Church taking this form.[69] It is known that Christians were persecuted at least intermittently under Domitian, and Pliny wrote on the incarceration of Christians at the beginning of the second century.[70] Further evidence for this practice in the second century appears throughout the literature of that period.[71] Therefore, a tradition of Paul persecuting the Church could easily have taken the form found in Acts of a man jailing Christians. We can hardly be too suspicious here: Acts undoubtedly contains pre-Lukan tradition, also on this point, but it does not reflect the genuine activities of Paul as a persecutor of Christians.

At this point the second question posed above should be dealt with. If Paul's call took place in or near Damascus, how could there have been a Christian congregation in that town? The answer is simple. It appears that the account Acts gives of the early Christian history is fragmentary. Not all developments are mentioned, not all characters described. Either the author of Acts did not have any details on the origin of the congregation in Damascus, or he did not consider the information he had interesting enough for his writing. This observation confirms the suspicion that the author is not really interested in an accurate description of the history of the early Christian communities, but rather in presenting a selection of

---

[69] See e.g. Mark 13,9.11 parr.
[70] Pliny, *Ep.* x,96.
[71] Cf. for instance Just., *Apol.*, II 2,11; Herm., *Sim.* IX,28; Lucian, *De morte Peregrini* 12.

events from that history, developing the plan of 1,8, and describing the divine origin of the growth of the movement as a whole from an inner-Jewish group to a new community of Jews and Gentiles alike. The commissioning of Paul by the High Priest may have been a means for the author to account for the fact that the persecutor Saul, who was situated in Jerusalem (7,58-8,3), experienced his call in or near Damascus. This last element was established above as reliable, and was definitely part of the pre-Lukan tradition on Paul's call that formed the basis for the account of this event in Acts 9. Therefore it is probable that the description of Saul in 9,1-2 is as redactional as that of 7,58-8,3.

If this is indeed the case, how is the use of the noun ὁδός to be interpreted? The book of Acts is the only writing from the early Christian movement in which this word is used for Christianity.[72] Acts mentions it a number of times without further specification: 19,9.23; 22,4; 24,14.22. But also 'the way of salvation' (16,17), 'of the Lord' (18,25) or 'of God' (18,26?) is used. In his ICC commentary, Barrett mentions a number of parallels from the literature of Qumran,[73] and draws the conclusion: 'The Way was understood (in the Qumran writings; LP) as strict observance of the Mosaic Law (...). This is not how even the most conservative Jewish Christian groups understood their "Way", but the two have in common the exact performance of what is understood to be the revealed will of God.'[74] Since the term ὁδός is found only in Acts as a reference to the Christian movement, it might be argued that it is an invention by the author of this book. Yet given that the terminology is the same as that found in the writings from Qumran, it is highly unlikely that it is. It is far more probable that the author has used a traditional designation for the Christian movement in this redactional passage.

It is now time to turn to the picture of the pre-Christian Paul as given in the two other accounts of Paul's call, viz. Acts 22 and 26. In these two chapters Paul describes his call in defence speeches. Given this literary character, the stories told in the speeches by Paul in cc. 22 and 26 are secondary to the account of ch. 9: they have been formed by the author of Acts out of a description in the third person of Paul's call. Nevertheless, they may contain some details that add to our information so far.

---

[72] See E. Repo, *Der "Weg" als Selbstbezeichnung des Urchristentums* (Helsinki: Suomalainen Tiedeakatemia 1964); S.V. McCasland, 'The Way', *JBL* 77 (1958), pp. 222-230.
[73] CD I,13; II,6; XX,18; 1QS VIII,12-15; IX,17-18; X,21; XI,13.
[74] Barrett, *Acts*, vol. 1, p. 448.

The beginning of Paul's speech in 22,3-5 does contain two new elements: Paul describes his birth in Tarsus and his education in Jerusalem. Neither of these elements is mentioned in ch. 9 or in Paul's letters. W.C. van Unnik has shown that the *auctor ad Theophilum* here uses a fixed scheme to depict Paul's place of birth and the education he received.[75] In consequence, it is very plausible that the description was created by the author. This observation, however, does not deny the possible influence of pre-Lukan tradition. The city of Tarsus is mentioned twice before in Acts, and these two instances presuppose that Paul lived in Tarsus. The first time is in 9,30, the final word in the chapter on what happened to Paul/Saul after his call. After depicting his flight from Damascus and his coming to Jerusalem, the author has Saul being sent off to Tarsus. It is in that place that he reappears in 11,25, when he and Barnabas commence their mission. Since Tarsus plays no part at all in the narrative of Acts, and no possible reason can be imagined for the author to invent Paul's birth and apparent residence in that city, the conclusion must be that Tarsus was mentioned in pre-Lukan tradition as the place of birth and residence of Paul. As there is no good reason to doubt this tradition, it may be taken as a fact that Paul was indeed born there.[76]

Tarsus must have influenced Paul to a high degree.[77] It was a prosperous city with flourishing trade and commercial activities. At the same time it was known as an important centre of Cynic-Stoic philosophy which probably influenced both Paul's views and his behaviour. Furthermore, it may not be a coincidence that Paul in his preaching of the gospel took trade-centres such as Tarsus as his base.[78] His provenance from Tarsus is thus an important piece of information from the Book of Acts.

In regard to Paul's education in Jerusalem, however, there is more reason to be suspicious. Time and again the author of Luke-Acts mentions

---

[75] W.C. van Unnik, 'Tarsus or Jerusalem. The City of Paul's Youth', in: *Sparsa Collecta. The Collected Essays of W.C. van Unnik*, vol. 1 (SNT 29; Leiden: Brill, 1973), pp. 259-320.

[76] On Paul's provenance from Tarsus, see e.g. K. Haacker, *Paulus. Der Werdegang eines Apostels* (SBS 171; Stuttgart: Katholisches Bibelwerk, 1997), pp. 21-27. There is no need here to explore the origins of Jerome's remark on Paul's provenance from Gishala: *Paulus apostolus, qui ante Saulus, extra numerum duodecim apostolorum de tribu Beniamin ex oppido Iudeae Giscalis fuit, quo a Romanis capto cum parentibus suis Tarsum Ciliciae commigravit* (*De viris illustribus* v,9).

[77] On Tarsus, see W.W. Gasque, 'Tarsus', *ABD* vol. 6, pp. 333-334; also H. Böhlig, *Die Geisteskultur von Tarsus im augusteischen Zeitalter mit Berücksichtigung der paulinischen Schriften* (FRLANT 19; Göttingen: Vandenhoeck & Ruprecht, 1913).

[78] We will come back to these issues in the next two chapters.

Jerusalem as the centre of the action. It is of great importance for him to locate Paul's education among the Pharisees of Jerusalem. The fact that Van Unnik has shown that Luke's introduction of Paul as being educated in Jerusalem is based on a fixed Hellenistic scheme[79] does not imply that the information originated in a reliable tradition. The mention of Gamaliel as Paul's teacher may have been based on a certain regard he had had for the Christians (cf. 5,37-38). Gamaliel may also have been mentioned because he was the prime leader of the Pharisees during the time Paul must have received his education.[80] Furthermore, for the author to mention precisely Gamaliel as Paul's teacher must have underlined his historical trustworthiness.

The third new element in Acts 22, compared to Acts 9, is the fact that Paul is said to speak 'in Hebrew' (= in Aramaic). This is fully in accordance with Paul's own remarks on being 'a Hebrew', discussed above (p. 140). It may not be surprising, but it is still important to note that the author of Acts thus confirms the picture of Paul as a Greek Jew speaking Aramaic.

The second passage in Acts in which Paul himself gives an account of his call (26,12-18) adds no new information to the reconstruction so far. In comparing the accounts in cc. 9 and 22 a new element is the fact that Paul presents himself as a Pharisee. He had also done this in 23,6, and therefore the addition is redactional. It coincides with Paul's own remark in Phil 3,5, and therefore does not add to our knowledge of Paul's period before his call.

It thus appears that the book of Acts contains some details about Paul in regard to his pre-Christian period. Firstly, the name 'Saul' is new compared to the letters of Paul. This name is not restricted to the period preceding Paul's call, and should for that reason be considered as the Aramaic equivalent for the Latin *Paulus*. Secondly, Acts presents us with the fact that Paul had been born in Tarsus. Both these facts appear to come from pre-Lukan tradition, and can be relied upon with a fair degree of certainty. As for the rest, the picture of the pre-Christian Paul either repeats data contained in the letters of Paul or reflects the redactional purposes of the *auctor ad Theophilum*. Only in the case of Paul's education in Jerusalem and his commissioning by the High Priest it is difficult to decide.

---

[79] Van Unnik, 'Tarsus or Jerusalem', p. 287.
[80] Gamaliel appears as such in various rabbinic traditions; cf. Strack-Billerbeck, vol. 2, pp. 636-639; see also Schürer *et al.*, *History*, vol. 2, pp. 367-368.

f. Evaluation

The passages in the letters, in which Paul explicitly speaks of his Jewish identity, all originate in discussions Paul had about the dividing line between Christians and Jews. Paul and his contemporaries had serious theological problems to face. What is the status of (fellow-) Jews who do not confess Jesus Christ as the risen Lord? And, of course: how should those who are not Jewish but confess Jesus as the Christ, God's eschatological envoy, be valued? These two questions are in fact two sides of the same coin. This basic problem faced by Paul was present throughout early Christianity and concerned the self-definition of the new religious community that centred around the confession of Jesus Christ. Is this a Jewish community? If so, what is the status of Gentiles within it? And: what is the central point of cohesion on which to build this community? Is it the combination of the Jewish Law and the confession of Jesus Christ as the risen Lord? Or is it just the latter?

In his assessment of his pre-Christian life Paul frequently speaks of this period with pride. Nevertheless, it is a pride that belongs to his past. Paul characterises himself as a Pharisee, as one who fervently strove to obey the Law and the traditions of his ancestors. This element recurs in the book of Acts. And yet, the words used in Gal 1,13-14 clearly indicate that for Paul this period is finished. His 'progression within Judaism' belongs to his former life. Nevertheless, he can still call himself an Israelite, a descendant of Abraham, a Hebrew. This is to be accounted for by the observation that, for Paul, the Christians were to be considered as the small, elect group that constitute the true Israel. Paul's progression within Judaism was his progression within the religion of the Pharisees, focused on the Mosaic Law as its centre. This *specific type* of Judaism belongs to his past. His present is focused on the confession of Christ as well as on the formation and preservation of the community that had this confession as its centre.

We should note that Paul refers to his 'zeal' for the traditional religion in relation to the fact that he had persecuted the 'church of God'. According to Hengel this zeal for the ancestral tradition and the Law brought Paul to persecute the Hellenistic Christians who confessed the crucified Jesus as the Messiah. Their confession was an outrage to those who seriously wanted to keep the commandments of the Law and it was because of this outrage that Paul tried to eradicate their views.[81] Although Hengel's

---

[81] Hengel, *Pre-Christian Paul*, pp. 63-86; see also e.g. Martyn, *Galatians*, pp. 161-163.

view is attractive, its foundation is not as solid as it seems. Hengel takes his evidence on the criticism of the Law by the earliest Hellenistic Christians basically from Acts 7, Stephen's speech. As we've seen in the previous chapter, this speech may indeed contain pre-Lucan material, but it is far from certain that this material genuinely reflects the pre-Pauline situation within the Hellenistic Christian community. Acts 7 simply cannot be used as evidence that the Hellenistic Christians in Jerusalem were indeed critical of the Law. This element in the picture of Acts may well be a retrojection originating in the last decades of the first century CE.

Although the evidence from Acts 7 does not allow us to conclude that Paul's persecution of the church aimed at the church's Law-free attitude, the second part of Hengel's solution is very plausible. Indeed in Gal 3,13 Paul does refer to the fact that a crucified Messiah was a folly for those who strictly observed the Mosaic Law (cf. 1 Cor 1-2).[82] The crucified preacher who proclaimed the coming Kingdom of God greatly differed from the various expectations of a messiah or eschatological agent that were current in Judaism of the time. He was not a national king, he did not cast away Israel's enemies, he was not a priestly figure, he did not come in great glory, and, worst of all, he had died by crucifixion. It was the fact that the Christians confessed precisely this man as the crucified messiah, that made Paul persecute them.[83] Interestingly enough, exactly this element is lacking in the portrayal given in Acts.

Paul's persecution of the church, as analysed here, has an important implication for the understanding of what Paul considered his call. The sheer fact that Paul persecuted the views of the earliest Christians implies that he was familiar with its confession. It was argued above, that Paul did not kill Christians, but instead tried to eradicate their views. Consequently Paul knew these views. He must have already known the christological confession of the Jesus movement before the great change in his life. This is an important observation in regard to the background of Paul's call on which the next section will dwell.

---

[82] B. Lindars, *New Testament Apologetic: the Doctrinal Significance of the Old Testament Quotations* (Philadelphia: Westminster Press, 1961), pp. 232-237, has argued that Gal 3,13 shows that the controversy surrounding Jesus regarded his claims, which his opponents interpreted as blasphemy. According to Lindars, Deut 21,23 and Josh 10,26-27 point out that a man was hanged because he was cursed, not *vice versa*. This curse could be evoked by blasphemy.

[83] For this reconstruction, see C. Dietzfelbinger, *Die Berufung des Paulus als Ursprung seiner Theologie* (WMANT 58; Neukirchen-Vluyn: Neukirchener Verlag, 1985), pp. 10-42.

2. Called by God

It is obvious from the New Testament data that Paul experienced a great change in his life. But how should we name that change? Was it a conversion or a call? No doubt the designation 'call' would come closest to the way Paul himself saw the change in his life.[84] He explicitly presents himself to the Corinthians and the Romans for instance as one who has been 'called to be an apostle' (1 Cor 1,1; Rom 1,1). But how should we understand the designation 'call'?

In his study of Paul, A.F. Segal presents the great change in his life as a conversion, but hastens to add that this is an *etic* term: an 'outside' term used to describe an event that in 'inside' terminology is labelled as a 'call'.[85] Paul himself, at the time that he wrote his letters, understood the decisive transformation in his life as a prophetic call,[86] and therefore, in his own words, he was 'called'. This does not mean, however, that Paul cannot be interpreted as a typical convert. Doing so brings along two important insights.

Firstly, research by psychologists shows that a convert is liable to view the period in his life that preceded the conversion through the lense of his converted existence. In other words: a convert tends to depict his pre-conversion state negatively because he judges it through the values he has come to recognise after his conversion.[87] This observation should make us aware of the difficulties we have to face in interpreting Paul's statements on his pre-Christian life. Paul presents that period of his life through the lense of his apostolic call.

Secondly, there is a profound sociological aspect to conversion. R. Stark has shown that conversion usually originates in personal contacts with members of the community of which the convert becomes a member.[88] The general rule is, that 'conversion to new, deviant religious groups

---

[84] See K. Stendahl, *Paul among Jews and Gentiles, and other Essays* (Philadelphia: Fortress Press, 1976), pp. 7-23 ('Call rather than Conversion'!). K.O. Sandnes, *Paul – One of the Prophets? A Contribution to the Apostle's Self-Understanding* (WUNT 43; Tübingen: Mohr, 1991), esp. pp. 48-70, argues that Paul models the description of his conversion experience in Galatians 1 on a prophetic call.

[85] Segal, *Paul the Convert*, esp. pp. 285-300; cf. p. 285: 'Paul's experience can be described as a conversion, though he himself used the vocabulary of transformation and prophetic calling to describe it. (…) Conversion must be considered an *etic* term in regard to Paul.'

[86] Stendahl, *Paul among Jews*, p. 12.

[87] For the analysis underlying this argument, see Segal, *Paul the Convert*, pp. 285-300.

[88] R. Stark, *The Rise of Christianity. A Sociologist Reconsiders History* (Princeton: Princeton University Press, 1996), pp. 13-21.

occurs when, other things being equal, people have or develop stronger attachments to members of the group than they have to nonmembers'.[89] Conversion happens through social interaction, not by a sudden, new perspective on things. This new perspective grows as a result of the interaction with members of the group that the convert joined and not the reverse. If this general rule can be applied to Paul too, it would mean that Paul did first experience some interaction with Christians before he converted.

These results from a social-scientific approach of the evidence raises the need of an evaluation. What do these general observations say about Paul? The propositions stated by psychology and sociology are built on the basis of generalisation, and Paul's case is obviously an individual case. Nevertheless, we can assume that the great transformation Paul experienced did not take place in a social vacuum. We may speak of Paul as a convert, using the *etic* or outside term, or mention the change in his life as a call, using the *emic* or inside term. But whichever option we choose, chances are that Paul's great transformation took place when he somehow stood in close contact with a group of followers of Jesus.

There is, unfortunately, very little Paul himself says about his call. The only passage in which he explicitly speaks about it is Gal 1,15-16, and there are a number of passages in 1 Corinthians in which he implicitly notifies his readers about this great change. What follows, is a brief discussion of each of these passages and a critical evaluation of the evidence. The passage Phil 3,7-11 will be left out of consideration here, because it does not give any evidence on what happened to Paul – instead, it describes the importance Paul attached to this call. Finally, the narrative portrayal of Paul's call in the book of Acts is discussed.

a. 1 Corinthians 9,1; 15,1-9

'(9,1) Am I not free? Am I not an apostle? Have I not seen Jesus our Lord?'

Paul defends himself against an attack on his attitude by presenting himself as an example of freedom tempered by the concern of love.[90] He builds his ἀπολογία (9,3) on a series of rhetorical questions that are

---

[89] Stark, *Rise*, p. 18.
[90] Cf. W.F. Orr, J.A. Walther, *1 Corinthians* (AB; Garden City: Doubleday, 1976), pp. 240-241. W. Schrage, *Der erste Brief an die Korinther (1 Kor 6,12-11,16)* (EKK; Düsseldorf: Benziger; Neukirchen-Vluyn: Neukirchener, 1995), p. 280, argues that Paul writes ch. 9 as an *exemplum*, thereby presenting himself as the example of freedom correctly used.

meant to confirm his status as a free apostle, who has seen the Lord Jesus.[91] This remark in itself could have pointed to any mystical experience of Jesus by Paul, at any given moment. It does not necessarily refer to Paul's call. Yet given the fact that Paul in 15,1-8 counts himself among the Easter-witnesses, exactly because the Lord had 'appeared' to him, it is improbable that in 9,1 Paul is referring to an experience other than his call. This experience must have included some kind of visual element, a vision of Christ, that convinced him that Jesus Christ is the Son of God.[92]

'(15,1) Now I would remind you, brothers and sisters, of the good news that I proclaimed to you, which you in turn received, in which also you stand, (2) through which also you are being saved, if you hold firmly to the message that I proclaimed to you – unless you have come to believe in vain. (3) For I handed on to you as of first importance what I in turn had received: that Christ died for our sins in accordance with the scriptures, (4) and that he was buried, and that he was raised on the third day in accordance with the scriptures, (5) and that he appeared to Cephas, then to the twelve. (6) Then he appeared to more than five hundred brothers and sisters at one time, most of whom are still alive, though some have died. (7) Then he appeared to James, then to all the apostles. (8) Last of all, as to one untimely born, he appeared also to me. (9) For I am the least of the apostles, unfit to be called an apostle, because I persecuted the church of God.'

In this passage Paul includes himself in the list of Easter-witnesses.[93] He is the last, untimely born, but still he is included. The image Paul uses

---

[91] Fee, *First Corinthians*, p. 393: 'Since a crisis of authority lies behind much of this letter (…) Paul takes this occasion (…) to hit it head-on.'

[92] Since Paul's seeing of the Lord is mentioned as a precondition for his apostolic work (cf. Schrage, *1 Korinther*, p. 287), the conclusion is inevitable that in 9,1 Paul speaks of the experience he had at his call. Fee, *First Corinthians*, p. 395, argues that the combination of 9,1 and 15,8 points out two things. Firstly, that Paul thought himself to have experienced more than just a vision; secondly, that Paul had received a special commission, since not everyone who had seen the Lord automatically became an apostle. On this latter observation, see below, pp. 177-185.

[93] On the structure of this passage and the traditional formula used in it, see J. Lambrecht, 'Line of Thought in 1 Cor 15,1-11', *Gregorianum* 72 (1991), pp. 655-670; O. Schwankl, 'Auf der Suche nach dem Anfang des Evangeliums. Von 1 Kor 15,3-5 zum Johannes-Prolog', *BZ* 40 (1996), pp. 39-60; M. Winger, 'Tradition, Revelation and Gospel. A Study in Galatians', *JSNT* 53 (1994), pp. 65-86; H. Conzelmann, *Der erste Brief an die Korinther* (KEK; Göttingen: Vandenhoeck und Ruprecht, 1981), pp. 305-309; P. von der Osten-Sacken, 'Die Apologie des paulinischen Apostolats', *ZNW* 64 (1973), pp. 245-262.

for himself, ἔκτρωμα, expresses Paul's hesitation: he should not have experienced such an appearance since he was not worthy of it.[94] Nevertheless, Paul does count himself as belonging to those to whom Christ had appeared.

In the opening verse of 1 Corinthians 15 Paul clearly starts the discussion of a new subject. He uses the same expression as in Gal 1,11: γνωρίζω ... ὑμῖν, ἀδελφοί (cf. also 1 Cor 12,3; 2 Cor 8,1). It is more or less a stock phrase Paul uses when he wants to point out something very clearly. In 1 Cor 15,1 Paul summarises the gospel as he preached it to the Corinthian congregation. This summary consists of an extensive formula: Χριστὸς ἀπέθανεν ὑπὲρ τῶν ἁμαρτιῶν ἡμῶν κατὰ τὰς γραφὰς καὶ ἐτάφη καὶ ἐγήγερται τῇ ἡμέρᾳ τρίτῃ κατὰ τὰς γραφὰς καὶ ὤφθη Κηφᾷ εἶτα τοῖς δώδεκα (vv. 3-4). This formula no doubt reflects pre-Pauline tradition, used and adapted by Paul in his preaching as a summary of the gospel.[95] Since in v. 5 the word ὅτι is used for the last time, it is probable that vv. 6-8 form an addition by Paul to the pre-Pauline formula that ended with the mention of the twelve.[96]

In a few words Paul passes on a great deal of important information. Firstly, Paul testifies to the existence of a group of 'the twelve'. Secondly, he mentions only Cephas (Peter) and James explicitly thereby indicating their prominent positions within the early Christian movement. Thirdly, Paul distinguishes between 'the twelve' and 'all the apostles'. This implies that the group of apostles was larger than the group of twelve. Fourthly, and for the present purpose the most important element in this passage, Paul describes that the risen Christ had appeared to him too. Paul does not state how, he merely mentions the fact that Christ had appeared to him. The word used, ὤφθη, is standard vocabulary in the description of appearances in visions or dreams.[97] Unfortunately, it states nothing concerning the nature of this appearance.

In vv. 9-11 Paul continues his argument with an interpretation of his own view of his call. The argument Paul uses here is the same as that in

---

[94] H.W. Hollander, G.E. van der Hout, 'The Apostle Paul calling himself an Abortion: 1 Cor. 15:8 within the Context of 1 Cor. 15:8-10', NT 38 (1996), pp. 224-236, conclude that 'Paul wanted his readers to know that his apostolate had its origin in an act of God's grace: he did not deserve it, nor did he ask for it, for in his own eyes he was no more than "a miscarriage".'

[95] Cf. Schwankl, 'Auf der Suche', pp. 41-44.

[96] Von der Osten-Sacken, 'Apologie', p. 247, interprets 15,6-8 as an 'Erweiterung der Paradosis'.

[97] See S. Kim, The Origin of Paul's Gospel (WUNT 2-4; Tübingen: Mohr, 2nd ed., 1984, [1]1981), pp. 55-66.

Galatians 1. Since Paul had persecuted the church (v. 9) he did not deserve to have Christ appear to him. Therefore, it is not by his own merit, but by the grace of God that Paul became an apostle (v. 10). To this grace Paul ascribes his efforts and the fact that he did more than any other apostle. Paul concludes his reference to the apostolic preaching of the gospel by the remark that both he and the other apostles preach through the grace of God, and that it is in this way that the Corinthians also had come to believe in Christ.

The summary given by Paul offers, so we may infer, an example of the gospel he preached. It furthermore affirms his own position as well as the existence of a group of apostles and the leading position of Peter and James. But it offers more than that. Paul introduces his summary with the words τὸ εὐαγγέλιον ὃ εὐηγγελισάμην ὑμῖν, ὃ καὶ παρέλαβετε (...). He then continues: παρέδωκα γὰρ ὑμῖν ἐν πρώτοις, ὃ καὶ παρέλαβον (...). The verbs used for the tradition of the gospel are εὐαγγελίζομαι, παραδίδωμι, and παραλαμβάνω. The first verb is often used by Paul as a description of the proclamation of the Christian kerygma.[98] It tells us nothing of Paul's view on his call. The other two verbs, however, do give us some information: παραδίδωμι and παραλαμβάνω are standard terms for the passing on of tradition.[99] A good example of the meaning of the former verb is given in Mark 7,3.13. Mark 7,3 contains an aside by the author on the reason why Pharisees and Jews generally wash their hands before eating: they do so in order to observe the tradition of the elders (παράδοσις τῶν πρεσβυτέρων). Jesus reacts to this custom by contrasting the human tradition with God's command (v. 9), and objects: you make 'void the word of God through your tradition that you have handed on' (τῇ παραδόσει ὑμῶν ᾗ παρεδώκατε).[100] Paul uses the same verb in 1 Cor 11,2 as he speaks of the tradition he himself had passed on to the Corinthians: ἐπαινῶ δὲ ὑμᾶς ὅτι (...) καθὼς παρέδωκα ὑμῖν, τὰς παραδόσεις κατέχετε. Here tradition-terminology is used to describe the instructions he had given to the congregation in Corinth. In 1 Cor 15,1-3 Paul combines this terminology with the standard term for the reception of tradition: παραλαμβάνω (cf. Gal 1,9.12; Phil 4,9; 1 Thess 2,13; 4,1). This is important since in 1 Cor 15,3 Paul uses the same verb for his own reception of the gospel: ὃ καὶ παρέλαβον. What exactly do these words say on Paul's call?

The verb παραλαμβάνω in itself says nothing on the origin of the object received. Yet in combination with παραδίδωμι it does: it is used in the sense of the receiving of human tradition. At this point, the words of 1 Cor 11,23 are illuminating. Here Paul speaks of the eucharistic tradition as he himself had 'received' it 'from the Lord'. He introduces the eucharistic formulae with the words ἐγὼ γὰρ παρέλαβον ἀπὸ τοῦ κυρίου, ὃ καὶ παρέδωκα ὑμῖν, ὅτι κτλ. The combination of the terms defines Paul as the intermediary between Christ and the Corinthian congregation. Paul uses the verb παραλαμβάνω to describe how he had received the eucharistic tradition. The words ἀπὸ κυρίου are intended to describe the origin of the tradition Paul had received, not the fact that it was the Lord who handed it to Paul.[101] If Paul had meant to describe the latter, he would have used the same preposition as in Gal 1,12, παρά. What Paul describes in 1 Cor 11,23 is that he received the tradition that ultimately comes from the Lord himself. Thus, the meaning of παραλαμβάνω in 11,23 is 'to receive tradition'. Hence, Paul's remark in 15,5 implies that he himself is the recipient of tradition, and Paul thus states that he has received the gospel through human instruction, something he explicitly denies in Gal 1,12. The three words ὃ καὶ παρέλαβον betray the fact that Paul did indeed depend upon pre-Pauline tradition. Paul heard the gospel by means of other Christians. He did not receive the credal formula he recites in vv. 3b-5 in some sort of vision, but from oral transmission by earlier Christians.

The observation that Paul must have received his gospel through tradition further gives credit to Stark's proposition of the social embeddedness of conversion. Remember the sociological approach: conversion is primarily a social phenomenon, caused by the fact that significant others went ahead of the convert on the same path. We still have no reason to conclude that Paul followed one or more of the people with whom he stood in close contact. But the evidence from 1 Corinthians 15 does indicate that Paul somehow depended on a Christian community for his inculturation in and his reception of the gospel. Paul betrays the fact that he received this gospel from others before him, and sociology implies that he became involved with those others already before his conversion. Unfortunately, we do not have any specific evidence to substantiate this view.

---

[101] Cf. Conzelmann, *1 Korinther*, pp. 238-239; Fee, *First Corinthians*, p. 548; Lang, *Korinther*, p. 150.

b. Galatians 1,15-16

'(15) But when God, who had set me apart before I was born and called me through his grace, was pleased (16) to reveal his Son within me,[102] so that I might proclaim him among the Gentiles, I did not confer with any human being (…)'

The information Paul gives here on his call is coloured in two ways. Firstly, Paul mentions this event as an element in his polemic against his opponents who, in his view, had bewitched the Galatians with a gospel that contained the necessity for circumcision. His description of his call is thus influenced by the rhetorical context. It is 'part of the apologetic narratio'.[103] Secondly, these verses have a retrospective character.[104] They do not give a detailed description of what exactly happened, but describe how Paul interpreted the meaning of his call in the light of what happened afterwards.

In these two essential verses Paul states three things on the meaning of his call: it resulted from the fact that God had 'set (Paul) apart' before his birth; that God had 'called (him) through his grace'; and that the implication of the revelation of Christ was that Paul would proclaim him among the nations. A few observations should be made here.

Firstly, the terminology for 'to set apart' (ἀφορίζω), also used by Paul in Rom 1,1, is probably reminiscent of Jer 1,5: 'Before I formed you in the womb I knew you, and before you were born I consecrated you; I appointed you a prophet to the nations.'[105] The similarities in thought are striking, notwithstanding the lack of verbal parallels: in both cases their fate was determined by God even before their birth, and in both cases this fate is to proclaim the Lord among the nations. The conclusion to be drawn is that Paul here wittingly characterises his own identity as comparable to that of Jeremiah.[106] By identifying his call with that of

---

[102] Translation LP; NRSV reads: 'to me'.

[103] Betz, *Galatians*, p. 69.

[104] Segal, *Paul the Convert*, p. 29: 'Thus, the accounts of Paul's and other ancient conversions, even the first-person accounts, are retrospective re-tellings of events, greatly enhanced by group norms learned and appropriated in the years prior to the writing.'

[105] Also the prophet Isaiah uses this terminology, this time however concerning the fate of the Servant of the Lord: 'The Lord called me before I was born, while I was in thy mother's womb he named me' (LXX Isa 49,1: ἐκ κοιλίας μητρός μου ἐκάλεσεν τὸ ὄνομά μου).

[106] Segal, *Paul the Convert*, pp. 13-14; S. Kim, *The Origin of Paul's Gospel* (WUNT 2-4; Tübingen: Mohr, 2nd ed., 1984), pp. 91-99, argues that Paul understood his call from the perspective of Isa 6 and 49,1-6. His argumentation, however, is far too complicated to be convincing. According to Sandnes, *Prophets*, pp. 59-68, Paul models

Jeremiah, Paul implies also that his task may be regarded as similar to that of the prophet. Thus, at the moment of writing his letter to the Galatians Paul apparently interpreted his call as a prophetic commission.

Secondly, Paul uses the words 'by grace' to describe his call. These words are Pauline vocabulary.[107] They describe the idea that Paul deemed himself unworthy of his call. The effect of Paul's description of his persecution of the church is that, because of his excessive offence against God, he now appears blessed by God to a high degree. In Old Testament tradition, many of those who are called deem themselves unworthy: Moses (Exod 3,11-12; 4,10-11.13), Gideon (Jdg 6,15), Saul (1 Sam 9,21), Isaiah (Isa 6,5), and Jeremiah (Jer 1,6).[108] Paul thus presents himself here by means of the literary motif of the unworthiness of the one called. By doing so, Paul underlines his argument that it was not by man that he received his call and his gospel, thereby claiming the authority he needed in the discussion with his opponents in Galatia.

Thirdly, it should be noted that the final clause ἵνα εὐαγγελίζωμαι αὐτὸν ἐν τοῖς ἔθνεσιν defines the purpose of the revelation Paul received. This purpose is that Paul should proclaim God's son among the nations. As noted above, this task forms a parallel to that of Jeremiah as described in Jer 1,5. At this point it is important to remember that here Paul is writing in retrospect. The explicit characterisation of his task as preaching among the nations, modelled on the example of Jeremiah, is absent in all but one of Paul's other letters. Only in Romans, probably the last letter he wrote, does Paul use the same characterisation (cf. Rom 1,1.5; 11,13). It therefore seems safe to conclude that only at the time when he wrote his letter to the Galatians Paul had come to interpret his task through the paradigm of Jeremiah. Paul implicitly compares his call to that of this particular prophet because he compares his task to that of Jeremiah: as Jeremiah did, Paul had to proclaim God's message to the nations and as was the case with Jeremiah, God had elected him to do so long before he himself was aware of that task.

The only information Paul gives on the event of his call is found in the temporal clause: ὅτε δὲ εὐδόκησεν ὁ θεός ... ἀποκαλύψαι τὸν υἱὸν αὐτοῦ ἐν ἐμοί.... The verb εὐδοκέω refers to the fact that it is by God's

---

his description of the event on Isa 49,1.5. Paul would have quoted these verses from memory, which explains the differences in words.

[107] Cf. Rom 1,5; 12,3; 15,15; 2 Cor 9,14; Gal 1,6; 2,9 – Betz, *Galatians*, p. 70, n. 138.

[108] This was pointed out to me by dr. H.W. Hollander, University of Leiden, whom I wish to thank here.

decision that Paul received a revelation. The same verb is used in 1 Cor 1,21 when Paul describes how God has decided to save the believers by means of the paradox of the cross. The object of God's pleasure is the revelation of his son. But how should the words ἐν ἐμοί be interpreted? Grammatically, there are three possibilities, viz. 'to me', 'within me', and 'by me'.[109] The last possibility would appear attractive if it were compared to 1 Cor 3,13 where Paul speaks of a revelation by means of fire (ἐν πυρὶ ἀποκαλύπτεται). Also Rom 1,17 seems to point in this direction, as Paul speaks of righteousness by means of the gospel (ἐν αὐτῷ ἀποκαλύπτεται). Yet, the final clause with ἵνα describes the effect of the revelation ἐν ἐμοί, and this clause 'favours the reference to an experience in itself affecting Paul only'.[110] Since the first interpretation ('to me') is expressed by a simple dative,[111] the second interpretation is probably the best. This interpretation comes close to the words of v. 12, where Paul states that he had received the gospel through a revelation of Jesus Christ. Hence, the information Paul gives on his call is that God has revealed his son 'within him'. The expression used is very rare,[112] and therefore significant. Paul applies it to express the fact that the great shift in his life was an event that took place within himself. There is a great risk of interpreting the evidence Paul gives here in a modern way as a statement on a psychological process. This would be a misinterpretation of Paul's words. The human mind, psychology, and psychological processes are modern inventions which Paul was unfamiliar with. What Paul expresses here, then, is not that the revelation of Christ was the result of a process within himself, but rather that it happened within himself as a result of an act of God. In Paul's view, it was God who revealed his son, and he did this *within* Paul. Yet from our modern day perspective we may safely regard this 'revelation within Paul' as a mystical experience that created such a deep and lasting impression, that it made Paul change his direction in a profound manner.

---

[109] BDR §220.1 mentions Gal 1,16 as an example of ἐν used for the simple dative. Moulton-Turner, *Grammar*, vol. 3, p. 264, interprets ἐν ἐμοί as 'pleonastically for the normal dative: *to me* (perhaps *through me*). Also M. Zerwick, *Biblical Greek. English Edition adapted from the Fourth Latin Edition by J. Smith S.J.* (Rome: Pontifical Institute, 1963, 3rd repr. 1987), §120, p. 41, favours the interpretation as a simple dative. Robertson, *Grammar*, p. 587, interprets ἐν ἐμοί as 'simply "in".'

[110] De Witt Burton, *Galatians*, p. 50.

[111] Cf. e.g. Matt 16,17; Luke 10,21-22; 1 Cor 14,30; Eph 3,5; Phil 3,15; *Vit. Ad.* 1; *T. Reub.* 3,15; *T. Jud.* 16,4; *T. Jos.* 6,6; *T. Ben.* 10,5; *Jos. Asen.* 16,14; 22,13; *3 Apoc. Bar.* 4,13-14; *Apoc. Ezra* 5,20; *Apoc. Sedr.* 2,1.

[112] See *Acts of Thomas* 25: ἀπεκάλυψάς σου τὴν ἀλήθειαν ἐν τοῖς ἀνθρώποις τούτοις.

Thus, the information Paul gives on his call is that he ascribes its origin to God, as well as describing its effect on his own person. He gives no information as to what exactly happened. The only indication that he is pointing to a certain moment and therefore to a distinct event, is his use of the aorist in εὐδόκησεν and ἀποκαλύψαι. As to the content of the revelation, the grammatical object is τὸν υἱὸν αὐτοῦ. What is revealed to Paul, then, is Jesus himself as the Son of God. This is Paul's short summary of the revelation to which he ascribes his Christian identity. According to Segal, Paul had a predisposition to mystical experiences,[113] and it was such an experience that changed Paul's identity. Indeed Paul's description of his call by the words ἐν ἐμοί emphasizes the fact that he is referring to such a mystical experience. It is remarkable, however, that he says nothing further on what exactly happened, but simply draws attention to the meaning of the event.

As said above, the content of the revelation Paul received is clearly defined: Jesus Christ as the Son of God. This revelation, then, is not the revelation of a fact, but of a person. This implies, that during Paul's transformation experience, it was somehow confirmed to him that the Christian confession he opposed – Jesus as the Christ as the Son of God – was in fact correct.[114] What exactly Paul experienced is not really important. It is the result in the form of Paul's interpretation of this experience that matters. This result is that for Paul Jesus Christ became the true Son of God and he himself became His servant.

c. Evaluation

The evidence Paul gives on his transformation calls for an evaluation: just as in the first section of this chapter Paul appears to contradict himself. In Galatians he strongly insists upon the divine origin of his call. He did not receive the gospel by the word of man, Paul argues. Yet in 1 Corinthians he states that he himself had also 'received' the gospel. As was argued above, the terminology points out that Paul was indeed dependent upon human instruction. How is this seeming dichotomy to be valued?

[113] Segal, *Paul the Convert*, pp. 34-71.
[114] Cf. Segal, *Paul the Convert*, p. 74, who argues that 'viewed from the perspective of social commitment, conversion resembles a new and conscious choice to socialize to a particular group – a resocialization.' This conscious choice can only be made if the convert knows the ideas of the group he is to join.

The solution may be simple. In his letter to the Galatians Paul argues in a polemical way. His own authority has been undermined by other preachers who had instructed the Galatians that they should keep the Mosaic Law and should therefore be circumcised. For Paul this means a severe threat to the freedom which, according to him, was brought about by Christ. Following this, Paul himself appears to be the object of discussion. If it was not by his opponents that Paul's personal status was brought into the discussion, then surely it was by Paul himself. The argumentative function of Paul's description of his past and his call is clear. Paul describes his life within Judaism and the fact that he persecuted the church of God. Then he mentions his transformation experience as evidence of the mercy God had shown him. Paul a former persecutor became the apostle to the Gentiles. For Paul it is of great importance that his position be as strong as possible. Therefore he argues that the origin of his proclamation of the gospel lay not within himself, but in God.

There can be no doubt that this emphasis on the divine origin of Paul's gospel is based on Paul's transformation experience. It was stated above that Galatians 1 gives no indication whatsoever as to the exact nature of the experience that changed Paul's life so profoundly. This is understandable, since Paul tries to argue that the origin of his transformation experience lies within God, not within himself. In Galatians 1 Paul is not interested in the way in which his call took place, but only in its divine origin. In his eagerness to prove his point, Paul makes a statement such as that of 1,12. The point of this verse is that it was not by human instruction that Paul had received his confirmation of the truth of the gospel, but that he had received it directly from Christ himself.

In 1 Corinthians the polemics are lacking. Even though Paul appears to defend his position throughout the letter, ch. 15 lacks the specific focus that influenced the description of Paul's past and his transformation experience in Galatians 1. Paul does commence 1 Corinthians 15 with a description of his own personal stand and his history. But this time, he presents himself as one of the apostles, with whom he shares the gospel (15,11!). The lack of polemics has led to a different description of Paul's past. What is at stake here is the content of the gospel, rather than its origin. Paul introduces the resurrection of Christ as the core of the gospel, on which everything else is built. Here he wants to emphasise the resurrection as the major point of agreement of his gospel with that preached by others. Since the origin of Paul's call is not at stake here, he can easily use the three words that reflect his position of dependence on pre-Pauline tradition: ὃ καὶ παρέλαβον.

What actually happened to Paul should be reconstructed in the following way. Paul was familiar with the Christian gospel in his pre-Christian days. It is the faith in this gospel that he persecuted, and therefore he knew its content. Paul must somehow have been involved with the followers of Jesus, before his call. This is the only sound reason for him to have taken notice of their views. At some point, probably in or near Damascus (cf. Gal 1,17: πάλιν ὑπέστρεψα εἰς Δαμασκόν), Paul had a visionary experience that had a deep impact on him. This experience changed him so profoundly that he joined the movement he had previously opposed so fiercely. There, he became socialised within the Christian movement. Paul had been familiar with the gospel in his pre-Christian days, but had not accepted it as the truth until the visionary experience changed his mind. He interpreted this experience as a call from God, and later he even equated his call with that of one of the prophets. For him this mystical experience was proof that the gospel he had previously persecuted was no human invention, as he had thought until then. Paul had found confirmation of the gospel and changed his life accordingly.

d. A Narrative Elaboration in the Book of Acts

The book of Acts describes the great change in Paul's life in three different versions. The first description is put in the third person and narrated by the author himself (9,1-30). The other two are recollections of this event in speeches by Paul, the first one in Hebrew before a Hebrew court (22,1-21), the second in Greek before a Graeco-Roman court (26,1-23).[115] Any attempt to locate historically trustworthy material in the descriptions of Paul's call in Acts must start with the acknowledgement of the fact that Acts 9 forms the basis for the two other accounts. In writing Acts 22 and 26 the author could rely on the description of Paul's call given previously in chapter 9, but of course this does not mean that the other two accounts cannot contain any additional data.[116]

[115] Cf. E. von Dobschütz, 'Die Berichte über die Bekehrung des Paulus', ZNW 29 (1930), pp. 144-147; D.M. Stanley, 'Paul's Conversion in Acts: Why the Three Accounts?', CBQ 15 (1953), pp. 315-338 (who assumes an original, Aramaic account by Paul himself of his conversion); A. Girlanda, 'De conversione Pauli in Actibus Apostolorum tripliciter narrata', VD 39 (1961), pp. 66-81.129-140.173-188; C.W. Hedrich, 'Paul's Conversion/Call: A Comparative Analysis of the Three Reports', JBL 100 (1981), pp. 415-432.

[116] Hedrich, 'Comparative Analysis', p. 432, states that 'Acts 9,1-19 is a traditional miracle story of Paul's conversion that has been adapted as a commissioning narrative by Luke. Acts 22,4-16 is Luke's edited version of the traditional legend and Acts 26,

The three passages describing the call of Paul all serve different literary purposes. The first one, in ch. 9, functions as the major introduction by the author of the second leading character of his book. The second and third are a presentation of this character defending himself first in Hebrew against a Jewish court (ch. 22) and then in Greek against a Greek-Jewish client king (ch. 26).[117]

It is very likely that the different versions of this episode are variations on one and the same pre-Lukan tradition. This tradition would probably have contained at least those elements that are common to the three accounts:[118]

- Paul as enemy of the Christians, envoy of the High Priest (9,2; 22, 4-5; 26,9-12);
- Damascus (9,3; 22,5; 26,12);
- light (9,3; 22,6; 26,13);
- voice: 'Saul, Saul, why are you persecuting me?' (9,4; 22,7; 26,14)
- conversation: 'Who are you, Lord?' 'I am Jesus, whom you are persecuting' (9,5; 22,8; 26,15);
- instruction (9,6; 22,10; 26,16-18);
- Paul's companions (9,7; 22,9; 26,13).

The final account is remarkably short in comparison to the other two. In 9,9 and 22,11 Paul is said to have been blinded by the light, an inconvenience that is taken away by Ananias. Since the entire episode with Ananias is left out in ch. 26, the blindness is not mentioned in this chapter either.

The elements summarised above must have formed the framework of the pre-Lukan tradition on Paul's call. However, the thus reconstructed tradition hardly adds anything to the material contained in Paul's letters. The location of the event – Damascus – is implicitly mentioned by Paul in Gal 1,17, and Paul himself mentioned his hostility towards the Christians before his call a number of times in his letters (see above). The elements added to the data from Paul's epistles are mainly narrative additions: Paul as an envoy of the High Priest is likely to be a narrative

---

12-18 is Luke's own abbreviated composition.' Burchard, *Dreizehnte Zeuge*, pp. 51-130, gives a detailed analysis of the three accounts of Paul's conversion, and identifies 26, 12-18 as coming from tradition independent from that of Acts 9.

[117] See Conzelmann, *Apostelgeschichte*, p. 59; Lüdemann, *Das frühe Christentum*, p. 115; Barrett, *Acts*, vol. 1, p. 444.

[118] For a synopsis and discussion of the three accounts, see e.g. Barrett, *Acts*, vol. 1, pp. 439-440; Lüdemann, *Das frühe Christentum*, pp. 118-119.

elaboration of the fact that Paul had, in his pre-Christian period, 'persecuted' the church of God. And the fact that Paul is said to have jailed
Christians is a more elaborate characterisation of Paul as a fierce opponent
of the Church. It was already argued above that this is unlikely to be a correct representation of what Paul exactly did when opposing the Christians.

The christophany as described in Acts 9 must have been the central
element in the pre-Lukan tradition on Paul's call. The narrative is not
unique; there are parallels to it. For instance, it appears that there are
some important similarities with the legend of Heliodoros as recounted
in 2 Maccabees 3.[119] And also the appearance of an angel to Aseneth as
described in Jos. Asen. 14,2-8 is described in terms similar to those used
in Acts.[120] Both Heliodoros and Aseneth are said to have fallen to the
floor. Heliodoros was blinded by the vision and the conversation between
Aseneth and the angel who appeared to her is highly comparable to that
between Saul and Jesus in Acts 9.

The description of the appearance of Christ is not given by Paul himself in his letters. This means that Paul was reluctant to describe what he
experienced. We are thus faced with the strange situation in which the person who had had the (visionary) experience under discussion, Paul, is silent
on what exactly happened, whereas the author of Acts, who is dependent
on later tradition, is able to give a detailed account of the event. There is
only one valid explanation: the tradition that forms the basis for the
description in Acts is a legendary narrative elaboration of the data already
given by Paul himself.[121] Therefore, Acts' description of Paul's experience
of his call has no historical value beyond the data given by Paul himself.

Things might be different for the second part of the narrative in Acts 9.
Paul is said to meet Ananias in Damascus (9,10-19).[122] This Ananias is

---

[119] Cf. H. Windisch, 'Die Christusepiphanie von Damascus und ihren religionsgeschichtlichen Parallellen', ZNW 31 (1932), pp. 1-9; Barrett, Acts, vol. 1, p. 441.

[120] Burchard, Dreizehnte Zeuge, pp. 59-88, compares Acts 9,1-19a with Jos. Asen. 1-21,
and concludes that 'Apg 9,1-19a ist der Form nach kein Text sui generis, sondern folgt
einer gegebenen Struktur. Sie steht in einer jüdisch-hellenistischen Tradition, die
Mysterienelemente, wahrscheinlich aus der Isisreligion, aufgenommen hatte.'

[121] Lüdemann, Das frühe Christentum, p. 121, comes to a comparable conclusion: '(...) die
Lukas vorliegende Tradition des Damaskusgeschehens ist eine Berufungsgeschichte,
die im wesentlichen mit den paulinischen Eigenzeugnissen übereinstimmt. Lukas hat sie
aus darstellerischen Gründen verdreifacht und sich in Apg 9 durch die Interpretation der
Berufung als Bekehrung von der historischen Wahrheit ein Stück weit entfernt.'

[122] Because the author introduces Ananias by means of a double vision – a technique used
in cc. 9 and 10 (Peter and Cornelius) – it is very probable that the combination of
Ananias and Paul is the result of the author's hand. He most likely had a tradition
concerning Ananias at his disposal, which he elaborated and adapted into the present

no doubt a figure also mentioned in pre-Lukan tradition.[123] Several elements in the story on Ananias may be identified as reflecting local tradition in Damascus. It is true that details may be made up to make the narrative appear more reliable, but there is no reason to assume that the author of Acts invented the 'street called Straight', the 'house of Judas', or Ananias. No doubt these elements were mentioned in pre-Lukan tradition, which is likely to have originated in Damascus itself. This does not mean, however, that the tradition is entirely reliable. It may well be that Ananias was a prominent member of the congregation of Damascus, and that the house of Judas in the street called Straight was an important centre of that community. The only conclusion to be drawn from the existence of such a pre-Lukan tradition on Paul's acceptance in Damascus, is that Paul had indeed become accepted in the Christian community of that city. After his call Paul probably joined the Christian congregation of Damascus, even if this may only have been for a short period.[124]

It thus appears that Acts contains pre-Lukan traditional material on the call of Saul/Paul. This material, however, largely consists of the same elements mentioned by Paul himself, to which a few narrative details have been added. Two of these additions, the tradition concerning Ananias, and that on Paul's preaching of the gospel in Damascus, are indicative of the fact that Paul joined the Christian community in Damascus after his call.[125] This observation is supported by the evidence from Gal 1,17, which states that Paul went to Arabia after his call and returned to Damascus afterwards.

---

narrative. A. Wikenhauser, 'Doppelträume', *Biblica* 29 (1948), pp. 100-111, gives 19 parallels from ancient literature in which this literary technique is used.

[123] Ananias must have been a prominent member of the congregation in Damascus; cf. 22,12; Pesch, *Apostelgeschichte*, vol. 1, p. 305. The author of Acts mentions him as a representative of the whole congregation; see Jervell, *Apostelgeschichte*, p. 282; J. Roloff, *Die Apostelgeschichte* (NTD; Göttingen: Vandenhoeck und Ruprecht, 1981), p. 150.

[124] Murphy-O'Connor, *Paul*, pp. 85-90, considers Damascus as the place where Paul learned his trade as an apprentice, and started his preaching of the gospel. On Paul's relation to the Christian community in Damascus, see Hengel, Schwemer, *Paul between Damascus and Antioch*, pp. 83-93.

[125] Lüdemann, *Das frühe Christentum*, pp. 121-125, argues that Paul's preaching of the gospel in Damascus is a traditional element in Acts 9,19b-25, but is undecisive in regard to Ananias (p. 120).

Conclusion

The intention of this chapter was to survey the evidence on Paul's pre-Christian life and his call as contained in his own letters and the book of Acts. What we found out can be summarised as follows.

Before he experienced his call, Paul was a Law-abiding Pharisee who fiercely opposed the views of the Jesus movement. In retrospect, Paul speaks of this period of his life as 'excessively persecuting the church of God'. It is not very likely however that Paul actually used violence, and there is no solid proof in his letters to assume this. Since his opposition to the Jesus movement was directed against the views of this movement, Paul must have been familiar with these views as well as with a number of persons within the movement.

At some time in or near Damascus Paul had a mystical experience that changed his life profoundly: it confirmed the faith he opposed. Although Paul states that he did not go to see anyone after his transformation experience, he did get involved with the church in Damascus where he was socialised in the Christian movement. The Pharisee had become a follower of Jesus. But what were the consequences for Paul? And how did he end up describing his own task as that of the apostle to the Gentiles? It is to these questions the next chapter turns.

CHAPTER FIVE

THE APOSTLE TO THE GENTILES

In the previous chapter it became clear that Paul did not receive any lengthy instruction from Christ on the road to Damascus in which his specific task was described. Rather, it is probable that the transformation experience Paul had in or near Damascus was the decisive *momentum* in a process. In retrospect Paul views this *momentum* as his call to be an apostle. But how and when did he come to regard his task as that of an apostle? And what did that mean to Paul?

In this chapter we will have to search the evidence on Paul's view of his apostolate. The first section is dedicated to the indications Paul himself gives in his letters. In the second section the notion of 'being sent' will be dealt with. Subsequently the relevant evidence from Acts on Paul's early period will be dealt with. Finally, we will search for clarity in regard to Paul's relation to the Gentiles.

1. Paul on his Apostolate

The first thing we should observe when dealing with Paul's own remarks on his apostleship is that he does not explicitly introduce himself as an apostle in all his letters. He does so in his epistles to the Romans, Corinthians, and Galatians, but in 1 Thessalonians, Philippians, and Philemon he does not present himself as such. The difference becomes clear when comparing the letter openings:

Rom 1,1   Παῦλος δοῦλος Χριστοῦ Ἰησοῦ, κλητὸς ἀπόστολος ἀφωρισμένος εἰς εὐαγγέλιον θεοῦ

1 Cor 1,1 Παῦλος κλητὸς ἀπόστολος Χριστοῦ Ἰησοῦ διὰ θελήματος θεοῦ

2 Cor 1,1 Παῦλος ἀπόστολος Χριστοῦ Ἰησοῦ διὰ θελήματος θεοῦ

Gal 1,1   Παῦλος ἀπόστολος οὐκ ἀπ' ἀνθρώπων οὐδὲ δι' ἀνθρώπου ἀλλὰ διὰ Ἰησοῦ Χριστοῦ

In these four opening formulas Paul explicitly presents himself as an apostle whose task was laid upon him by God or Christ himself. Note how different the other letter openings sound:

Phil 1,1   Παῦλος καὶ Τιμόθεος δοῦλοι Χριστοῦ Ἰησοῦ
1 Thess 1,1 Παῦλος (without any further characterisation)
Phlm   Παῦλος δέσμιος Χριστοῦ Ἰησοῦ.

The differences should be explained from the divergent contexts in which Paul wrote the respective letters. In the Corinthian correspondence, as well as in the epistle to the Galatians, Paul had to defend himself and his apostolate. In both cases Paul had to defend his authority over against competing preachers (Galatians) or the congregation itself (Corinthians). In his letter to the Romans Paul introduces himself to a congregation that does not yet know him and therefore he extensively describes his ideas as well as his view of his own task.

The other three letters were obviously written in different situations. The letter to Philemon originated from prison, hence the characterisation of Paul as 'a prisoner on behalf of Christ Jesus' (δέσμιος Χριστοῦ Ἰησοῦ).[1] Furthermore, Philemon is more of a private letter than an apostolic one, and as such it is not strange that Paul does not introduce himself as an apostle. But why would 1 Thessalonians and Philippians lack the introduction of Paul as an apostle in the opening formula? The reason must lie in the fact that Paul has no need to defend himself in these letters.[2] His apostolate was apparently not disputed in the communities of Thessalonica and Philippi.

This last observation is supported by evidence from 1 Thess 2,5-7. Paul, Silvanus, and Timothy remind the Thessalonians in 2,1-16 of how they had brought the gospel to them.[3] They point out the difference between the way they did act in Thessalonica during their ministry and the way they could have acted, by means of a short remark: δυνάμενοι ἐν βάρει εἶναι ὡς Χριστοῦ ἀπόστολοι. Paul and his companions could have claimed the authority of being 'apostles of Christ', but did not do so. This remark shows us Paul's refusal to excercise the rights he and his companions thought they could claim as apostles. This remark proves that already in his earliest letter Paul testifies to the existence of 'apostles of

---

[1] Cf. P. Stuhlmacher, *Der Brief an Philemon* (EKK; Zürich: Benziger; Neukirchen-Vluyn: Neukirchener, 1975), p. 29.

[2] For 1 Thessalonians, see e.g. I.H. Marshall, *1 and 2 Thessalonians* (NCB; London: Marshall, Morgan & Scott; Grand Rapids: Eerdmans, 1983), p. 48; for Philippians, see Fee, *Philippians*, p. 62.

[3] 1 Thessalonians was written by these three authors together. The church of Thessalonica had also been established by Paul, Silvanus, and Timothy together – see T. Holtz, *Der erste Brief an die Thessalonicher* (EKK; Düsseldorf: Benziger; Neukirchen-Vluyn: Neukirchener, 1986), pp. 13-14.

Christ' as a leading group of individuals. Furthermore it points out that Paul counts himself, as well as Silvanus and Timothy, among this group.[4] Since he obviously considers himself an apostle in his later letters, the conclusion should be that Paul did so throughout the period of his independent proclamation of the gospel. But how did Paul use the term?

To understand Paul's use of the title 'apostle' it is important to search for its origins.[5] There are two competing theories on this matter: either the notion of apostle derives from the synagogal institution of a *shaliach*[6] or the idea goes back to Jesus' commissioning of disciples as described in the material discussed in chapter three (cf. above, pp. 82-90).[7] The problem is that both options are difficult to prove. In regard to the *shaliach*-hypothesis we encounter the problem that there is no hint of evidence that the well developed administrative system of synagogue-communities and their regulations as found in rabbinic sources already existed before 70 CE. There were obviously Jewish communities throughout the Roman Empire and these communities were obviously committed to prayer, education, worship, and the interpretation of the Law. But if we decide to assume that synagogue institutions from the second and later centuries CE were already in use during the first century, we take an enourmous risk of letting an anachronism enter our reconstruction. Since

---

[4] Paul describes the proclamation of the gospel in Gal 2,8 as ἀποστολή. This word, used by Paul in only two other passages (Rom 1,5; 1 Cor 9,2), reveals that the apostolate had become a more or less fixed function within the Church. It refers to the office of apostle. This once again underlines the fact that Paul saw himself as an apostle in the official sense of the word, i.e. as one of the leading and prominent figures in the early Church; cf. K. Rengstorf, s.v. ἀπόστολος, *ThWNT* vol. 1, p. 447.

[5] On the use of the designation 'apostle' and the people it was used for, see Reinbold, *Propaganda und Mission*, pp. 32-116.

[6] See J. Roloff, 'Apostel, Apostolat, Apostolizität I', *TRE* vol. 3, pp. 430-445, esp. p. 432: 'Der jüdische Autorisationsbegriff *shaliach* gehört in den Zusammenhang von Rechtsvorstellungen, deren Wurzel im altsemitischen Botenrecht liegt (z.B. 1 Sam 25,40; 2 Sam 10,1ff.), und die in rabbinischer Zeit ihre prägnanteste Formulierung in dem Grundsatz gefunden haben "Der Gesandte eines Menschen ist wie dieser selbst" (... Ber 5,5).' The most extensive discussion and defense off the *shaliach*-hypothesis is given by K. Rengstorf, s.v. ἀπόστολος, *ThWNT*, vol. 1, esp. pp. 413-420; see also J.-A. Bühner, s.v. ἀπόστολος, *EWNT*, vol. 1, cols. 342-351, and the literature mentioned there.

[7] Formulated by e.g. T.W. Manson in his discussion of Luke 11,49-50: 'The term "apostles" has a technical ecclesiastical sense, which ought not to be read into the text here. Jesus used the Aramaic equivalent of the word, and – as I think – gave it as a name to certain of His disciples; but He used in in a wide sense to designate anyone who had a mission from God to men'; H.D.A. Major, T.W. Manson, C.J. Wright, *The Mission and Message of Jesus. An Exposition of the Gospels in the Light of Modern Research* (New York: Dutton and Co., 1938), p. 394. See the correction by C.K. Barrett, *The Signs of an Apostle. The Cato Lecture 1969* (Carlisle: Paternoster, 1996 = 1970), pp. 30-34.

we cannot be certain of the *shaliach*-institution prior to the second century, it is dangerous to take this exact function as the background to the Christian idea of apostleship. Seen from this perspective it would be safer to err on the side of caution and to look for an alternative reconstruction. Furthermore, in an extensive discussion of the matter W. Schmithals has scrutinised the differences between the *shaliach*-institution and the Christian notion of apostleship.[8] After noticing the many differences Schmithals concludes: 'If there were any two "sent ones" who had nothing to do with each other, they would have been the Christian apostle and the Jewish *Schaliach*.'[9] Unfortunately, Schmithals' alternative is even more speculative than the *shaliach*-hypothesis: according to him the origin of apostleship lies within Jewish Gnosticism. Since Schmithals' views of Gnosticism cannot be upheld, his reconstruction does not provide for a final solution either.

The alternative would be to search for the origin of the function of apostle within Jesus' ministry. In chapter three we have seen that the evidence on Jesus' commissioning of disciples should be traced back to the earliest layers of Christian tradition. But we have also seen that the reconstruction cannot pass the border of the Easter event: the commissioning narratives were taken as evidence that the earliest Christian preachers legitimised their actions by narrating their commissioning by Jesus. This means that some of those who regarded themselves as apostles claimed their status with an appeal to Jesus. But again the evidence does not lead to the solution needed: if we cannot be certain about Jesus' instruction of preachers supporting his ministry, we cannot use the commissioning traditions as evidence for the institution of apostleship.

The two leads that could possibly account for the origin of the Christian notion of apostleship therefore amount to nothing. We cannot regard the institution of *shaliach* as its historical background nor can we take a certain event during Jesus' ministry as its starting-point. Let us therefore commence at the other end and look into the earliest evidence: Paul's use of the word ἀπόστολος.

In two texts Paul uses the term ἀπόστολος to describe an envoy from a specific congregation: Phil 2,25 and 2 Cor 8,23. In Phil 2,25 Paul speaks about Epaphroditus, who was clearly sent as an envoy of the Philippians

---

[8] W. Schmithals, *The Office of Apostle in the Early Church* (Nashville, New York: Abingdon, 1969), pp. 98-110 [= *Das kirchliche Apostelamt* (Göttingen: Vandenhoeck& Ruprecht, 1961)].

[9] Schmithals, *Office of Apostle* p. 110.

(ὑμῶν δὲ ἀπόστολος).[10] And in 2 Cor 8,23 (ἀπόστολοι ἐκκλησιῶν) Paul mentions a number of 'brothers' who, as envoys of a number of congregations, accompany Titus on his task of collecting money.[11] These specific texts reflect the function of an ἀπόστολος as an envoy from a specific congregation. A similar use of the term is found in Rev 2,2; *Did.* 11,4-6 and also Acts' description of Paul's work together with Barnabas appears to reflect this practice of sending envoys (cf. below, pp. 185-190). In all these passages the word ἀπόστολος is apparently not used as a special title, but rather as a designation of an 'envoy'.

This specific non-titular use of the word ἀπόστολος is also attested by Josephus. In *Ant.* XVII,300 he describes a delegation of Jews who were sent to Rome in order to ask Augustus for autonomy. In his description of their coming to Rome, Josephus mentions this delegation (πρεσβεία) as an 'embassy' (ἀπόστολος): ἀφίκετο εἰς τὴν Ῥώμην πρεσβεία Ἰουδαίων, Οὐάρου **τὸν ἀπόστολον** αὐτῶν τῷ ἔθνει ἐπικεχωρηκότος, ὑπὲρ αἰτήσεως αὐτονομίας – 'There arrived at Rome a delegation of Jews, which Varus had permitted the nation to send, for the purpose of asking autonomy'.[12] Here, the word is used for the entire group and its use is evidently non-titular.

Next to this non-titular use of the word, Paul's letters also give evidence for the fact that within the early Christian movement the function of 'apostle' was growing more and more important. In the letter openings discussed above Paul employs the word in a way that is rather different from the category of envoys of a certain congregation. Paul presents himself as an ἀπόστολος, not of a certain congregation, but of Christ, according to the will of God. Obviously Paul did not invent this use of the term. This was already pointed out in the above. The evidence from 1 Thess 2,5-7 should be combined with 1 Cor 12,28-29, where Paul mentions 'the apostles' as the first and most prominent group of functionaries within the church. The apostles he mentions here are not envoys of congregations, but form a more or less well defined group, a group also mentioned in 15,7. As was argued in the discussion of 1 Cor 15,1-7,[13] Paul mentions the witnesses who had seen the Lord after his resurrection. He states a credal formula in 15,3b-5, and adds the apparitions to five-hundred

---

[10] Fee, *Philippians*, p. 276, interprets this type of apostle as 'one sent on behalf of the congregation to perform a given task'.

[11] Martin, *2 Corinthians*, p. 277: 'messengers appointed by the congregations'.

[12] Text and translation taken from LCL, R. Marcus, A. Wikgren, *Josephus*, vol. VIII.

[13] See above, pp. 163-166.

brothers, to 'James and all of the apostles', and to Paul himself. Since the apparition to Peter and the twelve is probably an element in the pre-Pauline formula Paul quoted in vv. 3b-5, the addition of the 'other apostles' in v. 7 leaves open the possibility that the twelve were also reckoned among the apostles. But 'the twelve' obviously did not coincide with 'the apostles'.

According to Hahn and others the apostles formed a privileged and important group whose status was linked to the fact that its members had shared in the Easter-appearances.[14] That the apostles indeed formed a more or less privileged group cannot be doubted. A number of times Paul hints at duties and privileges that he could have taken advantage of as an apostle. So, for instance, he mentions the fact that apostles were allowed to marry (1 Cor 9,5). Paul could have claimed the rights of an apostle (1 Thess 2,5-7), and he describes how he was, as an apostle, financially supported by the congregation of the Philippians (Phil 4,10-15; cf. 2 Cor 11,9). But whether this group was formed solely by those who shared the Easter-apparitions cannot be argued on the basis of 1 Cor 9,1 and 15, 1-9. Paul's remarks in 9,1 do seem to connect his vision of the Lord to his apostolate. In 15,6-7 Paul mentions two different groups who have experienced an apparition: a group of five-hundred, and 'all the apostles'. Paul apparently does not include the group of five-hundred brothers among the apostles, although the 500 did 'see the Lord'. Hence, there must have been an additional criterion for being an apostle. An apparition alone was not enough.

Unfortunately it is unclear what this additional criterion may have been. The Lukan concept of the twelve disciples who became the twelve apostles, fails the test (see esp. Luke 6,13). Paul himself gives evidence that Barnabas (1 Cor 9,5-6) and Andronikos and Junia (Rom 16,7)[15] were reckoned among the apostles. To look for the additional criterium in some connection with the historical Jesus does not settle the case either. No such connection can be attributed to Barnabas or Andronikos and Junia. So much is clear, that the group addressed as 'apostles' were the most prominent members of the early church. When Paul describes his visit to Jerusalem in Galatians 2, he mentions that he had a meeting with the leaders of the Jerusalem community, Peter (Cephas) and James, who were

[14] Thus for instance F. Hahn, 'Der Apostolat im Urchristentum. Seine Eigenart und seine Voraussetzungen', *KuD* 20 (1974), pp. 54-77; cf. also Roloff, *TRE* vol. 3, pp. 430-445.

[15] V. Fabrega, 'War Junia(s), der hervorragende Apostel (Röm. 16,7), eine Frau?', *JAC* 27/28 (1984-1985), pp. 47-64, has convincingly argued on the basis of patristic evidence, that Junia was a female apostle, whose name was later changed into the male Junias.

also reckoned among the apostles. And in summing up the different functions and tasks in the Christian community in 1 Corinthians 12, Paul mentions the apostolate as the first and most important function.

The only safe conclusion we can draw on the basis of this evidence is that the concept of 'apostle' was not clearly defined in the early days of the Christian movement.[16] There were at least two different concepts, viz. that of the envoy of a congregation and that of an 'Envoy of Christ'. This latter concept would ultimately grow into the prime criterion for authentic Christianity: apostolicity.

The difference in status between the two types of 'envoys' explains the difficulties Paul experienced in claiming the title of 'apostle'. According to N. Taylor Paul's Christian life should be divided into three stages.[17] It started with the period immediately following his call. For Paul this period would have been 'an unsettled time during which he was unable to become fully integrated into any Christian community'.[18] Subsequently Paul became a member of the church of Antioch that sent him out as an envoy together with Barnabas. Then the two were ἀπόστολοι τῆς ἐκκλησίας, with Barnabas acting as the *primus*, and Paul as the *secundus*.[19] When eventually Paul came to challenge Peter and Barnabas at the so-called 'Antioch-incident', his position within the Antiochene church became untenable. This was, according to Taylor, the birth of Paul's independent apostolate, even the origin of Paul's own specific definition of apostolate.

Taylor's thesis on Paul's career as an apostle may be somewhat speculative on a number of points,[20] but its general outline is well-reasoned. It is not only supported by the data on the title of 'apostle', but also by Paul's use of the word 'call', which is far from restricted to the call of an apostle only: every believer has been 'called'.[21] It furthermore helps

[16] Cf. Reinbold, *Propaganda und Mission*, p. 114: 'Die Überblick über die vorhandenen Daten zeigt mit aller Deutlichkeit, daß es einen klar umrissenen Begriff vom Wesen und den Aufgaben eines "Apostels" nicht gegeben hat.'
[17] See N. Taylor, *Paul, Antioch and Jerusalem. A Study in Relationships and Authority in Earliest Christianity* (JSNTSS 66; Sheffield: Sheffield Academic Press, 1992), *passim*; summary on pp. 222-226.
[18] Taylor, *Antioch*, p. 223.
[19] Cf. Taylor, *Antioch*, pp. 88-95; p. 94: 'There can be little doubt that Barnabas was the senior partner in the Antiochene apostolate...'
[20] For instance Taylor's view that Paul developed 'a theocentric self-identity' in order to 'compensate for his loss of dyadic identity and apostolic authority' (*Antioch*, p. 225) can by no means be substantiated.
[21] Rom 1,6-7; 8,28; 11,29; 1 Cor 1,2.24.26; 7,20; Phil 3,14; cf. Paul's use of the verb καλέω in Rom 8,30; 9,12.24; 1 Cor 1,9; 7,15.17.21.22; Gal 1,6.15; 5,13; 1 Thess 2,12; 4,7; 5,24.

to understand how Paul can acknowledge his own reception of the earliest Christian tradition in 1 Corinthians 15, while he also emphasises his independence from human instruction in Galatians 1.

Seen against this background, the troubles Paul experienced concerning his apostolate were caused in part by the fact that there was no fixed definition of the office of apostle. Due to this situation Paul could claim to be an apostle whereas at the same time his opponents could deny him his apostolic status. Paul did not belong to the circle of prominent members of the first Christian community in Jerusalem, and yet he claimed the same title after he left Antioch. But why did Paul claim this title? And what was the importance of 'being sent'?

2. The Notion of 'Being Sent'

In 1 Cor 1,17 Paul explicitly founds his mission, the fact that he was sent, in Christ himself: 'Christ did not send me to baptise, but to preach the gospel' (οὐ γὰρ ἀπέστειλέν με Χριστὸς βαπτίζειν ἀλλα εὐαγγελίζεσθαι). This remark by Paul is the only text in which he explicitly states that he considered himself as 'sent'. How does this notion relate to Paul's view of his work as an 'apostle', an envoy?

A survey of the use of ἀποστέλλω and its cognates is presented in the appendices to this book (pp. 261-290). Therefore we can summarise the evidence here. The verb ἀποστέλλω is used for the sending of a regular envoy who has to act on behalf of the one who sent him (Appendix 1, s.v. ἀποστέλλω, section 1). In a religious way it is used of God who 'sends' his envoys. This idea is already found in an early stratum of Christian tradition: Q 11,49 and 13,34 (cf. Appendix 1, s.v. ἀποστέλλω, section 3). Both texts express the idea that God sends his envoys to Jerusalem. The background to this idea is no doubt found in the LXX-usage of the same terminology for the 'sending' of prophets (Appendix 2, s.v. ἀποστέλλω). In similar fashion Jesus was seen as 'sent' by God (Appendix 1, s.v. ἀποστέλλω, section 4). This notion develops into the terminology used in Johannine writings of the Son who is sent by the Father (Appendix 1, s.v. ἀποστέλλω, section 4a, and s.v. πέμπω). Those who act on behalf of Jesus Christ see themselves as 'sent' by him, as ἀπόστολοι (Appendix 1, s.v. ἀπόστολος, sections 2 and 4.b-d).

The origin therefore of the Christian notion of 'apostle' lies in the concept of being sent by Jesus as Jesus was sent by God. The terminology with which this notion was expressed is derived from vocabulary found throughout the Septuagint (Appendix 2, s.v. ἀποστέλλω LXX). As is shown by the data in Appendix 2, this use reflects a prophetic awareness. The 'apostles' are sent by Jesus Christ as YHWH had sent his prophets. This observation fits in with the reconstruction made in the previous chapter of Paul's view of his call as a prophetic commissioning. Furthermore, the prophetic enthusiasm of the earliest Christian movement as a whole also accounts for the fact that there was no fixed definition of the vocabulary. The titular use of the term 'apostle' thus gradually came into existence out of the prophetic awareness within the Jesusmovement and early Christian groups. A non-titular use of the term is found in several passages where the noun ἀπόστολος is evidently used for an 'envoy' for instance of a specific congregation. It is this use of the word we encounter e.g. in Acts 14,4.14 on Paul and Barnabas as envoys of Antioch.[22]

3. The Evidence from Acts

In the above we have established that Paul's conversion to the early Christian movement came about as a decisive *momentum* within a longer process, and that he considered himself as an 'apostle' throughout the period in which he wrote his letters. Taylor's view of Paul's life was accepted as a likely reconstruction. Therefore we will now have to take a look at the way in which Paul's early period is treated in the Book of Acts. Paul himself does not say much on that part of his ministry, but the author of Acts at least pretends to have some more information than what we know from the letters. What does the Book of Acts say on (a) Paul's life after his 'call', on (b) Barnabas, on (c) Paul's relation to the congregation of Antioch, and on (d) the work Paul and Barnabas did together?

(a.) According to Acts, Paul joined the Christian community of Damascus immediately after his call, but he soon had to flee. Paul's preaching of the gospel is depicted in a way that will prove to be a pattern in the book of Acts: Paul takes his stand in the synagogue of Damascus, enrages a number of those present who subsequently decide to cast Paul out. Similar reactions of 'the Jews' are described in 13,45.50; 14,19;

---

[22] Pesch, *Apostelgeschichte*, vol. 2, p. 52, considers the use of ἀπόστολοι for Paul and Barnabas in Acts 14 as caused by the source the author apparently used: '"Aposteln", wie die Missionare als "Gesandte" der antiochenischen Gemeinde (vgl. 13,4) in der Quelle heißen.' – cf. also Barrett, *Acts*, vol. 1, pp. 666-667; Hahn, *Verständnis*, p. 134; H. Conzelmann, *Geschichte des Urchristentums* (GNT 5; Göttingen: Vandenhoeck & Ruprecht, 1969), p. 138.

17,13; 18,12; 21,27-32; 23,12-15. Given this stereotypical reaction of Paul's Jewish opponents in Acts 9,23-25 we could be tempted assume that this account is formed by the author as a redactional transition from Paul's stay in Damascus to his visit to Jerusalem. However, Paul himself gives us comparable evidence of an event at which he escaped from Damascus in a basket: 2 Cor 11,33. Given the fact that Paul mentions Damascus in Gal 1,17 as the place to which he returned after his call, it is likely that the escape described in this manner did indeed take place at the end of Paul's stay there. This event must have occurred before 40/41 CE, because is took place during the reign of the Nabatean king Aretas IV.[23] It is unclear whether the ἐθνάρχης of Aretas was the leader of the Nabatean commercial colony in Damascus,[24] or whether Damascus fell under Nabatean control at the moment Paul had to escape the city.[25] The situation is probably best summarised by D.F. Graf: 'the circumstances remain obscure, but the Jewish and Nabatean Arab community appear to have acted in concert against Paul.'[26]

A serious difficulty for the reconstruction of Paul's deeds after his call is formed by the obvious contradiction between Galatians and Acts. In Gal 1,17-22 Paul denies having gone to Jerusalem after his call. Instead, he describes how he went to Arabia and then returned to Damascus. He left the city only after three years to become acquainted with Peter (Cephas). On that occasion, according to Paul, he met James as well. Subsequently Paul visited Syria and Cilicia. The account given by Acts is very different from this one. After his call, Paul is said to have stayed in Damascus, to have fled from Damascus to Jerusalem, and to have returned to his hometown of Tarsus after that. H.-D. Betz has argued that Paul's denial of his visit to Jerusalem immediately after his description of his call (Gal 1,16-17), in combination with his oath of speaking the truth (Gal 1,20), is an attack on stories such as the tradition contained in Acts 9.[27] If he is

---

[23] See the excellent discussion by D.A. Campbell, 'An Anchor for Pauline Chronology: Paul's Flight from the "Ethnarch of King Aretas" (2 Corinthians 11:32-33)', *JBL* 121 (2002), pp. 279-302.

[24] Argued by E.A. Knauf, 'Zum *Ethnarchen* des Aretas 2 Kor 11,32', *ZNW* 74 (1983), pp. 145-147. According to Knauf, the ethnarch was the 'Vorsteher der nabatäischen Handelskolonie in Damaskus, der wohl zugleich die Interessen des nabatäischen Staates vertrat, (…) eine Art Konsul also.' (p. 147); see also J.-P Rey-Coquais, 'Syrie romaine, de Pompée à Dioclétien', *JRS* 68 (1978), pp. 44-73.

[25] See R. Jewett, *Dating Paul's Life* (Philadelphia: 1979), pp. 30-33; G.W. Bowersock, *Roman Arabia* (Cambridge MA: Harvard University Press, 1983), pp. 68-69.

[26] D.F. Graf, in *ABD* vol. 1, p. 375.

[27] Betz, *Galatians*, p. 73, suggests that Paul in Gal 1,16 'apparently denies such stories in order to defend the independence of his commission.'

right, and there is much that favours this conclusion,[28] the author of Acts would have depended on an old tradition on Paul, which in some form was already known in Paul's own day. We must also conclude then, that he neither had access to the first hand information given by Paul himself in Gal 1,17 nor to any oral information given by Paul on the subject. This disqualifies the still much adhered to theory that Acts was written by Luke, a former companion of Paul.

The above observation also has its consequences for 9,30. There Paul is said to have gone back to Tarsus, which is repeated in 11,25. That verse tells how Barnabas went to fetch Paul in order to go out on a missionary expedition with him. In all probability the remark on Paul's going to Tarsus is a redactional one: it places 'the brothers' in Caesarea, where the meeting between Peter and Cornelius occurred (c. 10), and gives a valid explanation for the absence of Paul in the period described in the passage 9,31-11,24. Since the author knew Tarsus to be Paul's hometown, he places him there in order to await his return to the scene.

(b.) What does the Book of Acts reveal about Barnabas? Two elements in the passage 9,26-30 are worth considering separately: the mention of Barnabas as the one by whom Paul was introduced into the circle of the movement in Jerusalem, and the conflict with the 'Hellenists'. Barnabas is introduced in Acts 4,36 as 'Joseph, who is called Barnabas'.[29] It is said of him that he was 'a Levite, a native from Cyprus'. Paul himself mentions Barnabas in two of his letters: 1 Cor 9,6; Gal 2,1.9.13. Acts 13,2 describes how Paul and Barnabas went out to preach the gospel together.[30] According to Acts, they continued working as a team until they parted company because of a disagreement over John Mark (15,36-41). It has already been argued above, that Galatians 2 describes the true reason why Paul and Barnabas split up: the so-called Antioch-incident.[31]

---

[28] The author of Acts is well known for the less than accurate way in which he reproduced the chronology of events (cf. for example the census of Augustus under Quirinius mentioned in Luke 2 or the mention of Theudas in Gamaliel's judgement of the Way. It is thus well imaginable that he did not check the traditions he received on Paul and other preachers within early Christianity.

[29] A prosopographic study of Barnabas is offered by Reinbold, *Propaganda und Mission*, pp. 84-106.

[30] For a thorough analysis of Acts' description of the so-called 'first missionary journey' (Acts 13-14), see C. Breytenbach, *Paulus und Barnabas in der Provinz Galatien. Studien zu Apostelgeschichte 13f.; 16,6; 18,23 und den Adressaten des Galaterbriefes* (AGAJU 38; Leiden [etc.]: Brill, 1996).

[31] See the discussion above (p. 000), and Taylor, *Antioch*, pp. 123-139. On the date of this incident, see A. Suhl, 'Der Beginn der selbständigen Mission des Paulus', *NTS* 38 (1992), pp. 430-447, who dates the incident to the year 47 at the latest.

What we are concerned with here, is the fact that Acts mentions Barnabas as the one who introduced Paul/Saul to the movement in Jerusalem. Since Paul categorically denies having gone to Jerusalem after his call, and does not speak of Barnabas as the one who led him there when he finally did, it is not very likely that this account in Acts reflects the true course of history.

(c.) The Christian community in Antioch has been discussed in chapter three. Here, it is important to recall that the Antiochene community is presented as the first group in which Jews and non-Jews lived together and were called 'Christians' (11,30). According to Acts Paul became a member of exactly this community. He was sent out by the congregation of Antioch as an envoy together with Barnabas. Acts depicts the persecution of the Hellenists in Jerusalem as the main source from which the congregation of Antioch grew (11,19-20; cf. above, pp. 129-132).[32] The introduction of Barnabas in Antioch is probably a redactional feature in Acts (11,22; cf. above):[33] the author intends to show the whole spread of the movement as having its origin in the community of Jerusalem. It is uncertain whether Barnabas indeed came from Jerusalem to Antioch. What is clear is that Paul became involved with Barnabas in Antioch.

(d.) The report on Barnabas and Paul in cc. 13-14 reveals the fact that Paul had indeed become involved in the congregation of Antioch. It is very likely that the core of Acts' portrayal of Barnabas and Paul as envoys of the congregation of Antioch is correct.[34] The two are presented as being sent from Antioch to the synagogues of Cyprus, Pamphylia, Pisidia, Galatia, and Attalia. The emphasis in the account of what is usually called the 'first missionary journey' lies on the fact that Barnabas and Paul acted as envoys of the Antiochene community, through whom God himself

---

[32] For the importance of the 'Hellenists' in relation to Antioch and Paul, see Räisänen, 'Hellenists', pp. 149-202. Räisänen concludes that the Hellenists formed a bridge between Hellenistic Judaism of the Dispersion and the Palestinian Jesus movement, and between Jesus' apocalyptic proclamation of a new temple and later writers critical of the temple cult as such. Räisänen's position is to be preferred above that of Hengel, *Between Jesus and Paul*, p. 29, who considers the Hellenists to be such a bridge but directly between Jesus and Paul, and adds that 'only this community can be called the "pre-Pauline Hellenistic community" in the full sense of the word.'

[33] In an attempt to show the divine origin of the spread of the gospel, Acts 11,20-26 puts the report of the gospel's transition of the boundaries of Judaism in biblicistic terminology: 11,21 cf. LXX 2 Sam 3,12; 11,22 cf. LXX Isa 5,9 – Haenchen, *Apostelgeschichte*, p. 310: 'Lukas berichtet in biblischem Stil vom Missionserfolg; das Wachstum der Gemeinde beweist, daß Gott mit dem Handeln dieser Männer einverstanden ist: somit ist die antiochenische Heidenmission von ihm anerkannt.'

[34] See Lüdemann, *Das frühe Christentum*, pp. 164.171-172.

'opened a door of faith' for the Gentiles (14,27).[35] During this journey they preached the gospel to the members of the Jewish synagogues, but it was welcomed by pagans rather than by Jews (cf. 13,48-52).

It is a remarkable feature of the journey of Barnabas and Paul, that they were sent out together on behalf of the congregation of Antioch. In Luke 10,1 the same author added a significant element to the Q-material on the commissioning of the seventy: they also were sent out two by two.[36] The same number plays an important part in Revelation 11, where the two eschatological prophets appear who are to be slain by the Beast. The background to the number two in Revelation 11, Mark 6,7, and Luke 10,1 should probably be sought in the legal tradition that *unus testis nullus testis*, which is put in positive terms in Deut 19,15: 'only on the evidence of two or three witnesses shall a charge be sustained'. Since this principle is explicitly referred to in Matt 18,16; 2 Cor 13,1; 1 Tim 5,19 and probably implicitly in John 8,17 it must have formed a widely accepted rule. The fact that Barnabas and Paul were sent out together, with John Mark as their aid (13,5), should therefore be seen against this background. This tradition on Barnabas and Paul thus reflects an early missionary practice in which two envoys of one community preach the gospel to another community.

The fact that Acts contains this tradition of the combined preaching of the gospel by Barnabas and Paul also reveals the progression Paul must have made within the Antiochene congregation.[37] Paul must have been a member of this church for some time before being sent out with Barnabas.[38] His testimony together with that of Barnabas must indeed have been aimed primarily at Jewish communities in Asia Minor. It was probably directed towards non-Jews after discovering that they were more inclined to accept the gospel. Thus the sequence that Acts gives of the proclamation of the gospel by Paul (proclamation in the synagogue – rejection by his Jewish audience – proclamation to pagans – acceptance by his pagan audience) has its origin in the first period of Paul's public ministry. Together with Barnabas he indeed acted as an envoy of the congregation of Antioch.

The outline of Paul's activities with Barnabas is simple: the two went to a number of towns where they visited the Jewish communities to proclaim the gospel. The places mentioned in Acts are Seleucia, Salamis

---

[35] The same terminology is also found in Paul: 1 Cor 16,9; 2 Cor 2,12.
[36] See also Mark 6,7; cf. above pp. 85-86.
[37] See Taylor, *Antioch*, pp. 88-95.
[38] Taylor, *Antioch*, p. 94: 'There can be little doubt that Barnabas was the senior partner in the Antiochene apostolate...'

in Cyprus, Paphos, Perge in Pamphylia, Antioch in Pisidia, Iconium, Lystra and Derbe. From there they returned through Lystra and Pisidian Antioch to Pamphylia, Attalia, and finally back to their base in Antioch. The reason why Barnabas and Paul moved on from one place to the next is either kept hidden or it is explicitly portrayed as being caused by severe opposition from 'the Jews' (13,45; 14,1-2.5-7.19-20). According to Acts, however, the main impetus for their actions is the Spirit. Barnabas and Paul are sent forth by the Spirit (13,4), and their actions are guided by the Spirit (13,9). Also the growth in the number of disciples is depicted as being caused by the Spirit (13,52).

It is probably a genuine historical feature of this account of Acts 13-14 that Barnabas and Paul met with serious opposition from within the Jewish communities they visited. It is due to the combination of this opposition and the fact that pagan sympathisers with Judaism easily accepted their gospel, that the author of Acts states in yet another programmatic verse (13,46): 'It was necessary that the word of God should be spoken first to you. Since you reject it and judge yourselves to be unworthy of eternal life, we are now turning to the Gentiles.' The implication that Barnabas and Paul consciously crossed the borders of the Jewish religion is probably too strong. Since the community of Antioch was a Christ-confessing group consisting of Jews and non-Jews alike, the divide had already been crossed at the time the two envoys were sent.

The evidence discussed in sections a.-d. urges us to draw a number of conclusions. Firstly, some time after his call Paul indeed became involved, in one way or another, in the Christian community of Antioch. He gradually achieved such a prominent position within this community, that he was sent out together with Barnabas. Secondly, the two envoys visited a number of settlements on Cyprus and in Asia Minor, as ἀπόστολοι τῆς ἐκκλησίας, envoys of the Antiochene community. As such they met with resistance among Jews and positive reception among pagan sympathisers with Judaism. Eventually Paul would come to defend the unity of these two types of believers 'in Christ' in such a way that it would lead to a parting of the ways between him and Barnabas. This point, the unity of Jew and Greek in Christ, would become his main focus throughout his post-Antiochene ministry.

4. Paul on the Gentiles

In Galatians 2 Paul describes how he came to an agreement with the apostles in Jerusalem. In the previous chapter Paul had given an account of his transformation experience and his interpretation of it. As was argued above, Paul in retrospect points to this experience as the moment of his call to be an apostle. He did not go to Jerusalem to those who were 'apostles before him' (1,17). It was later that he visited Peter on which occasion he also met with James.

In his description of this meeting Paul says nothing about any discussion he might have had or an agreement he might have made with Peter and James.[39] This is not so strange. The point Paul is making in Galatians 1 is his independence of the apostles in Jerusalem. In the early stage of his ministry Paul met them only once. Only after fourteen years did he return to them, this time together with Barnabas and Titus. On this occasion the content of his mission was discussed and this discussion resulted in the consensus that Peter, James, and John should direct their preaching of the gospel towards the Jews, and Paul and Barnabas towards Gentiles (2,7-9). Paul's remarks on the subject are extremely important, since they contain a great deal of information.

The previous section has reconstructed that Paul went to Jerusalem as an envoy of the congregation of Antioch. As such he accompanied Barnabas and Titus. The meeting Paul had in Jerusalem, which is probably to be identified as the so-called Apostolic Council described in Acts 15,[40] is thus important in a number of ways. It is important because it shows that Jerusalem and Antioch were the two most prominent centres of the Jesus movement. In these two centres two different attitudes towards the Mosaic Law predominated. The congregation in Jerusalem consisted of Law-abiding Jews, whereas the Antiochene church was evidently made up of a mixed group of Jews and non-Jews with a far more lenient attitude towards the Law. Within pluralistic Judaism of the period these different attitudes towards the Law would hardly have formed an exception. Yet

---

[39] The first visit to Jerusalem was probably not for the purpose of discussing problems that had arisen due to differences of opinion. It is more likely that Paul was instructed by Peter on Jesus – cf. Hengel, Schwemer, *Paul between Damascus and Antioch*, p. 146-150, who correctly characterise this meeting as 'a real encounter which was important for the further development of earliest Christianity' (p. 146).

[40] For a brief but instructive discussion on the identification of the conference described in Gal 2,1-10 and Acts 15, see Taylor, *Antioch*, pp. 52-54. Taylor mentions the possibility of identifying Gal 2,1-10 with either Acts 11,27-30 or 18,1-17, and rightly rejects both alternatives. According to Wedderburn, the Apostolic Decree can 'be regarded as a response to the problem thrown up by the quarrel at Antioch, and as legislation for Antioch and its immediate area of missionary influence.' – A.J.M. Wedderburn, 'The "Apostolic Decree": Tradition and Redaction', *NT* 35 (1993), pp. 362-389 (quotation from p. 389).

in this case both groups confessed Jesus as the Anointed One, God's ultimate eschatological envoy. Their shared confession raised the need for the churches of Jerusalem and Antioch to establish their common ground, and to develop a common minimum agreement in respect to the Law of Moses.

Apparently the congregation of Antioch recognised the primacy of the Jerusalem church, since they sent an embassy to discuss the problems in Jerusalem. Paul's membership of this embassy is an important detail. As was already argued above, Paul had become one of the more prominent members of the church of Antioch, so that now he was sent out to form an agreement on the difficult matter of the status of the Law.[41] Here we find the explanation why Paul did not go to Jerusalem for fourteen years after his call: he did not work independently during this period, but was rising to a leading position within the church of Antioch. Since he was embedded in this congregation, he had no need to consult the Jerusalem apostles on anything.

In his description of the meeting in Jerusalem, Paul mentions the agreement whereby the Antiochene church would proclaim the 'gospel for the uncircumcised', whereas the Jerusalem church would stick to the 'gospel for the circumcised' (2,7). Does this mean that there were two different 'gospels'? Does this mean that there was an agreement on a Law-abiding Christianity for Jews and a Law-free Christianity for Gentiles?

If there was any such agreement – which is difficult to prove – Paul denied its outcome. For him the Gospel concerning Christ was core of his activities.[42] The most explicit summary is given in 1 Cor 15,3b-5. This, no doubt, is an adequate summary of the proclamation Paul handed on to the Corinthians and others, and in 1 Cor 15,1 Paul himself characterises this proclamation as his εὐαγγέλιον. Paul can thus speak of 'my gospel'[43] or 'our gospel'[44] when describing the content of the proclamation he

---

[41] Cf. Gal 2,9, where the agreement is made between Peter, James, and John on the one hand, and Paul and Barnabas on the other.

[42] On this matter, see e.g. C.E.B. Cranfield, *The Epistle to the Romans* (ICC: Edinburgh: Clark, 1975), vol. 1, p. 54, n.2, who takes a stand against G. Friedrich's discussion of εὐαγγέλιον in the *ThDNT*. Friedrich argued that the word can either denote the act of proclaiming or the content of the proclamation. Cranfield: 'Is it not a preferable explanation of the data to say that in Paul εὐαγγέλιον always denotes the message of the good news, but that sometimes the context (...) may indicate that it is used in a slightly pregnant way, the thought of the message's proclamation (...) coming specially to the fore?'

[43] Rom 2,16; 16,25.

[44] 2 Cor 4,3; 1 Thess 1,5.

brought.[45] The content of this proclamation is God's decisive intervention in history through Christ: the Christ-event. This is expressed by the genitives Χριστοῦ and Θεοῦ.[46] But this gospel was, of course, not restricted to Paul; he shared it with the entire Jesus movement. The problem is that it said nothing on breaking or keeping the Law.

There can hardly have been any great differences in perception of the gospel between the congregations of Antioch and Jerusalem as to its content. Therefore, what must have made the difference between the 'gospel for the uncircumcised' and that 'for the circumcised' are the consequences drawn from the proclamation of the Christ-event. The Antiochene church was permitted to continue practising its more lenient attitude towards the Law, whereas the congregation in Jerusalem maintained a stricter approach. Although Acts 15,20 speaks of a number of cultic rules that would have formed the minimum of which the agreement consisted, Paul only mentions the remembrance of the poor.[47]

Clearly the compromise in Jerusalem, whatever its exact content, was not enough. It apparently resulted in two forms of the Christian movement: one in which observation of the Law remained an essential part and another in which not the Mosaic Law, but the confession of Jesus Christ became the central focus. These two forms of Christianity must have constituted the two extremes, and it is basically the conflict between these extremes that turned Paul into what he became after the incident at Antioch.[48]

Paul's account of the agreement between the two congregations is revealing in other respects as well. It proves that Peter/Cephas had a leading position within the earliest Jesus movement: it is Peter who had been primarily entrusted with the 'gospel for the circumcised', not James or John (Gal 2,9). Peter was probably able to claim this position because of his role among the followers of Jesus during the time before Jesus' death.

---

[45] Cf. 1 Cor 15,1; Gal 1,11; 1 Thess 2,9.

[46] Εὐαγγέλιον Χριστοῦ: Rom 15,19; 1 Cor 9,12; 2 Cor 2,12; 4,4 (εὐ. τῆς δόξης τοῦ Χρ.) 9,13; 10,14; Gal 1,7; Phil 1,27; 1 Thess 3,2; εὐαγγέλιον Θεοῦ: Rom 1,1; 15,16; 1 Thess 2,2.8.9.

[47] For this remembrance of the poor, see B. Beckheuer, *Paulus und Jerusalem* (EHS 23/611; Frankfurt am Main [etc.]: Peter Lang, 1997), pp. 52-97; Taylor, *Antioch*, pp. 116-122. According to Taylor, pp. 140-142, the Apostolic Decree was made not *at* but *after* the Council.

[48] In the present reconstruction the Apostolic Council is dated before the incident at Antioch. Although this is a matter of dispute, the majority of students of this topic appear to share this chronology; cf. G. Howard, *Paul: Crisis in Galatia. A Study in Early Christian Theology* (SNTSMS 35; Cambridge [etc.]: Cambridge University Press, 2nd ed., 1990), pp. 41-44; also Taylor, *Antioch*, pp. 123-139. A bibliography on the Apostolic Council is given by Jervell, *Apostelgeschichte*, pp. 386-388.

The position of Peter as one of the leading characters in the gospel traditions also points in this direction.[49] Paul's account of the incident in Antioch in Gal 2,11-14 is illustrative of the prominent position of Peter. Yet it also betrays the fact that there must have been a difference of opinion between Cephas/Peter and James. Peter at first sanctions the sharing of a table by Jewish and non-Jewish Christians. Only when a delegation from James comes to Antioch, does Peter withdraw. The fact that Peter at first actively participated in this table-communion proves that his views on this point were flexible. He acted contrary to the Jewish custom by joining non-Jews during their meals thereby showing his 'conformity to the practice of the Antiochene church'.[50]

Peter's lenient attitude changed, however, when a delegation from James (τινες ἀπὸ Ἰακώβου) arrived. Peter separated himself from his Gentile dinner-partners, because he feared the Law-abiding Jewish Christians (referred to by Paul as οἱ ἐκ περιτομῆς). Peter made the Jewish Christians in Antioch join him, together with Barnabas (2,13). In the perception of Paul, this was a matter of συνυποκρίνεσθαι, 'joining in the hypocrisy': according to him the Antiochene church's lenient attitude towards the Law was perfectly legitimate. Peter's action defied this legitimacy and confirmed the superiority of the Law-abiding Christians. For Paul this was very much a matter to be discussed: 'If you, though a Jew, live like a Gentile and not like a Jew, how can you compel the Gentiles to live like Jews?' (2,14). In Paul's view the Law had been superceded by Christ (2,18). It is clear that this incident pointed out '*the fundamental meaning and message of the gospel as Paul understood it*, namely, the constitution of all the Peoples of the world as the new Israel.'[51] It is indeed the 'one-ness of the new Israel' that was at stake for Paul in Antioch.[52] It was here that Paul decided in favour of this new Israel.

This incident in Antioch had great consequences. For Paul it meant that he could no longer remain in the church of Antioch, since he had taken a stand against the Jewish part of the congregation as well as against

---

[49] See E. Lohse, 'St. Peter's Apostleship in the Judgment of St. Paul, the Apostle to the Gentiles. An Exegetical Contribution to an Ecumenical Debate', *Gregorianum* 72 (1991), pp. 419-435; for a brief but instructive discussion of the NT evidence on Peter, see K.P. Donfried, s.v. 'Peter', *ABD* vol. 5, pp. 251-263.

[50] Taylor, *Antioch*, p. 131.

[51] D. Boyarin, *A Radical Jew. Paul and the Politics of Identity* (Contraversions 1; Berkeley [etc.]: University of California Press, 1994), p. 112 (italics Boyarin).

[52] Boyarin, *Radical Jew*, p. 112.

Barnabas.[53] Therefore the conflict signified the beginning of Paul's independent work as an apostle. Instead of being an ἀπόστολος τῆς ἐκκλησίας of the Antiochene community, Paul now became an independent ἀπόστολος Χριστοῦ. As such he must have left for Asia Minor in order to preach the gospel in its Law-free form.

The conflict presumably had its consequences for Paul's perception of the gospel too. Even more keenly than before Paul became the one to preach a Law-free gospel of Christ to which Greeks and Jews alike were invited. The fact that Paul considered the Mosaic Law to have been set aside by Christ, who had thus brought about a new freedom (cf. Gal 5,1), was absolutely fundamental to the rest of his ministry. This explains Paul's harsh reaction against Jewish Christians who wished to reintroduce the Law (e.g. Gal 5,1-12; Phil 3,2-4).

Also for the development of the Christian movement in general the incident in Antioch had great significance. A slumbering conflict had erupted and as a result Paul's own form of Christianity emerged: critical of the Law and open to Jews and Greeks alike. This 'new' movement broadened the spectrum at the other end of which was what we should probably identify as an early form of what later became known as the Ebionite Christians.[54] What started as a Jewish sect, now gradually turned into a Greek cult.[55] Between these two extremes there was a whole range of intermediate forms of the Christian movement. But it is questionable whether any other early Christian preacher would have been able to introduce the gospel to the heart of Greek culture as effectively as Paul did.

Paul's own view of his task as apostle to the Gentiles is stated explicitly only in his final letter, the epistle to the Romans. Before the relevant

---

[53] Taylor, *Antioch*, pp. 135-139; Taylor's position is summarised on p. 146: 'Paul's confrontation with Peter at Antioch left him isolated in that church and alienated him also from the Jerusalem church.'

[54] 'The Ebionites are described by the Fathers as Law-abiding Jews, who rejected Paul.' – W.L. Petersen, 'Ebionites, Gospel of the', *ABD* vol. 2, pp. 261-262; cf. also H.J. Schoeps, 'Ebionite Christianity', *JThS* 4 (1953), pp. 219-224; A.F.J. Klijn, G.J. Reinink, *Patristic Evidence for Jewish-Christian Sects* (SNT 36; Leiden: Brill, 1973), pp. 19-43. Irenaeus, *Adv. haer.* 1,26,2: *solo autem eo, quod est secundum Matthaeum, evangelio utuntur et apostolum Paulum recusant, apostatam eum legis dicentis.*

[55] On the distinction between sect and cult, cf. Stark, *Rise*, pp. 33-34. In Stark's words: sect movements 'occur by schism within a conventional religious body when persons desiring a more otherworldly version of the faith break away to "restore" the religion to a higher level of tension with its environment' whereas cult movements are 'new faiths': they 'always start small – someone has new religious ideas and begins to recruit others to the faith, or an alien religion is imported into a society where it then seeks recruits'.

passages can be discussed, a preliminary question has to be addressed, viz.: why does Paul speak of himself as 'apostle to the Gentiles' only in this letter? The answer must lie in the communicative situation of this particular letter. Paul wrote his letter to facilitate his visit to the congregation in Rome on his planned voyage to Spain (15,24.28). Thus he introduces himself by means of this letter in which he explicitly discusses the relationship of Greeks and Jews to Christ. It was this problem that had made Paul who he was, and it was a problem that was most certainly felt within the church of Rome.[56] By addressing precisely this fundamental topic in his letter, Paul was forced to write a more or less systematic essay in which he could present his solution to the problem. In this essay he could not entirely leave his own role out of consideration.

For Paul the Christ-event had brought about eschatological salvation for all who believe, Jews and Greeks alike (1,16-17). Paul establishes the fact that neither the Greeks nor the Jews have been able to achieve righteousness on their own: all are held by the power of sin (1,18-3,20). Salvation is brought about by Jesus Christ, and not by the deeds of men (cf. 3,21-26). Continuing on this theme, Paul gives the theological foundation for the universal meaning of the Christ-event. At the same time, Paul's theological reflections form a retrospective on his practice of preaching the gospel. Paul mentions his own task mainly in the opening and closing sections of the letter, as well as at the end of the instructive section (ch. 11). In the opening section Paul states that he has received his 'grace and his apostolate' εἰς ὑπακοὴν πίστεως ἐν πᾶσιν τοῖς ἔθνεσιν ὑπὲρ τοῦ ὀνόματος αὐτοῦ (= Χριστοῦ; 1,5). The goal of his apostolate is thus to promote 'obedience to faith' *among all* Gentiles, in the name of Christ. He repeats these words in 15,18, where he also describes his task as an apostle as one of leading the Gentiles to obedience, this time omitting the universalistic πᾶς. Here, it is said that Christ is the one who leads the Gentiles to obedience by means of Paul (δι' ἐμοῦ). For Paul, at the time he wrote this letter, being the apostle to the Gentiles meant trying to persuade Gentiles to obey the gospel which he thought had a universal significance. The same purpose is described in the secondary closing section of Romans, Rom 16,25-27.

---

[56] A.J.M. Wedderburn, *The Reasons for Romans* (Edinburgh: Clark, 1988), pp. 44-65, explains the situation of the congregation in Rome: This church would have originated in a Jewish group, which had taken a pagan course due to the edict of Claudius. At the time Paul wrote his letter, the Jewish inhabitants of Rome were returning, and thus a reconsideration of the social and theological structure of the congregation was necessary.

The fact that Paul describes the gospel as having consequences for Greek and Jew alike, i.e. as a universal event, implies that Paul's task as a messenger of the gospel had universal implications as well. This explains how Paul can speak of 'obedience to faith *among all* Gentiles' (1,5). Dunn correctly notes that Paul's use of ἐν 'probably also indicates Paul's recognition that "the obedience to faith" would be patchy so far as Gentile response was concerned.'[57] But all the same, the use of πᾶς does point to the universal meaning of the gospel.

That Paul considered himself as an 'apostle for the Gentiles', appears from 11,13: ὑμῖν δὲ λέγω τοῖς ἔθνεσιν. ἐφ ' ὅσον μὲν οὖν εἰμι ἐγὼ ἔθνων ἀπόστολος κτλ. In this passage Paul praises his mission as apostle to the Gentiles. He presents the rejection of Christ by the majority of Jews as resulting in the salvation of the world and the Gentiles, for it is as a result of this rejection that the Gentiles could share in the salvation brought about by God's intervention in history through Christ (11,11). In 11,12 Paul mentions his hope that the complete repentance of Israel would lead to even better things.[58] In vv. 15-16 he repeats his argument using different words. Israel's rejection had led to salvation for the world, and therefore their repentance must lead to something far better: the eschatological resurrection of the dead (ζωὴ ἐκ νεκρῶν). In vv. 13 and 14 Paul characterises the effect he hoped to achieve by his ministry: he hoped to provoke Israel's jealousy by converting the Gentiles. This jealousy would lead the Israelites to restore their relationship with God (cf. 10,19-21) so that they might come to faith.

Paul's description of the effect he hoped his apostolate would have should not be mistaken for the historical foundation of his ministry. In Rom 11,13-14 Paul describes his task as he interpreted it within the context of his communication to the church of Rome. This description is the result of theological reflection. It is not intended to present the programme that Paul had been carrying out throughout his active life as an apostle. Nevertheless, Paul does point out here that in his own eyes he has indeed

---

[57] J.D.G. Dunn, *Romans 1-8* (WBC; Dallas: Word Books, 1988), p. 18.

[58] In 11,12 πλήρωμα is either meant as the opposite of ἥττημα, indicating the fullness versus the reduction of the full number of elect (U. Wilckens, *Der Brief an die Römer* vol. 2 [EKK; Düsseldorf: Benziger; Neukirchen-Vluyn: Neukirchener, 1982], p. 243) or as an attempt by Paul to strive 'for effect (rather) than precision' (Dunn, *Romans 9-16*, p. 655). In both cases it implies a full conversion of Israel. The alternative, viz. to regard πλήρωμα as a description of the quality of obeying the gospel, is not convincing.

been sent to the Gentiles, that he keeps hoping for a full repentance of Israel, and that the gospel has universal significance.

Paul's hope for a full repentance of Israel is expressed in 11,25-32 as well. Here, he ends his discussion on the relationship between Israel and the Gentiles by a statement that summarises the problem. Part of Israel has 'hardened', i.e. refuses to accept Christ. According to Paul this situation will last until 'the fullness of the Gentiles has gone in' (v. 25). For the present enquiry it is very important to determine the meaning of these words. Does Paul speak of a universal conversion of Gentiles or does he refer to a limited elect group from among them?

Many interpreters of this passage take the words πλήρωμα ἐθνῶν as a reference to the full elect group from among the Gentiles. In apocalyptic writings the tradition is found of a fixed number of righteous who will be saved at God's final intervention in history.[59] The 'fullness of the Gentiles' would thus be this elect group taken from among the Gentiles. Yet an alternative interpretation appears more favourable. The contrast of the πλήρωμα ἐθνῶν and πᾶς Ἰσραήλ (v. 26) strongly supports the interpretation 'all of the Gentiles'. Furthermore, there are parallels in Paul's writing that also indicate this meaning. In 1 Cor 15,23-28 Paul expressly states the expectation that Christ will subdue every power on earth before handing over the kingship to God. This expectation is stated in cosmic terms. Such a description betrays the fact that Paul expected the *parousia* to be a cosmic, universal event, on which occasion the entire world would be involved. In the final words of the hymn in Phil 2,6-11 it is clearly stated that 'every knee will bend ..., and every tongue will confess that Jesus Christ is Lord.' It would be fully in accordance with these two lines to interpret the words πλήρωμα ἐθνῶν in a universalistic way as 'all Gentiles'.[60]

If the former observation is indeed correct, Paul implicitly mentions the view that is also found in e.g. Matt 28,19-20; Mark 13,10; 16,15, viz. of the need for a world-wide proclamation of the gospel. Yet contrary to the later texts mentioned, Paul does not present the proclamation of the gospel as a necessary precondition for the coming of the *parousia* (see esp. Mark 13,10) nor does he promote baptism in the 'name of the Father and the Son and the Holy Ghost' (Matt 28,19). Paul states no more than

---

[59] See *4 Ezra* 4,35-37; *2 Apoc. Bar.* 23,4; 30,2; 75,6; *Apoc. Abr.* 29,17; *1 Clem.* 2,4; 59,2; also Rev 6,11; 7,4; 14,1 – cf. Dunn, *Romans*, p. 680.

[60] Bauer, *Wörterbuch*, s.v. πλήρωμα gives a good example from Aelius Aristides: πλήρωμα ἐθνους, 'the entire people'.

the need for proclaiming the gospel, but it is only one step to move from Paul's position to Matthew's.

In Rom 15,15-16 Paul once again makes an important remark concerning his own task. The evidence from Romans 15 will be discussed at greater length in the next chapter. Here we should focus on Paul's attitude over against the Gentiles: Paul describes the churches he has founded as eschatological offerings to God. He depicts his activities as the apostle to the Gentiles in words taken from the context of the priestly service of a religious cult. Paul was appointed as apostle to the Gentiles by the grace of God 'to be a minister of Christ Jesus to the Gentiles in the priestly service of the gospel of God, so that the offering of the Gentiles may be acceptable, sanctified by the Holy Spirit.'[61] The point Paul is trying to make is the metaphorical description of the Gentiles as an eschatological offering to God. He describes his own activities by applying the language of priestly service to himself. This does not mean that Paul presents himself as a priest, but rather that he considers himself as the means through which the offering is made. Paul thus betrays his vision of his own task: he is the one through whom Christ directs his activities towards the Gentiles, and he is responsible for their conversion. This also appears from vv. 18-21: 'For I will not venture to speak of anything except what Christ has accomplished through me to win obedience from the Gentiles ... &c.' Again the aim of his activities is mentioned as 'obedience from the Gentiles' (cf. 1,5). He does so, wherever 'the name of Christ had not yet been mentioned' (15,20). Some interpreters take this evidence to conclude that Paul here refers to a missionary programme that may even have been a general apostolic plan, confirmed at the Apostolic Council.[62] This question will be dealt with in the next chapter; it may suffice here to note that in Rom 15,15-20 Paul does not describe the missionary programme he had been enacting ever since he started out as an independent envoy of

---

[61] On λειτουργέω Cranfield argues: 'That in the present verse it does have a sacral sense is strongly suggested by the context.' (*Romans*, vol. 2, p. 755). Cranfield seriously considers the option defended by Bengel and Barth, that Paul considers Jesus Christ as the priest, and therefore himself as a Levite, a *sacerdotis minister.*

[62] E.g. Wilckens, *Römer*, vol. 3, p. 120: 'Hinter Röm 15,19 steht eine heilsgeschichtliche Missionskonzeption; und man mag fragen, ob diese als solche nicht in den Verhandlungen des Apostelkonzils (vgl. Gal 2,9!) die Stunde ihrer Geburt – oder doch jedenfalls ihrer ersten offiziellen Markierung – und von daher gesamtkirchlich-ökumenische Geltung gewonnen hat. Wenn Paulus hier davon spricht, stellt er sich also gerade nicht mit seiner Mission exklusiv selbst heraus, sondern ordnet sie vielmehr in den übergreifenden Kontext einer universalen Evangeliums-Missions-Vorstellung ein, deren Geltung er als auch in Rom bekannt und anerkannt voraussetzen kann.'

Christ. Rather, he looks back on his work until that moment and describes the area he had been active in.[63]

For now we should conclude that, in his letter to the Romans, Paul describes his task as that of an 'apostle to the Gentiles' sent to proclaim the gospel where it has not yet been proclaimed. Paul is convinced of the gospel's universal implications, and regards himself as being commissioned to proclaim it to those who did not yet perceive it. Paul does not, however, give a neutral account of his ministry. Instead, he describes himself in this manner in an attempt to facilitate his access to the Roman church on his way to Spain. This means that Paul's presentation of his task in Romans is not a timeless description of his entire ministry, but it shows us the final stage of Paul's development. He describes his task as he had come to see it during the years of his independent ministry. Furthermore, Paul's description of the universal meaning of the gospel does entail a certain degree of reflection in Romans 15. Paul had obviously come to think about his own part in the play in which he was acting. In his perception the focus of his ministry was on preaching the gospel, just because he thought of the gospel as a divine imperative.[64] Obviously this was no new idea for Paul when he wrote to the Romans. The way in which he frased it was new, though. Thus in Paul's ministry we find the early stage of the development that would ultimately lead to the missionary command as it is given in Matthew 28.

Conclusion

For Paul's ministry his call was the first decisive *momentum*, but not the last. Only after the Antioch-incident did Paul come to develop a view of himself as the 'apostle to the Gentiles' who proclaimed a Law-free gospel on Jesus Christ and His importance for Jew and Greek alike.

As we have seen, Paul saw his task as that of a direct envoy of Christ, an ἀπόστολος Ἰησοῦ Χριστοῦ throughout the period of his independent ministry. Clearly, this implied a change over against his period as an Antiochene envoy with Barnabas. It is evident that there was no consensus on

---

[63] For this approach, see also L.J. Lietaert Peerbolte, 'Romans 15:14-29 and Paul's Missionary Agenda', in: P.W. van der Horst, M.J.J. Menken, G.C.M. van Oyen, J.F.M. Smit, *Persuasion and Dissuasion in Early Christianity, Ancient Judaism, and Hellenism* (CBET 33; Leuven, Paris, Dudley MA: Peeters, 2003).

[64] For the need to proclaim the gospel, see 1 Cor 9,16 (ἀνάγκη μοι ἐπίκειται). The need to obey is stated or assumed in Rom 1,5; 10,16; 15,18; 2 Cor 10,5; cf. the deutero-Pauline 2 Thess 1,8.

the exact meaning of the title 'apostle' by the time that Paul claimed it for himself. What is also clear is that by claiming this title Paul presented his task in direct continuity with the prophets of the Old Testament. They too saw themselves as 'sent' by God.

Paul's independent ministry was preceded by a period in which he functioned as an envoy from Antioch. Obviously, it is this period that taught Paul the unity of Jew and Greek in Christ. The Antioch incident described in Galatians 2 points out that Paul took a stand over against Barnabas, Peter, James and others in regard to the consequences he drew from this idea of a basic unity in Christ. In Paul's eyes this idea was more fundamental to the community of believers than the Mosaic Law. His departure from Antioch therefore did not mean that he broke with the gospel. Instead, it pointed him in a more extreme theological position that would make him start congregations of Jew and Greek alike, who would be 'one in Christ'.

CHAPTER SIX

PAUL THE MISSIONARY

In the previous chapters we have sought for the preconditions of Paul's ministry as well as its various stages and Paul's self-understanding. The one question that was left open is to be dealt with in this chapter: what exactly did Paul do? Did he go out and preach the gospel to all people he accidentally met? Did he carefully plan his operations to start a world-wide missionary movement? It is to these questions that this final chapter turns.

In looking for the answers to these questions several matters will have to be dealt with. First Paul's relation to 'his' churches will have to be scrutinised: how did Paul start them and how did he relate to them? Secondly, Paul's means of livelihood will be taken into account. As will be argued, Paul's manual labour enabled him to preach the gospel the way he did, and his choice to combine these activities was not an accidental one. Thirdly this chapter will deal with a very important phemomenon in Paul's ministry, namely his fellow workers. Since Paul did not work on his own, it is important to ask for their activities and the degree to which their activities were organised by Paul. After that section, we will search for the cities Paul visited, look for their characteristics and for the people Paul addressed. Finally, section five will search for the evidence of a theological programme Paul would have tried to fulfil, and it will argue that Paul's programmatic decision was his interpretation of his own task as that of a prophet.

Before setting out to achieve our purpose, one important preliminary observation on the use of the label 'mission' has to be made. According to Goodman's definition of proselytising mission the newly converted should not only change their views, but should also join the new social group whose views they come to share.[1] This view of proselytising mission puts the focus on the element of group-identity. Since Paul played an important part in the formation of early Christianity as an independent movement, his role must somehow have been decisive in the origin of Christian mission: this chapter will argue that it was Paul's attempt to

---

[1] See the discussion above, p. 5.

legitimate and define the identity of his churches as a group of believers in Christ that had a formative function within the Christian movement and its proselytising mission. This movement started out with Jesus' proclamation of God's kingdom, and continued with his followers' proclamation of the risen Christ. Paul's subsequent focus on the unity of the faithful in Christ not only legitimated that movement as a new social group,[2] but also redefined its proclamation of the gospel: faith in the gospel became tied up to participation in this new social group. It is at this stage that we find proselytising mission – new believers should not only change their views, but should also participate in the group that proclaimed their new faith. We will find that Paul not only tried to establish an ecclesiological definition of the new community 'in Christ', but that he thereby generated the phenomenon we know as proselytising Christian mission.

1. Paul and his Churches

a. Paul: Preacher and Founder of Christian Communities

It is evident that Paul founded new Christian communities. His letters testify to the fact that he did so at least in Philippi,[3] Thessalonica,[4] Athens,[5] Corinth,[6] Ephesus,[7] and a number of places in Galatia.[8] Yet how should this founding of communities be evaluated? Paul's letters unfortunately only reveal the fact *that* Paul stood at the basis of these congregations, whereas they are as good as silent on the question as to *how* he raised them. Did he purposely create a new community when he entered a new town? Or was the formation of a community an unforeseen result of his preaching of the gospel? The best way to find an answer is to take a closer look at those passages in which Paul explicitly describes his activities as a founder of congregations.

---

[2] The importance of this sociological dimension of Paul's ministry has rightly been argued by F. Watson, *Paul, Judaism and the Gentiles. A Sociological Approach* (SNTSMS 56; Cambridge [etc.]: Cambridge University Press, 1986); see his conclusions on pp. 177-181, and esp. p. 178: 'Paul's theoretical discussions of such themes as the law and works, grace and faith, election and promise, are thus to be regarded as *an attempt to letigimate the social reality of sectarian Gentile Christian communities in which the law was not observed.*'
[3] Phil 1,1; 1 Thess 2,2.
[4] Phil 4,16; 1 Thess 1,1.
[5] 1 Thess 3,1.
[6] 1 Cor 1,1; 2 Cor 1,1.
[7] 1 Cor 15,32; 16,8.
[8] 1 Cor 16,1; Gal 1,2.

A methodological observation should be made first. It concerns the access we have to the process of the formation of Christian congregations. In his 1994 monograph on Paul, M. Pesce argued that Paul's ministry should be reconstructed as having consisted of two stages.[9] The first stage would be the period in which Paul preached the gospel, and the second stage that in which he had to come to the aid of the newly formed congregations by admonishing them with his apostolic advice. According to Pesce, Paul's letters should all be placed within the second period of his ministry. For this reason they do not offer direct access to Paul's preaching of the gospel and the subsequent formation of the communities that resulted from this activity. Although the evidence from Paul's letters points out that these two stages cannot be separated by a clear line of division, Pesce's model does present us with a good explanation for the fact that Paul's letters should probably all be dated to the second half of his Christian existence. In Pesce's approach Paul's remarks on his founding of the various congregations are coloured by later developments. His letters were primarily intended to provide solutions to the problems that had appeared after his departure from the congregation(s) he wrote to. In writing to them, Paul looks back on their beginnings from the point of view that he had developed in the meantime.

Once we admit that Paul's letters give us only indirect evidence on the process of the formation of congregations, we should also recognise that they do contain a number of references that are important in this respect. The vocabulary Paul uses to describe the activities out of which the congregations had grown, is revealing on the way he views his task. It consists of the verbs εὐαγγελίζομαι and κηρύσσω, and the metaphors 'planting', 'having fruit', 'building', 'foundation', 'entrance', and the 'opening of a door'. But first of all, Paul's use of the word ἔργον as a description of his ministry is important.

On a number of occasions Paul refers to his ministry as an ἔργον. Thus he addresses the congregation of the Corinthians and identifies it as his ἔργον, the 'result of my work'[10] (1 Cor 9,1). When he recommends Timothy to the Corinthians, Paul describes him as one who fulfils the same task for the Lord as he, Paul, himself does: τὸ γὰρ ἔργον κυρίου ἐργάζεται ὡς κἀγώ (1 Cor 16,10). The genitive τοῦ κυρίου is probably a subjective genitive ('work by the Lord'), as it would also be in Phil

[9] M. Pesce, Le due fasi della predicazione di Paolo. Dall'evangelizzazione alla guida della communità (Studi biblici 22; Bologna: Edzioni dehoniane, 1994).
[10] Fee, First Corinthians, pp. 394-395.

2,30.[11] It is for this reason that Paul can speak of the Corinthian congregation as he does in 1 Cor 3,5-9: it is God himself who induces the growth,
who is the origin of the congregation.[12] Paul refers to the existence of the
congregation in Rom 14,20 as τὸ ἔργον τοῦ θεοῦ.

Paul's use of the noun ἔργον as a description for his preaching activities implies that he regarded what he did as a task imposed on him by
Christ or God. The fact that he can refer to the Corinthian congregation
as his ἔργον (1 Cor 9,1) and to the congregation of the Romans as the
ἔργον of God (Rom 14,20), shows that Paul was convinced that his activities were aimed at the formation of Christian congregations. But as soon
as this observation is made, one has to admit that Paul did not focus on
the formation of congregations as a goal in itself, but rather as part of the
proclamation of the gospel. The evidence is clear in this respect.

When referring to his preaching activities, Paul often uses the verb
εὐαγγελίζομαι. In his description of the goal of his call in Gal 1,16 Paul
mentions his task as εὐαγγελίζεσθαι αὐτὸν (sc. τὸν υἱὸν τοῦ θεοῦ) ἐν
τοῖς ἔθνεσιν. This means that in this important retrospect,[13] Paul focuses
on the preaching of the gospel as the main element in his ministry. Hence,
Paul refers to his first activities among the Galatians as εὐαγγελίζεσθαι:
Gal 1,8.9.11; 4,13. Also in the Judean rumour on Paul his activity is
described as εὐαγγελίζεσθαι (sc. τὴν πίστιν ἥν ποτε ἐπόρθει; Gal
1,23). The object of Paul's preaching is either defined as τὸ εὐαγγέλιον
(1,11), or τὴν πίστιν (1,23), or the verb is used in an absolute manner.
Paul's use of the verb in his letter to the Galatians corresponds to that in
his other letters. He will preach among the Romans (Rom 1,15), and he
states that he has preached where the name of Christ was still unknown
(Rom 15,20). Also in the Corinthian correspondence Paul describes his
activities as εὐαγγελίζομαι in an absolute manner (1 Cor 1,17; 9,16; 2
Cor 10,16), or with the gospel as its object (1 Cor 9,18; 15,1-2; 2 Cor
11,7 – 'the gospel of God'). Hence for Paul the character of his work can
be summarised as 'preaching the gospel'.

More or less as a synonym for this expression Paul uses the verb
κηρύσσω. Just as he 'preaches' the gospel (of God), Paul can describe
his task as 'proclaiming the gospel (of God)': 1 Thess 2,9; Gal 2,2. Also

---

[11] This appears e.g. from the terminology of συνεργοί for those who work together with
Paul: all συνεργοί – including Paul himself – are submitted to the one who is the true
origin of the ἔργον, viz. God. Cf. below, p. 231.
[12] See also Paul's use of ἔργον in 1 Cor 3,13-15.
[13] Cf. above, pp. 167-170.

κηρύσσω can be used in an absolute way (1 Cor 9,27; 15,11), but more frequently Paul uses the verb with Christ as the direct object: 1 Cor 1,23 (Χριστὸν ἐσταυρωμένον); 15,12 (Χριστὸς ... ἐκ νεκρῶν ἐγήγερται); 2 Cor 1,19 (ὁ τοῦ θεοῦ ... υἱὸς Ἰησοῦς Χριστός [sc. εἶναί]); 4,5 (Ἰησοῦν Χριστὸν κύριον); 11,4 (Ἰησοῦν).

The fact that Paul uses these two verbs to describe his activities reveals that for him the preaching of the gospel, the proclamation of the Christ event, was *the* central activity.[14]

Strangely enough there is only one passage in which Paul explicitly describes the task of the preacher. In Rom 9,30-11,36 Paul discusses the problem of the status of Israel. The difficulty he faces is expressed in 9,30-31: 'Gentiles, who did not strive for righteousness, have attained it, that is righteousness through faith; but Israel, who did strive for the righteousness that is based on the Law, did not succeed in fulfilling that Law.' In 10,3 Paul points out that the real problem is: '...being ignorant of the righteousness that comes from God, and seeking to establish their own, they (= Israel; LP) have not submitted to God's righteousness (i.e. Christ; LP).' Paul mentions the confession of Jesus as Lord and the faith in his resurrection from the dead as the basis for salvation (10,9). Then, he states that because of this one Lord there is no difference between Jew and Greek, a statement he stresses by a quotation from LXX Joel 3,5: 'everyone who calls on the name of the Lord shall be saved'. By quoting these words shortly after the mention of the confession of Jesus as Lord, Paul defines the κύριος mentioned in Joel as Christ, not God. He subsequently describes the necessary preconditions for calling on the name of the Lord (10,14-15): 'But how are they to call on one in whom they have not believed? And how are they to believe in one of whom they have never heard? And how are they to hear without someone to proclaim him (χωρὶς κηρύσσοντος)? And how are they to proclaim him (κηρύξωσιν) unless they are sent (ἐὰν μὴ ἀποσταλῶσιν)? As it is written "How beautiful are the feet of those who bring good news (τῶν εὐαγγελιζομένων τὰ ἀγαθά)".' This passage clearly identifies Paul's role as that of the preacher sent by God to proclaim Christ in order that the recipients of the proclamation may come to believe in Christ, and will thus be saved. The quotation from Isa 52,7[15] is part of

---

[14] In 2 Cor 5,11 and Gal 1,10 Paul uses the verb πείθω as a description of his preaching of the gospel. Apparently Paul did think of the preaching of the gospel as a need to convince people.

[15] The words are 'closer to the MT than to the LXX' – Cranfield, *Romans*, vol. 2, p. 525; see also Wilckens, *Römer*, vol. 2, pp. 228-229, who regards the words as 'ein freies Zitat'.

a chain of scriptural quotations,[16] and as such it testifies to Paul's understanding of his apostolic preaching activity through the focus of this
prophecy by Isaiah.[17] The two verses quoted above also point out that
Paul regarded his preaching activity, like that of his fellow Christian
preachers, as a necessary condition for the salvation of those who did not
yet know Christ. The remark that the preachers can only proclaim Christ
if they are *sent*, indicates that for Paul the activity of proclaiming the
gospel starts with God.[18] It is God who commissions the preachers, and
their preaching starts out as a 'mission': they are sent by God. According to Dunn, the link of Paul's view of himself as preacher with
ἀποστέλλω 'is not accidental': the preacher – whether labeled as κῆρυξ
or ἀπόστολος – is a 'spokesman for another, not as someone with his
own message auhorised by himself'.[19]

Although Paul's words in Rom 10,14-15 are highly influenced by the
rhetoric of the passage as a whole, they do reflect Paul's view of the task
of the preacher, including his own. Paul regarded it as his task to preach
the gospel to those who had not yet heard it, in order that they might be
saved. Furthermore, the words discussed indeed betray Paul's idea of
being sent by God to perform this specific task. These observations further stress the importance of the question of Paul's relationship to the
communities he founded. If Paul's preaching had the effect he hoped for,
and new Christians were 'born' (Phlm 10), they would form a community.
It is in regard to the process of founding these communities that Paul uses
the metaphors 'entrance', the 'opening of a door', 'planting', 'having fruit',
'foundation', and 'building'.

In the first letter to the Thessalonians Paul refers to his reception
among them: all believers in Macedonia and Achaia testify ὁποίαν
εἴσοδον ἔσχομεν πρὸς ὑμᾶς (1,9). Unfortunately, this description with
εἴσοδος gives us no evidence of how Paul saw his task among the Thessalonians. The word 'can mean either (1) a place through which one

---

[16] Paul quotes Isa 52,7; 53,1 and Ps 19,5 on the task of the preacher; subsequently he cites
Deut 32,21 and Isa 65,1.2 as a description of Israel's refusal to harken to the messenger
of the Lord. Cf. O. Michel, *Der Brief an die Römer* (KEK; Göttingen: Vandenhoeck&
Ruprecht, 14th ed., 1978), pp. 332-333.

[17] Thus Cranfield, *Romans*, vol. 2, p. 535: 'Paul does not refer directly to his own apostolic ministry or the preaching of other Christian evangelists, but by appealing to Isa
52.7 he both points to it indirectly and at the same time gives the scriptural attestation
of its true significance.'

[18] See Appendix I, nrs. 3-4.

[19] Dunn, *Romans 9-16*, p. 621. Dunn refers to 1 Cor 15,9-11; 2 Cor 4,5; 11,4; and Gal 2,2
to underline his observation.

enters or (2) the act of entering. The second can be extended to include "visit", and this seems to be the meaning of the same word in 2,1; that meaning is also possible here.'[20] The accent in Paul's use of the term is on the effect of his visit, which is presented in the sequel πῶς ἐπεστρέψατε κτλ.[21] By using the word 'entrance' Paul obviously does not refer to a fixed community into which he entered, but rather to the consequences of his coming to Thessalonica. What Paul presents here as these consequences is not so much the formation of a congregation, as the turning away from idols and the confessing of Jesus Christ.[22] The point Paul is making is that the reception of the gospel among the Thessalonians was exemplary among the Macedonians and the Achaians.[23]

A metaphor closely related to that of the 'entrance' is the 'opening of a door'. In 1 Cor 16,9 Paul mentions his positive expectations concerning the acceptance of the gospel in Ephesus by stating that 'a door has been opened for me'. Paul uses the same metaphor in 2 Cor 2,12, where he says that in Troas (the Troad?)[24] his preaching was successful: θύρας μοι ἀνεῳγμένης ἐν κυρίῳ κτλ. The same expression is used in a slightly different manner in Col 4,3 and Acts 14,27 where in both cases a genitive construction explains the object that the 'door' leads to (θύρα τοῦ λόγου, Col 4,3; θύρα πίστεως, Acts 14,27). Paul, however, uses the expression in an absolute manner, which raises the question of what the intended meaning may be. It is very likely that a literal explanation of how indeed doors were opened at the preaching of the gospel misses the point.[25] The

---

[20] *Translator's Handbook*, p. 14.

[21] Cf. *Translator's Handbook*, p. 14: 'However, the word for "what kind of", together with the rest of verses 9-10, suggests that Paul's deepest concern is neither with the fact of their entering Thessalonica, nor with anything special about the way in which they entered, nor even with the personal friendliness with which some of the Thessalonians welcomed them, but with the results of their visit, that is, with what happened as a consequence of their entering.'

[22] On the Gentiles, see ch. 5 above.

[23] C.A. Wanamaker, *The Epistle to the Thessalonians. A Commentary on the Greek Text* (NIC; Grand Rapids: Eerdmans; Exeter: Paternoster, 1990), p. 84: 'The way in which the Thessalonians had received and responded to the Pauline mission under very trying circumstances had probably become a piece of missionary propaganda used to demonstrate the truth of the Christian message to others.'

[24] For the question whether Paul refers to Troas or the Troad – the region surrounding the city –, see M.E. Thrall, *The Second Epistle to the Corinthians* vol. 1 (ICC; Edinburgh: Clark, 1994), p. 184-185. Thrall mentions a number of texts that indicate that ἡ Τρῳάς was used for the region rather than for the town.

[25] *Pace* Thrall, *2 Corinthians*, p. 184. The reference to Diogenes Laertius, *Vit. Phil.* VI,86 (Crates as a Θυρεπανοίκτης), advanced by Windisch and mentioned by a.o. Thrall (p. 184, n.390) misses the point.

expression is clearly metaphorically intended, and may for that reason be better explained by later rabbinical parallels in which 'to open a door' means 'to create an opportunity'.[26] This meaning, however, does not fit in with the context of 2 Cor 2,12. There, Paul describes how he came to Troas εἰς τὸ εὐαγγέλιον τοῦ Χριστοῦ: 'on behalf of the gospel of Christ' or 'to proclaim the gospel'. Whichever possibility is correct, the goal of the journey was evangelism.[27] If by the use of the metaphor 'the opening of a door' Paul refers to the possibility of success, it is not very likely that he would have left Troas (or the Troad) immediately after having seen such a possibility. Paul's remark in vv. 12-13 only makes sense if the meaning of the metaphor is, that Paul indeed had been successful. Paul clearly states that he left for Macedonia immediately *after* he had been successful at Troas, not *before* the proclamation of the gospel. Thus, the meaning of the metaphor 'a door being opened' in 2 Cor 2,12 is that it expresses the successful proclamation of the gospel.

This meaning fits very well within the context of 1 Cor 16,9. There Paul writes that he will wait before leaving Ephesus, because his proclamation of the gospel is achieving success, but there are many opponents. Unfortunately, the metaphor 'the opening of a door' says nothing on how Paul saw his work in relation to the founding of a community of Christians.

The three metaphors we have left – 'building', 'foundation', and 'planting' – again speak of the effect of the preaching of the gospel without expressing anything as to the method of the proclamation. It is remarkable that these metaphors are all used in two chapters: 1 Corinthians 3 and Romans 15. In his exposition in 1 Cor 1,10-3,23 Paul warns the Corinthians about the divisions in their congregation. The problem of the factions in Corinth is well known: there were apparently three different groups within the congregation appealing to Apollos, Paul, and Cephas.[28] Paul's argument in 1,10-3,23 is that none of these so-called leaders really means anything, only Christ. Paul depicts his own role in Corinth, together with that of Apollos, as only of relative importance (3,5-9). In this attempt to show the Corinthians that only God really matters, Paul uses the metaphor of planting, watering, and growing. 'I planted,

---

[26] Cf. Strack-Billerbeck, vol. 3, pp. 484-485.
[27] See Thrall, *2 Corinthians*, p. 183.
[28] The existence of a fourth group, the so-called 'Christ party' is debatable. In the present author's opinion, the conclusion to the argument as a whole (3,21-23) points out that there were but three parties: that of Apollos, that of Paul, and that of Cephas.

Apollos watered, but God gave the growth. So neither the one who plants nor the one who waters is anything, but only God who gives the growth' (3,6-7). This metaphor expresses the fact that human envoys of God all stand at the same level, whereas the only true origin of the Corinthians' faith is God himself. It has been noted that the Qumran community defined itself as an 'everlasting plantation'.[29] Yet this is no real parallel to the metaphor used by Paul, for in 1 Cor 3,5-9 the focus is not on the congregation as the plantation, but on the question as to who stands at the foundation of the congregation.

The use of this metaphor of planting and growing points out that for Paul it was God who did the real work. For Paul the foundation and growth of a congregation did not depend on his efforts, but on God. This view, however, does not give us any new information on how Paul saw his own task in relation to the founding of congregations. It does state that Paul was the one who started the congregation in Corinth, but remains silent on how he did it.

The same problem exists concerning the metaphor used in the passage after the one previously discussed: 1 Cor 3,10-17. Here, Paul states the same view but in other words.[30] It was he who had laid the foundation, and this foundation is the essential part of the building. Thus Paul presents his gospel of Jesus Christ as the starting-point for the community. He presents this in such a way that it becomes clear that Paul himself was responsible for the fact that this solid foundation had been laid. Yet again the metaphor does not inform us *how* Paul had done his work.

The metaphor of building is also used in Rom 15,20. Paul writes to the Romans about his travel plans (cf. below, pp. 244-254), and reveals something of his own view of his task. He mentions the fact that he does not want to bring the gospel where someone has been ahead of him, and does so by using the metaphor of building: 'Thus I make it my ambition to proclaim the good news, not where Christ has already been named, so that

---

[29] 1QS VIII,5; cf. 1QH XIV,15; XVI,6.20. The link with the Qumran community is suggested for instance by Conzelmann, *1 Korinther*, p. 99, n. 43, who immediately adds: 'Das Bild ist aber darüber hinaus allgemein jüdisch, s. Bill. I 720f., (zu Mt 3,10). Röm 11,16-24; Od Sal 38, 17ff.'

[30] H.W. Hollander, *1 Korintiërs I* (T&T; Kampen: Kok, 1996), p. 53-54, points out that the two metaphors of 'planting' and 'building' are often used side by side. He mentions Deut 20,5-6; Jer 1,10; 18,9; 24,6; Wis 49,7; Philo, *De Virt.* 29; *Leg. All.* 1,48 as examples. Furthermore, the metaphor of building was also used by Philo in *De Gig.* 30; *De Conf. Ling.*5; 87; *De Mut. Nom.* 211; and by Epictetus, *Diss.* II,15,8.

I do not build on someone else's foundation etc...' (v. 20). This again points out that Paul regarded his task to be the proclamation of the gospel, rather than to build the community resulting from this proclamation. Paul apparently saw himself as the 'architect' (1 Cor 3,10), the founder who laid the basis for others to continue his work.

Two more elements in Paul's relationship to the congregations he founded should be looked into: Paul's baptism of the house of Stephanas in Corinth, and the way in which Paul describes the effect of the newly founded congregations.

Two remarks in 1 Corinthians (1,16 and 16,15) indicate that Paul did indeed practice baptism, but only occasionally. In 1,16 Paul speaks of the fact that in Corinth he had baptised 'the house of Stephanas', but he hastens to add that he does not recall having baptised others as well. He then continues with the remark that Christ 'did not send me to baptise, but to preach the gospel' (οὐ γὰρ ἀπέστειλέν με Χριστὸς βαπτίζειν ἀλλὰ εὐαγγελίζειν; v. 17). From 16,15 we may infer that the baptism of the house of Stephanas was indeed the only baptism Paul performed as well as the first in this region.

The fact that Paul baptised the members of this house means that Paul did act like for instance Philip. Philip apparently preached the gospel and baptised the newly converted, and along with him it is likely that others practiced this combination of proclamation and baptism as well. Paul had apparently done the same thing, but for some reason stopped practising baptism.[31] The use of the aorist in 1 Cor 1,16 points out that Paul refers to one single event. Paul did indeed baptise the first house(hold) he converted, but subsequently left the baptising to others, perhaps even the members of that household.[32]

Since Paul obviously did not regard the practice of baptism as his main task, we should ask what effects he hoped to achieve by founding new communities. The answer may be deduced from the manner in which Paul speaks of the effect of the Christian life of 'his' communities. In 1 Thess 1,7-9 Paul praises the faith of the Thessalonian con-

---

[31] For Paul's views of baptism and baptising, see J.D.G. Dunn, *Baptism in the Holy Spirit. A Re-examination of the New Testament Teaching on the Gift of the Spirit in Relation to Pentacostalism Today* (Philadelphia: Westminster, 1970), pp. 103-151.

[32] Schrage, *1 Korinther*, p. 157: 'Jedoch scheint er selbst nur die ersten Glieder einer Gemeinde getauft zu haben, was zweifellos nicht nur für Korinth gilt. Wer anstelle des Apostels die Taufe in den Missionsgemeinden vollzogen hat, läßt sich nicht sagen. Man kann auf Silvanus und Timotheus raten, aber auch vermuten, daß der Ortsgemeinde selbst überlassen blieb, neue Glieder zu taufen.'

gregation, not merely in a literary appraisal, but as an example for all believers to follow. Their example was so good, that it should be followed by all who heard of it. Thus, the very existence of the Christian community of Thessalonica should contribute to the further spread of the gospel. It is very likely that here we meet one of the most important reasons why Paul founded communities: once they exist, they contribute to a further spread of the gospel. Furthermore, an additional reason is so very obvious that we could be tempted to forget it: no ancient personality would express his religion merely in private.[33] Religious observances were always embedded in the specific social context of a group.[34] Therefore, Paul's relationship with 'his' communities must also have been highly influenced by these two objectives: firstly, the believers were thought to be part of a larger community, the group of people 'in Christ', and secondly, Paul obviously had the wish that the prosperous Christian life of these communities would further enable the spread of the gospel.

b. The New Community in Christ

It appears that for Paul the most fitting description of this new identity was 'being in Christ', whereas the community as a whole was identified by him as an ἐκκλησία. These two characterisations betray much of Paul's view of the new congregations.[35]

It is by the words ἐν χριστῷ that Paul most often expresses the Christian character of a person or congregation.[36] This particular expression was used by Paul himself to signify the relationship of the individual

---

[33] The social embeddedness of ancient personalities is argued by e.g. Malina, Neyrey, *Portraits of Paul*, pp. 154-176, where the authors deal with ancient personalities as 'group oriented persons'. For a further analysis of the social character of first-century personality, see B.J. Malina, *The New Testament World. Insights from Cultural Anthropology* (Louisville: Westminster John Knox Press, 3rd rev. ed., 2001, ¹1981), pp. 58-80.

[34] A clear presentation of the influence of corporate thought on the early Christian movement is given by D.G. Powers, *Salvation through Participation. An Examination of the Notion of the Believers' Corporate Unity with Christ in Early Christian Soteriology* (CBET 29; Leuven: Peeters, 2001).

[35] For Paul's view of his communities, see A. Chister, 'The Pauline Communities', in: M. Bockmuehl, M.B. Thompson (eds.), *A Vision for the Church. Studies in Early Christian Ecclesiology* (FS Sweet; Edinburgh: Clark, 1997), pp. 105-120.

[36] Paul uses this expression 52 times: Rom 3,24; 6,11.23; 8,1.2.39; 9,1; 12,5; 15,17; 16,3.7.9.10; 1 Cor 1,2.4.30; 3,1; 4,10.15.17; 15,18.19.31; 16,24; 2 Cor 2,17; 3,14; 5,17.19; 12,2.19; Gal 1,22; 2,4.17; 3,14.26.28; Phil 1,1.13.26; 2,1.5; 3,3.14; 4,7.19.21; 1 Thess 2,14; 4,16; 5,18; Phlm 8.20.23.

believer, as well as that of the community as a whole, to the living Christ. As such it denotes a local, mystical area in which the believers live, governed by Christ.[37] If Paul is describing what was probably his own vision in 1 Cor 12,2 he addresses the vision to a 'man in Christ' (ἄνθρωπος ἐν χριστῷ). Similarly, the Christian congregations in Judea are mentioned as the ἐκκλησίαι ... ἐν Χριστῷ ['Ιησοῦ] (1 Thess 2,14; Gal 1,22). Paul describes the Christians as ἅγιοι ἐν Χριστῷ (Phil 1,1), ἡ ἐκκλησία τοῦ θεοῦ, κλητοὶ ἅγιοι (1 Cor 1,2). Paul has 'begotten' the Corinthians 'in Christ' (1 Cor 4,15), just as he can speak of the Christian slave Onesimus as a father of his son (Phlm 10). Paul sends a greeting to his fellow-worker 'in Christ', Urbanus (Rom 16,9; cf. v. 10), and speaks of the Christian identity of Andronicus and Junia (Junias?) as of 'being in Christ' (Rom 16,7). In his first letter to the Corinthians Paul stresses their identity as people 'in Christ': ὑμεῖς ἐστε ἐν Χριστῷ (1,30). In his polemic against the Corinthian pomposity, Paul argues that he could not address them as adults, but had to speak to them as 'infants in Christ' νήπιοι ἐν Χριστῷ (3,1; cf. the ironic remark in 4,10). At the end of the argument in cc. 1-4 of 1 Corinthians Paul underlines the fact that it is he who has led the Corinthians to their Christian state: ἐν γὰρ Χριστῷ 'Ιησοῦ διὰ τοῦ εὐαγγελίου ἐγὼ ὑμᾶς ἐγέννησα (4,15). The same terminology of 'being in Christ' is used in 1 Thess 4,16, when Paul describes how the Christians who have died will be raised by Christ. The words he uses here are οἱ νεκροὶ ἐν Χριστῷ.

Thus for Paul the present state of the Christians is 'in Christ'. This is a state of near salvation, for it is through Christ that they will eventually be saved at God's final intervention in history.[38] Because of the fact that the believers *now already* know that they will be saved, they can live as eschatological ἐκκλησία even though the final change has *not yet* been

---

[37] For this description of the formula ἐν χριστῷ, see A. Deissmann's classic *Die neutestamentliche Formel "in Christo Jesu"* (Marburg: Elwert, 1892), pp. 97-98. In his words: 'Die von Paulus unter Benutzung eines vorhandenen Profangebrauches geschaffene Formel ἐν χριστῷ 'Ιησοῦ charakterisiert das Verhältnis des Christen zu Jesus Christus als ein lokal aufzufassendes Sichbefinden in dem pneumatischen Christus.' Deissmann gives a thorough survey of the contemporary pagan Greek usage of the preposition ἐν with a personal singular as the background to Paul's formula. See also W.D. Davies, *Paul and Rabbinic Judaism. Some Rabbinic Elements in Pauline Theology* (London: SPCK, 1962 = 1948 with additional comments), esp. pp. 86-110.

[38] This eschatological state of bliss 'in Christ' reminds Paul of the first intervention of God in history, viz. the creation: cf. L.J. Lietaert Peerbolte, 'Man, Woman, and the Angels in 1 Cor 11:2-16', in: Gerard P. Luttikhuizen (ed.), *The Creation of Man and Woman. Interpretations of the Biblical Narratives in Jewish and Christian Traditions* (TBN 3; Leiden [etc.]: Brill, 2000), pp. 76-92, esp. pp. 76-80.

brought about. In this intermediary, eschatological state of being, the Christians are marked out by Paul as a new creation: ὥστε εἴ τις ἐν Χριστῷ, καινὴ κτίσις (2 Cor 5,17). Within this community the laws of death and sin have been defeated and the new, spiritual law of Christ has freed its members (Rom 8,2). This spiritual freedom is most markedly present in Paul's idea that there is no longer any difference in status between the various members of the community: 'there is no longer Jew or Greek, there is no longer male and female; πάντες γὰρ ὑμεῖς εἰς ἐστε ἐν Χριστῷ Ἰησοῦ' (Gal 3,28; cf. 5,6).

Owing to the fact that through Christ God himself builds the entire community of those who are 'in Christ', Paul can say that for the Christians the love of God in Christ surpasses all powers: 'For I am convinced that neither death, nor life, nor angels, nor rulers, nor things present, nor things to come, nor powers, nor heights, nor depth, nor anything else in all creation, will be able to separate us from the love of God in Christ Jesus our Lord' (ἀπὸ τῆς ἀγάπης τοῦ θεοῦ τῆς ἐν Χριστῷ Ἰησοῦ τῷ κυρίῳ ἡμῶν – Rom 8,38-39). In his instruction to the Thessalonians Paul describes the ideal spiritual life of the congregation: 'Rejoice always, pray without ceasing, give thanks in all circumstances: for this is the will of God in Christ Jesus for you' (τοῦτο γὰρ τὸ θέλημα θεοῦ ἐν Χριστῷ Ἰησοῦ εἰς ὑμᾶς – 1 Thess 5,16-18). Paul thus describes the community that has grown out of the confession of Jesus Christ as one in which God, through Christ, reigns, or at least, should reign.

There are two passages in which Paul explicitly contrasts the present state of being 'in Christ' with the future state of being 'with Christ/the Lord'. Christ, for Paul, is the heavenly Lord whose power builds up the community that Paul has founded. Therefore, the Christians are now ἐν Χριστῷ. But at the *parousia* this will change. They will be united with the Lord and will therefore live *with* him: σὺν χριστῷ/κυρίῳ. The most evident expression of this thought is found in 1 Thess 4,17. In the previous verses Paul describes the events at the end and now he adds that, after the dead in Christ will have been resurrected and the living transformed, 'we will be with the Lord forever' (οὕτως πάντοτε σὺν κυρίῳ ἐσόμεθα). The expression σὺν Χριστῷ εἶναι is used in Phil 1,23, where Paul states that he longs for his death, so that he may be with Christ. The purport of this remark is most likely the idea that Paul hopes to be resurrected in heaven as an individual, righteous martyr immediately after his death.[39]

---

[39] Holleman, *Resurrection and Parousia*, pp. 194-195.

The two passages quoted point out, that for Paul there is a clear change of perspective: *now* the saints are 'in Christ', and *then* they will be 'with Christ'.

In being 'in Christ' the community should cling to the correct, apostolic instruction given by Paul, for in Paul's eyes it is through this instruction that genuine Christian life is accomplished (cf. 1 Cor 4,17: τὰς ὁδοὺς μου τὰς ἐν Χριστῷ ['Ιησοῦ]). This observation is important, for it points out the responsibility Paul thought he held over against the congregations he had founded.

Nevertheless, this observation does not imply that the apostle's responsibility is the only factor in the life of the congregation. The main impulse should come not from man, but from the Spirit. For Paul, life 'in Christ' is defined by unity with the Spirit. The two ideas – living 'in Christ' and 'in the Spirit' – are closely related. As R. Bultmann put it: '...das πνεῦμα (ist) die eschatologische Gabe (...), die ἀπαρχή (Rm 8,23), der ἀρραβών (2 Kr 1,22; 5,5). Denn damit ist ja gesagt, daß das Leben des Glaubenden bestimmt ist durch die Zukunft, die für ihn Ursprung und Kraft wie Norm ist. (...) Wie die eschatologische Existenz ein εἶναι ἐν Χριστῷ genannt werden kann (...), so ein εἶναι ἐν πνεύματι (Rm 8,9), und ohne Unterschied des Sinnes wechseln damit die Wendungen πνεῦμα Χριστοῦ ἔχειν, Χριστὸς ἐν ὑμῖν (V.9f.).'[40] Inspired by the Spirit, the Christian congregation lives as the eschatological ἐκκλησία. Within this ἐκκλησία the Spirit rules those who are 'justified in the name of the Lord Jesus Christ and in the Spirit of our God' (1 Cor 6,11). Paul envisages the gift of the Spirit as such a corporate reality that he can say to the Corinthians (1 Cor 3,16): 'Do you not know that you (pl.) are God's temple and that God's Spirit dwells in you (pl.)?' But at the same time the various *charismata* that define life within the congregation all come from the same Spirit: '...there are varieties of gifts, but the same Spirit' (1 Cor 12,4: τὸ δε αὐτὸ πνεῦμα).

Life according to the Spirit coincides with life according to the will of God. In Rom 5,5 Paul gives but one solid foundation for steadfastness in one's life as a Christian: '... God's love has been poured into our hearts through the Holy Spirit that has been given to us (διὰ πνεύματος ἁγίου τοῦ δοθέντος ἡμῖν)'. The effect of the gift of the Spirit is mentioned in 8,2: 'the law of the Spirit of life in Christ Jesus has set you free from the law of sin and of death.' Because of this, those 'in Christ' do not live

---

[40] Bultmann, *Theologie*, pp. 336-337.

'according to the flesh, but according to the Spirit' (8,4; cf. vv. 9-27). Time and again Paul mentions the Spirit as the fundamental power that inspires the Christian congregation (cf. e.g. also Gal 3,5.14; 4,6; 5,5).

The local congregation in which the Christians live together 'in Christ' is described by Paul as ἐκκλησία.[41] K. Berger has shown that Paul used the word in more or less the same way as it was used by Hellenistic-Jewish groups.[42] According to him, the word later developed into the favourite definition of the way in which the Christian movement as a whole understood itself, especially because Jesus himself had founded the *qahal* or *ekklesia* of God within Israel.[43] H. Merklein has argued that the development went the other way round: the congregation in Jerusalem would have understood itself, and the Christian movement in general, as the ἐκκλησία τοῦ θεοῦ.[44] Paul then introduced a new understanding of the term by also applying it to local congregations. He recognised the local communities as independent ἐκκλησίαι that formed part of the larger, general ἐκκλησία. Although Berger's interpretation appears to reflect a natural development, Merklein has a very strong argument in Paul's description of the period in which he persecuted 'the Church of God' (Gal 1,13; Phil 3,6). In these instances Paul clearly uses the term ἐκκλησία in a general way, referring not to one specific local community but to the Christian movement in general. This proves that already quite early, the movement as a whole was known and understood as 'the gathering of God'.

Paul's understanding of the Christian communities as ἐκκλησίαι is therefore based on a perception of the early Christian movement as held by others in the movement as well. The large number of Hellenistic sources mentioned by Berger in which the word ἐκκλησία is used, clearly points out that the term was a common word for a gathering at the instigation of a king or his delegate. In Berger's analysis there is a close connection between the gathering of the faithful in the ἐκκλησία, and

---

[41] Paul uses the word ἐκκλησία 42 times. It is evident that for him a congregation of Christians is to be identified as an ἐκκλησία: Rom 16,1.4.5.23; 1 Cor 1,2; 4,17; 6,4; 7,17; 10,32; 11,16.18.22; 12,28; 14,4.5.12.19.23.28.33.34.35; 15,9; 16,1.19; 2 Cor 1,1; 8,1.18.19.23.24; 11,8.28; 12,13; Gal 1,2.13.22; Phil 3,6; 4,15; 1 Thess 1,1; 2,14; Phlm 2.

[42] K. Berger, 'Volksversammlung und Gemeinde Gottes: zu den Anfängen der christlichen Verwendung von "Ekklesia"', *ZTK* 73 (1976), pp. 167-207.

[43] Berger, 'Volksversammlung', p. 187-201. Esp. p. 198: 'Die Auffassung ist ohne Zweifel zunächst, daß durch Jesus der qahal bzw. die Ekklesia Gottes begründet ist, und zwar *in* Israel.'

[44] Merklein, 'Ekklesia Gottes', pp. 48-70.

their future gathering in the βασιλεία.[45] If this is correct, the fact that the early Christian movement defined itself as the ἐκκλησία τοῦ θεοῦ is exemplary of its eschatological self-understanding. But even if Berger is wrong, and there is no connection between the two terms, it is clear that the use of ἐκκλησία as a designation for the Christian movement betrays a strong eschatological awareness: in Paul's words the gathering of the faithful is the gathering of the κλητοὶ ἅγιοι (Rom 1,6; 1 Cor 1,2; cf. 1 Cor 1,26).[46]

In summa, Paul sees the Christian congregation – whether local or general – as the eschatological ἐκκλησία inspired by the Spirit of God. Within this community the Spirit rules as the 'first instalment' (2 Cor 1,22), the promise of the final sanctification that will be brought about at the *parousia*. But did Paul regard the Christian congregation in this manner from the outset of his ministry or did he arrive at this view at a later stage? Unfortunately our answer can only be tentative since we have no direct proof from the period preceding the writing of Paul's letters. Yet the fact that Paul refers to the 'Church of God' as the object of his persecution (cf. above) does indicate that the Christian movement understood itself to be an eschatological gathering quite early. It is indeed very likely that the earliest movement saw itself as the eschatological קהל יהוה, and that Paul accepted this view applying it to the local communities in the way reconstructed by Merklein.[47]

Paul's view of this 'Church of God' had great social consequences: according to him, God himself had included the Gentiles in this group. It was precisely this topic that caused the split between Paul and Barnabas in Antioch. At the incident after which their ways parted, Paul stood up in favour of the unity of the community 'in Christ' (Gal 2,11). Here, Paul argued from the standpoint that there is no distinction between Jew and Gentile in Christ because the Law had been set aside by Christ (cf. 2,15-21). The social consequences of the gospel are named explicitly in

---

[45] Berger, 'Volksversammlung', pp. 201-207; esp. p. 204: 'Ekklesia und Basileia treten daher erst da zeitlich, nicht aber in ihrer inneren Zuordnung, auseinander, wo die Ekklesia Gottes aufgrund des Heilswerkens Jesu schon bestehen kann – oder auch umgekehrt: Wenn man davon ausgehen kann, daß im hellenistischen Judenchristentum Ekklesia Gottes eine von jüdischen Gemeinden übernommene Bezeichnung ist (also nie die erst zukünftige Versammlung bezeichnete), dann treten Ekklesia und Basileia deshalb auseinander, weil die Basileia eine erst zukünftige Größe ist.'

[46] In Berger's view this is already a 'Gruppenbezeichnung' – 'Volksversammlung', p. 190.

[47] Cf. Merklein, 'Ekklesia Gottes'. For the Hebrew קהל or the Aramaic קהלא as the most probable background to the terminology of ἐκκλησία, cf. K.L. Schmidt in: *ThWNT*, vol. 3, pp. 502-539, esp. pp. 505-512.

Gal 3,28 (cf. 5,6; Rom 10,12; 1 Cor 12,13),[48] where Paul mentions three opposing pairs that have been overcome 'in Christ': Jew and Greek, slave and free man, and male and female. In Rom 10,12 Paul limits himself to the first pair of these three, and in 1 Cor 12,13 he mentions the first two pairs. According to H.-D. Betz, Gal 3,28 defines 'the religious, cultural, and social consequences of the Christian baptismal initiation'.[49] All differences between the baptised become irrelevant, since the unity in Christ is all that matters.[50] It seems that Paul in this respect was highly influenced by Cynic-Stoic thoughts.[51]

The unity of the Christian congregation, established through baptism, is also the subject of 1 Cor 12,12-27, where Paul uses the metaphor of the 'body of Christ'.[52] This metaphor is used to express the oneness of the body and the multipicity of its parts. In v. 13 Paul states that 'in one Spirit we have all been baptised into one body'. It is only in v. 27 that Paul uses the expression σῶμα Χριστοῦ. Since Paul uses this metaphor only on this single occasion, it is impossible to state that Paul saw 'the church' as 'the body of Christ'. Apparently Paul thought of this metaphor as a fitting way to express the unity of the members of the Christian congregation in Corinth.[53]

Paul's defence of the unity of the believers in Christ established a new kind of Israel and raised the need to rethink the relationship of this group to the Israel that rejected Christ. Seen from this perspective, it is remarkable that Paul mentions the relationship with Israel in only two of his letters: Galatians and Romans. Here he points out, between the lines, that

---

[48] Cf. Betz, *Galatians*, pp. 189-201; F.G. Downing, *Cynics, Paul and the Pauline Churches. Cynics and Christian Origins II* (London, New York: Routledge, 1998), p. 278, speaks of Gal 3,28 as a 'very Cynic-sounding baptismal slogan.'

[49] Betz, *Galatians*, p. 189. Following Windisch's theory, Betz considers the phrase οὔτε Ἰουδαῖος οὔτε Ἕλλην to have its origin in hellenistic Jewish mission (*Galatians*, p. 191).

[50] According to Betz, *Galatians*, pp. 198-201, the background of the distinction between ἄρσεν καὶ θῆλυ should be sought in the myth of the androgynous, primordial man.

[51] See Downing, *Cynics, Paul and the Pauline Churches*, pp. 1-25, and Engberg-Pedersen, *Paul and the Stoics*, passim, who convincingly argues that Paul's pattern of thought was thoroughly influenced by the Stoic system.

[52] In 1 Cor 6,15 Paul also seems to point to such a metaphor, but there he does not explicitly use it. Furthermore, the focus in 6,15 is rather different from that in 12,12-27 – cf. Fee, *First Corinthians*, p. 258: 'This usage, however, moves in a completely different direction from that in 12:12-26, where the "body" refers to the church, and the concern is with the relationship of the "members" to one another. Here the concern is with one's relationship to the Lord himself.'

[53] The background to the metaphor is unclear. Perhaps the eucharistic language of 10, 16-17 and 11,23-29 led Paul to use this metaphor.

for him the Christian movement should be interpreted as a true or spiritual Israel (Rom 9,6; 11,25-26; Ἰσραὴλ τοῦ θεοῦ = καινὴ κτίσις – Gal 6,15-16; cf. 1 Cor 10,18).

The existence of the community of Qumran proves that another minority within Judaism also regarded itself as the true faithful. It will not be far from the truth to state that the early Christian movement started as a similar minority group to the Qumran community. This group performed the cultic rituals in a much stricter way than mainstream Judaism did in the temple of Jerusalem, and thus understood itself to be the eschatological remnant of the chosen people, the true Israel.[54] The Christian movement focused on the Christ event which was not accepted by the majority of Judaism. It is a natural form of self-justification that this movement came to think of itself as the truly faithful part of Israel. At a later stage in the development the new group of Christians came to be dominated by the presence of Gentiles. But at the time Paul was writing his letters this was not yet the case. For him the Christian movement broke up the boundaries of Judaism, but did not begin a new religion. The new community was a new form of Israel, in direct continuity with that which had preceded it, divided from the past by the death and resurrection of Christ, and opened up for the Gentiles by God himself.

Notwithstanding Paul's active part in defining the new, Christian community, he was not interested in the formation of this new group as a goal in itself. It was the proclamation of the gospel, the Christ event, that really mattered to Paul.[55] The congregations he founded were the natural result of the fact that a group of people had come to believe in the gospel, and they were a means of facilitating its further spread.[56] The eschatological core of their faith meant that these communities were waiting for

---

[54] This phrase does not imply that this 'mainstream Judaism' was a single group that held the same views and shared the same rituals. It merely aims at comparing the minority with the majority.

[55] This is also the conclusion of D.N. Howell, jr., 'Mission in Paul's Epistles: Genesis, Pattern, and Dynamics', in: W.J. Larkin jr., J.F. Williams (eds.), *Mission in the New Testament. An Evangelical Approach* (ASMS 27; Maryknoll: Orbis, 1998), pp. 63-91, who on p. 91 states: 'The essential core of the Pauline mission, however, is not found in its genesis, strategic pattern, or underlying dynamics. Paul's self-understanding as God's apostle is as one "set apart for the gospel of God" (Rom. 1:1). It is the *message* – the gospel of God – that defines and determines the man and his mission.'

[56] P. Bowers has argued that Paul's founding of communities should not be seen as a means for further spread of the gospel, but unfortunately Bowers fails to identify the nature of both Paul's mission and the missionary component in the existence of the Christian communities. He argues that the Pauline congregations were not missionary in character since they were not directed outwardly, but wrongly assumes that Paul's

the *parousia* so that the faithful might be united with the Lord. But sooner or later it became apparent that the *parousia* was being delayed and the congregations had to adapt to a long-term and independent stay in this aeon. It was during this process of adjustment that Paul was asked to admonish the congregations he had founded. This brought a more pastoral touch to his relationship with 'his' congregations.[57]

In Paul's perception of the Christian movement the focus is on the idea that Christians were one in Christ and formed a community prefiguring the New Creation. Paul thus raised communities that were to form an image of the eschatological newness of life, but this was not the prime goal of his work. His prime goal was the proclamation of the gospel and the communities he founded were a necessary means to achieve that goal.

2. Paul's Independence – Means of Livelihood

Now that it has been established how Paul regarded the Christian movement and his own task in regard to the spread of the gospel, we should ask more specifically how he performed this task. The first part of the answer is to be sought in Paul's economic independence from the congregations that resulted from his preaching, and the second in his relationship with his co-workers.

The contribution of Paul's congregations to the further spread of the gospel can be witnessed in the support they gave to Paul on a number of occasions. In two passages in his letters Paul explicitly speaks of this kind of assistance. In Phil 4,15-16 Paul mentions his support by the Philippians during his stay in Thessalonica, and in 2 Cor 11,7-11 Paul speaks of 'other churches' that had been supporting him when he was in Corinth. The terminology Paul uses in 2 Cor 11,8 is rather strong:

---

missionary approach did consist of such an outward attitude – P. Bowers, 'Church and Mission in Paul', *JSNT* 44 (1991), pp. 89-11.

[57] In Pesce's view this pastoral touch to the relationship between Paul and his churches is to be identified as the apostolic responsibility Paul held towards these congregations. It even leads Pesce to deny the occasional character of Paul's letters – cf. Pesce, *Due fasi*, e.g. p. 12. Pesce here wrongly assumes that the gospel Paul preached already contained instructions for the existence of the Christian community: 'Anzitutto, la guida delle comunità consiste nel sorvegliare che la vita cristiana si svolga secondo il progetto impostato con l'evangelizzazione e la fondazione delle comunità e perciò le risposte dell'apostolo non costruiscono *ex novo* e tanto meno a caso, ma si richiamano sempre ai principi fondamentali del vangelo, alle fondamentali norme di vita etica, comunitaria e liturgica che egli ha lasciato alla comunità, a quei fondamentali orientamenti per la vita cristiana che egli sempre consegna ai neoconvertiti come bussola per la vita.'

ἐσύλησα, 'robbed', and ὀψώνιον, 'payment'. Apparently Paul confronts the Corinthians with a strong reproach: he could have been paid by them, but instead he took money from other congregations. The plural 'other congregations' (ἄλλας ἐκκλησίας) points out that the support did not come from just one community, but from a number of them. In Phil 4,15-16 Paul refers to the fact that 'in the early days of the preaching of the gospel' (ἐν ἀρχῇ τοῦ εὐαγγελίου) no congregation supported him other than that of the Philippians. Since 2 Cor 11,9 mentions the 'brothers from Macedonia', it is certain that the church of Philippi supported Paul both during his stay in Thessalonica (Phil 4,15), and while he was in Corinth (2 Cor 11,8-9). The plural in 2 Cor 11,8 may also point to the congregation of Thessalonica supporting Paul in Corinth together with the Philippians, but this is not certain.

It thus appears that Paul sometimes received support from congregations he had previously founded. This support was surely intended to facilitate Paul's preaching the gospel. This is an important observation that should not be overlooked: apparently Paul did not accept money from the congregation he was in the process of founding, but he did receive occasional support from churches he had already formed. The money Paul took was therefore intended not as a favour in return for his preaching of the gospel, but as a contribution to its further spread. Paul's accepting of support was therefore missionary in character in so far as it aimed at the further spread of the gospel. Apart from accepting money from congregations he had previously founded, it appears that Paul was also incidentally supported by wealthy individuals. Acts 16,14-15 suggests that Lydia from Thyatira sustained Paul during his stay in Neapolis, and from 18,1-3 it appears that Prisca and Aquila did the same.

The support given by congregations or wealthy acquaintances did not, however, provide for all Paul's needs. Evidence shows that Paul made his own living by working with his hands, and that he barely succeeded at that: in 1 Cor 4,11-12, for instance, Paul mentions his manual labour in line with a description of his hunger and thirst, thereby pointing out the difficult circumstances in which he had to live.[58]

In an article published in 1974 G. Theissen argued that two types of 'missionaries' existed in the early Christian movement: wandering charismatics and organisers of communities.[59] The first type is presented by

---

[58] See also e.g. 2 Cor 6,5; 11,27; Phil 4,12. Rhetorical as these passages may be, there must be some truth in their description of the hardships Paul had to endure.

[59] Theissen, 'Legitimation und Lebensunterhalt'.

Theissen as a charismatic, ascetic missionary, preaching the coming of the Kingdom of God and acting within the Palestinian context. He presents the second type as the missionary who acts within the Graeco-Roman context, planning a missionary route and preaching the Christian gospel. According to Theissen Paul and Barnabas should be identified as examples of this second type.[60] And also in his ministry without Barnabas, Paul would have worked by consciously planning his attempts to found new congregations.[61]

Theissen's article is important for a number of reasons. Firstly, he appears to make an illustrative differentiation between the two types of early Christian preachers. And secondly, the way in which Theissen defines Paul as an example of the second type of 'missionary' points out that for him Romans 15 is a programmatic description of Paul's method. Both of these points are worth further consideration. The interpretation of Romans 15 will be considered below. Here we will deal with the first point.

The distinction between wandering charismatics and organisers of communities offers a helpful characterisation. Theissen describes the first type as heralds of the kingdom of God who preach the ultimate intervention of God in history in a 'quietist' manner.[62] These preachers depend for their food and drink upon the gifts they receive from the people who welcome them. According to Theissen this type of preacher was 'free' in the Cynic way: the true wise man was free from the care for his own life and could therefore act as the true, pious envoy of the god (cf. e.g. Epictetus, *Diss.* III,22,46-48).[63] These preachers could not regard Paul as free, since he supported his preaching by his own manual labour. This is one of the reasons that Theissen regards Paul as a preacher of a different type, namely as an organiser of congregations.

---

[60] Theissen, 'Legitimation und Lebensunterhalt', p. 200 [209]: 'Protagonisten der hellenistischen Mission aber wurden Barnabas und Paulus. Sie begannen mit einer planmäßigen Mission hellenistischer Mittelmeerstädte.'
[61] Theissen, 'Legitimation und Lebensunterhalt', p. 204-205 [213-214]: 'Paulus vertritt damit einen Typus Missionars, der sich als zielstrebiger 'Gemeindeorganisator' charakterisieren läßt, der Neuland gewinnen will, vom Judentum getrennte selbständige Gruppen gründet, anstatt schon bestehende Sympathisantengruppen 'abzugrasen'. Er hat sich vorgenommen, so die ganze 'Welt' bis Spanien hin zu missionieren. Alle Überlegungen sind diesem großen Werk untergeordnet.' Theissen clearly bases his view of Paul on his interpretation of Romans 15. For this, see the discussion of that chapter below, pp. 245-254.
[62] Theissen, 'Legitimation und Lebensunterhalt', p. 194 [203], characterises the Jesus movement as the quietistic wing of a movement of messianic prophets.
[63] Theissen, 'Legitimation und Lebensunterhalt', p. 208 [217].

It will be argued below that Paul did not work on the basis of a well-developed missionary programme as much as Theissen believes him to do. And it is doubtful whether Paul should be identified primarily as an 'organiser of congregations'. But nevertheless Theissen's distinction is helpful: it stresses the fact that Paul did not proclaim the gospel at random, but helped to form local communities that would have to contribute to the further spread of the gospel.

The fact that Paul had to defend himself against the reproach of not being free becomes clear from 1 Cor 9,1-23. In this pericope Paul defends himself against a criticism by at least part of the Corinthian congregation. He argues that the way in which he preaches the gospel shows that he is free through the gospel. Paul could lean on the Corinthian congregation for his livelihood, but he refused to do so (vv. 6.13-15). In this respect Paul argues that it is he who is free, since it is by his own free choice that he works (v. 19). In his argument Paul makes some important statements on the nature of his ministry. He mentions the fact that the preaching of the gospel was not just some pastime for him but sheer necessity: 'an obligation is laid on me, and woe to me if I do not proclaim the gospel' (v. 16). For Paul the proclamation of the gospel was apparently an obligation that came forth from his call – he *had* to proclaim the good news.[64] Having said this, Paul turns to his method: nothing should prevent him from spreading the gospel. 'We endure anything rather than put an obstacle in the way of the gospel of Christ' (v. 12). Thus Paul proclaims the gospel 'free of charge' (v. 18) in order to ease its spread.

It is by way of illustration that Paul subsequently states that he has become 'as a Jew' for the Jews, and like one without the Law for those without the Law (vv. 19-23). His proclamation of the gospel did obviously not aim exclusively at Gentiles, but also at Jews. Hence the remark in Gal 2,7 on the 'gospel for the uncircumcised' should be interpreted as reflecting the *prime* aim of his proclamation of the gospel, not the *only*.

Apart from this, the vv. 19-23 point out that Paul adapted himself to his audience. Among Jews he acted 'as a Jew' and among pagans 'as a pagan'. There can be no other reason for Paul to act in this manner than to facilitate the acceptance of the gospel. Acting as a pagan before a Jewish audience would create an enormous obstacle for the success of the gospel, and so would the reverse. It is this that Paul wanted to avoid at all costs (v. 12!).

---

[64] For the formulation ἀνάγκη μοι ἐπίκειται see Homer, *Illiad* VI,458; *Sib. Or.* III,572.

From the pericope 1 Cor 9,19-23 a number of important observations can thus be derived: Paul regarded the proclamation of the gospel as an obligation imposed on him by his call; he adapted himself to the situation in which he proclaimed it, acting like a Jew among Jews and like a pagan among pagans; and, finally, Paul took care of his own livelihood.[65]

Regarding the nature of Paul's manual labour his letters are silent. The Book of Acts, however, does give us some information. Acts 18, 1-3 explicitly mentions that Paul worked together with Priscilla and Aquila, since they were all 'tentmakers' (σκηνοποιοί). The passage obviously contains elements that were taken from earlier tradition – the edict of Claudius that 'all Jews should leave Rome' and the fact that Priscilla, Aquila, and Paul shared the same profession. As has been argued above, the report in 18,2 is trustworthy in that such an expulsion from Rome did indeed take place.[66] Paul's greeting of Prisca (= Priscilla) and Aquila in Rom 16,3 points out he knew these two people and that they were Jews who then lived in Rome. Therefore the report that they had come to Corinth on account of the expulsion should be considered reliable. The same observation should be made concerning their profession: 18,3 is the only time that Paul is mentioned as a σκηνοποιός, and this fact has no implications at all for the redaction of Acts.

In the early church Paul's occupation was evidently undisputed. John Chrysostom for instance refers to Paul as 'that σκηνοποιός, the teacher of the world'.[67] The nature of this occupation, however, is not undisputed. For a long time scholars have thought that Paul worked with linen, to produce tents.[68] In his contribution to Kittel's *ThWNT*, however, W. Michaelis

---

[65] In 1 Thess 4,11 Paul praises the virtue of 'working by your own hands'; 1 Thess 2,9 and 1 Cor 4,12 further attest to the fact that Paul performed manual labour.

[66] See above, and Levinskaya, *Diaspora Setting*, pp. 168-182.

[67] Ὁ σκηνοποιὸς ἐκεῖνος, ὁ τῆς οἰκουμένης διδάσκαλος. This description is followed by a long eulogy on Paul who is addressed with numerous titles, among them: ὁ γῆν καὶ θάλασσαν καθάπερ ὑπόπτερος περιδραμών (...) ὁ νυμφαγωγὸς τοῦ Χριστοῦ, ὁ τῆς ἐκκλησίας φυτουργός, ὁ σοφὸς ἀρχιτέκτων etc. See John Chrysostom, *De petitione matris filiorum Zebedei* 3, Migne PG 48, col 772.

[68] See for instance A. Deissmann, *Paulus. Eine kultur- und religionsgeschichtliche Skizze* (Tübingen: Mohr Siebeck, 2nd ed. 1925), p. 40, who clearly interprets Paul's manual work as that of a linen weaver ('an den Webstuhl'). Deissmann's verdict, however, is still valuable: Paul was 'ein einfacher Mann, der in seinem Handwerk als Geselle um Lohn arbeitete und darin die wirtschaftliche Grundlage seiner Existenz hatte.' We may question whether Paul was as 'common' as Deissmann argued, but the bottom line of his view is still correct.

has argued that Paul and Aquila were in fact leather-workers.[69] This interpretation is followed by most scholars, and is likely to be correct.[70]

Paul did not choose this occupation by accident. There are indications
that he purposely modelled his ministry in this manner. In a short but
compelling monograph R.F. Hock has drawn attention to the importance
of Paul's profession.[71] According to Hock tentmaking was the ideal occupation for Paul: it enabled him to maintain his financial independence,
to stay on the road, and at the same time did not prevent him from discussing the gospel. 'The requisite knives and awls, incidentally, would
have made tentmaking an easily portable trade, a fact that helps explain
Paul's eventual use of his trade as his means of support during his travels as a missionary.'[72] Hock argues that the tentmaker's workshop must
have been a place for discussion and proclamation of the gospel.[73] An
important new element he introduces into the discussion is that Paul's
choice to work with his hands should not be interpreted from the rabbinical ideal of the labouring pious, but rather from the point of view of
Greek philosophers who provided for themselves by labouring in artisan's workshops. According to Hock this was one of the four options
they could choose from in order to support their teaching.[74] Hock raises
serious doubts about the interpretation of Paul's work as reflecting the
rabbinic ideal of combining Torah and trade: 'such a position has problems not only because of doubts about Paul's rabbinic training but also
because of the likelihood that the rabbinic ideal itself arose only after the
time of Paul.'[75] The alternative Hock proposes for the interpretation of
Paul's artisanship is far more plausible: 'Intellectually, his plying a trade
means that he came into contact with a tradition of philosophy – in large
part Cynic – that addressed itself to the question of suitable occupations
and trades for the urban poor, that made the workshop one of its settings
for doing philosophy, and that in the figure of Simon the shoemaker made

---

[69] *ThWNT*, vol. 7, pp. 394-396.
[70] For an adequate analysis, see R.F. Hock, 'Paul's Tentmaking and the Problem of his
Social Class', *JBL* 97 (1978), pp. 555-564, and idem, 'The Workshop as a Social
Setting for Paul's Missionary Preaching', *CBQ* 41 (1979), pp. 438-450.
[71] Hock, *Social Context*, cf. above, p. 76.
[72] Hock, *Social Context*, p. 25.
[73] Hock, *Social Context*, pp. 26-49.
[74] These four ways are: 1) finding a patron; 2) being paid for his teachings; 3) begging;
and 4) working – cf. Hock, *Social Context*, pp. 52-59; see also Downing, *Cynics, Paul
and the Pauline Churches*, pp. 192-194.
[75] Hock, *Social Context*, p. 66.

the artisan-philosopher the embodiment of its ideals of self-sufficiency and freedom.'[76]

It has already been argued in chapter two that the closest parallel to Paul's proclamation of the gospel is the teaching of travelling philosophers, mostly Cynics, who proclaimed their views in a comparable manner to Paul.[77] It now again appears that Paul's ministry is similar to a certain attitude among Cynic philosophers, who sometimes also laboured with their hands in order to remain independent. Thus, we may assume that Paul in this respect used a model for his ministry that had already been formed by philosophers: Paul worked as an artisan, thereby creating his own financial independence as well as the opportunity to proclaim the gospel.[78]

This observation is yet another indication that Paul was influenced by popular Greek philosophers. It has been noted by many scholars that Paul frequently uses ideas, patterns, and style elements that were current among Greek, mainly Cynic-Stoic, philosophers.[79] Already in antiquity an anonymous author regarded Paul and the great Stoic Seneca as congenial minds to such an extent that he wrote a pseudepigraphous correspondence between the two.[80] Paul's mastery of the style of the catalogues of hardships is another well-known example.[81] And careful comparison of Paul's

---

[76] Hock, *Social Context*, p. 68.

[77] Cf. above, pp. 76-78.

[78] Apparently, Paul's opponents argued that Paul was not really free (cf. 1 Cor 9,1.15-18; 2 Cor 11-13): he had to work for his support. Paul's reply is, that exactly this work enabled him to maintain his freedom. On this conflict, see Hock, *Social Context*, pp. 50-65; Theissen, 'Legitimation und Lebensunterhalt', p. 204-205 [213-214]. Theissen argues that Paul already during his period with Barnabas modelled his ministry after the philosophic tradition of αὐταρκία (cf. Phil 4,11; Socrates in Diog. Laert., *Vit. Phil.* II,24), and the philosophic idea of ἐλευθερία (cf. Epictetus, *Diss.* III,22,48).

[79] See Downing, *Cynics, Paul and the Pauline Churches*, who on pp. 50-249 points out numerous parallels between Paul and the Cynics. Downing's way had been paved especially by A.J. Malherbe, who in e.g. his *Paul and the Popular Philosophers* (Minneapolis: Fortress, 1989) has drawn attention to the many similarities between Paul and popular Greek philosophers. Cf. also H.-D. Betz, *Der Apostel Paulus und die sokratische Tradition. Eine exegetische Untersuchung zu seiner "Apologie" 2 Korinther 10-13* (BhTh 45; Tübingen: Mohr, 1972), who on pp. 65-69 argues that the fact that Paul described his defence in 1 Corinthians 10-13 as τολμᾶν is best compared with the frank speech of the Cynics.

[80] Cf. J.K. Elliott, *The Apocryphal New Testament. A Collection of Apocryphal Christian Literature in an English Translation* (Oxford: Clarendon, 1993), pp. 547-553. In the seventh letter Seneca comments upon a number of Paul's letters: 'I admit that I enjoyed reading your letters to the Galatians, to the Corinthians, and to the Acheans.'

[81] J.T. Fitzgerald, *Cracks in an Earthen Vessel. An Examination of the Catalogues of Hardships in the Corinthian Correspondence* (SBLDS 99; Atlanta: Scholars Press, 1988) has shown that Paul 'borrowed' the style of the catalogue of hardships from the

thoughts with the ideas of popular philosophers of his day reveals even more similarities.[82] This complementary evidence indicates that Paul has modelled his preaching of the gospel after the example of popular philosophers. He must have become acquainted with Cynic philosophers and their ideas in the town of his birth, Tarsus, which was a famous centre of Cynic and Stoic philosophy.[83]

In this section it was shown that Paul provided for his own livelihood by labouring as a tentmaker, and that he did so on purpose. In the previous section it appeared that Paul was supported by congregations that he had founded earlier or by individuals with whom he had become acquainted. Thus something of a method appears to be evolving: Paul took care of his needs by working and by accepting support from others. This method enabled Paul to proclaim the gospel where it had not yet been heard, in a way that would most effectively contribute to its growth. But the most remarkable thing is that Paul did not work on his own – he organised a group of fellow workers around him.

3. The Fellow Workers

Paul was supported in his proclamation of the gospel by a certain group of co-workers, 'fellow workers' (συνεργοί) in Christ. This specific group is a selection of all those people Paul mentions in his letters. The names listed below are presented by Paul as somehow related to him, and those 'fellow-workers' whose names have come down to us through Paul's letters form a group within this group.

People connected to Paul, mentioned in the letters[84]

1. Achaicus (1 Cor 16,17; not in Acts)
2. Ampliatus (Rom 16,8; not in Acts)
3. Andronicus (Rom 16,7; not in Acts)
4. Apelles (Rom 16,10; not in Acts)
5. Apollos (1 Cor 1,12; 3,4.5.6.22; 4,6; 16,12; Acts 18,24; 19,1)

---

philosophers of his day. In Fitzgerald's conclusion, Paul presents the circumstances in which he worked in the way philosophers would present the circumstances the ideal sage had to confront. '(...) Paul in 1 and 2 Corinthians frequently depicts himself in terms typically used to describe the ideal philosopher, and his use of *peristasis* catalogues is an integral part of this *Selbstdarstellung*.' – *Cracks*, p. 204.

[82] See e.g. Malherbe, *Popular Philosophers*, pp. 91-119.
[83] On Tarsus, see above, p. 157.
[84] The list is presented in alphabetical order, which says nothing on the relation these people had with Paul.

6. Apphia (Phlm 2; not in Acts)
7. Aquila (Rom 16,3; 1 Cor 16,1; Acts 18,2.18.26)
8. Archippus (Phlm 2; not in Acts)
9. Aristarchos from Macedonia (Phlm 24; Acts 19,29; 20,4; 27,2)
10. Aristobulus (Rom 16,10; not in Acts)
11. Asyncritus (Rom 16,14; not in Acts)
12. Barnabas (1 Cor 9,6; Gal 2,1.9.13; Acts 4,36; 9,27; 11,22.30; 12,25; 13,1.2.7.43.46.50; 14,12.14; 15,2.12.22.25.35.36.37.39)
13. Chloe (1 Cor 1,11; not in Acts)
14. Clement (Phil 4,3; not in Acts)
15. Crispus (1 Cor 1,14; Acts 18,8)
16. Demas (Phlm 24; not in Acts)
17. Epaenetus (Rom 16,5; not in Acts)
18. Epaphras (Phlm 23; not in Acts)
19. Epaphroditus (Phil 2,25; 4,18; not in Acts)
20. Erastos (Rom 16,23; Acts 19,22)
21. Euodia (Phil 4,2; not in Acts)
22. Fortunatus (1 Cor 16,17; not in Acts)
23. Gaius (Rom 16,23; 1 Cor 1,14); Gaius from Macedonia (Acts 19,20) and Gaius from Derbe (Acts 20,4)
24. Hermas (Rom 16,14; not in Acts)
25. Hermes (Rom 16,14; not in Acts)
26. Herodion (Rom 16,11; not in Acts)
27. Jason (Rom 16,21; Acts 17,5.6.7.9)
28. Julia (Rom 16,15; not in Acts)
29. Junia (Rom 16,7; not in Acts)
30. Lucius (Rom 16,21; Acts 13,1)
31. Luke (Phlm 24;; not in Acts)
32. Mark (Phlm 24; probably another Mark than Barnabas' nephew, mentioned in Acts 12,12.25; 15,37.39)
33. Mary (Rom 16,6; not in Acts)
34. Narcissus (Rom 16,11; not in Acts)
35. Nereus and his sister (Rom 16,15; not in Acts)
36. Olympas (Rom 16,15; not in Acts)
37. Onesimus (Phlm 10; not in Acts)
38. Patrobas (Rom 16,15; not in Acts)
39. Philemon (Phlm 1; not in Acts)
40. Philologus (Rom 16,15; not in Acts)
41. Phlegon (Rom 16,14; not in Acts)
42. Phoebe (Rom 16,1; not in Acts)
43. Prisca (Rom 16,3; 1 Cor 16,1; 'Priscilla' in Acts 18,2.18.26)
44. Quartus (Rom 16,23; not in Acts)
45. Rufus (Rom 16,13; not in Acts, but Mark 15,21?)
46. Silvanus (2 Cor 1,19; 1 Thess 1,1; 'Silas' in Acts 15,22.27.32.40; 16,19.25.29; 17,4.10.14.15; 18,5)
47. Sosipater (Rom 16,21; not in Acts)
48. Sosthenes (1 Cor 1,1; Acts 18,7)
49. Stachys (Rom 16,9; not in Acts)

50. Stephanas (1 Cor 1,16; 16,15.17; not in Acts)
51. Syntyche (Phil. 4,2; not in Acts)
52. Tertius (Rom 16,22; not in Acts)
53. Timothy (Rom 16,21; 1 Cor 4,17; 16,10; 2 Cor 1,1.19; Phil 1,1; 2,19; 1 Thess 1,1; 3,2.6; Phlm 1; Acts 16,1; 17,14.15; 18,5; 19,22; 20,4)
54. Titus (2 Cor 2,13; 7,6.13.14; 8,6.16.23; 12,18; Gal 2,1.3)
55. Tryphaena (Rom 16,12; not in Acts)
56. Tryphosa (Rom 16,12; not in Acts)
57. Urbanus (Rom 16,9; not in Acts)

In his 1979 monograph W.-H. Ollrog has examined the phenomenon of the group of co-workers surrounding Paul.[85] In his reconstruction Paul joined the congregation of Antioch in order to be sent out as an apostle by that congregation. At this stage of his ministry Paul assisted Barnabas who must have headed the mission. After the incident at Antioch Paul must have continued the proclamation of the gospel on his own, at first with the assistance of Silvanus (called 'Silas' in Acts), and later with the aid of Timothy. According to Ollrog, it is no accident that the one in whom Paul apparently put most of his trust, Timothy, was the first non-Jewish fellow worker to side with Paul.

Only during his independent ministry did Paul decide to focus on one town rather than go from one town to another. This kind of local preaching of the gospel is identified by Ollrog as *Zentrumsmission*: mission aimed at one specific centre that would lead to a further spread of the gospel to the regions surrounding it.[86] It was at this stage of his ministry that Paul was helped by his fellow-workers in Christ. Paul uses the term συνεργός to describe these colleagues in the proclamation of the gospel.[87] The noun does not denote a hierarchic relationship, but rather the fact that the συνεργοί co-operate in the proclamation of the gospel.

---

[85] H.W. Ollrog, *Paulus und seine Mitarbeiter. Untersuchungen zu Theorie und Praxis der paulinischen Mission* (WMANT 50; Neukirchen-Vluyn: Neukirchener Verlag, 1979).

[86] 'Er wanderte nicht mehr von Ort zu Ort, als reisender Herold nicht lange verweilend, um am Ende zum Ausgangspunkt, der Muttergemeinde, zurückzukehren. Sondern er gründete nur in einer Stadt in einer Provinz, gewöhnlich in der Provinzhauptstadt, eine Gemeinde, blieb dort möglichst so lange, bis die Gemeinde auf eigenen Beine zu stehen vermochte, und reiste dann zur nächsten (Haupt-)Stadt weiter.' p. 126. See also Reinbold, *Propaganda und Mission*, p. 212: 'Paulus gründet, sofern es die Umstände zulassen, im Zentrum der Region eine Ekklesia, begleitet sie gerade so lange, bis sie in der Lage ist, selbständig zu existieren, und zieht weiter.'

[87] See Rom 16,3.9.21; 1 Cor 3,9; 2 Cor 1,24; 8,23; Phil 2,25; 4,3; 1 Thess 3,2; Phlm 1.24.

The co-workers preach the gospel together with Paul. The designation συνεργός is formed on the basis of the awareness of a common ἔργον.[88]

The group under discussion must have consisted of at least those persons attested as συνεργοί in Paul's letters:[89] Aristarchus, Clement, Demas, Epaphroditus, Luke, Mark, Philemon, Prisca and Aquila, Timothy, Titus, and Urbanus. Reinbold correctly argues that to this list a number of others should definitely be added: Silvanus/Silas, Archippus, Epaphras, Euodia and Syntyche, and Trophimus.[90]

In Ollrog's reconstruction this group of fellow workers is of the utmost importance for Paul's mission. They were envoys of Pauline congregations who acted on behalf of these in assisting Paul in his missionary work.[91] These envoys were sent out by their congregations for a certain, fixed period. During this period they had to do missionary work for Paul. According to Ollrog this system formed the core of the Pauline mission. It grew out of a combination of the charismatic wandering missionaries (*Wandermission*) and the Hellenistic missionary system of the *shaliach* who was sent as an envoy of a particular congregation.[92]

Although Ollrog's thesis has many attractive elements, there are three major problems with it. The first of these concerns his use of the concept of *shaliach*. In the previous chapter it was argued that the existence of the *shaliach*-institution cannot be proved before 70 CE. This means that the ease with which Ollrog defined the background of the institution of fellow workers cannot be upheld. We simply cannot regard these co-workers as *shelichim*.

---

[88] In Ollrog's words: 'Συνεργός ist, wer mit Paulus zusammen als Beauftragter Gottes am gemeinsamen "Werk" der Missionsverkündigung arbeitet. (…) Das Wort definiert sich von der gemeinsamen Arbeit her, vom ἔργον; nicht vom Teamgedanken, vom Zusammensein in der Arbeit, dem συν-Sein. Der Begriff beschreibt in erster Linie nicht die Form der Zusammenarbeit, sondern ihren gemeinsamen *Inhalt*.' – Ollrog, *Mitarbeiter*, p. 67.

[89] For an individual analysis of these fellow-workers, see Reinbold, *Propaganda und Mission*, pp. 213-224.

[90] Reinbold, *Propaganda und Mission*, p. 213.

[91] Cf. Ollrog, *Mitarbeiter*, p. 79: 'Hinweise darauf, daß einzelne Titulierungen sich zu "Ämtern" verfestigt hätten, ergeben sich nicht. Die bisherigen Überlegungen führen also zu dem einheitlichen Ergebnis, daß die Mitarbeiter des Paulus in der Mission mitarbeiteten. Ihre Arbeit versteht Paulus als Missionsarbeit. Was sie dabei im einzelnen taten, bleibt offen. Daraus legt sich die Vermutung nahe, daß die Mitarbeiter in ihrer Arbeit keine bestimmten, festgelegten Aufgaben wahrnahmen, die zu bestimmten "Ämtern" hätten gerinnen können, sondern daß sie jeweils unterschiedliche und wechselnde, durch die verschiedenen Missionssituationen und -erfordernisse bedingte Funktionen ausübten.'

[92] Ollrog, *Mitarbeiter*, pp. 150-161.

The second problem is related to the first: Ollrog so much perceives the function of the συνεργοί as that of an office, that he implicitly presents the term συνεργός as a transformation of the institution of the *shaliach*. Ollrog defines the term as a 'terminus technicus für die mit [Paulus] in der Missionsarbeit stehenden Personen'.[93] This view is rightly criticised by Reinbold, who argues that Ollrog overinterprets the evidence.[94] Indeed Paul's use of the vocabulary of συνεργός and συνεργέω is far less fixed than Ollrog takes it to be.[95]

The third difficulty arises when Ollrog, like so many others, assumes that Paul based his ministry on the concept of a worldwide mission.[96] This assumption is based on the interpretation of Rom 15,14-24 as a programmatic statement. As will be argued below, this is not the most likely interpretation of that passage.

Nevertheless, even if Ollrog misrepresents the character of the Pauline mission as being planned on the basis of a universal programme and as using and transforming the office of a *shaliach*, the fact remains that the Pauline mission was an activity not of one single man, but of a group of people. Indeed, Barnabas, Silvanus, and Timothy would have acted as Paul's closest associates, and Apollos, Prisca and Aquila, and Titus were examples of related 'missionaries'.[97] Furthermore, Ollrog puts together a second element in Paul's ministry, namely its form. According to Ollrog, Paul started as a wandering preacher who proclaimed the gospel, probably as an envoy of the congregation in Antioch. Later he became a more urbanised preacher, deciding to stay in one town for a certain period, directing his activities from that town, and having contact with fellow workers – 'colleagues in Christ' – who also preached the gospel. This reconstruction fits in well with the one presented in this study.

---

[93] Ollrog, *Mitarbeiter*, p. 84.

[94] Reinbold, *Propaganda und Mission*, pp. 213-214.

[95] Reinbold, *Propaganda und Mission*, p. 214, mentions the use of this terminology by Paul in 1 Cor 3,9 and 1 Thess 3,2, where Paul labels himself, together with Apollos and Timothy, as συνεργοὶ [τοῦ] θεοῦ, and adds Rom 8,28; 1 Cor 16,16; 2 Cor 1,24; 6,1 to his counter-evidence.

[96] See e.g. Ollrog, *Mitarbeiter*, p. 125: 'Es war nicht die augeklügelte Organisation, das Delegiertensystem und die Konzentrierung der Kräfte, durch welche die Mitarbeitermission ihre faszinierende Stoßkraft erhielt, sondern die Art der konkreten Verantwortlichkeit für die Mission, also die theologische Motivation, das Selbstverständnis der Gemeinden als handelnder Teile *am weltweiten Missionsauftrag* (ital. LP).'

[97] E.E. Ellis, 'Paul and his Co-Workers', *NTS* 17 (1970-71), pp. 437-453, points out that Paul was assisted in his ministry by a group known as the ἀδελφοί, and that others were involved in Paul's activities as well. Ellis concludes that '(…) "the brothers" in Pauline literature fairly consistently refers to a relatively limited group of workers, some of whom have the Christian mission and/or ministry as their primary occupation' – p. 447.

It now appears that Paul worked within the setting of a team. He started building a new congregation with the help of his fellow workers, financially supported by previous acquaintances and congregations as well as by his own manual labour. All these elements together indicate that Paul did not aim at large audiences, addressing them with missionary speeches, but rather focused on individual contacts. Several recent studies point in this direction, and correctly so. Ollrog, Reinbold, and Stark, for instance, have all stressed the importance of social networks and mission through individual contacts.[98] On the basis of the analysis made here we should stress their conclusion that Paul indeed employed the method labeled by Ollrog and Reinbold as centripetal mission (*Zentrumsmission*): Paul traveled to a certain town, made himself a living there, and used the social networks available to him in order to spread the gospel to attract new believers. After a new congregation had been formed, he went on to the next town. In the next section these towns Paul visited will be dealt with.

4. Paul's Audience: the Cities and the People

The next question to be addressed is the most obvious one, but perhaps the most difficult one to answer: which towns did Paul visit and who did he aim his activities at?

Unfortunately, two complexes of difficulties blur our sight here. Firstly, there is the problem that Paul himself hardly talks about the cities he visited. He speaks about the congregations he writes to, he admonishes them, and occasionally he gives a glimpse at his travel-plans. But more often than not Paul is silent on where he is staying and what he exactly he is doing. The latter is more easy to guess than the former, but we don't find too much evidence in his letters.

Secondly, there is the problem of Hellenistic Diaspora Judaism. We do have information on the variety of forms of Diaspora Judaism, but again not much. For instance, we don't really know whether there was any

---

[98] Ollrog, *Mitarbeiter*, p. 130, argues: 'Durch den normalen Kontakt mit der heidnischen Umwelt, durch die mannigfachen Berührungen des täglichen Lebens und die grundsätzliche Offenheit gegenüber den Nichtchristen entstand also eine gewissermaßen natürliche missionarische Wirkung, bewußt zwar, aber nicht eigentlich geplant oder sogar organisiert.' See also Reinbold, *Propaganda und Mission*, pp. 200-202, who refers to S.K. Stowers, 'Social Status, Public Speaking and Private Teaching', *NT* 26 (1984), pp. 59-82. Reinbold quotes from Stowers' conclusion: 'We may conclude that the widespread picture of Paul the public orator, sophist or street-corner preacher is a false one.' (Reinbold, p. 202 = Stowers, p. 81). See also Stark, *Rise*, who argues throughout his book that Christianity spread first and foremost through social networks.

institution we can label as a 'synagogue'.[99] Did the author of Acts refer to such an institution as comparable to the synagogues we meet in post-200 CE evidence? Or was it actually something different?

Having stated these two problems, we may start our reconstruction of the towns Paul went to on the basis of the letters.[100] The cities mentioned here are mostly places in which Paul founded communities of believers. The letters testify to the fact that Paul successively visited at least Damascus,[101] Jerusalem,[102] Antioch,[103] Philippi,[104] Thessalonica,[105] Athens,[106] Corinth,[107] Ephesus,[108] Cenchraea,[109] Troas (or the Troad)[110] and – probably – Rome.[111] The provinces Paul mentions as the areas of his ministry are Galatia,[112] Asia,[113] Macedonia,[114] and Achaia.[115] There is no evidence that he ever reached Illyricum or Spain.[116] It is probably no accident that the cities mentioned by Paul all share a number of fea-

---

[99] For a rather optimistic view, see L.I. Levine, *The Ancient Synagogue. The First Thousand Years* (New Haven, London: Yale University Press, 2000), esp. pp. 42-73 (on Pre-70 Judea) and 74-123 (on The Pre-70 Diaspora). A more careful evaluation is given by A. Runesson, *The Origins of the Synagogue. A Socio-Historical Study* (Coniectanea Biblica New Testament Steries 37; Stockholm: Almqvist&Wiksell, 2001), esp. pp. 169-235 ('The First Century Synagogue'), who sums up the diversity of names and institutions found in evidence on the first century CE. For a thorough presentation of the evidence, see A.T. Kraabel, 'The Diaspora Synagogue: Archaeological and Epigraphical Evidence', in: *ANRW* 2:19,1 (1979), pp. 477-510, and P.R. Trebilco, *Jewish communities in Asia Minor* (SNTSMS 69; Cambridge [etc.]: Cambridge University Press, 1991).

[100] The exact chronology of Paul's ministry cannot be dealt with here. Others have given valuable reports on that topic; cf. esp. R. Jewett, *A Chronology of Paul's Life* (Philadelphia: Fortress, 1979). Riesner, *Frühzeit*, pp. 31-203, gives a detailed analysis of the chronology of Paul's early ministry. For an elaborate discussion, see A. Suhl, 'Paulinische Chronologie im Streit der Meinungen', in: W. Haase, *ANRW II Principat* 26/2 (1995), pp. 939-1188.

[101] 2 Cor 11,32; Gal 1,17.

[102] Rom 15,19.25.26.31; 1 Cor 16,3; Gal 1,17.18; 2,1; 4,25.26.

[103] Gal 2,11.

[104] Phil 1,1; 1 Thess 2,2.

[105] Phil 4,16; 1 Thess 1.

[106] 1 Thess 3,1.

[107] 1 Cor 1,2; 2 Cor 1,1.23.

[108] 1 Cor 15,32; 16,8.

[109] Rom 16,1.

[110] 2 Cor 2,12.

[111] Rom 1,7.15.

[112] See 1 Cor 16,1 ('the churches of Galatia'); Gal 1,2.

[113] Rom 16,5.19; 2 Cor 1,8.

[114] Rom 15,26; 16,5; 2 Cor 1,16; 2,13; 7,5; 8,1; 9,2; 11,9; Phil 4,15; 1 Thess 1,7.8; 4,10.

[115] Rom 15,26; 16,15; 2 Cor 1,1; 9,2; 11,10; 1 Thess 1,7.8.

[116] Both are mentioned in Romans 15; Illyricum: 15,19; Spain: 15,24.28. On this passage, see below.

tures: the presence of a Jewish community is attested for most of these cities,[117] and they were all important centres of commerce and trade. This similarity must somehow explain the fact that Paul turned to precisely these towns: his special interest must have resulted from this specific combination.[118]

In regard to the first point there is a problem with Philippi, Thessalonica, Athens, and Corinth: the presence of a Jewish community has not been attested for this period by any other evidence than the writings of Paul and the book of Acts.[119] Neither archeological nor epigraphic remains of a Jewish community in Paul's day have been found. This does not automatically imply that there were no Jewish settlements in these towns at the time Paul was active there, but it does mean that we have a lack of evidence. As J. Murphy-O'Connor puts it: 'Information on Greek Jewry is virtually non-existent, so as regards the community at Corinth we are forced to extrapolate from what is known elsewhere in the Diaspora.'[120] The same approach is valid for Thessalonica, Philippi, and Athens. It is likely that there were Jewish residents in these cities, but since they left no discernible traces we can only assume this.[121] Nevertheless, it cannot be by accident that Paul addresses the Thessalonians as well as the Corinthians as 'former pagans' (1 Thess 1,9; 1 Cor 12,2),

---

[117] See Juster, *Les Juifs*, vol. 1, pp. 180-209.

[118] In the opening address of the 2002 SBL Annual Meeting at the Humboldt Universität of Berlin, C. Breytenbach has argued that the spread of Christian communities throughout the Roman Empire was connected to that of Jewish settlements until the fourth century. A similar case is made by Stark, *Rise*, 49-71, who argues that cultural continuity between Judaism and Christianity, the existence of accomodated forms of Judaism, and Jewish networks throughout the area supplied for the conditions for a mission to the Jews to succeed.

[119] This gives rise to analyses as made by C. Koukouli-Chrysantaki who, commenting on the inscription by Nikostratos Aurelios Oxycholoios (Philippi Museum Inv. No. Λ1529), argues that: 'This tombstone dates from much later than Saint Paul's time (sc. 3rd cent.; LP), but is serves as an important archaeological commentary on the Acts of the Apostles, offering the first epigraphical evidence of the existence of an organized Jewish community in the city of Philippi in the late third century CE.' The problem with this kind of reasoning is, that it overlooks the possibility of a post-Christian origin for this Jewish community. See C. Koukouli-Chrysantaki, 'Colonia Iulia Augusta Philippensis', in: C. Bakirtzis, H. Koester (eds.), *Philippi at the Time of Paul and after His Death* (Harrisburg: Trinity Press, 1998), pp. 5-35, esp. pp. 28-35 (quotation from p. 34).

[120] J. Murphy-O'Connor, *St. Paul's Corinth. Texts and Archaeology* (GNS 6; Delaware: Glazier, 1983), p. 80.

[121] It is in this manner that W. Elliger, *Paulus in Griechenland. Philippi, Thessaloniki, Athen, Korinth* (SBS 92/93; Stuttgart: Katholisches Bibelwerk, 1978), pp. 47-50, reconstructs the 'place of prayer' in Philippi mentioned in Acts 16,13.

something he also does when writing to the Galatians (Gal 4,8). The new believers Paul writes to in these letters obviously came from the pagan community of the towns rather than from the Jewish. Nevertheless, the fact that Paul refers to the Jewish Bible time and again, also in the letters to the Thessalonians, the Corinthians, and the Galatians, at least presupposes some knowledge on the part of the recipients with this Scripture. Such knowledge would have been impossible to acquire had there not been any Jewish community at hand. Therefore we have to suppose that Paul did indeed use the network of Jewish settlements throughout his ministry, and that such settlements either directly provided for a part of his audience or indirectly created the circumstances for Paul to work in by attracting pagans to their Jewish heritage.

The second reason for Paul to choose the cities under discussion is no doubt their economic prominence. Paul obviously wanted to work in these towns for the same reason he chose Corinth and Ephesus as important centres for his activities:[122] the infrastructure provided him with many people who could be reached by the gospel, and who, if convinced by Paul, could in turn proclaim the Good News along the trade routes they or their acquaintances would follow.[123] If Paul preached the gospel in cities with many travellers, those of them who came to accept the gospel would pass it on on their way home. The effect of preaching in an important trade centre was far greater than that of preaching in an ordinary town or village.

To this brief reconstruction based on the letters, we should add the evidence from Acts on Paul's independent ministry, i.e. his activities after he broke with Barnabas. Here we will have to focus our attention on what are usually described as the second and third missionary journeys Paul undertook together with Silas (16,1-21,14). It is remarkable that this part of the book of Acts also presents to us a Paul who in the first place aims at a Jewish audience. There is no change in Paul's behaviour when compared to his ministry with Barnabas (13,1-14,28): Paul preaches the gospel in Philippi and on the Sabbath day wishes to do so at the Jewish

---

[122] On Corinth see esp. R.M. Rothaus, *Corinth: The First City of Greece. An Urban History of Late Antique Cult and Religion* (RGRW 139; Leiden [etc.]: Brill, 2000). On Ephesus see W. Thiessen, *Christen in Ephesus. Die historische und theologische Situation in vorpaulinischer und paulinischer Zeit und zur Zeit der Apostelgeschichte und der Pastoralbriefe* (TANZ 12; Tübingen, Basel: Francke, 1995), and H. Koester (ed.), *Ephesos, Metropolis of Asia. An Interdisciplinary Approach to Archaeology, Religion, and Culture* (HTS 41; Valley Forge: Trinity, 1995).

[123] J. Murphy-O'Connor on Ephesus, in: *ABD* vol. 1, p. 1139: 'In addition to excellent communications, the extraordinary number of visitors (...) created the possibility of converts who could carry the gospel back to their homelands.'

place of prayer outside the town (16,13). He preaches at the synagogues of Thessalonica and Beroea (17,1-14), Corinth (18,5-17), and Ephesus (19,8-12). Time and again Paul meets with fierce opposition from Jews. He and Silas are imprisoned in Philippi after the members of the Jewish synagogue had taken action against them (16,19-40). They meet with similar opposition in Thessalonica, where Paul and Silas are cast out of town (17,5-9), and in Beroea where the Jews from Thessalonica came 'to stir up and incite the crowds' (17,13). The subsequent episode at Corinth is of great importance within the narrative of Acts as a whole. It is here that Paul leaves the synagogue where he has proclaimed that Jesus is the Anointed One, to continue his preaching in the house of a godfearer, Titus Justus (18,1-11). Next, Paul is brought before Gallio by Jewish opponents but their plan does not succeed (18,12-16). After Paul leaves Corinth, he heads towards Ephesus where he 'went into the synagogue and had a discussion with the Jews' (18,19). It is after Paul's visit to Jerusalem, recounted in 18,22, that his stay at Ephesus is described at length (19,1-40). Here he met with opposition not only from Jews, but also from Greeks (see esp. 19,23-40). But again, Paul's preaching of the gospel takes place within the synagogue. Then, Paul goes from Ephesus to Corinth and subsequently onward to Troas (20,1-6), where he miraculously raises the dead Eutychus (20,7-12). After this event Paul leaves for Assos and Mitylene, eventually to come to Caesarea (21,8) and Jerusalem (21,17).

In summa, the places Paul visits in Acts 16-21 are the following: Derbe, Lystra (16,1), Phrygia and **Galatia**, not Asia (16,6), Mysia, not Bithynia (16,7), **Troas** (16,8), Samothrace, Neapolis (16,11), **Philippi** (16,12), Amphipolis, Apollonia, **Thessalonica** (17,1), Beroea (17,10), **Athens** (17,15), **Corinth** (18,1), **Cenchreae** (18,18), **Ephesus** (18,19), Caesarea, **Jerusalem**, **Antioch** (18,22), Galatia/Phrygia (18,23), **Ephesus** (19,1), Macedonia, Achaia, Paul stays in **Asia** (Ephesus) to prepare for his visit to Jerusalem (19,21), **Macedonia** (20,1), Greece (=**Achaia?**) (20,2), **Macedonia** (20,3), Philippi, **Troas** (20,6), Assos, Mitylene (20,14), Chios, Samos, Miletus (20,15), Cos, Rhodes, Patara (21,1), Cyprus, Syria, Tyre (21,3), Ptolemais (21,7), Caesarea (21,8), **Jerusalem** (21,17). After Jerusalem, Paul eventually ends up in **Rome** (28,14.16). The cities and provinces printed in bold are also mentioned by Paul himself. In the account of Acts these cities and provinces are the centres of Paul's ministry; the others are mentioned as stations along the road.

It is important to note that the author of Acts does not describe Paul's journeys through Syria, Cilicia, Asia Minor, Greece and Palestine as the result of a planned outline Paul himself had made before starting off. He primarily presents Paul and his fellow workers as inspired and driven on by the Spirit. In 16,6-10 it is the Spirit that first prevents Paul from going to Asia and Bithynia and subsequently Paul has a dream of the man calling him to come over to Macedonia. Dreams were considered as a divine source of information, and therefore Paul's dream is introduced in the narrative as a divine sign. The divine origin of Paul's actions as described in 16,6-10 is a means by which the author underlines the fact that Paul was commissioned by God himself to go out on his travels. Remarkably enough, the Spirit does not figure in the description of Paul's travels in cc. 16-19 in the prominent role it was assigned in the earlier and later chapters of Acts: the Spirit is mentioned anew in 20,23, when Paul mentions it as the one who gives him the strength to await his fate, and in 13,4 it was explicitly stated that the Spirit had sent Paul and Barnabas on their journey.

Guidance by the Spirit is not the only reason Acts mentions for Paul to move on. A number of times the author describes how Paul had to escape the aggressive opposition of either Jewish or pagan antagonists. In 17,10 it is told how Paul and Silas were sent from Thessalonica to Beroea to escape a group of Jewish opponents. Unfortunately, Paul's opponents in Thessalonica come to hear about his preaching the gospel in Beroea, and arrive to make trouble – once again Paul has to flee, this time to Athens. Later, when Paul plans to go to Syria from Greece, he is forced to change his plans and heads for Macedonia.

In all other instances in cc. 16-21 Paul's moving from one place to another is described in a neutral way without an apparent reason being given. This is an important observation. The author of Acts reconstructs Paul's travels on the basis of the traditions he had received, but describes them in a matter-of-fact style in which it is taken for granted that Paul moves from one place to another. No underlying plan is described, and Paul's activities are depicted within the literary framework of Acts as aiming to present the divine origin and growth of the Christian movement: Paul moves on either because the Spirit urges him to or because human opposition does so. In both cases Gamaliel's analysis is valid: from the author's perspective the movement comes from God and nothing can be done against it. It thus appears that the picture given in Acts is highly literary in character: Paul is pushed forward by the Spirit, he preaches to Jews who reject his gospel, and subsequently to Gentiles.

Not only the way in which Paul moves on in the Book of Acts is consciously formed as literature, the use of the travel motif itself is not by accident either. W.L. Knox already argued, that the author of Acts used the form of a travel story to describe the actions of Paul in an engaging manner.[124] This approach to the travel sections of Acts is appealing because it explains why the author presented Paul's ministry in the form of a travel narrative: this was a popular and attractive genre, also used for instance to describe the ministry of Apollonius of Tyana. The same author used the same genre for an important part of the gospel of Luke.[125] Yet to conclude as Knox did that the appealing nature of the genre is the only reason why Paul's ministry is described as it is in cc. 16-21 is pushing the evidence too far. There can be no doubt that the author of Acts had various traditions at his disposal concerning Paul's travels. Either he incorporated some kind of source in the 'we-passages', as is often argued, and obviously had written evidence for Paul's travels at his disposal, or he used oral traditions concerning Paul.[126] Either way, the evidence from Acts confirms what we already knew on the basis of Paul's letters, namely that he travelled.

Having seen that Paul travelled through great parts of Asia Minor, Macedonia, and Greece, the question should be raised: who did Paul aim his preaching of the gospel at? In the previous sections it was argued that Paul made use of his occupation and his fellow workers to reach for his audience. We should now ask who belonged to this audience.

It is remarkable that Acts, throughout the book, describes Paul as proclaiming the gospel in the synagogues of the places he visited.[127] There are two reasons to be suspicious of this picture. The first is that Acts obviously tries to mask the rupture in Paul's ministry. At first Paul and Barnabas indeed visited synagogues during their travels, and they obviously did so because they had been sent as envoys of the Antiochene con-

---

[124] W.L. Knox, *The Acts of the Apostles* (Cambridge: University Press, 1948), p. 55: 'Such stories, whether true or fictitious, appealed to the popular taste by providing a variety of scenes and adventures with plenty of marvels thrown in. The travelling philosopher was a well-known phenomenon and Paul's missions could be described in this light in a form which was true as far as it went, while at the same time it contained an element of miracle and adventure to suit the popular taste, combined with valuable propaganda on behalf of Christianity in an interesting and readable form.'

[125] Luke 9,51-19,27: the 'travel section'.

[126] Vielhauer, *Geschichte*, p. 392, e.g., is rather certain about the use of the itinerary: 'als Quellenschrift läßt sich nur das Itinerar einigermaßen nachweisen; es ist nicht als ganzes dem Buch eingelegt, sonder gibt den "roten Faden" für 13,4-21,18 ab.' For a careful discussion of the evidence, see V. Fusco, *Da Paolo a Luca. Studi su Luca-Atti* vol. 1 (SB 124; Brescia: Paideia, 2000), pp. 57-84, and the book Fusco discusses: J. Wehnert, *Die Wir-Passagen der Apostelgeschichte. Ein lukanisches Stilmittel aus jüdischen Tradition* (GTA 40; Göttingen: Vandenhoeck&Ruprecht, 1989).

[127] See Acts 13,14.15.43; 14,1; 17,1.10.17; 18,4.7.8.17.19.26; 19,8.

gregation. In the latter part of his ministry Paul travels on his own, not as an envoy, and this is one of the reasons his status is disputed by some of his opponents.[128] We cannot automatically assume that, at this stage of his ministry, Paul continued to enter synagogues in the same way he had done as an envoy from Antioch. The second reason to be suspicious of the picture given by Acts is that Paul himself explicitly describes how he preached the gospel to the Gentiles.[129] Also the evidence on the Apostolic Council, as found in Galatians and in Acts,[130] points out that Paul was sent not to Jews, but to Gentiles. As a result, the description Acts offers of Paul's independent ministry cannot be interpreted as compelling evidence that Paul aimed his proclamation of the gospel primarily at Jewish synagogues to be thrown out and re-direct his activities at Gentiles.[131] This does not mean that Paul did not include Jews at all in his audience; it merely indicates that we cannot base our reconstruction for this part of Paul's ministry on the Book of Acts.

If we turn to Paul's own letters for a reconstruction of his audience we encounter a methodological difficulty: these letters are directed inward, and reflect the situation that resulted from Paul's preaching of the gospel. Therefore they do not automatically shed light on Paul's activities out of which these congregations grew. The audience Paul addresses within the newly formed Christian congregations he raised need not coincide with the audience he aimed his preaching at. Nevertheless, some conclusions can be drawn from a number of clues Paul gives.

Firstly, it is important to note that Paul occasionally refers to his readers as 'former pagans'. In 1 Thess 1,9 Paul explicitly notes that the Thessalonians 'turned away from the idols toward the living and true God'.[132] This remark cannot refer to a Jewish audience. A similar observation holds for the extensive discussion of the consumption of meat that had been sacrificed to idols in 1 Corinthians 8. Paul's remark in 8,7 implies that the consumption of this kind of meat was habitual among at least some of the Corinthians. Therefore, not only the believers in Thessalonica can be identified as former pagans, but also those in Corinth. Furthermore,

---

[128] See e.g. 1 Cor 9,1; 2 Cor 11-13; Gal 1,10-12.
[129] See Rom 11,13 (ἐθνῶν ἀπόστολος); 11,25; 15,16.18; Gal 2,2.8-9; 1 Thess 2,16.
[130] Gal 2,8-9, cf. Acts 15,1-29.
[131] See Hengel, Schwemer, *Paul between Damascus and Antioch*, p. 128: 'That the Jews launch attacks on Paul seems almost to be something like a fixed theme in Luke, though it was historically well grounded in Paul's life (...)'.
[132] On 'the living God', see Breytenbach, *Paulus und Barnabas*, pp. 60-65, who correctly argues: 'Paulus greift hier Traditionelles auf', p. 65, n. 69.

the discussions in Galatians and Philippians on the introduction of the Mosaic Law for pagans clearly points out that there were indeed pagans among the believers in those congregations. Thus Paul addresses the believers in Thessalonica, Corinth, Galatia, and Philippi as people from a pagan background. Since the letter to the Romans is addressed to a congregation that Paul did not start, and the letter to Philemon gives no description of the congregation this Philemon belonged to, we must say that the evidence Paul gives on 'his' congregations explicitly points to a pagan origin of these groups.

Secondly, we do have indications in the letters that not all Christians within the congregations mentioned were former pagans. The discussion on the relation to Israel as given by Paul in e.g. Galatians 4 points out that this problem is not merely a problem to Paul, but also to the congregations he wrote to. Furthermore, Paul often uses arguments from Scripture, citing passages from the Septuagint or even translating directly from the Hebrew. Paul must have assumed the recipients of his letters would at least understand these arguments. In order to do so, the recipients must have been familiar with the Jewish Scriptures Paul quotes from.

Seen from this perspective the evidence indicates that Paul's preaching activities reached for pagans and Jews alike. It is not by chance that Paul explains his ministry as becoming a Jew to Jews and a pagan to pagans (1 Cor 9,19-23). This observation implies that the pagans Paul reached for may have belonged to the category of sympathisers with Judaism discussed in chapter one. However, we cannot be sure of this on the basis of the data in Paul's letters.

Another way to approach the question of the identity of Paul's audience is to study the opposition Paul apparently met with. Several passages in the letters as well as in Acts refer to this phenomenon. Not only was Paul's position internally debated among at least the communities 'in Christ' in Corinth and Galatia, he also met with fierce external opposition from both Jews and Gentiles who rejected his message. The letter to the Philippians was written whilst Paul was in custody, and his epistle to the Thessalonians clearly reflects a situation of oppression (1 Thess 3,3-4). On a number of occasions Paul refers in his letters to difficult situations, usually in general terms (cf. Rom 2,9; 5,3; 8,35; 2 Cor 1,4.8; 2,4; 6,4; 7,4; 8,2; 12,10). But especially in the catalogue of hardships of 2 Cor 11,23-29, Paul appears to relate a number of actual events at which he was oppressed by his external opponents.

In an article in 1928 A. Fridrichsen pointed out the similarities of the catalogue of hardships in 2 Cor 11,23-32 to similar ones in for instance

Plutarch.[133] In 1929 he added the observation that Paul in this passage willingly uses the style of *res gestae*, presenting his hardships as a *cursus honorum*. Thus Paul 'boasts in his weaknesses', i.e. he presents all the hardships he has endured as evidence of his trustworthiness.[134] In 1964 Georgi drew attention to these catalogues of hardships once again, this time in connection with Paul's opponents in 2 Corinthians. Georgi has argued that *peristasis* catalogues were an important element within the Cynic-Stoic diatribe, and functioned to point out the divine inspiration of the philosopher: notwithstanding all his sufferings, he could still instruct people on the divine truth.[135] In a more recent discussion of the catalogues of hardships J.T. Fitzgerald gives weight to Georgi's thesis that Paul frequently uses this style when describing the circumstances in which he preached the gospel.[136] According to Fitzgerald, these catalogues were often used in Graeco-Roman literature 'for the depiction and demonstration of the sage's various qualities as the ideal philosopher'.[137] Fitzgerald's monograph points out that in his catalogues of hardships Paul applies a style element commonly used to depict the ideal philosopher who in his mind conquers all hardships he has to face.[138]

In 2 Cor 11,23-29, however, something more is at stake than rhetoric only. Here Paul sums up the perils he has endured during his preaching of the gospel. He does so in order to demonstrate the value of his ministry to recipients of the letter. Although Paul uses a common style element here, a number of the perils he mentions do reflect the actual opposition Paul encountered. The 'dangers' he describes here are put in relatively general terms: dangers from rivers, bandits, dangers from his own people, from Gentiles, from the city or the desert. But especially the θάνατοι, the 'mortal dangers' elaborated in vv. 24-25, appear to describe a number of actual incidents in which Paul was threatened. Paul mentions that he was lashed five times, stoned once, beaten with a rod three times, and shipwrecked three times. The lashings and the stoning must have

---

[133] A. Fridrichsen, 'Zum Stil des Paulinischen Peristasenkatalogs 2 Cor. 11,23ff.', *SO* 7 (1928), pp. 25-29.

[134] A. Fridrichsen, 'Peristasenkatalog und *res gestae*. Nachtrag zu 2 Cor. 11,23ff', *SO* 8 (1929), pp. 78-82.

[135] Georgi, *Gegner*, pp. 192-200.

[136] Fitzgerald, *Cracks*, p. 203: 'It has been shown that *peristasis* catalogues are essentially "catalogues of circumstances", with the circumstances envisioned either "good" or "bad" or both.'

[137] Fitzgerald, *Cracks*, p. 203.

[138] Unfortunately, Fitzgerald does not discuss the catalogue of 2 Cor 11,23-29. For a discussion of the style and genre of this pericope, see Martin, *2 Corinthians*, pp. 368-372.

been inflicted on Paul by Jews, whereas the beating with a rod was a Roman punishment.[139] Interpreters often try to reveal the exact circumstances in which these punishments were inflicted on Paul.[140] Unfortunately, there is not enough evidence to discover which actual events Paul is referring to here. Yet the relevance of this passage within our reconstruction of Paul is evident. It proves that he did indeed meet with fierce resistance, from both Jews and Gentiles. This in turn indicates that Paul proclaimed the gospel to Jew and Gentile alike.

The resistance against Paul's gospel not only points out that Paul addressed a mixed audience, it is also relevant for a different matter: due to the violent opposition Paul describes he must have been forced to leave a number of the places where he worked. After a conflict so fierce that it ended in a flogging, beating, or even stoning, Paul was hardly liable to be able to continue preaching the gospel. Such a beating, flogging, or stoning would no doubt have caused him to move on.

The book of Acts indeed presents us with a number of forced departures from towns where Paul worked. Acts 14,19-20 speaks of a stoning in Lystra (perhaps the incident referred to by Paul in 2 Cor 11,25), and 17,1-10 speaks of Paul's flight from Thessalonica (cf. 17,15; 20,3). It has been argued above that the theme of oppression leading to a further spread of the gospel is an important feature in the redaction of Acts.[141] Judging from the evidence of Paul's letters, Paul did meet with fierce opposition, and therefore in this respect the incidents described in Acts may be considered more or less reliable: even if the accounts may not be fully accurate concerning the exact nature of the events, they probably do give a more or less reliable characterisation of Paul's ministry.

Having stated this, we should note that in the Book of Acts Paul primarily faces Jewish opposition: this is the case in Philippi, Thessalonica, and Beroea, but also later on in the book. After the clearly redactional turning-point in 18,5-7, Paul directs his attention towards Gentiles rather

---

[139] Deut 25,2-3 prescribes 40 lashes as a punishment, but in order to safeguard the victim from having too many lashes, the custom developed that the punisher was to stop at 39; cf. *mMak* 3,10; Strack-Billerbeck, vol. 3, pp. 527-530. On the time of those beatings and the Roman character of the beating with rods, see Martin, *2 Corinthians*, pp. 376-377. On the latter also: R. Bultmann, *2 Korinther*, p. 217.

[140] W. Meeks, e.g., has argued that Paul received the 39 lashes on five occasions in the 'silent years' of his ministry, when Paul apparently aimed his proclamation of the gospel at Jewish audiences – *First Urban Christians*, p. 26. Unfortunately, the point cannot be decided, since we simply do not have any information to match these punishments with; see Martin, *2 Corinthians*, p. 377.

[141] See p. 102.

than Jews. Nevertheless, he has to face Jewish opposition again – members of the synagogue bring him before Gallio, who subsequently releases Paul. After the beating of Sosthenes is reported, Paul leaves Corinth for Ephesus. Again it is Jewish opposition that forces him to leave. By means of the subsequent episode at Ephesus, the author points out that Paul also had to face Greek opposition: his conflict with Demetrius leads to an uproar after which Paul leaves Ephesus. In his analysis of Acts Lüdemann has convincingly argued that the uproar at Ephesus was formed following a pagan tradition into which Paul and his companions would have been inserted by the author of Acts.[142] In consequence, the picture of the opposition Paul met at Ephesus is fully redactional.

If we relate this clearly redactional element in Acts to the evidence found in the letters, the conclusion lies at hand that the author of Acts downplays the Greek and Roman opposition against Paul for literary and apologetical reasons. The over-all picture cannot be taken away: Paul met with opposition from Jew and Gentile alike, which proves that he preached his gospel to both categories. Therefore, the conclusion to this section should be that Paul travelled and worked in the cities mentioned above, aiming his proclamation at both groups of potential believers. This observation raises the final question: did Paul work on the basis of an all-encompassing missionary programme?

5. Paul's Missionary Programme

Throughout the history of Christianity Paul's travels were interpreted as an attempt to fulfil a missionary programme or even command given directly by Jesus.[143] In chapter three, however, it was argued that the missionary command by Jesus, as narrated by Matt 28,16-20, should be interpreted as an example of 'Gemeindebildung', and that the commissioning of disciples by Jesus in synoptic tradition reflects a post-Easter habit rather than an encompassing missionary programme held by Jesus. Furthermore, the reports on Paul's conversion as given by Paul and the author of Acts, were labelled as later retrospectives on the great change in Paul's life. These observations entail that Paul's ministry did not rest upon any missionary command by Jesus himself, either during his earthly ministry or at moment he 'called' Paul. Therefore the

---

[142] Lüdemann, Das frühe Christentum, pp. 223-228.
[143] See e.g. above, p. 2.

question of whether Paul worked on the basis of a missionary programme, and if so, where he took that programme from, becomes all the more relevant.

We should depart from the observation that Paul indicates to have planned his work to a certain extent. Several times in his letters Paul refers to a plan to visit a congregation. When writing 1 Corinthians Paul obviously planned to visit the congregation (1 Cor 4,19; 11,34; 16,5-9). Later he describes his reluctance to visit Corinth again, after his previous visit had turned out to be a disaster (2 Cor 12,14.20-21). He even cancelled a visit to Corinth for this reason (2 Cor 1,15-24). In the letter to the Thessalonians, Paul points out that he had wanted to return earlier, but had been held against his will from doing so (1 Thess 2,18). He stresses the fact that he looks forward to visiting them again (3,6.10). Also to the Romans he mentions the fact that he had already been planning to visit them at an earlier stage (Rom 1,9-13; 15,22-23).

The passages mentioned are proof of the fact that Paul planned his visits ahead. His remark in 2 Cor 2,12-13 even points to the fact that he intended to proclaim the gospel in Troas, but changed his plans because he could not find Titus. Thus Paul makes clear that he indeed planned his ministry ahead to a certain degree. But are incidental plans like these enough evidence for the interpretation of Paul's work as being based on a world-wide missionary programme?

The pericope that is usually referred to as a crown witness for the existence of such a programme is Rom 15,14-29.[144] This passage contains some important information on how Paul saw his own task at the time of writing his letter to the Romans, and therefore it is worth while discussing it at some length.

In Rom 15,16 Paul defines the purpose of the 'grace given to me by God' as 'being a minister of Jesus Christ to the Gentiles in the priestly service of the gospel of God, so that the offering of the Gentiles may be acceptable, sanctified by the Holy Spirit.' The words χάρις ἡ δοθεῖσά μοι are a description of Paul's state as a believer: he is accepted by God in grace. The same description is used elsewhere by Paul of himself[145] or others.[146] Often interpreters of Romans consider the phrase to be a

---

[144] See e.g. F.F. Bruce, *Paul. Apostle of the Free Spirit*, (Carlisle: Paternoster, 1995 = rev. ed. 1980, ¹1977), p. 314: 'For another thing, Rome in his mind was a halting place, or at best an advance base, on his way to Spain, where he planned to repeat the programme which he had just completed in the Aegean world (Romans 15: 23f.).'

[145] Rom 12,3; 1 Cor 3,10; Gal 2,9.

[146] 1 Cor 1,4; 2 Cor 8,1.

description of the special apostolic call Paul had received, and point at Gal 1,5; 2,9 to underline this.[148] Indeed it appears at first sight as if Paul is speaking of a special grace that only he had received. This interpretation could be supported by a reference to 1 Cor 15,10: 'by the grace of God I am what I am, and his grace toward me has not been in vain' (χάριτι δὲ θεοῦ εἰμι ὅ εἰμι, καὶ ἡ χάρις αὐτοῦ οὐ κένη ἐγενήθη). Yet the fact that Paul uses the word χάρις for all Christians, also in the exact same phrase ἡ χάρις ἡ δοθεῖσά μοι/ὑμῖν (1 Cor 1,4; 2 Cor 8,1), indicates that the state of grace is not so much the apostolic state as the state of *all believers*.

The purport of vv. 15-16 is therefore, that Paul as a believer saw his destiny as being the one to offer the Gentiles to God through his preaching of the gospel. The language Paul uses in this pericope is evidently cultic. Although λειτουργός is a profane term, ἱερουργέω, προσφορά, and εὐπρόσδεκτος are words with a cultic meaning. The description of Paul's task is no doubt modelled after Isa 66,20:

MT:

and they will bring all of your brothers	והביאו את כל אחיכם
from all of the nations	מכל הגוים
an offering to the Lord	מנחה ליהוה
on horses and on chariots,	בסוסים וברכב
and on litters and on mules	ובצבים ובפרדים
and on dromedaries	ובכרכרות
to my holy mountain Jerusalem,	על הר קדשי ירושלם
says the Lord,	אמר יהוה
just like the children of Israel	כאשר יביאו בני
bring an offering	ישראל את המנחה
in a clean vessel to the house of the Lord.	בכלי טהור בית יהוה

LXX:

καὶ ἄξουσιν τοὺς ἀδελφοὺς ὑμῶν ἐκ πάντων τῶν ἐθνῶν δῶρον κυρίῳ μεθ' ἵππων καὶ ἁρμάτων ἐν λαμπήναις ἡμιόνων μετὰ σκιαδίων εἰς τὴν ἁγίαν πόλιν Ἰερουσαλήμ, εἶπεν κύριος, ὡς ἂν ἐνέγκαισαν οἱ υἱοὶ Ἰσραήλ ἐμοὶ τὰς θυσίας αὐτῶν μετὰ ψαλμῶν εἰς τὸν οἶκον κυρίου.

In this verse the idea is that the dispersed members of Israel will be gathered as an offering for the Lord from among the Gentiles. Paul's use of the imagery signifies an important shift: in his description the Gentiles

---

[147] See e.g. Michel, *Römer*, p. 456; H. Schlier, *Der Römerbrief* (HThK; Freiburg [etc.]: Herder, 1977), p. 429.

themselves are an offering to the Lord. It is therefore worth the effort to take a look at contemporary literature in which the eschatological fate of the Gentiles is described. Did Paul make use of any earlier re-interpretation of Isa 66,20 or not?

Contemporary Jewish literature shows a number of possibilities in regard to the fate of the Gentiles. In for instance *As. Mos.* 10 the eschatological redemption of Israel is described without even a single mention of the Gentiles. Apparently their fate was totally irrelevant to the author. Many others shared this idea.[148] If the Gentiles are described, however, they are often wiped out by God and his people. The enemies of Israel were to be defeated at the final intervention of God in history, and they would be punished severely (cf. *4 Ezra* 12,33; 13,49; *2 Apoc. Bar.* 13,6.11; 40,1; 58,1-2; 70,7; also 1QM XVIII,1-5). Often it is Israel itself that will judge the Gentiles and inflict a punishment upon them (LXX Dan 7,22; *Jub.* 32,19; Wis 3,8; 1QpHab v,4; 1QH IV,26; 1QM VI,6; XI,13-14; 1QS v,6-7). Only occasionally is a 'conversion' of Gentiles described (*1 Enoch* 10,21; 48,4-5; 90,33-36; Tob 14,6; cf. LXX Gen 49,10). A far more important element within the apocalyptic expectations of the final intervention of God is the hope for the return of Jews from all over the world to their own land, Israel.[149] In *Pss. Sol.* 17,30-31 two elements are combined, viz. the return of the Dispersed to Israel, and the recognition by the Gentiles of Israel's king as a divine ruler. The king will not only rule over Israel, but also over the Gentiles:

> καὶ ἕξει λαοὺς ἐθνῶν δουλεύειν αὐτῷ ὑπὸ τὸν ζυγὸν αὐτοῦ (...)
> καὶ καθαριεῖ Ἰερουσαλὴμ ἐν ἁγιασμῷ ὡς καὶ τὸ ἀπ᾽ ἀρχῆς
> ἔρχεσθαι ἔθνη ἀπ᾽ ἄκρου τῆς γῆς ἰδεῖν τὴν δόξαν αὐτοῦ φέρον-
> τες δῶρα τοὺς ἐξησθενηκότας υἱοὺς αὐτῆς καὶ ἰδεῖν τὴν δόξαν
> κυρίου, ἣν ἐδόξασεν αὐτὴν ὁ θεός.

In Paul's view we find a fusion of the expectation of the gathering of the dispersed Jews from among the Gentiles, as found in Isaiah 66,[150] and the

---

[148] See also the verdict by Bousset, Gressmann, *Religion*, p. 234: 'Im ganzen und großen kann man nämlich sagen, daß das Schicksal der Völker die Apokalyptiker nicht beschäftigt.'

[149] P. Volz, *Die Eschatologie der jüdischen Gemeinde im neutestamentlichen Zeitalter* (Tübingen: Mohr Siebeck, 1934), p. 344: 'Es gehört zum Inventar der nationalen Eschatologie, daß auch die zerstreuten Juden in die Heimat zurückkehren und am Heil teilnehmen werden.' For a description see pp. 344-348, and also Bousset, Gressmann, *Religion*, pp. 236-238. See among many other ancient witnesses to this expectation: *1 Enoch* 57,1; *2 Macc* 2,18; *Pss. Sol.* 8,28; 11,2-6; 17,12.18.31; *4 Ezra* 12,34; 13, 40-48; *Apoc. Abr.* 31,1; *T. Naph.* 8,3; *T. Ash.* 7,7; *Shmone Esre* 10.

[150] See also *1 Enoch* 90,32; *Pss. Sol.* 11; cf. Bousset, Gressmann, *Religion* pp. 236-237.

tradition of the eschatological 'conversion' of Gentiles, found in e.g. *Psalm of Solomon* 17.[151] At the time he wrote his letter to the Romans, Paul recognised his own ministry in the description of Isa 66,20. His perception of what he was doing did, however, lead Paul to change the purport of that verse. He did not see himself as the one who brought about the gathering of the dispersed Jews, but as the servant bringing the Gentiles themselves as an offering. Paul obviously transforms the traditional expectation of the eschatological gathering of all of Israel to the idea of a gathering of Gentiles as an eschatological offering before the Lord: it is only in Paul's words that the Gentiles themselves form the offering.[152] In Isa 66,20 they bring the dispersed Jews as an offering, and in *Pss. Sol.* 17,30-31 the Gentiles bring presents.[153] In presenting the Gentiles as an offering Paul has created a new idea. Since this idea is found nowhere else in Paul's writings, it cannot be held to have formed the basis for Paul's work throughout his ministry, but must be interpreted as an *ad hoc* invention by Paul by the time he wrote his letter to the Romans.

Does this conclusion mean that we have found Paul's 'missionary programme'? Unfortunately, we cannot say that. What we found is Paul's interpretation of his task at the time he wrote his last letter preserved for us. A careful consideration of the evidence points out that this interpretation cannot be identified as a 'missionary programme'.

The influence of Isaiah 66 on Paul has been reconstructed by R. Riesner in his 1994 monograph on the early period of Paul.[154] According to Riesner,

---

[151] It is remarkable that both in Rom 15,16 and in *Pss.Sol.* 17,30 the ἁγιασμός plays an important part. Since this important element is far less prominent in Isa 66,20, the conclusion must be that Paul has been influenced by a tradition we also find in *Psalm of Solomon* 17.

[152] Schlier, *Römerbrief*, pp. 430-431. Esp. 431: 'Jetzt, da die Gerechtigkeit setzende und durchsetzende Bundestreue Gottes sich in Jesus Christus ereignet hat (Röm 3,21 ff.; vgl. 15,8) und so "der Tag des Heils", den der Prophet verheißen hat (2 Kor 6,2), gekommen ist und sich seine Gegenwart im Evangelium erweist, jetzt wird das Opfer nicht mehr im Tempel zu Jerusalem durch rituellen Vollzug dargebracht, sondern die Völker, deren sich das apostolische Evangelium bemächtigt hat, sind das Opfer, "geheiligt durch den Heiligen Geist", der im Evangelium wirksam ist, und so das Opfer, das Gott angenehm ist.'

[153] In *Pss. Sol.* 17,32 the Gentiles bring δῶρα (plural!) to Jerusalem. Paul's language is closer to Isaiah's: Paul regards the Gentiles themselves as 'an offering' (προσφορά). In Isaiah the word used is מנחה – 'gift' (LXX δῶρον). Paul thus introduces a cultic element that is absent from both Isaiah and *Pss. Sol.* 17,32, but makes the same identification that is made in Isa 66,20.

[154] Riesner, *Frühzeit*, esp. pp. 216-225. R.D. Aus, 'Paul's Travel Plans to Spain and the "Full Number of the Gentiles" of Rom. xi 25', *NT* 21 (1979), pp. 232-262, had already proposed to interpret Spain as the Tarshish of Isa 66,20.

it is very likely that Paul in preparing his journey to Rome and subsequently to Spain, read the prophecy of Isaiah as a description of his own task.[155] Riesner argues that Paul was influenced by this prophecy in the geographic modelling of his mission. In Riesner's view, Paul's contemporaries interpreted the places mentioned in Isa 66,19 as 1. Tarsus (Cilicia), 2. Lybia (Cyrene), 3. Lydia (Asia Minor), 4. Cappadocia or Mysia, 5. the Causasus or Bithynia, 6. Greece and Macedonia, and 7. the far West.[156] According to Riesner, this area can be summarised as 'half a circle from Jerusalem to Illyricum' (Rom 15,19). Paul would have left some of the areas mentioned in Isaiah out of his plans because others had already been there ahead of him. The evangelisation of Italy and North-Africa has already been taken care of by others.[157] On the other hand, Paul would have refused to visit for instance the province of Thrace, because this area is not mentioned in Isaiah.

Notwithstanding the ingenious and careful character of his attempt, Riesner cannot prove his point with certainty. If Riesner's hypothesis is correct, Paul would have modelled his travels on the geographic programme of Isa 66,19. There are, however, three major problems with this view. Firstly, Riesner's reconstruction of the interpretation of the areas mentioned in Isaiah may be probable, but it is not certain. The identification of the areas Paul visited with the areas in Isaiah remains speculative. Secondly, even if the identification is correct it has still to be explained why Paul left a number of these regions untouched. And thirdly, Paul mentions the prophecy of Isaiah 66 in only one pericope in which he looks back on his ministry up to that moment. As a result, it is far more likely that in Rom 15,24-29 Paul is not reviewing his travels in the context of a programme that he had planned to carry out. In stead, he looks back on his ministry up to that moment, concludes that his work is

---

[155] Riesner is very careful not to suggest that Paul's entire ministry was modelled after the prophecy of Isa 66,18-21: 'Es soll hier weder behauptet werden, daß sich die paulinischen Missionspläne von vornherein an Jes. 66,19 orientierten, noch daß in dieser Prophetie der einzige oder wichtigste Grund für die vom Apostel beschrittenen Routen liegt.' Nevertheless, Riesner does try to find out 'ob Paulus an entscheidenden Stationen seines Weges *auch* von dieser alttestamentlichen Missionsweissagung beeinflußt wurde.' – Riesner, *Frühzeit*, pp. 224-225. Riesner's attempt to interpret Paul from the perspective of Isaiah does lead him to the speculative theory that Paul would have interpreted the light he saw at his conversion as the messianic light signifying the beginning of the eschatological gathering of the nations – *Frühzeit*, p. 211. Riesner overlooks the fact that the only light near Damascus we know of is mentioned by the author of Acts, not by Paul.

[156] Riesner, *Frühzeit*, p. 224.

[157] See Riesner's discussion with F.F. Bruce, *Frühzeit*, pp. 271-272.

done in the vast area between Jerusalem and Illyricum, and then mentions his plan to visit Spain from Rome.

The fact that Paul describes the effect of his call in retrospect, rather than its intention at the outset, is further stressed by a grammatical observation. Paul's use of ὥστε in v. 19 is consecutive, and not final: in combination with an infinitive ὥστε describes the effect of an action either as it has already occurred or as it is hoped to be. In Paul's day ὥστε was also used with a final meaning,[158] but only in combination with the subjunctive (cf. 1 Cor 5,8). Since its use is consecutive in all cases where Paul uses it with an infinitive,[159] it is highly unlikely that Rom 15,19 would form an exception. In consequence, Rom. 15,19 should be taken as describing the effect of his actions *after the fact*. It thus appears that Paul is looking back on his preaching activities up to that moment. He describes that he has 'fulfilled the gospel' in the whole area between Jerusalem and Illyricum. The expression Paul uses reflects his view of his task: the expression πληροῦν τὸ εὐαγγέλιον, a *hapax legomenon* within the corpus of the New Testament, probably means 'to fulfil the assignment of preaching the good news'.[160] In this case the perfect tense is evidence of the fact that for Paul this assignment had been completed in the area mentioned.

The observation that Paul considered his work done in the area between Jerusalem and Illyricum is remarkable, but revealing. It is evident that by the time he wrote his letter to the Romans Paul had not brought about the Christianisation of the whole of Asia Minor, and therefore he must have had the major cities in mind. Apparently the gospel had been preached in these cities, either by Paul himself or by others. Paul obviously aimed at a gradual spread of the gospel from the centres where it had already been proclaimed. Paul and his colleagues had lit a number of candles, so to speak, and trusted that these would spread the fire.[161] This observation coincides with the reconstruction made above of Paul's ministry: he focused on a number of towns, centres of trade and commerce, so that the gospel would subsequently spread of its own accord.

---

[158] Moulton, *Grammar* vol. 3, p. 106: 'In Hellenistic colloquial speech there was much overlapping in the use of ἵνα (or ὅπως) and ὥστε (or ὡς); so much that ἵνα (ὅπως) are even used with the inf. and ὥστε with subj., with their final and consecutive rôles respectively reversed.'

[159] Rom 7,6; 1 Cor 1,7; 5,1; 13,2; 2 Cor 1,8; 2,7; 3,7; 7,7; Phil 1,13; 1 Thess 1,7-8.

[160] Michel, *Römer*, p. 460, paraphrases these words as though Paul boasts that 'er habe den ganzen Osten des Mittelmeergebietes mit dem Evangelium von der Messias erfüllt.' For πληροῦν as 'to fulfil an assignment': Wilckens, *Römer* vol. 3, p. 119.

[161] Harnack, *Mission und Ausbreitung*, p. 64: 'Voraussetzung ist dabei, daß sich nach rechts und links von der flammenden Linie das Feuer von selbst verbreiten wird.'

Apart from confirming the observation made above concerning Paul's method, Rom 15,20-21 also explicitly states that Paul did not take the gospel to places where it had already been brought by someone else. The quotation from LXX Isa 52,15 points out that Paul saw it as his task to proclaim the gospel to those who had not yet heard it. The fact that Paul did not direct his activities towards those congregations where others had already preached the gospel is only a natural result of this view. This cannot be taken as evidence for a 'missionary plan',[162] but merely supports the view that Paul was driven by one thing, namely the need to proclaim the gospel. In Paul's communication with the congregation of Rome, this remark also illustrates the fact that Paul did not intend to come to Rome in order to preach the gospel. His plan was to use Rome as a base for his journey to Spain.

Rather than reflecting the geographical programme of Paul's ministry, the description of his work in Romans 15 was influenced by the collection for the poor that Paul was about to deliver in Jerusalem. It was probably the eschatological connotation of this collection for Jerusalem brought Paul on the trail of interpreting his ministry by means of Isaiah 66.[163]

In view of the previous observations, the question arises as to whether Paul had any specific reason for planning a journey to Spain.[164] In this respect Riesner's attempt to interpret Paul's ministry from the perspective of Isaiah 66 is valuable. Even if it cannot be proved that Paul tried to fulfil a missionary programme described in Isaiah, the universalistic tendencies Paul shares with Isaiah cannot be neglected. As was already argued above, Paul interpreted the gospel as a message with universal implications. It is this universal purpose of the gospel that Paul found reflected in Isaiah.[165] In 15,20-21 Paul describes his principle of not pro-

---

162 See also R. Allen, *Missionary Methods: St. Paul's or Ours?* (London: World Dominion Press, 1953), p. 15: 'It is quite impossible to maintain that St. Paul deliberately planned his journeys beforehand, selected certain strategic points at which to establish his Churches and then actually carried out his designs.'

163 See Beckheuer, *Paulus und Jerusalem*, pp. 218-224.

164 The exact fate of Paul in his final years is unknown. *1 Clem.* 5,5-7 however may not be used as evidence that Paul did indeed reach Spain. If Clement's τέρμα τῆς δύσεως points to Spain, it is more likely to refer to Rom 15,24.28 than to an event otherwise unattested – cf. Bruce, *Paul*, pp. 446-448; *pace* H. Löhr, 'Zur Paulus-Notiz in 1 Clem 5,5-7', in: F. W. Horn (ed.), *Das Ende des Paulus. Historische, theologische und literaturgeschichtliche Aspekte* (BZNW 106; Berlin, New York: De Gruyter, 2001), pp. 197-213. For a discussion of other reconstructions of Paul's plan to visit Spain, see B. Wander, 'Warum wollte Paulus nach Spanien? Ein forschungs- und motivgeschichtlicher Überblick', in: Horn (ed.), *Das Ende des Paulus*, pp. 175-195.

165 On Paul's use of Isaiah in his letter to the Romans, see J. Ross Wagner, *Heralds of the Good News. Isaiah and Paul <in Concert> in the Letter to the Romans* (SNT 101;

claiming the gospel where it had already been brought, underlining his point of view by means of a quotation from Isa 52,15. It is no accident that here Paul quotes from a passage in Isaiah that clearly describes the universal implication of God's salvation – the first part of the verse Paul quotes says 'many nations will be amazed by him' (LXX: οὕτως θαυμά-σονται ἔθνη πολλὰ ἐπ' αὐτῷ...).

Paul's plan to visit Spain must have found its origin in his wish to preach the gospel where it had not yet been brought. This wish in turn originated in Paul's perception of the gospel as a proclamation with uni-versal significance. In Paul's eyes the coming judgement would extend to the entire cosmos and it was only by means of the confession of Jesus Christ as the Lord, that man would be saved (cf. 1 Thess 1,10). Paul's wish to visit Spain therefore ultimately originated in his interpretation of the gospel as a necessary and universal means for salvation rather than in his reading of Isaiah. More likely Paul read Isaiah because there he found the confirmation of his ideas on the universal importance of the gospel.

This universal significance of the gospel is implicitly present through-out the letters of Paul. Time and again he stresses its saving function for believers, hereby pointing out that according to him, only faith in Christ would lead to salvation at the coming ultimate intervention of God in history. This thought is expressed in some of the earliest known words of Paul, 1 Thess 1,10. There, Paul explains the function of Christ: he will save the believers from the coming wrath. The same thought is expressed in Rom 5,9-10, and inferred in e.g. Rom 10,9.13; 1 Cor 1,18; 5,5; 10,33; 2 Cor 2,15; and 1 Thess 2,16. Especially 1 Cor 15,2 is explicit in this respect: it is the gospel that saves people.

It thus appears that in Romans 15, too, Paul is shown to act on the basis of the universal significance of the gospel. Somewhat later this idea was expressed in a conditional form in Mark 13,10 (καὶ εἰς πάντα τὰ ἔθνη πρῶτον δεῖ κηρυχθῆναι τὸ εὐαγγέλιον). And one step further in the development of this thought, Matt 28,19-20 formulated the mission-ary command by Jesus (πορευθέντες οὖν μαθητεύσατε πάντα τὰ ἔθνη, βαπτίζοντες αὐτοὺς εἰς τὸ ὄνομα τοῦ πατρὸς καὶ τοῦ υἱοῦ καὶ τοῦ ἁγίου πνεύματος κτλ.).

Leiden [etc.]: Brill, 2002), passim. On Romans 15, see pp. 307-340. Wagner correctly concludes to a 'complex and dynamic interrelationship of scripture, theology, and mis-sion within a particular cultural and historical context' (p. 357) as far as Paul's use of Isaiah is concerned.

Together with the universal significance of the gospel, there is another element in Paul's words in Romans 15 that may be extended to Paul's ministry as a whole: his description of himself in terms of a prophet. It was argued above that Paul only gradually came to see himself as an independent apostle. In his description of his call in Gal 1,15 Paul had used language referring to Jer 1,5 and Isa 49,1 (cf. pp. 167-168). Now, in Romans 15, Paul uses Isaiah 66 to depict the nature of his ministry. Apparently Paul interpreted his ministry in the terms of that of a prophet, although he never explicitly identifies himself as such.[166]

Paul's words in Rom 15,19 show that he acted as a prophet, by performing 'signs and wonders', 'inspired by the Spirit'. According to Dunn, the expression σημεῖα καὶ τέρατα is used quite frequently in the LXX as 'a traditional way of referring to the miracles of the Exodus'.[167] The use of this terminology by Paul would show how he interpreted the 'eschatological exodus of the gospel out of Palestine into the world as of the same epochal significance as the original Exodus'.[168] According to W.A. Meeks, however, the terminology σημεῖα καὶ τέρατα has been influenced by two *loci classici* on the coming of a prophet as Moses – Deut 13,2-6 and 18,18-22.[169] Meeks has shown that the performance of signs and wonders was regarded as a characteristic of such a prophet like Moses. Therefore, it is more likely that Paul in this passage presents his apostolic task as that of a prophet, rather than referring to the 'original Exodus'.

This prophetic aspect of Paul's apostolic task is also implied by the inspiration of the Spirit Paul mentions (ἐν δυνάμει πνεύματος; v. 19). That the combination of this inspiration with the performing of signs and wonders was not a new invention of Paul's at the time he wrote his letter

---

[166] K.O. Sandnes, *Paul – One of the Prophets?*, explains how Paul thought of himself in terms of a prophet, while at the same time he never explicitly labels himself as such; cf. esp. pp. 242-244.

[167] J.D.G. Dunn, *Romans 9-16*, pp. 862-863, mentions 'Exod 7,39; 11,9-10; Deut 4,34; 6,22; 7,19; 11,3; 26,8; 29,3; 34,11; Neh 9,10; Pss 78,43; 135,9; Jer 32,20-21; Wisd Sol 10,16; Bar 2,11; see also Isa 8,18; 20,3; Dan 4,2-3; 6,27; Wisd Sol 8,8; Philo, *Mos.* 1,95; *Spec.Leg.* 2,218; TDNT 7,16-17.221'.

[168] Dunn, *Romans 9-16*, pp. 862-863.

[169] Meeks, *Prophet-King*, pp. 162-164, discusses the feature of the 'signs and wonders' in traditions based on Moses. See esp. p. 163: 'The emphasis on "signs and wonders" in Moses' mission led to a similar emphasis in the expectation of the "prophet like Moses" or of a *Moses redivivus*. This is especially clear in Josephus' description of Theudas and the other "magicians" (like Theudas, they doubtless called themselves "prophets") who promised or actually attempted to perform miracles in the wilderness.' According to Meeks 'the performance of "signs and wonders" must have been a fundamental characteristic of the mission of the prophet like Moses.' (p. 164).

to the Romans, is evident from 1 Cor 2,4 (ἐν ἀποδείξει πνεύματος καὶ δυνάμεως) and 1 Thess 1,5 (τὸ εὐαγγέλιον ... ἐν λόγῳ ... καὶ ἐν δυνάμει καὶ ἐν πνεύματι ἁγίῳ κτλ.). Also in his defence against the so-called 'super-apostles' in 2 Cor 12,12, Paul refers to the fact that he had performed 'the signs of a true apostle' among the Corinthians, 'with utmost patience, signs and wonders and mighty works' (ἐν πάσῃ ὑπομονῇ, σημείοις τε καὶ τέρασιν καὶ δυνάμεσιν).[170] Paul could not have written this specific defence if he had not indeed been active as a prophetic miracle-worker among the Corinthians.[171]

Paul thus considered himself to be inspired by the Spirit whose power enabled him to perform signs and wonders. This is an important observation, for it characterises Paul's view of his apostleship as directly related to the task of a prophet. Paul makes a difference between prophets and apostles in 1 Cor 12,28-29, but this does not mean that for him his apostolic task was not *related* to that of a prophet: both were envoys, sent by God and guided by the Spirit. Since Paul describes his call in Gal 1,15-17 in the terms used in the call of Jeremiah, it would seem that Paul indeed saw himself having a prophetic task: he had to proclaim the gospel of God in a way comparable to that in which the prophets proclaimed God's will in ancient times. This observation means that we did find the theological root of Paul's missionary endeavours: he considered himself as sent like a prophet, and read the prophets of old from his own perspective of one commissioned to proclaim the Christ event.

Conclusion

Throughout his ministry Paul considered the proclamation of the gospel, the Christ event, to be his prime task. He was called and urged by God

---

[170] In Heb 2,4 it is said that 'the message declared through angels was valid' (v. 2), and that this message was one of salvation (σωτηρία; v. 3). This salvation was proclaimed by the apostles (= those who had heard him [the Lord; LP]), and their proclamation was underlined by God himself 'by signs and wonders and various miracles, and by gifts of the Holy Spirit' (σημείοις τε καὶ τέρασιν καὶ ποικίλαις δυνάμεσιν καὶ πνεύματος ἁγίου μερισμοῖς). Apparently, the performing of signs (and wonders and miracles) and the inspiration by the Spirit counted as attributes of an apostle not only for Paul, but within the entire early Christian movement.

[171] On Paul as a performer of miracles, see S. Schreiber, *Paulus als Wundertäter. Redaktionsgeschichtliche Untersuchungen zur Apostelgeschichte und den authentischen Paulusbriefen* (BZNW 79; Berlin, New York: De Gruyter, 1996), esp. part C, pp. 160-234. Remarkably enough Schreiber takes no interest in a possible prophetic background of the performing of signs and wonders by Paul.

to proclaim Christ. As a result of Paul's proclamation of the gospel, new communities developed consisting of Jews and pagans alike. Paul 'planted' these communities, helped them reflect on their identity and shape their lives. Paul's view of these new communities was that they formed the beginning of the 'new creation' that God was about to establish. There is every reason to consider Paul's aim with these communities as missionary: these communities of those who confessed Christ as the Lord would contribute to the further spread of the gospel.

Paul focused his activities primarily on cities that could enhance the possibilities for further proclamation of the gospel due to their economic status. By proclaiming the gospel and raising communities in trade centres, Paul hoped to light a fire that would subsequently spread on its own accord. During the second stage of his ministry, i.e. the period after the incident at Antioch, Paul worked as an independent preacher, supported by either a congregation he had previously founded or by his own artisanship. In this respect, Paul shows himself to be influenced by the example he knew of Cynic-Stoic philosophers who often carried out their teaching in a similar way.

Although Paul laid great store on his independence, he did not work alone. Paul was aided by a number of fellow-workers who formed a web around him. This circle of 'colleagues' developed from the interaction between Paul and his congregations. With this 'team' Paul aimed his proclamation of the gospel at both Jew and Gentile, although the latter group appears to have been his prime focus. Given the fact that Paul often refers to the Septuagint in discussions with his new congregations, the conclusion lies at hand that his 'converts' came from Greek Jewry and from Graeco-Roman sympathisers with Judaism many of whom would have understood themselves as adherents to traditional Graeco-Roman cults rather than as 'God-fearers' (cf. Paul's stress on the worship of idols in 1 Thess 1,9 and the problems he discusses in 1 Corinthians 8-11).

Paul appears to have spent a great deal of his time on the move. Sometimes this was because of heavy resistance against Paul and his gospel, sometimes because of Paul's wish to visit a congregation he had founded earlier, and sometimes because he wanted to move on to another area that had not yet heard the gospel. Paul explicitly states to have worked solely *in terram incognitam evangelii* – in places where the gospel had not yet been heard. This desire did not originate in a world-wide missionary programme, but in the universal imperative of the gospel itself, as Paul understood it. For Paul the gospel was the necessary means of salvation, and those who had not yet heard it could not be saved from the coming judgement. Paul combined this interpretation of the gospel with a view of his own task as that of a prophet commissioned by God himself. It is the combination of these factors that turned Paul into what he ultimately became: a missionary.

PAUL'S PROCLAMATION OF THE GOSPEL

In the above it appeared that Paul's ministry brought about an important change in the early Christian movement. Seen from the perspective of contemporary religious propaganda, Paul's missionary work should be interpreted in the following manner.

The phenomenon of proselytising mission cannot be traced back to either Jewish or pagan cults in the pre-Christian era. Various forms of religious propaganda were practised in Paul's day, both by Jews and by pagans. Yet traces of an active, proselytising mission, aimed at the conversion of a person or group who would subsequently join a new religious group and adopt this new group's views, have not been found in pre-Christian sources.

The missionary command of Matt 28,16-20 should, however, be recognised as evidence for such a proselytising attitude. This indicates that at the end of the first century at least some Christians did practice this type of mission. Paul's ministry should therefore be situated in the early stage of the development that led to this proselytising attitude.

It has been argued above that the early Christian movement originated in Jesus' proclamation of the nearness of the Kingdom of God. Synoptic evidence shows that early in the Jesus tradition, probably after Jesus' death and the experience of his resurrection by his followers, those followers told the account of a commissioning of disciples to support Jesus' proclamation. They too were to announce the coming of the Kingdom: they were heralds of the New Age. Jesus was regarded as vindicated by God through his resurrection. His followers therefore continued his proclamation of the Kingdom, but due to the change in circumstances the content of their proclamation came to change too. The Christ event became the most important element of this proclamation, and Christ's death and resurrection were announced as the inauguration of the Kingdom. The accent within the proclamation thus shifted from Jesus' message of the Kingdom that *was about* to come to the belief that the Kingdom *had already started* to arrive in Jesus Christ.

The proclamation of the Christ event led to the formation of 'Christian' communities. The earliest communities were formed by Jews, and soon by Jews and Gentiles alike. The focus of these communities was on the confession of Jesus Christ as Lord. The new movement understood itself as the קהל יהוה, the eschatological congregation of the true Israel.

After his transformation experience, Paul somehow came to join the Antiochene community that consisted of Jews and Gentiles. Paul became involved in the proclamation of the Christ event, and was sent out together with Barnabas to related Jewish communities on Cyprus and in Asia Minor. After an agreement had been reached in Jerusalem on the status of mixed communities (the so-called 'Apostolic Council'), Paul took a stand opposite to that of Peter and Barnabas at the incident in Antioch. Paul's choice was to regard pagans as full members of the new community, and therefore to give more weight to Christ than to the Mosaic Law. This incident caused Paul and Barnabas to split up, and occasioned the start of Paul's independent ministry.

During his independent ministry, Paul came to regard himself as an 'apostle of Jesus Christ'. As such, it is the proclamation of the gospel that drove him. This proclamation of the gospel was aimed at those who had not yet heard the Good News, Jew and Gentile alike. During his ministry most of Paul's attention went to Gentiles, but this does not mean that Paul left Jewish communities untouched.

As a result of Paul's proclamation of the gospel, new communities grew. Paul regarded these communities as proof of the power of the gospel, as raised by God himself. By applying the general idea of ἐκκλησία τοῦ θεοῦ to every individual community, Paul made a major contribution to the self-awareness of these new churches. For him, however, the communities he founded were not the ultimate goal of his ministry, but a means to a further spread of the gospel.

In the method Paul used for the fulfilling of his task – the proclamation of the gospel – Paul was supported by wealthy individuals or congregations he (or others) had previously founded. Next to that Paul provided for his own livelihood by working as an artisan. In this respect, as in so many others, he was influenced by popular Greek philosophers. The urge to preach the gospel where it had not yet been heard drove Paul on from one town to another, but he did not move on before the community he had started had become religiously self-supporting. Not only did Paul do his very best to maintain his independence and to raise viable new congregations, he also formed a 'team' of fellow workers around him who could support his activities. Furthermore, he sought out his territory with care: the cities he chose for his missionary purposes enabled him to perform his artisanship, but also enabled the congregations he founded to further the spread of the gospel in a natural way. They were to function as examples and could thereby enhance the spread of the gospel.

It has been mentioned a number of times throughout this book that Paul apparently used some of the techniques that were also practised by popular Greek philosophers. His preaching of the gospel in the workshop was interpreted against the background of philosophic tradition rather than as the result of a rabbinic ideal. Yet the intention and effect of Paul's preaching of the gospel were not at all comparable to those of a philosopher. Whereas the latter intended to raise new philosophers or at least to give some new insight to his pupils concerning their world, Paul aimed at 'saving people' (cf. 1 Cor 9,22). In his own perception Paul likened his task to that of a prophet, although he did not explicitly identify himself as such. His ministry resulted in the growth of congregations, and these congregations were to attract new believers and thus to contribute to a further spread of the gospel.

Theologically, the core of Paul's mission was formed by the universal implications of the Christ event: in Paul's eyes the confession of Christ was a necessary condition for salvation. God would reject those who did not confess Christ as the Lord at the coming universal judgement. In this respect, some of Paul's earliest recorded words continued to function as the only real programme he had: 1 Thess 1,9-10. Paul considered the final intervention of God and his judgement of the entire cosmos as being near. At this event, only those who confessed Jesus would be saved. For Paul, this defined the need for him to preach the gospel. He considered the acceptance of the gospel as a necessary condition for man to be saved. Paul's task was, therefore, to enable the spread of the gospel to reach as many people as possible, because he considered himself commissioned to do so.

The accent in Paul's ministry was thus on the proclamation of the gospel. Nonetheless, Paul's great significance for later developments lies primarily in his founding of congregations, and in his definition of their identity. For Paul the Christian movement was not just some group of people agreeing on one or two major issues – it meant a 'new creation' 'in Christ'. Although Paul still expected the ultimate defeat of the present aeon to come, he did consider the new aeon to have already begun within the community-in-Christ. With the growing independence of these congregations, and their eventual separation from Jewish communities, the

Sitz im Leben of the gospel's proclamation changed. It is in fact Paul's notion of the identity of the congregation-in-Christ as the beginning of the new creation, which ultimately formed the backbone for the idea that a convert should join the new social group of Christians in order to be saved. It is only a small shift in accent, but this shift does signify the birth of a Christian proselytising mission. Paul may not even have realised it, but he was indeed the first missionary.

APPENDIX 1:
'MISSION'-TERMINOLOGY
IN THE NEW TESTAMENT

Here the use of ἀποστέλλω and its cognates in the New Testament is presented together with a survey of πέμπω.

ἀποστέλλω to send (132)
Matt 2,16; 8,31; 10,5.16.40; 11,10; 13,41; 14,35; 15,24; 20,2; 21,1.3.34.36-37; 22,3-4.16; 23,34.37; 24,31; 27,19; Mark 1,2; 3,14.31; 4,29; 5,10; 6,7.17.27; 8,26; 9,37; 11,1.3; 12,2-6.13; 13,27; 14,13; Luke 1,19.26; 4,18.43; 7,3.20.27; 9,2.48.52; 10,1.3.16; 11,49; 13,34; 14,17.32; 19,14.29.32; 20,10.20; 22,8.35; 24,49; John 1,6.19.24; 3,17.28.34; 4,38; 5,33.36.38; 6,29.57; 7,29.32; 8,42; 9,7; 10,36; 11,3.42; 17,3.8.18.21.23.25; 18,24; 20,21; Acts 3,20.26; 5,21; 7,14.34-35; 8,14; 9,17.38; 10,8.17.20.36; 11,11.13.30; 13,15; 15,27.33; 16,35-36; 19,22; 26,17; 28,28; Rom 10,15; 1 Cor 1,17; 2 Cor 12,17; 2 Tim 4,12; Heb 1,14; 1 Pet 1,12; 1 John 4,9-10.14; Rev 1,1; 5,6; 22,6.

1. An envoy is sent to perform a task on behalf of the sender

Matt 2,16
Τότε Ἡρῴδης ἰδὼν ὅτι ἐνεπαίχθη ὑπὸ τῶν μάγων ἐθυμώθη λίαν, καὶ **ἀποστείλας** ἀνεῖλεν πάντας τοὺς παῖδας τοὺς ἐν Βηθλέεμ καὶ ἐν πᾶσι τοῖς ὁρίοις αὐτῆς ἀπὸ διετοῦς καὶ κατωτέρω, κατὰ τὸν χρόνον ὃν ἠκρίβωσεν παρὰ τῶν μάγων.

Matt 14,35
καὶ ἐπιγνόντες αὐτὸν οἱ ἄνδρες τοῦ τόπου ἐκείνου **ἀπέστειλαν** εἰς ὅλην τὴν περίχωρον ἐκείνην καὶ προσήνεγκαν αὐτῷ πάντας τοὺς κακῶς ἔχοντας

Matt 22,16
καὶ **ἀποστέλλουσιν** αὐτῷ τοὺς μαθητὰς αὐτῶν μετὰ τῶν Ἡρῳδιανῶν λέγοντες· διδάσκαλε, οἴδαμεν ὅτι ἀληθὴς εἶ καὶ τὴν ὁδὸν τοῦ θεοῦ ἐν ἀληθείᾳ διδάσκεις καὶ οὐ μέλει σοι περὶ οὐδενός· οὐ γὰρ βλέπεις εἰς πρόσωπον ἀνθρώπων,

Matt 27,19
Καθημένου δὲ αὐτοῦ ἐπὶ τοῦ βήματος **ἀπέστειλεν** πρὸς αὐτὸν ἡ γυνὴ αὐτοῦ λέγουσα· μηδὲν σοὶ καὶ τῷ δικαίῳ ἐκείνῳ· πολλὰ γὰρ ἔπαθον σήμερον κατ᾽ ὄναρ δι᾽ αὐτόν.

Mark 3,31
Καὶ ἔρχεται ἡ μήτηρ αὐτοῦ καὶ οἱ ἀδελφοὶ αὐτοῦ καὶ ἔξω
στήκοντες **ἀπέστειλαν** πρὸς αὐτὸν καλοῦντες αὐτόν.

Mark 6,17
Αὐτὸς γὰρ ὁ Ἡρῴδης **ἀποστείλας** ἐκράτησεν τὸν Ἰωάννην καὶ
ἔδησεν αὐτὸν ἐν φυλακῇ διὰ Ἡρῳδιάδα τὴν γυναῖκα Φιλίππου
τοῦ ἀδελφοῦ αὐτοῦ, ὅτι αὐτὴν ἐγάμησεν·

Mark 6,27
καὶ εὐθὺς **ἀποστείλας** ὁ βασιλεὺς σπεκουλάτορα ἐπέταξεν
ἐνέγκαι τὴν κεφαλὴν αὐτοῦ. καὶ ἀπελθὼν ἀπεκεφάλισεν αὐτὸν ἐν
τῇ φυλακῇ

Mark 8,26
καὶ **ἀπέστειλεν** αὐτὸν εἰς οἶκον αὐτοῦ λέγων· μηδὲ εἰς τὴν κώμην
εἰσέλθῃς.

Mark 12,13
Καὶ **ἀποστέλλουσιν** πρὸς αὐτόν τινας τῶν Φαρισαίων καὶ τῶν
Ἡρῳδιανῶν ἵνα αὐτὸν ἀγρεύσωσιν λόγῳ.

Luke 7,3
ἀκούσας δὲ περὶ τοῦ Ἰησοῦ **ἀπέστειλεν** πρὸς αὐτὸν πρεσβυτέρους
τῶν Ἰουδαίων ἐρωτῶν αὐτὸν ὅπως ἐλθὼν διασώσῃ τὸν δοῦλον
αὐτοῦ.

Luke 7,20
παραγενόμενοι δὲ πρὸς αὐτὸν οἱ ἄνδρες εἶπαν· Ἰωάννης ὁ
βαπτιστὴς **ἀπέστειλεν** ἡμᾶς πρὸς σὲ λέγων· σὺ εἶ ὁ ἐρχόμενος ἢ
ἄλλον προσδοκῶμεν;

Luke 14,32
εἰ δὲ μή γε, ἔτι αὐτοῦ πόρρω ὄντος πρεσβείαν **ἀποστείλας** ἐρωτᾷ
τὰ πρὸς εἰρήνην.

Luke 19,14
οἱ δὲ πολῖται αὐτοῦ ἐμίσουν αὐτὸν καὶ **ἀπέστειλαν** πρεσβείαν
ὀπίσω αὐτοῦ λέγοντες· οὐ θέλομεν τοῦτον βασιλεῦσαι ἐφ᾽ ἡμᾶς.

Luke 24,49
καὶ [ἰδοὺ] ἐγὼ **ἀποστέλλω** τὴν ἐπαγγελίαν τοῦ πατρός μου ἐφ᾽
ὑμᾶς· ὑμεῖς δὲ καθίσατε ἐν τῇ πόλει ἕως οὗ ἐνδύσησθε ἐξ ὕψους
δύναμιν.

John 1,19
Καὶ αὕτη ἐστὶν ἡ μαρτυρία τοῦ Ἰωάννου, ὅτε **ἀπέστειλαν** [πρὸς
αὐτὸν] οἱ Ἰουδαῖοι ἐξ Ἱεροσολύμων ἱερεῖς καὶ Λευίτας ἵνα
ἐρωτήσωσιν αὐτόν· σὺ τίς εἶ;

John 1,24
Καὶ ἀπεσταλμένοι ἦσαν ἐκ τῶν Φαρισαίων.

John 5,33
ὑμεῖς ἀπεστάλκατε πρὸς Ἰωάννην, καὶ μεμαρτύρηκεν τῇ ἀληθείᾳ·

John 7,32
ἤκουσαν οἱ Φαρισαῖοι τοῦ ὄχλου γογγύζοντος περὶ αὐτοῦ ταῦτα, καὶ ἀπέστειλαν οἱ ἀρχιερεῖς καὶ οἱ Φαρισαῖοι ὑπηρέτας ἵνα πιάσωσιν αὐτόν.

John 11,3
ἀπέστειλαν οὖν αἱ ἀδελφαὶ πρὸς αὐτὸν λέγουσαι· κύριε, ἴδε ὃν φιλεῖς ἀσθενεῖ.

John 18,24
ἀπέστειλεν οὖν αὐτὸν ὁ Ἄννας δεδεμένον πρὸς Καϊάφαν τὸν ἀρχιερέα.

Acts 5,21
ἀκούσαντες δὲ εἰσῆλθον ὑπὸ τὸν ὄρθρον εἰς τὸ ἱερὸν καὶ ἐδίδασκον. Παραγενόμενος δὲ ὁ ἀρχιερεὺς καὶ οἱ σὺν αὐτῷ συνεκάλεσαν τὸ συνέδριον καὶ πᾶσαν τὴν γερουσίαν τῶν υἱῶν Ἰσραὴλ καὶ ἀπέστειλαν εἰς τὸ δεσμωτήριον ἀχθῆναι αὐτούς.

Acts 7,14
ἀποστείλας δὲ Ἰωσὴφ μετεκαλέσατο Ἰακὼβ τὸν πατέρα αὐτοῦ καὶ πᾶσαν τὴν συγγένειαν ἐν ψυχαῖς ἑβδομήκοντα πέντε.

Acts 8,14
Ἀκούσαντες δὲ οἱ ἐν Ἱεροσολύμοις ἀπόστολοι ὅτι δέδεκται ἡ Σαμάρεια τὸν λόγον τοῦ θεοῦ, ἀπέστειλαν πρὸς αὐτοὺς Πέτρον καὶ Ἰωάννην,

Acts 9,38
ἐγγὺς δὲ οὔσης Λύδδας τῇ Ἰόππῃ οἱ μαθηταὶ ἀκούσαντες ὅτι Πέτρος ἐστὶν ἐν αὐτῇ ἀπέστειλαν δύο ἄνδρας πρὸς αὐτὸν παρακαλοῦντες· μὴ ὀκνήσῃς διελθεῖν ἕως ἡμῶν.

Acts 10,8
καὶ ἐξηγησάμενος ἅπαντα αὐτοῖς ἀπέστειλεν αὐτοὺς εἰς τὴν Ἰόππην.

Acts 10,17
Ὡς δὲ ἐν ἑαυτῷ διηπόρει ὁ Πέτρος τί ἂν εἴη τὸ ὅραμα ὃ εἶδεν, ἰδοὺ οἱ ἄνδρες οἱ ἀπεσταλμένοι ὑπὸ τοῦ Κορνηλίου διερωτήσαντες τὴν οἰκίαν τοῦ Σίμωνος ἐπέστησαν ἐπὶ τὸν πυλῶνα,

Acts 10,20
ἀλλὰ ἀναστὰς κατάβηθι καὶ πορεύου σὺν αὐτοῖς μηδὲν διακρινό-
μενος ὅτι ἐγὼ **ἀπέσταλκα** αὐτούς.

Acts 10,36
τὸν λόγον [ὃν] **ἀπέστειλεν** τοῖς υἱοῖς Ἰσραὴλ εὐαγγελιζόμενος
εἰρήνην διὰ Ἰησοῦ Χριστοῦ, οὗτός ἐστιν πάντων κύριος,

Acts 11,11
καὶ ἰδοὺ ἐξαυτῆς τρεῖς ἄνδρες ἐπέστησαν ἐπὶ τὴν οἰκίαν ἐν ᾗ
ἦμεν, **ἀπεσταλμένοι** ἀπὸ Καισαρείας πρός με.

Acts 11,13
ἀπήγγειλεν δὲ ἡμῖν πῶς εἶδεν [τὸν] ἄγγελον ἐν τῷ οἴκῳ αὐτοῦ
σταθέντα καὶ εἰπόντα· **ἀπόστειλον** εἰς Ἰόππην καὶ μετάπεμψαι
Σίμωνα τὸν ἐπικαλούμενον Πέτρον,

Acts 11,30
ὃ καὶ ἐποίησαν **ἀποστείλαντες** πρὸς τοὺς πρεσβυτέρους διὰ
χειρὸς Βαρναβᾶ καὶ Σαύλου.

Acts 13,15
μετὰ δὲ τὴν ἀνάγνωσιν τοῦ νόμου καὶ τῶν προφητῶν **ἀπέστειλαν**
οἱ ἀρχισυνάγωγοι πρὸς αὐτοὺς λέγοντες· ἄνδρες ἀδελφοί, εἴ τίς
ἐστιν ἐν ὑμῖν λόγος παρακλήσεως πρὸς τὸν λαόν, λέγετε.

Acts 15,27
ἀπεστάλκαμεν οὖν Ἰούδαν καὶ Σιλᾶν καὶ αὐτοὺς διὰ λόγου ἀπαγ-
γέλλοντας τὰ αὐτά.

Acts 15,33
ποιήσαντες δὲ χρόνον ἀπελύθησαν μετ᾽ εἰρήνης ἀπὸ τῶν ἀδελφῶν
πρὸς τοὺς **ἀποστείλαντας** αὐτούς.

Acts 16,35
Ἡμέρας δὲ γενομένης **ἀπέστειλαν** οἱ στρατηγοὶ τοὺς ῥαβδούχους
λέγοντες· ἀπόλυσον τοὺς ἀνθρώπους ἐκείνους.

Acts 16,36
ἀπήγγειλεν δὲ ὁ δεσμοφύλαξ τοὺς λόγους [τούτους] πρὸς τὸν
Παῦλον ὅτι **ἀπέσταλκαν** οἱ στρατηγοὶ ἵνα ἀπολυθῆτε· νῦν οὖν
ἐξελθόντες πορεύεσθε ἐν εἰρήνῃ.

Acts 19,22
ἀποστείλας δὲ εἰς τὴν Μακεδονίαν δύο τῶν διακονούντων αὐτῷ,
Τιμόθεον καὶ Ἔραστον, αὐτὸς ἐπέσχεν χρόνον εἰς τὴν Ἀσίαν.

2 Cor 12,17
μή τινα ὧν **ἀπέσταλκα** πρὸς ὑμᾶς, δι᾽ αὐτοῦ ἐπλεονέκτησα ὑμᾶς;

2 Tim 4,12
Τύχικον δὲ **ἀπέστειλα** εἰς Ἔφεσον.

Rev 1,1
Ἀποκάλυψις Ἰησοῦ Χριστοῦ ἣν ἔδωκεν αὐτῷ ὁ θεὸς δεῖξαι τοῖς
δούλοις αὐτοῦ ἃ δεῖ γενέσθαι ἐν τάχει, καὶ ἐσήμανεν **ἀποστείλας**
διὰ τοῦ ἀγγέλου αὐτοῦ τῷ δούλῳ αὐτοῦ Ἰωάννῃ,

2. Jesus sends his disciples/envoys

Matt 10,5
Τούτους τοὺς δώδεκα **ἀπέστειλεν** ὁ Ἰησοῦς παραγγείλας αὐτοῖς
λέγων· εἰς ὁδὸν ἐθνῶν μὴ ἀπέλθητε καὶ εἰς πόλιν Σαμαριτῶν μὴ
εἰσέλθητε·

Matt 10,16
Ἰδοὺ ἐγὼ **ἀποστέλλω** ὑμᾶς ὡς πρόβατα ἐν μέσῳ λύκων· γίνεσθε
οὖν φρόνιμοι ὡς οἱ ὄφεις καὶ ἀκέραιοι ὡς αἱ περιστεραί.

Matt 21,1
Καὶ ὅτε ἤγγισαν εἰς Ἱεροσόλυμα καὶ ἦλθον εἰς Βηθφαγὴ εἰς τὸ
ὄρος τῶν ἐλαιῶν, τότε Ἰησοῦς **ἀπέστειλεν** δύο μαθητὰς

Matt 21,3
καὶ ἐάν τις ὑμῖν εἴπῃ τι, ἐρεῖτε ὅτι ὁ κύριος αὐτῶν χρείαν ἔχει·
εὐθὺς δὲ **ἀποστελεῖ** αὐτούς.

Mark 3,14
καὶ ἐποίησεν δώδεκα [οὓς καὶ ἀποστόλους ὠνόμασεν] ἵνα ὦσιν
μετ᾽ αὐτοῦ καὶ ἵνα **ἀποστέλλῃ** αὐτοὺς κηρύσσειν

Mark 6,7
Καὶ προσκαλεῖται τοὺς δώδεκα καὶ ἤρξατο αὐτοὺς **ἀποστέλλειν**
δύο δύο καὶ ἐδίδου αὐτοῖς ἐξουσίαν τῶν πνευμάτων τῶν
ἀκαθάρτων,

Mark 11,1
Καὶ ὅτε ἐγγίζουσιν εἰς Ἱεροσόλυμα εἰς Βηθφαγὴ καὶ Βηθανίαν
πρὸς τὸ ὄρος τῶν ἐλαιῶν, **ἀποστέλλει** δύο τῶν μαθητῶν αὐτοῦ

Mark 11,3
καὶ ἐάν τις ὑμῖν εἴπῃ· τί ποιεῖτε τοῦτο; εἴπατε· ὁ κύριος αὐτοῦ
χρείαν ἔχει, καὶ εὐθὺς αὐτὸν **ἀποστέλλει** πάλιν ὧδε.

Mark 14,13
καὶ **ἀποστέλλει** δύο τῶν μαθητῶν αὐτοῦ καὶ λέγει αὐτοῖς· ὑπάγετε
εἰς τὴν πόλιν, καὶ ἀπαντήσει ὑμῖν ἄνθρωπος κεράμιον ὕδατος
βαστάζων· ἀκολουθήσατε αὐτῷ

Luke 9,2
καὶ **ἀπέστειλεν** αὐτοὺς κηρύσσειν τὴν βασιλείαν τοῦ θεοῦ καὶ ἰᾶσθαι [τοὺς ἀσθενεῖς],

Luke 9,52
καὶ **ἀπέστειλεν** ἀγγέλους πρὸ προσώπου αὐτοῦ. καὶ πορευθέντες εἰσῆλθον εἰς κώμην Σαμαριτῶν ὡς ἑτοιμάσαι αὐτῷ·

Luke 10,1
Μετὰ δὲ ταῦτα ἀνέδειξεν ὁ κύριος ἑτέρους ἑβδομήκοντα [δύο] καὶ **ἀπέστειλεν** αὐτοὺς ἀνὰ δύο [δύο] πρὸ προσώπου αὐτοῦ εἰς πᾶσαν πόλιν καὶ τόπον οὗ ἤμελλεν αὐτὸς ἔρχεσθαι.

Luke 10,3
ὑπάγετε· ἰδοὺ **ἀποστέλλω** ὑμᾶς ὡς ἄρνας ἐν μέσῳ λύκων.

Luke 19,29
Καὶ ἐγένετο ὡς ἤγγισεν εἰς Βηθφαγὴ καὶ Βηθανία[ν] πρὸς τὸ ὄρος τὸ καλούμενον Ἐλαιῶν, **ἀπέστειλεν** δύο τῶν μαθητῶν

Luke 19,32
ἀπελθόντες δὲ οἱ **ἀπεσταλμένοι** εὗρον καθὼς εἶπεν αὐτοῖς.

Luke 22,8
καὶ **ἀπέστειλεν** Πέτρον καὶ Ἰωάννην εἰπών· πορευθέντες ἑτοιμάσατε ἡμῖν τὸ πάσχα ἵνα φάγωμεν.

Luke 22,35
Καὶ εἶπεν αὐτοῖς· ὅτε **ἀπέστειλα** ὑμᾶς ἄτερ βαλλαντίου καὶ πήρας καὶ ὑποδημάτων, μή τινος ὑστερήσατε; οἱ δὲ εἶπαν· οὐθενός.

John 4,38
ἐγὼ **ἀπέστειλα** ὑμᾶς θερίζειν ὃ οὐχ ὑμεῖς κεκοπιάκατε· ἄλλοι κεκοπιάκασιν καὶ ὑμεῖς εἰς τὸν κόπον αὐτῶν εἰσεληλύθατε.

John 17,18
καθὼς ἐμὲ **ἀπέστειλας** εἰς τὸν κόσμον, καγὼ **ἀπέστειλα** αὐτοὺς εἰς τὸν κόσμον·

Acts 9,17
Ἀπῆλθεν δὲ Ἀνανίας καὶ εἰσῆλθεν εἰς τὴν οἰκίαν καὶ ἐπιθεὶς ἐπ' αὐτὸν τὰς χεῖρας εἶπεν· Σαοὺλ ἀδελφέ, ὁ κύριος **ἀπέσταλκέν** με, Ἰησοῦς ὁ ὀφθείς σοι ἐν τῇ ὁδῷ ᾗ ἤρχου, ὅπως ἀναβλέψῃς καὶ πλησθῇς πνεύματος ἁγίου.

Acts 26,17
ἐξαιρούμενός σε ἐκ τοῦ λαοῦ καὶ ἐκ τῶν ἐθνῶν εἰς οὓς ἐγὼ **ἀποστέλλω** σε

1 Cor 1,17
οὐ γὰρ **ἀπέστειλέν** με Χριστὸς βαπτίζειν ἀλλὰ εὐαγγελίζεσθαι,
οὐκ ἐν σοφίᾳ λόγου, ἵνα μὴ κενωθῇ ὁ σταυρὸς τοῦ Χριστοῦ.

3. God sends multiple envoys, prophets

Matt 11,10
οὗτός ἐστιν περὶ οὗ γέγραπται· ἰδοὺ ἐγὼ **ἀποστέλλω** τὸν ἄγγελόν
μου πρὸ προσώπου σου, ὃς κατασκευάσει τὴν ὁδόν σου ἔμπροσθέν
σου.

Matt 23,34 (= Q 11,49)
Διὰ τοῦτο ἰδοὺ ἐγὼ **ἀποστέλλω** πρὸς ὑμᾶς προφήτας καὶ σοφοὺς
καὶ γραμματεῖς· ἐξ αὐτῶν ἀποκτενεῖτε καὶ σταυρώσετε καὶ ἐξ
αὐτῶν μαστιγώσετε ἐν ταῖς συναγωγαῖς ὑμῶν καὶ διώξετε ἀπὸ
πόλεως εἰς πόλιν·

Matt 23,37 (= Q 13,34)
Ἰερουσαλὴμ Ἰερουσαλήμ, ἡ ἀποκτείνουσα τοὺς προφήτας καὶ
λιθοβολοῦσα τοὺς **ἀπεσταλμένους** πρὸς αὐτήν, ποσάκις ἠθέλησα
ἐπισυναγαγεῖν τὰ τέκνα σου, ὃν τρόπον ὄρνις ἐπισυνάγει τὰ
νοσσία αὐτῆς ὑπὸ τὰς πτέρυγας, καὶ οὐκ ἠθελήσατε.

Mark 1,2
Καθὼς γέγραπται ἐν τῷ Ἠσαΐᾳ τῷ προφήτῃ· ἰδοὺ **ἀποστέλλω** τὸν
ἄγγελόν μου πρὸ προσώπου σου, ὃς κατασκευάσει τὴν ὁδόν σου·

Luke 7,27
οὗτός ἐστιν περὶ οὗ γέγραπται· ἰδοὺ **ἀποστέλλω** τὸν ἄγγελόν μου
πρὸ προσώπου σου, ὃς κατασκευάσει τὴν ὁδόν σου ἔμπροσθέν
σου.

Luke 11,49 (= Q 11,49)
διὰ τοῦτο καὶ ἡ σοφία τοῦ θεοῦ εἶπεν· **ἀποστελῶ** εἰς αὐτοὺς
προφήτας καὶ ἀποστόλους, καὶ ἐξ αὐτῶν ἀποκτενοῦσιν καὶ
διώξουσιν,

Luke 13,34 (= Q 13,34)
Ἰερουσαλὴμ Ἰερουσαλήμ, ἡ ἀποκτείνουσα τοὺς προφήτας καὶ
λιθοβολοῦσα τοὺς **ἀπεσταλμένους** πρὸς αὐτήν, ποσάκις ἠθέλησα
ἐπισυνάξαι τὰ τέκνα σου ὃν τρόπον ὄρνις τὴν ἑαυτῆς νοσσιὰν
ὑπὸ τὰς πτέρυγας, καὶ οὐκ ἠθελήσατε.

John 1,6
Ἐγένετο ἄνθρωπος, **ἀπεσταλμένος** παρὰ θεοῦ, ὄνομα αὐτῷ
Ἰωάννης·

John 3,28
αὐτοὶ ὑμεῖς μοι μαρτυρεῖτε ὅτι εἶπον [ὅτι] οὐκ εἰμὶ ἐγὼ ὁ Χριστός,
ἀλλ᾿ ὅτι **ἀπεσταλμένος** εἰμὶ ἔμπροσθεν ἐκείνου.

Acts 7,34
ἰδὼν εἶδον τὴν κάκωσιν τοῦ λαοῦ μου τοῦ ἐν Αἰγύπτῳ καὶ τοῦ
στεναγμοῦ αὐτῶν ἤκουσα, καὶ κατέβην ἐξελέσθαι αὐτούς· καὶ
νῦν δεῦρο **ἀποστείλω** σε εἰς Αἴγυπτον.

Acts 7,35
Τοῦτον τὸν Μωϋσῆν ὃν ἠρνήσαντο εἰπόντες· τίς σε κατέστησεν
ἄρχοντα καὶ δικαστήν; τοῦτον ὁ θεὸς [καὶ] ἄρχοντα καὶ
λυτρωτὴν **ἀπέσταλκεν** σὺν χειρὶ ἀγγέλου τοῦ ὀφθέντος αὐτῷ ἐν
τῇ βάτῳ.

Rom 10,15
πῶς δὲ κηρύξωσιν ἐὰν μὴ **ἀποσταλῶσιν**; καθὼς γέγραπται· ὡς
ὡραῖοι οἱ πόδες τῶν εὐαγγελιζομένων [τὰ] ἀγαθά.

1 Pet 1,12
οἷς ἀπεκαλύφθη ὅτι οὐχ ἑαυτοῖς ὑμῖν δὲ διηκόνουν αὐτά, ἃ νῦν
ἀνηγγέλη ὑμῖν διὰ τῶν εὐαγγελισαμένων ὑμᾶς [ἐν] πνεύματι ἁγίῳ
ἀποσταλέντι ἀπ᾽ οὐρανοῦ, εἰς ἃ ἐπιθυμοῦσιν ἄγγελοι παρακύψαι.

Rev 5,6
Καὶ εἶδον ἐν μέσῳ τοῦ θρόνου καὶ τῶν τεσσάρων ζῴων καὶ ἐν
μέσῳ τῶν πρεσβυτέρων ἀρνίον ἑστηκὸς ὡς ἐσφαγμένον ἔχων
κέρατα ἑπτὰ καὶ ὀφθαλμοὺς ἑπτὰ οἵ εἰσιν τὰ [ἑπτὰ] πνεύματα τοῦ
θεοῦ **ἀπεσταλμένοι** εἰς πᾶσαν τὴν γῆν.

Rev 22,6
Καὶ εἶπέν μοι· οὗτοι οἱ λόγοι πιστοὶ καὶ ἀληθινοί, καὶ ὁ κύριος
ὁ θεὸς τῶν πνευμάτων τῶν προφητῶν **ἀπέστειλεν** τὸν ἄγγελον
αὐτοῦ δεῖξαι τοῖς δούλοις αὐτοῦ ἃ δεῖ γενέσθαι ἐν τάχει.

3a God sends an angel

Luke 1,19
καὶ ἀποκριθεὶς ὁ ἄγγελος εἶπεν αὐτῷ· ἐγώ εἰμι Γαβριὴλ ὁ
παρεστηκὼς ἐνώπιον τοῦ θεοῦ καὶ **ἀπεστάλην** λαλῆσαι πρὸς σὲ
καὶ εὐαγγελίσασθαί σοι ταῦτα·

Luke 1,26
Ἐν δὲ τῷ μηνὶ τῷ ἕκτῳ **ἀπεστάλη** ὁ ἄγγελος Γαβριὴλ ἀπὸ τοῦ
θεοῦ εἰς πόλιν τῆς Γαλιλαίας ᾗ ὄνομα Ναζαρὲθ

4. God sends Jesus

Matt 10,40
Ὁ δεχόμενος ὑμᾶς ἐμὲ δέχεται, καὶ ὁ ἐμὲ δεχόμενος δέχεται τὸν
ἀποστείλαντά με.

Matt 15,24
ὁ δὲ ἀποκριθεὶς εἶπεν· οὐκ **ἀπεστάλην** εἰ μὴ εἰς τὰ πρόβατα τὰ ἀπολωλότα οἴκου Ἰσραήλ.

Mark 9,37
ὃς ἂν ἓν τῶν τοιούτων παιδίων δέξηται ἐπὶ τῷ ὀνόματί μου, ἐμὲ δέχεται· καὶ ὃς ἂν ἐμὲ δέχηται, οὐκ ἐμὲ δέχεται ἀλλὰ τὸν **ἀποστείλαντά** με.

Luke 4,18
πνεῦμα κυρίου ἐπ᾿ ἐμὲ οὗ εἵνεκεν ἔχρισέν με εὐαγγελίσασθαι πτωχοῖς, **ἀπέσταλκέν** με, κηρύξαι αἰχμαλώτοις ἄφεσιν καὶ τυφλοῖς ἀνάβλεψιν, **ἀποστεῖλαι** τεθραυσμένους ἐν ἀφέσει,

Luke 4,43
ὁ δὲ εἶπεν πρὸς αὐτοὺς ὅτι καὶ ταῖς ἑτέραις πόλεσιν εὐαγγελίσασθαί με δεῖ τὴν βασιλείαν τοῦ θεοῦ, ὅτι ἐπὶ τοῦτο **ἀπεστάλην**.

Luke 9,48
καὶ εἶπεν αὐτοῖς· ὃς ἐὰν δέξηται τοῦτο τὸ παιδίον ἐπὶ τῷ ὀνόματί μου, ἐμὲ δέχεται· καὶ ὃς ἂν ἐμὲ δέξηται, δέχεται τὸν **ἀποστείλαντά** με· ὁ γὰρ μικρότερος ἐν πᾶσιν ὑμῖν ὑπάρχων οὗτός ἐστιν μέγας.

Luke 10,16
Ὁ ἀκούων ὑμῶν ἐμοῦ ἀκούει, καὶ ὁ ἀθετῶν ὑμᾶς ἐμὲ ἀθετεῖ· ὁ δὲ ἐμὲ ἀθετῶν ἀθετεῖ τὸν **ἀποστείλαντά** με.

John 3,34
ὃν γὰρ **ἀπέστειλεν** ὁ θεὸς τὰ ῥήματα τοῦ θεοῦ λαλεῖ, οὐ γὰρ ἐκ μέτρου δίδωσιν τὸ πνεῦμα.

John 5,38
καὶ τὸν λόγον αὐτοῦ οὐκ ἔχετε ἐν ὑμῖν μένοντα, ὅτι ὃν **ἀπέστειλεν** ἐκεῖνος, τούτῳ ὑμεῖς οὐ πιστεύετε.

John 6,29
ἀπεκρίθη [ὁ] Ἰησοῦς καὶ εἶπεν αὐτοῖς· τοῦτό ἐστιν τὸ ἔργον τοῦ θεοῦ, ἵνα πιστεύητε εἰς ὃν **ἀπέστειλεν** ἐκεῖνος.

John 7,29
ἐγὼ οἶδα αὐτόν, ὅτι παρ᾿ αὐτοῦ εἰμι κἀκεῖνός με **ἀπέστειλεν**.

John 8,42
εἶπεν αὐτοῖς ὁ Ἰησοῦς· εἰ ὁ θεὸς πατὴρ ὑμῶν ἦν ἠγαπᾶτε ἂν ἐμέ, ἐγὼ γὰρ ἐκ τοῦ θεοῦ ἐξῆλθον καὶ ἥκω· οὐδὲ γὰρ ἀπ᾿ ἐμαυτοῦ ἐλήλυθα, ἀλλ᾿ ἐκεῖνός με **ἀπέστειλεν**.

John 10,36
ὃν ὁ πατὴρ ἡγίασεν καὶ **ἀπέστειλεν** εἰς τὸν κόσμον ὑμεῖς λέγετε
ὅτι βλασφημεῖς, ὅτι εἶπον· υἱὸς τοῦ θεοῦ εἰμι;

John 11,42
ἐγὼ δὲ ᾔδειν ὅτι πάντοτέ μου ἀκούεις, ἀλλὰ διὰ τὸν ὄχλον τὸν
περιεστῶτα εἶπον, ἵνα πιστεύσωσιν ὅτι σύ με **ἀπέστειλας.**

John 17,3
αὕτη δέ ἐστιν ἡ αἰώνιος ζωὴ ἵνα γινώσκωσιν σὲ τὸν μόνον
ἀληθινὸν θεὸν καὶ ὃν **ἀπέστειλας** Ἰησοῦν Χριστόν.

John 17,8
ὅτι τὰ ῥήματα ἃ ἔδωκάς μοι δέδωκα αὐτοῖς, καὶ αὐτοὶ ἔλαβον καὶ
ἔγνωσαν ἀληθῶς ὅτι παρὰ σοῦ ἐξῆλθον, καὶ ἐπίστευσαν ὅτι σύ
με **ἀπέστειλας.**

John 17,18
καθὼς ἐμὲ **ἀπέστειλας** εἰς τὸν κόσμον, καγὼ **ἀπέστειλα** αὐτοὺς
εἰς τὸν κόσμον·

John 17,21
ἵνα πάντες ἓν ὦσιν, καθὼς σύ, πάτερ, ἐν ἐμοὶ καγὼ ἐν σοί, ἵνα καὶ
αὐτοὶ ἐν ἡμῖν ὦσιν, ἵνα ὁ κόσμος πιστεύῃ ὅτι σύ με **ἀπέστειλας.**

John 17,23
ἐγὼ ἐν αὐτοῖς καὶ σὺ ἐν ἐμοί, ἵνα ὦσιν τετελειωμένοι εἰς ἕν, ἵνα
γινώσκῃ ὁ κόσμος ὅτι σύ με **ἀπέστειλας** καὶ ἠγάπησας αὐτοὺς
καθὼς ἐμὲ ἠγάπησας.

John 17,25
πάτερ δίκαιε, καὶ ὁ κόσμος σε οὐκ ἔγνω, ἐγὼ δέ σε ἔγνων, καὶ
οὗτοι ἔγνωσαν ὅτι σύ με **ἀπέστειλας**·

John 20,21
εἶπεν οὖν αὐτοῖς [ὁ Ἰησοῦς] πάλιν· εἰρήνη ὑμῖν· καθὼς **ἀπέσταλκέν**
με ὁ πατήρ, καγὼ πέμπω ὑμᾶς.

Acts 3,20
ὅπως ἂν ἔλθωσιν καιροὶ ἀναψύξεως ἀπὸ προσώπου τοῦ κυρίου
καὶ **ἀποστείλῃ** τὸν προκεχειρισμένον ὑμῖν χριστόν Ἰησοῦν,

Acts 3,26
ὑμῖν πρῶτον ἀναστήσας ὁ θεὸς τὸν παῖδα αὐτοῦ **ἀπέστειλεν** αὐτὸν
εὐλογοῦντα ὑμᾶς ἐν τῷ ἀποστρέφειν ἕκαστον ἀπὸ τῶν πονηριῶν
ὑμῶν.

4a The Father sends the Son

John 3,17
οὐ γὰρ ἀπέστειλεν ὁ θεὸς τὸν υἱὸν εἰς τὸν κόσμον ἵνα κρίνῃ τὸν κόσμον, ἀλλ᾽ ἵνα σωθῇ ὁ κόσμος δι᾽ αὐτοῦ.

John 5,36
Ἐγὼ δὲ ἔχω τὴν μαρτυρίαν μείζω τοῦ Ἰωάννου· τὰ γὰρ ἔργα ἃ δέδωκέν μοι ὁ πατὴρ ἵνα τελειώσω αὐτά, αὐτὰ τὰ ἔργα ἃ ποιῶ μαρτυρεῖ περὶ ἐμοῦ ὅτι ὁ πατήρ με ἀπέσταλκεν.

John 6,57
καθὼς ἀπέστειλέν με ὁ ζῶν πατὴρ καγὼ ζῶ διὰ τὸν πατέρα, καὶ ὁ τρώγων με κακεῖνος ζήσει δι᾽ ἐμέ.

1 John 4,9
ἐν τούτῳ ἐφανερώθη ἡ ἀγάπη τοῦ θεοῦ ἐν ἡμῖν, ὅτι τὸν υἱὸν αὐτοῦ τὸν μονογενῆ ἀπέσταλκεν ὁ θεὸς εἰς τὸν κόσμον ἵνα ζήσωμεν δι᾽ αὐτοῦ.

1 John 4,10
ἐν τούτῳ ἐστὶν ἡ ἀγάπη, οὐχ ὅτι ἡμεῖς ἠγαπήκαμεν τὸν θεὸν ἀλλ᾽ ὅτι αὐτὸς ἠγάπησεν ἡμᾶς καὶ ἀπέστειλεν τὸν υἱὸν αὐτοῦ ἱλασμὸν περὶ τῶν ἁμαρτιῶν ἡμῶν.

1 John 4,14
καὶ ἡμεῖς τεθεάμεθα καὶ μαρτυροῦμεν ὅτι ὁ πατὴρ ἀπέσταλκεν τὸν υἱὸν σωτῆρα τοῦ κόσμου.

5. Jesus sends forth demons

Matt 8,31
οἱ δὲ δαίμονες παρεκάλουν αὐτὸν λέγοντες· εἰ ἐκβάλλεις ἡμᾶς, ἀπόστειλον ἡμᾶς εἰς τὴν ἀγέλην τῶν χοίρων.

Mark 5,10
καὶ παρεκάλει αὐτὸν πολλὰ ἵνα μὴ αὐτὰ ἀποστείλῃ ἔξω τῆς χώρας.

6. The Son of Man sends his angels

Matt 13,41
ἀποστελεῖ ὁ υἱὸς τοῦ ἀνθρώπου τοὺς ἀγγέλους αὐτοῦ, καὶ συλλέξουσιν ἐκ τῆς βασιλείας αὐτοῦ πάντα τὰ σκάνδαλα καὶ τοὺς ποιοῦντας τὴν ἀνομίαν

Matt 24,31
καὶ **ἀποστελεῖ** τοὺς ἀγγέλους αὐτοῦ μετὰ σάλπιγγος μεγάλης, καὶ
ἐπισυνάξουσιν τοὺς ἐκλεκτοὺς αὐτοῦ ἐκ τῶν τεσσάρων ἀνέμων
ἀπ' ἄκρων οὐρανῶν ἕως [τῶν] ἄκρων αὐτῶν.

Mark 13,27
καὶ τότε **ἀποστελεῖ** τοὺς ἀγγέλους καὶ ἐπισυνάξει τοὺς ἐκλεκτοὺς
[αὐτοῦ] ἐκ τῶν τεσσάρων ἀνέμων ἀπ' ἄκρου γῆς ἕως ἄκρου
οὐρανοῦ.

7. 'Sending' in parables

Matt 20,2
συμφωνήσας δὲ μετὰ τῶν ἐργατῶν ἐκ δηναρίου τὴν ἡμέραν
ἀπέστειλεν αὐτοὺς εἰς τὸν ἀμπελῶνα αὐτοῦ.

Matt 21,34
ὅτε δὲ ἤγγισεν ὁ καιρὸς τῶν καρπῶν, **ἀπέστειλεν** τοὺς δούλους
αὐτοῦ πρὸς τοὺς γεωργοὺς λαβεῖν τοὺς καρποὺς αὐτοῦ.

Matt 21,36
πάλιν **ἀπέστειλεν** ἄλλους δούλους πλείονας τῶν πρώτων, καὶ
ἐποίησαν αὐτοῖς ὡσαύτως.

Matt 21,37
ὕστερον δὲ **ἀπέστειλεν** πρὸς αὐτοὺς τὸν υἱὸν αὐτοῦ λέγων·
ἐντραπήσονται τὸν υἱόν μου.

Matt 22,3
καὶ **ἀπέστειλεν** τοὺς δούλους αὐτοῦ καλέσαι τοὺς κεκλημένους
εἰς τοὺς γάμους, καὶ οὐκ ἤθελον ἐλθεῖν.

Matt 22,4
πάλιν **ἀπέστειλεν** ἄλλους δούλους λέγων· εἴπατε τοῖς κεκλημένοις·
ἰδοὺ τὸ ἄριστόν μου ἡτοίμακα, οἱ ταῦροί μου καὶ τὰ σιτιστὰ
τεθυμένα καὶ πάντα ἕτοιμα· δεῦτε εἰς τοὺς γάμους.

Mark 4,29
ὅταν δὲ παραδοῖ ὁ καρπός, εὐθὺς **ἀποστέλλει** τὸ δρέπανον, ὅτι
παρέστηκεν ὁ θερισμός.

Mark 12,2
καὶ **ἀπέστειλεν** πρὸς τοὺς γεωργοὺς τῷ καιρῷ δοῦλον ἵνα παρὰ
τῶν γεωργῶν λάβῃ ἀπὸ τῶν καρπῶν τοῦ ἀμπελῶνος·

Mark 12,3
καὶ λαβόντες αὐτὸν ἔδειραν καὶ **ἀπέστειλαν** κενόν.

Mark 12,4
καὶ πάλιν **ἀπέστειλεν** πρὸς αὐτοὺς ἄλλον δοῦλον· κακεῖνον ἐκεφαλίωσαν καὶ ἠτίμασαν.

Mark 12,5
καὶ ἄλλον **ἀπέστειλεν**· κακεῖνον ἀπέκτειναν, καὶ πολλοὺς ἄλλους, οὓς μὲν δέροντες, οὓς δὲ ἀποκτέννοντες.

Mark 12,6
ἔτι ἕνα εἶχεν υἱὸν ἀγαπητόν· **ἀπέστειλεν** αὐτὸν ἔσχατον πρὸς αὐτοὺς λέγων ὅτι ἐντραπήσονται τὸν υἱόν μου.

Luke 14,17
καὶ **ἀπέστειλεν** τὸν δοῦλον αὐτοῦ τῇ ὥρᾳ τοῦ δείπνου εἰπεῖν τοῖς κεκλημένοις· ἔρχεσθε, ὅτι ἤδη ἕτοιμά ἐστιν.

Luke 20,10
καὶ καιρῷ **ἀπέστειλεν** πρὸς τοὺς γεωργοὺς δοῦλον ἵνα ἀπὸ τοῦ καρποῦ τοῦ ἀμπελῶνος δώσουσιν αὐτῷ· οἱ δὲ γεωργοὶ ἐξαπέστειλαν αὐτὸν δείραντες κενόν.

Luke 20,20
Καὶ παρατηρήσαντες **ἀπέστειλαν** ἐγκαθέτους ὑποκρινομένους ἑαυτοὺς δικαίους εἶναι, ἵνα ἐπιλάβωνται αὐτοῦ λόγου, ὥστε παραδοῦναι αὐτὸν τῇ ἀρχῇ καὶ τῇ ἐξουσίᾳ τοῦ ἡγεμόνος.

8. Miscellaneous texts

John 9,7
καὶ εἶπεν αὐτῷ· ὕπαγε νίψαι εἰς τὴν κολυμβήθραν τοῦ Σιλωάμ (ὃ ἑρμηνεύεται **ἀπεσταλμένος**). ἀπῆλθεν οὖν καὶ ἐνίψατο καὶ ἦλθεν βλέπων.

Acts 28,28
γνωστὸν οὖν ἔστω ὑμῖν ὅτι τοῖς ἔθνεσιν **ἀπεστάλη** τοῦτο τὸ σωτήριον τοῦ θεοῦ· αὐτοὶ καὶ ἀκούσονται.

Heb 1,14
οὐχὶ πάντες εἰσὶν λειτουργικὰ πνεύματα εἰς διακονίαν **ἀποστελλόμενα** διὰ τοὺς μέλλοντας κληρονομεῖν σωτηρίαν;

ἀποστολή task, apostleship (4)
Acts 1,25; Rom 1,5; 1 Cor 9,2; Gal 2,8

Acts 1,25
λαβεῖν τὸν τόπον τῆς διακονίας ταύτης καὶ **ἀποστολῆς** ἀφ᾽ ἧς
παρέβη Ἰούδας πορευθῆναι εἰς τὸν τόπον τὸν ἴδιον.

Rom 1,5
δι᾽ οὗ ἐλάβομεν χάριν καὶ **ἀποστολὴν** εἰς ὑπακοὴν πίστεως ἐν
πᾶσιν τοῖς ἔθνεσιν ὑπὲρ τοῦ ὀνόματος αὐτοῦ,

1 Cor 9,2
εἰ ἄλλοις οὐκ εἰμὶ ἀπόστολος, ἀλλά γε ὑμῖν εἰμι· ἡ γὰρ σφραγίς
μου τῆς **ἀποστολῆς** ὑμεῖς ἐστε ἐν κυρίῳ.

Gal 2,8
ὁ γὰρ ἐνεργήσας Πέτρῳ εἰς **ἀποστολὴν** τῆς περιτομῆς ἐνήργησεν
καὶ ἐμοὶ εἰς τὰ ἔθνη,

ἀπόστολος apostle (80)
Matt 10,2; Mark 3,14; 6,30; Luke 6,13; 9,10; 11,49; 17,5; 22,14; 24,10;
John 13,16; Acts 1,2.26; 2,37.42-43; 4,33.35-37; 5,2.12.18.29.40; 6,6;
8,1.14.18; 9,27; 11,1; 14,4.14; 15,2.4.6.22-23; 16,4; Rom 1,1; 11,13;
16,7; 1 Cor 1,1; 4,9; 9,1-2.5; 12,28-29; 15,7.9; 2 Cor 1,1; 8,23; 11,5.13;
12,11-12; Gal 1,1.17.19; Eph 1,1; 2,20; 3,5; 4,11; Phil 2,25; Col 1,1;
1 Thess 2,7; 1 Tim 1,1; 2,7; 2 Tim 1,1.11; Titus 1,1; Heb 3,1; 1 Pet 1,1;
2 Pet 1,1; 3,2; Jude 1,17; Rev 2,2; 18,20; 21,14

1. One who is sent (in a general sense)

Luke 11,49
διὰ τοῦτο καὶ ἡ σοφία τοῦ θεοῦ εἶπεν· ἀποστελῶ εἰς αὐτοὺς
προφήτας καὶ **ἀποστόλους**, καὶ ἐξ αὐτῶν ἀποκτενοῦσιν καὶ
διώξουσιν,

John 13,16
ἀμὴν ἀμὴν λέγω ὑμῖν, οὐκ ἔστιν δοῦλος μείζων τοῦ κυρίου αὐτοῦ
οὐδὲ **ἀπόστολος** μείζων τοῦ πέμψαντος αὐτόν.

Rev 2,2
οἶδα τὰ ἔργα σου καὶ τὸν κόπον καὶ τὴν ὑπομονήν σου καὶ ὅτι οὐ
δύνῃ βαστάσαι κακούς, καὶ ἐπείρασας τοὺς λέγοντας ἑαυτοὺς
ἀποστόλους καὶ οὐκ εἰσὶν καὶ εὗρες αὐτοὺς ψευδεῖς,

2. Disciples sent by Jesus

Matt 10,2
Τῶν δὲ δώδεκα ἀποστόλων τὰ ὀνόματά ἐστιν ταῦτα· πρῶτος Σίμων ὁ λεγόμενος Πέτρος καὶ Ἀνδρέας ὁ ἀδελφὸς αὐτοῦ, καὶ Ἰάκωβος ὁ τοῦ Ζεβεδαίου καὶ Ἰωάννης ὁ ἀδελφὸς αὐτοῦ,

Mark 3,14
καὶ ἐποίησεν δώδεκα [οὓς καὶ ἀποστόλους ὠνόμασεν] ἵνα ὦσιν μετ' αὐτοῦ καὶ ἵνα ἀποστέλλῃ αὐτοὺς κηρύσσειν

Mark 6,30
Καὶ συνάγονται οἱ ἀπόστολοι πρὸς τὸν Ἰησοῦν καὶ ἀπήγγειλαν αὐτῷ πάντα ὅσα ἐποίησαν καὶ ὅσα ἐδίδαξαν.

Luke 6,13
καὶ ὅτε ἐγένετο ἡμέρα, προσεφώνησεν τοὺς μαθητὰς αὐτοῦ, καὶ ἐκλεξάμενος ἀπ' αὐτῶν δώδεκα, οὓς καὶ ἀποστόλους ὠνόμασεν·

Luke 9,10
Καὶ ὑποστρέψαντες οἱ ἀπόστολοι διηγήσαντο αὐτῷ ὅσα ἐποίησαν. Καὶ παραλαβὼν αὐτοὺς ὑπεχώρησεν κατ' ἰδίαν εἰς πόλιν καλουμένην Βηθσαϊδά.

Luke 17,5
Καὶ εἶπαν οἱ ἀπόστολοι τῷ κυρίῳ· πρόσθες ἡμῖν πίστιν.

3. **Envoys sent by a congregation**

Acts 14,4
ἐσχίσθη δὲ τὸ πλῆθος τῆς πόλεως, καὶ οἱ μὲν ἦσαν σὺν τοῖς Ἰουδαίοις, οἱ δὲ σὺν τοῖς ἀποστόλοις.

Acts 14,14
Ἀκούσαντες δὲ οἱ ἀπόστολοι Βαρναβᾶς καὶ Παῦλος διαρρήξαντες τὰ ἱμάτια αὐτῶν ἐξεπήδησαν εἰς τὸν ὄχλον κράζοντες

2 Cor 8,23
εἴτε ὑπὲρ Τίτου, κοινωνὸς ἐμὸς καὶ εἰς ὑμᾶς συνεργός· εἴτε ἀδελφοὶ ἡμῶν, ἀπόστολοι ἐκκλησιῶν, δόξα Χριστοῦ.

Phil 2,25
Ἀναγκαῖον δὲ ἡγησάμην Ἐπαφρόδιτον τὸν ἀδελφὸν καὶ συνεργὸν καὶ συστρατιώτην μου, ὑμῶν δὲ ἀπόστολον καὶ λειτουργὸν τῆς χρείας μου, πέμψαι πρὸς ὑμᾶς,

4. 'Apostle(s)'

a. *'Apostle' without a qualifying genitive construction*

Luke 22,14
Καὶ ὅτε ἐγένετο ἡ ὥρα, ἀνέπεσεν καὶ οἱ **ἀπόστολοι** σὺν αὐτῷ.

Luke 24,10 ἦσαν δὲ ἡ Μαγδαληνὴ Μαρία καὶ Ἰωάννα καὶ Μαρία ἡ Ἰακώβου καὶ αἱ λοιπαὶ σὺν αὐταῖς. ἔλεγον πρὸς τοὺς **ἀποστόλους** ταῦτα,

Acts 1,2
ἄχρι ἧς ἡμέρας ἐντειλάμενος τοῖς **ἀποστόλοις** διὰ πνεύματος ἁγίου οὓς ἐξελέξατο ἀνελήμφθη.

Acts 1,26
καὶ ἔδωκαν κλήρους αὐτοῖς καὶ ἔπεσεν ὁ κλῆρος ἐπὶ Μαθθίαν καὶ συγκατεψηφίσθη μετὰ τῶν ἕνδεκα **ἀποστόλων**.

Acts 2,37
Ἀκούσαντες δὲ κατενύγησαν τὴν καρδίαν εἶπόν τε πρὸς τὸν Πέτρον καὶ τοὺς λοιποὺς **ἀποστόλους·** τί ποιήσωμεν, ἄνδρες ἀδελφοί;

Acts 2,42
Ἦσαν δὲ προσκαρτεροῦντες τῇ διδαχῇ τῶν **ἀποστόλων** καὶ τῇ κοινωνίᾳ τῇ κλάσει τοῦ ἄρτου καὶ ταῖς προσευχαῖς.

Acts 2,43
ἐγίνετο δὲ πάσῃ ψυχῇ φόβος, πολλά τε τέρατα καὶ σημεῖα διὰ τῶν **ἀποστόλων** ἐγίνετο.

Acts 4,33
καὶ δυνάμει μεγάλῃ ἀπεδίδουν τὸ μαρτύριον οἱ **ἀπόστολοι** τῆς ἀναστάσεως τοῦ κυρίου Ἰησοῦ, χάρις τε μεγάλη ἦν ἐπὶ πάντας αὐτούς.

Acts 4,35
καὶ ἐτίθουν παρὰ τοὺς πόδας τῶν **ἀποστόλων**, διεδίδετο δὲ ἑκάστῳ καθότι ἄν τις χρείαν εἶχεν.

Acts 4,36
Ἰωσὴφ δὲ ὁ ἐπικληθεὶς Βαρναβᾶς ἀπὸ τῶν **ἀποστόλων**, ὅ ἐστιν μεθερμηνευόμενον υἱὸς παρακλήσεως, Λευίτης, Κύπριος τῷ γένει,

Acts 4,37
ὑπάρχοντος αὐτῷ ἀγροῦ πωλήσας ἤνεγκεν τὸ χρῆμα καὶ ἔθηκεν πρὸς τοὺς πόδας τῶν **ἀποστόλων**.

Acts 5,2
καὶ ἐνοσφίσατο ἀπὸ τῆς τιμῆς, συνειδυίης καὶ τῆς γυναικός, καὶ ἐνέγκας μέρος τι παρὰ τοὺς πόδας τῶν **ἀποστόλων** ἔθηκεν.

Acts 5,12
Διὰ δὲ τῶν χειρῶν τῶν **ἀποστόλων** ἐγίνετο σημεῖα καὶ τέρατα πολλὰ ἐν τῷ λαῷ. καὶ ἦσαν ὁμοθυμαδὸν ἅπαντες ἐν τῇ στοᾷ Σολομῶντος,

Acts 5,18
καὶ ἐπέβαλον τὰς χεῖρας ἐπὶ τοὺς **ἀποστόλους** καὶ ἔθεντο αὐτοὺς ἐν τηρήσει δημοσίᾳ.

Acts 5,29
ἀποκριθεὶς δὲ Πέτρος καὶ οἱ **ἀπόστολοι** εἶπαν· πειθαρχεῖν δεῖ θεῷ μᾶλλον ἢ ἀνθρώποις.

Acts 5,40
καὶ προσκαλεσάμενοι τοὺς **ἀποστόλους** δείραντες παρήγγειλαν μὴ λαλεῖν ἐπὶ τῷ ὀνόματι τοῦ Ἰησοῦ καὶ ἀπέλυσαν.

Acts 6,6
οὓς ἔστησαν ἐνώπιον τῶν **ἀποστόλων**, καὶ προσευξάμενοι ἐπέθηκαν αὐτοῖς τὰς χεῖρας.

Acts 8,1
Σαῦλος δὲ ἦν συνευδοκῶν τῇ ἀναιρέσει αὐτοῦ. Ἐγένετο δὲ ἐν ἐκείνῃ τῇ ἡμέρᾳ διωγμὸς μέγας ἐπὶ τὴν ἐκκλησίαν τὴν ἐν Ἱεροσολύμοις, πάντες δὲ διεσπάρησαν κατὰ τὰς χώρας τῆς Ἰουδαίας καὶ Σαμαρείας πλὴν τῶν **ἀποστόλων**.

Acts 8,14
Ἀκούσαντες δὲ οἱ ἐν Ἱεροσολύμοις **ἀπόστολοι** ὅτι δέδεκται ἡ Σαμάρεια τὸν λόγον τοῦ θεοῦ, ἀπέστειλαν πρὸς αὐτοὺς Πέτρον καὶ Ἰωάννην,

Acts 8,18
ἰδὼν δὲ ὁ Σίμων ὅτι διὰ τῆς ἐπιθέσεως τῶν χειρῶν τῶν **ἀποστόλων** δίδοται τὸ πνεῦμα, προσήνεγκεν αὐτοῖς χρήματα

Acts 9,27
Βαρναβᾶς δὲ ἐπιλαβόμενος αὐτὸν ἤγαγεν πρὸς τοὺς **ἀποστόλους** καὶ διηγήσατο αὐτοῖς πῶς ἐν τῇ ὁδῷ εἶδεν τὸν κύριον καὶ ὅτι ἐλάλησεν αὐτῷ καὶ πῶς ἐν Δαμασκῷ ἐπαρρησιάσατο ἐν τῷ ὀνόματι τοῦ Ἰησοῦ.

Acts 11,1
Ἤκουσαν δὲ οἱ **ἀπόστολοι** καὶ οἱ ἀδελφοὶ οἱ ὄντες κατὰ τὴν
Ἰουδαίαν ὅτι καὶ τὰ ἔθνη ἐδέξαντο τὸν λόγον τοῦ θεοῦ.

Acts 15,2
γενομένης δὲ στάσεως καὶ ζητήσεως οὐκ ὀλίγης τῷ Παύλῳ καὶ
τῷ Βαρναβᾷ πρὸς αὐτούς, ἔταξαν ἀναβαίνειν Παῦλον καὶ
Βαρναβᾶν καί τινας ἄλλους ἐξ αὐτῶν πρὸς τοὺς **ἀποστόλους** καὶ
πρεσβυτέρους εἰς Ἰερουσαλὴμ περὶ τοῦ ζητήματος τούτου.

Acts 15,4
παραγενόμενοι δὲ εἰς Ἰερουσαλὴμ παρεδέχθησαν ἀπὸ τῆς
ἐκκλησίας καὶ τῶν **ἀποστόλων** καὶ τῶν πρεσβυτέρων, ἀνήγγειλάν
τε ὅσα ὁ θεὸς ἐποίησεν μετ' αὐτῶν.

Acts 15,6
Συνήχθησάν τε οἱ **ἀπόστολοι** καὶ οἱ πρεσβύτεροι ἰδεῖν περὶ τοῦ
λόγου τούτου.

Acts 15,22
Τότε ἔδοξε τοῖς **ἀποστόλοις** καὶ τοῖς πρεσβυτέροις σὺν ὅλῃ τῇ
ἐκκλησίᾳ ἐκλεξαμένους ἄνδρας ἐξ αὐτῶν πέμψαι εἰς Ἀντιόχειαν σὺν τῷ Παύλῳ καὶ Βαρναβᾷ, Ἰούδαν τὸν καλούμενον
Βαρσαββᾶν καὶ Σιλᾶν, ἄνδρας ἡγουμένους ἐν τοῖς ἀδελφοῖς,

Acts 15,23
γράψαντες διὰ χειρὸς αὐτῶν· Οἱ **ἀπόστολοι** καὶ οἱ πρεσβύτεροι
ἀδελφοὶ τοῖς κατὰ τὴν Ἀντιόχειαν καὶ Συρίαν καὶ Κιλικίαν
ἀδελφοῖς τοῖς ἐξ ἐθνῶν χαίρειν.

Acts 16,4
Ὡς δὲ διεπορεύοντο τὰς πόλεις, παρεδίδοσαν αὐτοῖς φυλάσσειν
τὰ δόγματα τὰ κεκριμένα ὑπὸ τῶν **ἀποστόλων** καὶ πρεσβυτέρων
τῶν ἐν Ἱεροσολύμοις.

Rom 1,1
Παῦλος δοῦλος Χριστοῦ Ἰησοῦ, κλητὸς **ἀπόστολος** ἀφωρισμένος
εἰς εὐαγγέλιον θεοῦ,

Rom 16,7
ἀσπάσασθε Ἀνδρόνικον καὶ Ἰουνιᾶν τοὺς συγγενεῖς μου καὶ
συναιχμαλώτους μου, οἵτινές εἰσιν ἐπίσημοι ἐν τοῖς **ἀποστόλοις**,
οἳ καὶ πρὸ ἐμοῦ γέγοναν ἐν Χριστῷ.

1 Cor 4,9
δοκῶ γάρ, ὁ θεὸς ἡμᾶς τοὺς **ἀποστόλους** ἐσχάτους ἀπέδειξεν ὡς
ἐπιθανατίους, ὅτι θέατρον ἐγενήθημεν τῷ κόσμῳ καὶ ἀγγέλοις
καὶ ἀνθρώποις.

1 Cor 9,1
Οὐκ εἰμὶ ἐλεύθερος; οὐκ εἰμὶ **ἀπόστολος**; οὐχὶ Ἰησοῦν τὸν κύριον ἡμῶν ἑόρακα; οὐ τὸ ἔργον μου ὑμεῖς ἐστε ἐν κυρίῳ;

1 Cor 9,2
εἰ ἄλλοις οὐκ εἰμὶ **ἀπόστολος**, ἀλλά γε ὑμῖν εἰμι· ἡ γὰρ σφραγίς μου τῆς ἀποστολῆς ὑμεῖς ἐστε ἐν κυρίῳ.

1 Cor 9,5
μὴ οὐκ ἔχομεν ἐξουσίαν ἀδελφὴν γυναῖκα περιάγειν ὡς καὶ οἱ λοιποὶ **ἀπόστολοι** καὶ οἱ ἀδελφοὶ τοῦ κυρίου καὶ Κηφᾶς;

1 Cor 12,28
Καὶ οὓς μὲν ἔθετο ὁ θεὸς ἐν τῇ ἐκκλησίᾳ πρῶτον **ἀποστόλους**, δεύτερον προφήτας, τρίτον διδασκάλους, ἔπειτα δυνάμεις, ἔπειτα χαρίσματα ἰαμάτων, ἀντιλήμψεις, κυβερνήσεις, γένη γλωσσῶν.

1 Cor 12,29
μὴ πάντες **ἀπόστολοι**; μὴ πάντες προφῆται; μὴ πάντες διδάσκαλοι; μὴ πάντες δυνάμεις;

1 Cor 15,7
ἔπειτα ὤφθη Ἰακώβῳ εἶτα τοῖς **ἀποστόλοις** πᾶσιν·

1 Cor 15,9
Ἐγὼ γάρ εἰμι ὁ ἐλάχιστος τῶν **ἀποστόλων** ὃς οὐκ εἰμὶ ἱκανὸς καλεῖσθαι **ἀπόστολος**, διότι ἐδίωξα τὴν ἐκκλησίαν τοῦ θεοῦ·

2 Cor 11,5
Λογίζομαι γὰρ μηδὲν ὑστερηκέναι τῶν ὑπερλίαν **ἀποστόλων**.

2 Cor 12,11
Γέγονα ἄφρων, ὑμεῖς με ἠναγκάσατε. ἐγὼ γὰρ ὤφειλον ὑφ' ὑμῶν συνίστασθαι· οὐδὲν γὰρ ὑστέρησα τῶν ὑπερλίαν **ἀποστόλων** εἰ καὶ οὐδέν εἰμι.

2 Cor 12,12
τὰ μὲν σημεῖα τοῦ **ἀποστόλου** κατειργάσθη ἐν ὑμῖν ἐν πάσῃ ὑπομονῇ, σημείοις τε καὶ τέρασιν καὶ δυνάμεσιν.

Gal 1,1
Παῦλος **ἀπόστολος** οὐκ ἀπ' ἀνθρώπων οὐδὲ δι' ἀνθρώπου ἀλλὰ διὰ Ἰησοῦ Χριστοῦ καὶ θεοῦ πατρὸς τοῦ ἐγείραντος αὐτὸν ἐκ νεκρῶν,

Gal 1,17
οὐδὲ ἀνῆλθον εἰς Ἱεροσόλυμα πρὸς τοὺς πρὸ ἐμοῦ **ἀποστόλους**, ἀλλὰ ἀπῆλθον εἰς Ἀραβίαν καὶ πάλιν ὑπέστρεψα εἰς Δαμασκόν.

Gal 1,19
ἕτερον δὲ τῶν **ἀποστόλων** οὐκ εἶδον εἰ μὴ Ἰάκωβον τὸν ἀδελφὸν τοῦ κυρίου.

Eph 2,20
ἐποικοδομηθέντες ἐπὶ τῷ θεμελίῳ τῶν **ἀποστόλων** καὶ προφητῶν, ὄντος ἀκρογωνιαίου αὐτοῦ Χριστοῦ Ἰησοῦ,

Eph 3,5
ὃ ἑτέραις γενεαῖς οὐκ ἐγνωρίσθη τοῖς υἱοῖς τῶν ἀνθρώπων ὡς νῦν ἀπεκαλύφθη τοῖς ἁγίοις **ἀποστόλοις** αὐτοῦ καὶ προφήταις ἐν πνεύματι,

Eph 4,11
Καὶ αὐτὸς ἔδωκεν τοὺς μὲν **ἀποστόλους**, τοὺς δὲ προφήτας, τοὺς δὲ εὐαγγελιστάς, τοὺς δὲ ποιμένας καὶ διδασκάλους,
1 Tim 2,7
εἰς ὃ ἐτέθην ἐγὼ κῆρυξ καὶ **ἀπόστολος**, ἀλήθειαν λέγω οὐ ψεύδομαι, διδάσκαλος ἐθνῶν ἐν πίστει καὶ ἀληθείᾳ.

2 Tim 1,11
εἰς ὃ ἐτέθην ἐγὼ κῆρυξ καὶ **ἀπόστολος** καὶ διδάσκαλος,

Heb 3,1
Ὅθεν, ἀδελφοὶ ἅγιοι, κλήσεως ἐπουρανίου μέτοχοι, κατανοήσατε τὸν **ἀπόστολον** καὶ ἀρχιερέα τῆς ὁμολογίας ἡμῶν Ἰησοῦν,

2 Pet 3,2
μνησθῆναι τῶν προειρημένων ῥημάτων ὑπὸ τῶν ἁγίων προφητῶν καὶ τῆς τῶν **ἀποστόλων** ὑμῶν ἐντολῆς τοῦ κυρίου καὶ σωτῆρος,

Rev 18,20
Εὐφραίνου ἐπ᾽ αὐτῇ, οὐρανὲ καὶ οἱ ἅγιοι καὶ οἱ **ἀπόστολοι** καὶ οἱ προφῆται, ὅτι ἔκρινεν ὁ θεὸς τὸ κρίμα ὑμῶν ἐξ αὐτῆς.

b. *Apostle of Christ Jesus: ἀπόστολος Χριστοῦ Ἰησοῦ*

1 Cor 1,1
Παῦλος κλητὸς **ἀπόστολος Χριστοῦ Ἰησοῦ** διὰ θελήματος θεοῦ καὶ Σωσθένης ὁ ἀδελφὸς

2 Cor 1,1
Παῦλος **ἀπόστολος Χριστοῦ Ἰησοῦ** διὰ θελήματος θεοῦ καὶ Τιμόθεος ὁ ἀδελφὸς τῇ ἐκκλησίᾳ τοῦ θεοῦ τῇ οὔσῃ ἐν Κορίνθῳ σὺν τοῖς ἁγίοις πᾶσιν τοῖς οὖσιν ἐν ὅλῃ τῇ Ἀχαΐᾳ,

Eph 1,1
Παῦλος ἀπόστολος Χριστοῦ Ἰησοῦ διὰ θελήματος θεοῦ τοῖς ἁγίοις
τοῖς οὖσιν [ἐν Ἐφέσῳ] καὶ πιστοῖς ἐν Χριστῷ Ἰησοῦ,

Col. 1,1
Παῦλος ἀπόστολος Χριστοῦ Ἰησοῦ διὰ θελήματος θεοῦ καὶ
Τιμόθεος ὁ ἀδελφὸς

1 Tim 1,1
Παῦλος ἀπόστολος Χριστοῦ Ἰησοῦ κατ' ἐπιταγὴν θεοῦ σωτῆρος
ἡμῶν καὶ Χριστοῦ Ἰησοῦ τῆς ἐλπίδος ἡμῶν

2 Tim 1,1
Παῦλος ἀπόστολος Χριστοῦ Ἰησοῦ διὰ θελήματος θεοῦ κατ'
ἐπαγγελίαν ζωῆς τῆς ἐν Χριστῷ Ἰησοῦ

Rev 21,14
καὶ τὸ τεῖχος τῆς πόλεως ἔχων θεμελίους δώδεκα καὶ ἐπ' αὐτῶν
δώδεκα ὀνόματα τῶν δώδεκα ἀποστόλων τοῦ ἀρνίου.

c. *Apostle of Jesus Christ:* ἀπόστολος Ἰησοῦ Χριστοῦ

Titus 1,1
Παῦλος δοῦλος θεοῦ, ἀπόστολος δὲ Ἰησοῦ Χριστοῦ κατὰ πίστιν
ἐκλεκτῶν θεοῦ καὶ ἐπίγνωσιν ἀληθείας τῆς κατ' εὐσέβειαν

1 Pet 1,1
Πέτρος ἀπόστολος Ἰησοῦ Χριστοῦ ἐκλεκτοῖς παρεπιδήμοις διασ-
πορᾶς Πόντου, Γαλατίας, Καππαδοκίας, Ἀσίας καὶ Βιθυνίας,

2 Pet 1,1
Συμεὼν Πέτρος δοῦλος καὶ ἀπόστολος Ἰησοῦ Χριστοῦ τοῖς
ἰσότιμον ἡμῖν λαχοῦσιν πίστιν ἐν δικαιοσύνῃ τοῦ θεοῦ ἡμῶν καὶ
σωτῆρος Ἰησοῦ Χριστοῦ,

Jude 1,17
ὑμεῖς δέ, ἀγαπητοί, μνήσθητε τῶν ῥημάτων τῶν προειρημένων
ὑπὸ τῶν ἀποστόλων τοῦ κυρίου ἡμῶν Ἰησοῦ Χριστοῦ

d. *Apostle of Christ*

Rom 11,13
ὑμῖν δὲ λέγω τοῖς ἔθνεσιν· ἐφ' ὅσον μὲν οὖν εἰμι ἐγὼ ἐθνῶν
ἀπόστολος, τὴν διακονίαν μου δοξάζω,

2 Cor 11,13
οἱ γὰρ τοιοῦτοι ψευδαπόστολοι, ἐργάται δόλιοι, μετασχηματιζό-
μενοι εἰς **ἀποστόλους Χριστοῦ**.

1 Thess 2,7
δυνάμενοι ἐν βάρει εἶναι ὡς **Χριστοῦ ἀπόστολοι**. ἀλλὰ ἐγενήθημεν νήπιοι ἐν μέσῳ ὑμῶν, ὡς ἐὰν τροφὸς θάλπῃ τὰ ἑαυτῆς τέκνα,

ἐξαποστέλλω to send away, send forth, destroy (13)
is twice used by Paul for the 'sending' of the Son or the Spirit of the Son:

Gal 4,4
ὅτε δὲ ἦλθεν τὸ πλήρωμα τοῦ χρόνου, **ἐξαπέστειλεν** ὁ θεὸς τὸν
υἱὸν αὐτοῦ, γενόμενον ἐκ γυναικός, γενόμενον ὑπὸ νόμον,

Gal 4,6
Ὅτι δέ ἐστε υἱοί, **ἐξαπέστειλεν** ὁ θεὸς τὸ πνεῦμα τοῦ υἱοῦ αὐτοῦ
εἰς τὰς καρδίας ἡμῶν κρᾶζον· ἀββα ὁ πατήρ.

Once it is used for Paul who is sent to the Gentiles by Christ:

Acts 22,21
ὅτι ἐγὼ εἰς ἔθνη μακρὰν **ἐξαποστελῶ** σε.
Once this verb expresses the sending of an angel:

Acts 12,11
Καὶ ὁ Πέτρος ἐν ἑαυτῷ γενόμενος εἶπεν· νῦν οἶδα ἀληθῶς ὅτι
ἐξαπέστειλεν [ὁ] κύριος τὸν ἄγγελον αὐτοῦ καὶ ἐξείλατό με ἐκ
χειρὸς Ἡρῴδου καὶ πάσης τῆς προσδοκίας τοῦ λαοῦ τῶν Ἰουδαίων.

πέμπω to send (79)
Matt 2,8; 11,2; 14,10; 22,7; Mark 5,12; Luke 4,26; 7,6.10.19; 15,15;
16,24.27; 20,11-13; John 1,22.33; 4,34; 5,23-24.30.37; 6,38-39.44;
7,16.18.28.33; 8,16.18.26.29; 9,4; 12,44-45.49; 13,16.20; 14,24.26;
15,21.26; 16,5.7; 20,21; Acts 10,5.32-33; 11,29; 15,22.25; 19,31; 20,17;
23,30; 25,25.27; Rom 8,3; 1 Cor 4,17; 16,3; 2 Cor 9,3; Eph 6,22;
Phil 2,19.23.25.28; 4,16; Col 4,8; 1Thess 3,2.5; 2Thess 2,11; Titus 3,12;
1 Pet 2,14; Rev 1,11; 11,10; 14,15.18; 22,16.

Is used for the sending of envoys or helpers. Apart from Luke 20,13 and
Rom 8,3 the use of πέμπω for the sending of Jesus by God is specifically
Johannine:

Luke 20,13
εἶπεν δὲ ὁ κύριος τοῦ ἀμπελῶνος· τί ποιήσω; **πέμψω** τὸν υἱόν
μου τὸν ἀγαπητόν· ἴσως τοῦτον ἐντραπήσονται.

John 1,33
καγὼ οὐκ ᾔδειν αὐτόν, ἀλλ᾽ ὁ **πέμψας** με βαπτίζειν ἐν ὕδατι
ἐκεῖνός μοι εἶπεν· ἐφ᾽ ὃν ἂν ἴδῃς τὸ πνεῦμα καταβαῖνον καὶ μένον
ἐπ᾽ αὐτόν, οὗτός ἐστιν ὁ βαπτίζων ἐν πνεύματι ἁγίῳ.

John 4,34
λέγει αὐτοῖς ὁ Ἰησοῦς· ἐμὸν βρῶμά ἐστιν ἵνα ποιήσω τὸ θέλημα
τοῦ **πέμψαντός** με καὶ τελειώσω αὐτοῦ τὸ ἔργον.

John 5,23
ἵνα πάντες τιμῶσι τὸν υἱὸν καθὼς τιμῶσι τὸν πατέρα. ὁ μὴ τιμῶν
τὸν υἱὸν οὐ τιμᾷ τὸν πατέρα τὸν **πέμψαντα** αὐτόν.

John 5,24
Ἀμὴν ἀμὴν λέγω ὑμῖν ὅτι ὁ τὸν λόγον μου ἀκούων καὶ πιστεύων
τῷ **πέμψαντί** με ἔχει ζωὴν αἰώνιον καὶ εἰς κρίσιν οὐκ ἔρχεται,
ἀλλὰ μεταβέβηκεν ἐκ τοῦ θανάτου εἰς τὴν ζωήν.

John 5,30
Οὐ δύναμαι ἐγὼ ποιεῖν ἀπ᾽ ἐμαυτοῦ οὐδέν· καθὼς ἀκούω κρίνω,
καὶ ἡ κρίσις ἡ ἐμὴ δικαία ἐστίν, ὅτι οὐ ζητῶ τὸ θέλημα τὸ ἐμὸν
ἀλλὰ τὸ θέλημα τοῦ **πέμψαντός** με.

John 5,37
καὶ ὁ **πέμψας** με πατὴρ ἐκεῖνος μεμαρτύρηκεν περὶ ἐμοῦ. οὔτε
φωνὴν αὐτοῦ πώποτε ἀκηκόατε οὔτε εἶδος αὐτοῦ ἑωράκατε,

John 6,38
ὅτι καταβέβηκα ἀπὸ τοῦ οὐρανοῦ οὐχ ἵνα ποιῶ τὸ θέλημα τὸ ἐμὸν
ἀλλὰ τὸ θέλημα τοῦ **πέμψαντός** με.

John 6,39
τοῦτο δέ ἐστιν τὸ θέλημα τοῦ **πέμψαντός** με, ἵνα πᾶν ὃ δέδωκέν μοι
μὴ ἀπολέσω ἐξ αὐτοῦ, ἀλλὰ ἀναστήσω αὐτὸ [ἐν] τῇ ἐσχάτῃ ἡμέρᾳ.

John 6,44
οὐδεὶς δύναται ἐλθεῖν πρός με ἐὰν μὴ ὁ πατὴρ ὁ **πέμψας** με
ἑλκύσῃ αὐτόν, καγὼ ἀναστήσω αὐτὸν ἐν τῇ ἐσχάτῃ ἡμέρᾳ.

John 7,16
ἀπεκρίθη οὖν αὐτοῖς [ὁ] Ἰησοῦς καὶ εἶπεν· ἡ ἐμὴ διδαχὴ οὐκ
ἔστιν ἐμὴ ἀλλὰ τοῦ **πέμψαντός** με·

John 7,18
ὁ ἀφ' ἑαυτοῦ λαλῶν τὴν δόξαν τὴν ἰδίαν ζητεῖ· ὁ δὲ ζητῶν τὴν δόξαν τοῦ **πέμψαντος** αὐτὸν οὗτος ἀληθής ἐστιν καὶ ἀδικία ἐν αὐτῷ οὐκ ἔστιν.

John 7,28
ἔκραξεν οὖν ἐν τῷ ἱερῷ διδάσκων ὁ Ἰησοῦς καὶ λέγων· καμὲ οἴδατε καὶ οἴδατε πόθεν εἰμί· καὶ ἀπ' ἐμαυτοῦ οὐκ ἐλήλυθα, ἀλλ' ἔστιν ἀληθινὸς ὁ **πέμψας** με, ὃν ὑμεῖς οὐκ οἴδατε·

John 7,33
εἶπεν οὖν ὁ Ἰησοῦς· ἔτι χρόνον μικρὸν μεθ' ὑμῶν εἰμι καὶ ὑπάγω πρὸς τὸν **πέμψαντά** με.

John 8,16
καὶ ἐὰν κρίνω δὲ ἐγώ, ἡ κρίσις ἡ ἐμὴ ἀληθινή ἐστιν, ὅτι μόνος οὐκ εἰμί, ἀλλ' ἐγὼ καὶ ὁ **πέμψας** με πατήρ.

John 8,18
ἐγώ εἰμι ὁ μαρτυρῶν περὶ ἐμαυτοῦ καὶ μαρτυρεῖ περὶ ἐμοῦ ὁ **πέμψας** με πατήρ.

John 8,26
πολλὰ ἔχω περὶ ὑμῶν λαλεῖν καὶ κρίνειν, ἀλλ' ὁ **πέμψας** με ἀληθής ἐστιν, καγὼ ἃ ἤκουσα παρ' αὐτοῦ ταῦτα λαλῶ εἰς τὸν κόσμον.

John 8,29
καὶ ὁ **πέμψας** με μετ' ἐμοῦ ἐστιν· οὐκ ἀφῆκέν με μόνον, ὅτι ἐγὼ τὰ ἀρεστὰ αὐτῷ ποιῶ πάντοτε.

John 9,4
ἡμᾶς δεῖ ἐργάζεσθαι τὰ ἔργα τοῦ **πέμψαντός** με ἕως ἡμέρα ἐστίν· ἔρχεται νὺξ ὅτε οὐδεὶς δύναται ἐργάζεσθαι.

John 12,44
Ἰησοῦς δὲ ἔκραξεν καὶ εἶπεν· ὁ πιστεύων εἰς ἐμὲ οὐ πιστεύει εἰς ἐμὲ ἀλλὰ εἰς τὸν **πέμψαντά** με,

John 12,45
καὶ ὁ θεωρῶν ἐμὲ θεωρεῖ τὸν **πέμψαντά** με.

John 12,49
ὅτι ἐγὼ ἐξ ἐμαυτοῦ οὐκ ἐλάλησα, ἀλλ' ὁ **πέμψας** με πατὴρ αὐτός μοι ἐντολὴν δέδωκεν τί εἴπω καὶ τί λαλήσω.

John 13,16
ἀμὴν ἀμὴν λέγω ὑμῖν, οὐκ ἔστιν δοῦλος μείζων τοῦ κυρίου αὐτοῦ οὐδὲ ἀπόστολος μείζων τοῦ **πέμψαντος** αὐτόν.

John 13,20
ἀμὴν ἀμὴν λέγω ὑμῖν, ὁ λαμβάνων ἄν τινα **πέμψω** ἐμὲ λαμβάνει, ὁ δὲ ἐμὲ λαμβάνων λαμβάνει τὸν **πέμψαντά** με.

John 14,24
ὁ μὴ ἀγαπῶν με τοὺς λόγους μου οὐ τηρεῖ· καὶ ὁ λόγος ὃν ἀκούετε οὐκ ἔστιν ἐμὸς ἀλλὰ τοῦ **πέμψαντός** με πατρός.

John 14,26
ὁ δὲ παράκλητος, τὸ πνεῦμα τὸ ἅγιον, ὃ **πέμψει** ὁ πατὴρ ἐν τῷ ὀνόματί μου, ἐκεῖνος ὑμᾶς διδάξει πάντα καὶ ὑπομνήσει ὑμᾶς πάντα ἃ εἶπον ὑμῖν [ἐγώ].

John 15,21
ἀλλὰ ταῦτα πάντα ποιήσουσιν εἰς ὑμᾶς διὰ τὸ ὄνομά μου, ὅτι οὐκ οἴδασιν τὸν **πέμψαντά** με.

John 15,26
"Οταν ἔλθῃ ὁ παράκλητος ὃν ἐγὼ **πέμψω** ὑμῖν παρὰ τοῦ πατρός, τὸ πνεῦμα τῆς ἀληθείας ὃ παρὰ τοῦ πατρὸς ἐκπορεύεται, ἐκεῖνος μαρτυρήσει περὶ ἐμοῦ·

John 16,5
Νῦν δὲ ὑπάγω πρὸς τὸν **πέμψαντά** με, καὶ οὐδεὶς ἐξ ὑμῶν ἐρωτᾷ με· ποῦ ὑπάγεις;

John 16,7
ἀλλ᾽ ἐγὼ τὴν ἀλήθειαν λέγω ὑμῖν, συμφέρει ὑμῖν ἵνα ἐγὼ ἀπέλθω. ἐὰν γὰρ μὴ ἀπέλθω, ὁ παράκλητος οὐκ ἐλεύσεται πρὸς ὑμᾶς· ἐὰν δὲ πορευθῶ, **πέμψω** αὐτὸν πρὸς ὑμᾶς.

John 20,21
εἶπεν οὖν αὐτοῖς [ὁ Ἰησοῦς] πάλιν· εἰρήνη ὑμῖν· καθὼς ἀπέσταλκέν με ὁ πατήρ, καγὼ **πέμπω** ὑμᾶς.

Rom 8,3
Τὸ γὰρ ἀδύνατον τοῦ νόμου ἐν ᾧ ἠσθένει διὰ τῆς σαρκός, ὁ θεὸς τὸν ἑαυτοῦ υἱὸν **πέμψας** ἐν ὁμοιώματι σαρκὸς ἁμαρτίας καὶ περὶ ἁμαρτίας κατέκρινεν τὴν ἁμαρτίαν ἐν τῇ σαρκί,

2 Thess 2,11 speaks of the sending by God of the force of deceit:

καὶ διὰ τοῦτο **πέμπει** αὐτοῖς ὁ θεὸς ἐνέργειαν πλάνης εἰς τὸ πιστεῦσαι αὐτοὺς τῷ ψεύδει,

and **Rev 22,16** mentions the messenger sent by Jesus to bear witness to the churches:

Ἐγὼ Ἰησοῦς **ἔπεμψα** τὸν ἄγγελόν μου μαρτυρῆσαι ὑμῖν ταῦτα ἐπὶ ταῖς ἐκκλησίαις. ἐγὼ εἰμι ἡ ῥίζα καὶ τὸ γένος Δαυίδ, ὁ ἀστὴρ ὁ λαμπρὸς ὁ πρωϊνός.

APPENDIX 2:
'MISSION'-TERMINOLOGY
IN THE SEPTUAGINT

In this second appendix the use of 'mission'-terminology in the LXX is presented. What follows are concordant surveys of the use of ἀποστέλλω and its cognates as well as πέμπω. It appears that the verb ἀποστέλλω was often used for prophets or other envoys who were regarded as messengers on behalf of God. Is is often stated that these envoys were 'sent' by God.

ἀποστέλλω to send (647)
Gen 8,7-8; 19,13; 20,2; 21,14; 24,7.40; 26,27; 27,45; 28,5; 30,25; 31,4; 32,4.6.19.27; 37,13-14.32; 38,17.20.23.25; 41,8.14; 42,4.16; 43,4-5.8.14; 44,3; 45,5.7-8.23.27; 46,5.28; Exod 2,5; 3,10.13-15; 4,13.28; 5,22; 7,16; 8,24; 9,15.27; 10,10; 15,7.10; 23,20.27-28; Lev 16,10; 25,21; 26,22; Num 13,2.16-17.27; 14,36; 16,12.28-29; 20,14.16; 21,6.21.32; 22,5.10.15.37.40; 24,12; 31,4.6; 32,8; Deut 1,22; 2,26; 7,20; 19,12; 22,7; 28,8; 29,21; 32,24; 34,11; Josh 1,16; 2,1.3; 6,25; 7,2.22; 8,3.9; 10,3.6; 11,1; 14,7.11; 22,13; 23,5; 24,9.28; Judg 3,15; 4,6; 9,31; 11,12.14.17.19.28; 13,8; 16,18; 21,10.13; 1 Sam 4,4; 5,8; 6,2.21; 9,16; 11,3.7; 12,8.11; 15,1.18.20; 16,1.11-12.19.22; 19,11.14-15.20-21; 20,12.21.31; 21,3; 22,11; 25,5.14.25.32.39-40; 26,4; 30,26; 31,9; 2 Sam 2,5; 3,12.15.21-23.26; 5,11; 8,10; 9,5; 10,2-3.5-7.16; 11,1.3-6.14.18. 27-12,1; 12,25.27; 13,7.27; 14,2.29.32; 15,10.12.36; 17,16; 18,2.29; 19,12.15; 22,15.17; 24,13; 1 Kgs 1,44.53; 2,29.42; 5,15-16.22-23.28; 7,1; 9,27; 12,18.20.24; 15,20; 18,10.19-20; 19,2; 20,8.11.14; 21,2.5-7.9.17; 2 Kgs 1,2.6.9.11.13.16; 2,2.4.6.16-17; 4,22; 5,6-8.10.22; 6,9-10.13-14.23.32; 7,13-14; 8,9; 9,17.19; 10,1.5.7.21; 11,4; 12,19; 14,8-9.19; 16,7-8.10-11; 17,4.13.25-26; 18,14.17.27; 19,2.4.9.16.20; 20,12; 22,3.15.18; 23,1.16; 24,2; 1 Chron 8,8; 10,9; 13,2; 14,1; 18,10; 19,2-6.8.16; 21,12.15; 2 Chron 2,2.6-7.10.12.14; 6,34; 7,10.13; 8,18; 10,3.18; 16,2-4; 17,7; 24,19.23; 25,15.17-18.27; 28,16; 30,1; 32,9.21.31; 34,8.23.26.29; 35,21; 36,5.10.15; 1 Esdr 1,43.48; 6,7; 8,19.43.45; 9,51; Ezra 4,11.17-18; 5,5-7; 6,13; 7,14; 8,16; Neh 2,6.9; 6,2-5.8.12.19; 8,10.12; Esth 1,22; 3,13; 4,4-5; 8,5; 16,16; 9,19; Judith 1,7; 3,1; 4,4; 6,2; 7,18.32; 8,10.31; 9,9; 11,7.14.16.19.22; 12,6; 14,5; 15,4; 16,14;

Tob 2,12; 3,17; 8,12; 12,14.20; 1 Macc 1,29.44; 3,27.35.39; 5,10.38.48; 6,60; 7,7.9-10.19.26-27; 8,10.17.20.22; 9,1.35.60.70; 10,3.15.17.20.25.51. 69.89; 11,9.17.41-44.58; 12,1-3.7-8.10.16.19.26.45.49; 13,11.14.16.18-19.21.25.34-35.37; 14,2.20-21.24; 15,1.17.26.28; 16,18-21; 2 Macc 1,20; 2,15; 3,7; 4,19-21.23; 8,9.11; 11,6; 12,43; 14,39; 15,22-23; 3 Macc 3,25; 5,11; Ps 58,1; 77,25; 104,17.20; 106,20; 110,9; 147,4.7; Prov 9,3; 21,8; 25,13; 26,6.13; Eccl 11,1; Song 5,4; Job 1,5.11; 2,5; 5,10; 8,4; 38,35; 40,11; Wis 12,8; 16,18; Sir 15,9; 34,6; 48,18; Ps. Sol. 7,4; Hos 5,13; Zech 2,12-13; 6,15; Mal 3,22; Isa 6,6.8; 9,7; 10,6.16; 14,12; 16,1.8; 18,2; 19,20; 20,1; 33,7; 36,2.12; 37,2.4.9.17.21; 39,1; 43,14; 48,16; 57,9; 58,6; 61,1; Jer 2,10; 7,25; 9,16; 14,3.14-15; 16,16; 19,14; 21,1; 23,21.32.38; 24,10; 25,4.9; 30,8; 31,12; 32,15-17.27; 33,5.12.15; 34,3.15-16; 35,9.15; 36,1.3.9.25.28.31; 41,10.14; 42,15; 43,14.21; 44,3.7.15.17; 45,14; 46,14; 47,1.5.14; 49,5-6.20-21; 50,1-2.10; 51,4; Bar 1,7.10.14.21; 3,33; Lam 1,13; Ezek 7,7; 13,6; 30,11; 39,6; Dan 3,2.95; 4,13.23.25.37; 10,11; 13,29; 14,37.

In a large number of these passages it is God who sends an envoy to either the people of Israel, a king or an enemy. Many of the important persons in Israel's history are 'sent' by God. Moses for instance is 'sent' to the people of Israel (Ex 3,13-15; Num 16,28-29) as well as to the Pharao of Egypt (Ex 7,16). Prophets in general are sent to Israel or the king. This is especially manifest in the books of Samuel, but also in the prophets Jeremiah and Isaiah. See for instance:

> Isa 6,8 – Isaiah's commissioning: καὶ ἤκουσα τῆς φωνῆς κυρίου λέγοντος τίνα ἀποστείλω καὶ τίς πορεύσεται πρὸς τὸν λαὸν τοῦτον· καὶ εἶπα ἰδού εἰμι ἐγώ· ἀπόστειλόν με
> Isa 48,16 – καὶ νῦν κύριος ἀπέσταλκέν με καὶ τὸ πνεῦμα αὐτοῦ
> Isa 61,1 – πνεῦμα κυρίου ἐπ' ἐμέ, οὗ εἵνεκεν ἔχρισέν με· εὐαγγελίσασθαι πτωχοῖς ἀπέσταλκέν με, ἰάσασθαι τοὺς συντετριμμένους τῇ καρδίᾳ, κηρύξαι αἰχμαλώτοις ἄφεσιν καὶ τυφλοῖς ἀνάβλεψιν
> Jer 14,14-15 – on false prophets who are not 'sent' by YHWH;
> Jer 19,14 – Jeremiah is sent by YHWH;
> Jer 42,15 – καὶ ἀπέστειλα πρὸς ὑμᾶς τοὺς παῖδάς μου τοὺς προφήτας λέγων ἀποστράφητε ἕκαστος ἀπὸ τῆς ὁδοῦ αὐτοῦ τῆς πονηρᾶς κτλ.

A programmatic summary of the idea found in Jer 42,15 is given in 2 Chron 36,15, which describes how God has sent prophets and messengers out of mercy for his people: καὶ ἐξαπέστειλεν κύριος ὁ θεὸς τῶν πατέρων αὐτῶν ἐν χειρὶ προφητῶν ὀρθρίζων καὶ ἀποστέλλων τοὺς ἀγγέλους αὐτοῦ, ὅτι ἦν φειδόμενος τοῦ λαοῦ αὐτοῦ καὶ τοῦ ἁγιάσματος αὐτοῦ.

This brief presentation of evidence from the LXX shows that the idea that God 'sent' prophets and messengers on behalf of his people is deeply rooted in the literature of Israel. It is therefore not at all strange that the early Christians used the verb ἀποστέλλω and its cognates to express their idea that God (or Christ) had given them a special message to preach. In fact, the sheer use of this terminology points at a prophetic awareness within the Jesus-movement as well as in the earliest Christian groups.

ἀποστολή task (11)
Deut 22,7; 1 Kgs 5,14; 1 Esdr 9,51.54; 1 Macc 2,18; 2 Macc 3,2; Ps 77,49; Eccl 8,8; Song 4,13; Jer 39,36; Bar 2,25.

The **noun ἀπόστολος** is not used in the LXX.

ἐξαποστέλλω to send away, send forth, destroy (266)
Gen 3,23; 8,10.12; 19,29; 25,6; 26,29.31; 31,27.42; 32,14; 45,1.24; Exod 3,12.20; 4,21.23; 5,1-2; 6,1.11.13; 7,2.14.16.26-27; 8,4.16-17.25.28-9,2; 9,7.13-14.17.28.35; 10,3-4.7.20.27; 11,1.10; 13,15.17; 14,5; 18,27; 21,26-27; 24,5; Lev 14,7.53; 16,21-22.26; 18,24; 20,23; 26,25; Num 5,2-4; 13,3; Deut 9,23; 15,12-13.18; 21,14; 22,19.29; 24,1.3-4; 28,20; Josh 2,21; 22,6-7; 24,12; Judg 1,25; 2,6; 3,18; 5,15; 6,8.14.35; 7,8.24; 9,23; 11,7.17.38; 12,9; 15,5; 18,2; 19,25.29-30; 20,6.12.48; 1 Sam 5,10-11; 6,3.6.8; 9,19.26; 10,25; 13,2; 16,20; 19,17; 20,5.13.22.29; 2 Sam 3,14.24; 10,4; 11,12; 13,16-17; 1 Kgs 2,25; 8,66; 11,21-22; 12,24; 15,12.18-19; 16,28; 21,34; 2 Kgs 3,7; 5,5.24; 8,12; 11,12; 15,37; 24,2; 2 Chron 36,15; 1 Esdr 1,25; 3,14; 4,4.44.57; Esth 4,15; 8,10; 9,19-20.22; Tob 5,18; 10,8-9.11; 1 Macc 6,12; 11,62; 12,46; 2 Macc 6,1; 14,12.27; 3 Macc 4,4; 6,27; Ps 17,15.17; 19,3; 42,3; 56,4; 77,45.49; 80,13; 103,10.30; 104,26.28; 105,15; 109,2; 134,9; 143,6-7; 151,4; Job 12,19; 14,20; 22,9; 30,11; 39,3; Wis 9,10; Ps. Sol. 17,12; Hos 8,14; Amos 1,4.7.10.12; 2,2.5; 4,10; 7,10; 8,11; Mic 1,14; 6,4; Joel 2,19.25; 4,13; Obad 1,1.7; Hag 1,12; Zech 1,10; 2,15; 4,9; 7,2.12; 8,10; 9,11; Mal 2,2.4.16; 3,1; Isa 27,8; 50,1; 66,19; Jer 1,7; 3,1.8; 7,25; 8,17; 15,1; 24,5; 25,18; 27,33; 28,2; 33,22; 35,16; 41,9.14.16; Bar 4,11.37; 6,61; Ezek 2,3; 3,5-6; 5,16-17; 13,20; 14,13.21; 17,7.15; 23,16.40; 31,4

πέμπω to send (22)

Gen 27,42; 1 Esdr 2,20; Ezra 4,14; 5,17; Neh 2,5; Esth 8,5; 1 Macc 13,17; 2 Macc 1,20; 3,38; 4,44; 5,18.24; 11,17; 11,32.34.36.37; 14,19; 3 Macc 5,42; Wis 9,10.17; 12,25.

BIBLIOGRAPHY

a. Sources (Editions and Translations)

1. Bible

Old Testament:

Elliger, K., Rudolph, W. (eds.), *Biblia Hebraica Stuttgartensia* (Stuttgart: Deutsche Bibelstiftung, 1977).

Septuagint:

Rahlfs, A. (ed.), *Septuaginta* (Stuttgart: Deutsche Bibelgesellschaft, 1935).

New Testament:

Nestle, E., Aland, K. (eds.), *Novum Testamentum graece* (Stuttgart: Deutsche Bibelstiftung, 27th ed., 1993).

Latin Vulgate:

Weber, R., Fischer, B. (eds.), *Biblia Sacra* (Stuttgart: Deutsche Bibelgesellschaft, 1969).

For the translation of biblical passages the New Revised Standard Version is used, unless otherwise indicated.

2. Judaica and Graeco-Roman Sources

Pseudepigrapha are quoted from J.H. Charlesworth (ed.), *The Old Testament Pseudepigrapha*, 2 vols. (New York: Doubleday, 1983). For Qumran texts reference is made to F. García Martínez, F., *The Dead Sea Scrolls Translated. The Qumran Texts in English* (Leiden, New York, Köln: Brill, 1994), and F. García Martínez, E.J.C. Tigchelaar, *The Dead Sea Scrolls* Study Edition 2 vols. (Leiden [etc.]: Brill; Grand Rapids: Eerdmans, 1997.1998).

Flavius Josephus, Philo of Alexandria and other ancient authors are referred to in the LCL-edition, unless otherwise indicated. For Josephus,

De Bello Judaico, the edition of Michel and Baurnfeind was used: O. Michel, O. Bauernfeind, *Flavius Josephus: De Bello Judaico* (Darmstadt: Wissenschaftliche Buchgesellschaft, 1959).

b. Modern Authors

Abramowski, L., 'Die Entstehung der dreigliedrichen Taufformel – ein Versuch', *ZTK* 81 (1984), pp. 417-446.

Allen, R., *Missionary Methods: St. Paul's or Ours?* (London: World Dominion Press, 1953.

Attridge, H.W., 'Josephus and his Works', in: M.E. Stone (ed.), *Jewish Writings of the Second Temple Period* (CRINT 2,2; Assen: Van Gorcum; Philadelphia: Fortress Press, 1984), pp. 185-232.

Aus, R.D., 'Paul's Travel Plans to Spain and the "Full Number of the Gentiles" of Rom. xi 25', *NT* 21 (1979), pp. 232-262.

Axenfeld, K., 'Die jüdische Propaganda als Vorläuferin und Wegbereiterin des Christentums', in: idem *et alii*, (eds.), *Missionswissenschaftliche Studien* (FS Warneck; Berlin: Warneck, 1904).

Bamberger, B.J., *Proselytism in the Talmudic Period* (New York: KTAV, 1968 = Hebrew Union College Press, 1939).

Barnikol, E., *Die vor- und frühchristliche Zeit des Paulus* (Kiel: Mühlau 1929).

Baron, S.W., 'Population', *Encyclopaedia Judaica* vol. 13 (Jerusalem: Keter, 1971), cols. 866-903.

Barrett, C.K., *A Critical and Exegetical Commentary on the Acts of the Apostles*, 2 vols. (ICC; Edinburgh: Clark, 1994.1998).

——, *The Signs of an Apostle. The Cato Lecture 1969* (Carlisle: Paternoster, 1996 = 1970).

Barth, G., *Der Brief an die Philipper* (ZB; Zürich: Theologischer Verlag, 1979).

Barth, G., *Die Taufe in frühchristlicher Zeit* (BtS 4; Neukirchen-Vluyn: Neukirchener Verlag, 1981).

Barnett, P.W., 'Jewish mission in the era of the New Testament and the apostle Paul', in: P. Bolt, M. Thompson (eds.), *The Gospel to the Nations. Perspectives on Paul's Mission* (Leicester: Apollos; Downers Grove: Intervarsity, 2000), pp. 263-283.

Baur, F.C., *Paulus, der Apostel Jesu Christi. Sein Leben und Wirken, seine Briefe und seine Lehre* (Leipzig: Fues, 2nd ed., 1866).

——, *Apollonius von Tyana und Christus. Ein Beitrag zur Religionsgeschichte der ersten Jahrhunderte nach Christus* (Hildesheim: Olms, 1966 = Leipzig 1876).

Becker, J., Luz, U., *Die Briefe an die Galater, Epheser und Kolosser* (NTD; Göttingen, Vandenhoeck&Ruprecht, 18th ed., 1998).

Becker, J., *Paulus. Der Apostel der Völker* (Tübingen: Mohr, 2nd rev. ed. 1992, ¹1989).

Beckheuer, B., *Paulus und Jerusalem. Kollekte und Mission im theologischen Denken des Heidenapostels* (EHS 22/611; Frankfurt a.M. [etc]: Lang, 1997).

Beker, J.C., *Paul the Apostle: the Triumph of God in Life and Thought* (Philadelphia: Fortress Press, 1980).

Berger, K., 'Volksversammlung und Gemeinde Gottes: zu den Anfängen der christlichen Verwendung von "Ekklesia"', *ZTK* 73 (1976), pp. 167-207.

——, *Theologiegeschichte des Urchristentums. Theologie des Neuen Testaments* (UTB; Tübingen, Basel: Franke, 2nd rev. ed., 1995).

Betz, H.-D., *Der Apostel Paulus und die sokratische Tradition. Eine exegetische Untersuchung zu seiner "Apologie" 2 Korinther 10-13* (BhTh 45; Tübingen: Mohr, 1972).

——, *Galatians: a Commentary on Paul's Letter to the Churches in Galatia* (Hermeneia; Philadelphia: Fortress Press, 1979).

Bickerman, E., 'Consecratio', in W. den Boer (ed.), *Le culte des souverains dans l'empire romain* (EAC 19; Geneva: Fondation Hardt, 1973), pp. 3-25.

Böhlig, H., *Die Geisteskultur von Tarsus im augusteischen Zeitalter mit Berücksichtigung der paulinischen Schriften* (FRLANT 19; Göttingen: Vandenhoeck & Ruprecht, 1913).

Boll, F., 'Der Lebensalter', *Neue Jahrbücher für den klassiken Altertum* 31 (1913), pp. 89-91.

Borgen, P., 'Philo of Alexandria', in M.E. Stone (ed.), *Jewish Writings of the Second Temple Period. Apocrypha, Pseudepigrapha, Qumran Sectarian Writings, Philo, Josephus* (CRINT 2,2; Assen: Van Gorcum; Philadelphia: Fortress Press, 1984), pp. 233-282.

Bornkamm, G., *Paulus* (UB 119D; Stuttgart [etc.]: Kohlhammer, 1969).

Bousset, W., Gressmann, H., *Die Religion des Judentums im späthellenistischen Zeitalter* (HNT 21; Tübingen: Mohr, 1926, 4th ed., 1966).

Bowers, P., 'Paul and Religious Propaganda in the First Century', *NT* 22 (1980), pp. 316-323.

——, 'Church and Mission in Paul', *JSNT* 44 (1991), pp. 89-11.

Bowersock, G.W., *Roman Arabia* (Cambridge MA: Harvard University Press 1983).

Box, H. *Philonis Alexandrini In Flaccum* (London, New York, Toronto: Oxford University Press, 1939).

Boyarin, D., *A Radical Jew. Paul and the Politics of Identity* (Contraversions 1; Berkeley [etc.]: University of California Press, 1994).

Braude, W.G., *Jewish Proselyting in the First Five Centuries of the Common Era, the Age of the Tannaim and Amoraim* (BUS 6; Providence: Brown University, 1950).

Braun, H., *Qumran und das Neue Testament*, vol. 2 (Tübingen: Mohr, 1966).

Breytenbach, C., *Paulus und Barnabas in der Provinz Galatien. Studien zu Apostelgeschichte 13f.; 16,6; 18,23 und den Adressaten des Galaterbriefes* (AGAJU 38; Leiden [etc.]: Brill, 1996).

Brooks, O.S., 'Matthew 28, 16-20 and the Design of the First Gospel', *JSNT* 10 (1981), pp. 2-18.

Bruce, F.F., *The Acts of the Apostles. The Greek Text with Introduction and Commentary* (Grand Rapids: Eerdmans, 1951, repr. 1986).

——, *The Book of Acts* (Grand Rapids: Eerdmans, 1951, rev. ed., 1988).

——, *Paul. Apostle of the Free Spirit*, (Carlisle: Paternoster, rev. ed. 1980 = 1995, [1]1977).

Buckler, W.H., Calder, W.M., Cox, C.W.M., 'Monuments from Iconium, Lycaonia and Isauria', *JRS* 14 (1924), pp. 24-84.

Bühner, J.-A., s.v. ἀπόστολος, *EWNT*, vol. 1, cols. 342-351.

Bultmann, R., *Der zweite Brief an die Korinther* (KEK; Göttingen: Vandenhoeck & Ruprecht, 1976).

Burchard, C., *Der dreizehnte Zeuge. Traditions- und kompositionsgeschichtliche Untersuchungen zu Lukas' Darstellung der Frühzeit des Paulus* (FRLANT 104; Göttingen: Vandenhoeck & Ruprecht, 1970).

——, *Joseph und Aseneth* (JSHRZ; Gütersloh: Mohn, 1983).

Burkert, W., *Ancient Mystery Cults* (Cambridge Mass., London: Harvard University Press; 1987).

Cadbury, H.J., 'Names for Christians and Christianity in Acts', *Beginnings* vol. 5, pp. 375-392.

Campbell, D.A., 'An Anchor for Pauline Chronology: Paul's Flight from the "Ethnarch of King Aretas" (2 Corinthians 11:32-33)', *JBL* 121 (2002), pp. 279-302.

Carrez, M., *La deuxième épitre de Saint Paul aux Corinthiens* (CNT; Geneva: Labor et Fides, 1986).

Chister, A., 'The Pauline Communities', in: M. Bockmuehl, M.B. Thompson (eds.), *A Vision for the Church. Studies in Early Christian Ecclesiology* (FS Sweet; Edinburgh: Clark, 1997), pp. 105-120.

Clauss, M., *Cultores Mithrae. Die Anhängerschaft des Mithras-Kultes* (HABES 10; Stuttgart: Steiner, 1992).

Coggins, R.J., 'The Samaritans and Acts', *NTS* 28 (1982), pp. 423-434.

Cohen, S.J.D., *The Beginnings of Jewishness. Boundaries, Varieties, Uncertainties* (Berkeley [etc.]: University of California Press, 1999).

Collins, J.J., *The Sibylline Oracles of Egyptian Judaism* (SBLDS 13; Missoula: SBL, 1972).

Conzelmann, H., *Geschichte des Urchristentums* (GNT 5; Göttingen: Vandenhoeck & Ruprecht, 1969).

——, *Die Apostelgeschichte* (HNT; Tübingen: Mohr, 2nd ed., 1972).

——, *Der erste Brief an die Korinther* (KEK; Göttingen: Vandenhoeck und Ruprecht, 1981).

Cranfield, C.E.B., *The Epistle to the Romans*, 2 vols. (ICC: Edinburgh: Clark, 1975.1979).

Crossan, J.D., *The Historical Jesus. The Life of a Mediterranean Jewish Peasant* (San Francisco: Harper, 1991).

Cullmann, O., 'Le caractère eschatogique du devoir missionaire et de la conscience apostolique de S. Paul. Étude sur le κατέχον (—ων) de 2 Thess 2,6.7', *RHPR* 16 (1936), pp. 210-245

Dalbert, P., *Die Theologie der hellenistisch-jüdischen Missionsliteratur unter Ausschluss von Philo und Josephus* (TF 4; Hamburg-Volksdorf: Reich, 1954).

Daniel, J.L., 'Anti-Semitism in the Hellenistic-Roman Period', *JBL* 98 (1979), pp. 45-65.

Davies, W.D., Allison jr., D.C., *The Gospel according to Saint Matthew*, 3 vols. (ICC; Edinburgh: Clark, 1988-1997).

Davies, W.D., *Paul and Rabbinic Judaism. Some Rabbinic Elements in Pauline Theology* (London: SPCK, 1962 = 1948 with additional comments).

De Jonge, M., *Christology in Context. The Earliest Christian Response to Jesus* (Philadelphia: Westminster, 1988).

——, *God's Final Envoy. Early Christology and Jesus' Own View of His Mission* (Grand Rapids, Cambridge: Eerdmans, 1998).

De Witt Burton, E., *A Critical and Exegetical Commentary on the Epistle to the Galatians* (ICC; Edinburgh: Clark, 1921).

Deichgräber, R., *Gotteshymnus und Christushymnus. Untersuchungen zu Form, Sprache und Stil der frühchristlichen Hymnen* (SUNT 5; Göttingen: Vandenhoeck & Ruprecht, 1967).

Deissmann, A., *Die neutestamentliche Formel "in Christo Jesu"* (Marburg: Elwert, 1892).

——, *Paulus. Eine kultur- und religionsgeschichtliche Skizze* (Tübingen: Mohr Siebeck, 2nd ed. 1925).

Derwacter, F.M., *Preparing the Way for Paul. The Proselyte Movement in Later Judaism* (New York: Macmillan, 1930).

Devisch, M., 'La relation entre l'évangile de Marc et le document Q', in: M. Sabbe (ed.), *L'évangile selon Marc. Tradition et rédaction* (BETL 34; Leuven: Peeters/University Press, 1988), pp. 59-91.

Dibelius, M., *An die Thessalonicher I, II* (HNT; Tübingen: Mohr, 3rd ed., 1937).

——, 'Die Apostelgeschichte als Geschichtsquelle', in: idem, *Aufsätze zur Apostelgeschichte* hrsg. von H. Greeven (FRLANT 42; Göttingen: Vandenhoeck&Ruprecht; 1951), pp. 91-95.

——, 'Die Bekehrung des Cornelius', in: idem, *Aufsätze zur Apostelgeschichte* (ed. by H. Greeven; FRLANT 60; Berlin: Evangelische Verlagsanstalt, 1951), pp. 96-107.

——, Kümmel, W.G., *Paulus* (SG 1160; Berlin: De Gruyter, 4th ed. 1970).

Dietzfelbinger, C., *Die Berufung des Paulus als Ursprung seiner Theologie* (WMANT 58; Neukirchen-Vluyn: Neukirchener Verlag, 1985).

Dinkler, E., 'Philippus und der ΑΝΗΡ ΑΙΘΙΟΨ', in: E.E. Ellis, E. Gräßer, *Jesus und Paulus* (FS Kümmel; Göttingen: Vandenhoeck & Ruprecht, 1975), pp. 85-95,

Donaldson, T.L., 'Israelite, Convert, Apostle to the Gentiles: The Origin of Paul's Gentile Mission', in: R.N. Longenecker (ed.), *The Road from Damascus. The Impact of Paul's Conversion on His Life, Thought, and Ministry* (MNTS 2; Grand Rapids: Eerdmans, 1997), pp. 62-84.

——, *Paul and the Gentiles. Remapping the Apostle's Convictional World* (Minneapolis: Fortress, 1997).

Donfried, K.P., 'Peter', *ABD* vol. 5, pp. 251-263.

Downing, F.G., *Christ and the Cynics* (JSOTM 4; Sheffield: JSOT Press, 1988).

——, *Cynics, Paul and the Pauline Churches. Cynics and Christian Origins II* (London, New York: Routledge, 1998).

Dunand, F., *Le culte d'Isis dans le bassin oriental de la Mediterranée*, 3 vols (EPROER 26; Leiden [etc.]: Brill, 1973).

——, *Isis. Mère des Dieux* (Paris: Errance, 2000).

Dunn, J.D.G., *Baptism in the Holy Spirit. A Re-examination of the New Testament Teaching on the Gift of the Spirit in Relation to Pentacostalism Today* (Philadelphia: Westminster, 1970).

——, *Romans 1-8* (WBC; Dallas: Word Books, 1988).

——, *Romans 9-16* (WBC; Dallas: Word Books, 1988).

——, *A Commentary on the Epistle to the Galatians* (BNTC; London: Black, 1993).

296 PAUL THE MISSIONARY

——, *The Theology of Paul the Apostle* (Edinburgh: Clark; Grand Rapids: Eerdmans, 1998).

Dzielska, M., *Apollonius of Tyana in Legend and History* (PRSA 10; Roma: Bretschneider, 1986).

Edelstein, E.J., Edelstein, L., *Asclepius, A Collection and Interpretation of the Testimonies*, 2 vols. (TD 2; Baltimore: John Hopkins Press, 1945) [= Baltimore, London: John Hopkins University Press, 1998].

Elliger, W., *Paulus in Griechenland. Philippi, Thessaloniki, Athen, Korinth* (SBS 92/93; Stuttgart: Katholisches Bibelwerk, 1978).

Elliott, J.K., *The Apocryphal New Testament. A Collection of Apocryphal Christian Literature in an English Translation* (Oxford: Clarendon, 1993).

Ellis, E.E., 'Paul and his Co-Workers', *NTS* 17 (1970-71), pp. 437-453.

Engberg-Pedersen, T., *Paul and the Stoics* (Louisville: Westminster John Knox; Edinburgh: Clark, 2000).

Fabrega, V., 'War Junia(s), der hervorragende Apostel (Röm. 16,7), eine Frau?', *JAC* 27/28 (1984-1985), pp. 47-64.

Fee, G.D., *The first Epistle to the Corinthians* (NIC; Grand Rapids: Eerdmans, 1987).

——, *Paul's Letter to the Philippians* (NIC; Grand Rapids: Eerdmans, 1995).

Feldman, L.H., *Jew and Gentile in the Ancient World. Attitudes and Interactions from Alexander to Justinian* (Princeton: Princeton University Press, 1993).

Feldtkeller, A., *Identitätssuche des syrischen Urchristentums. Mission, Inkulturation und Pluralität im ältesten Heidenchristentum* (NTOA 25; Göttingen: Vandenhoeck&Ruprecht; Freiburg Schw.: Universitätsverlag, 1993).

Ferguson, E., *Backgrounds of Early Christianity* (Grand Rapids: Eerdmans, 2nd ed., 1993).

Fishwick, D., 'The Development of Provincial Ruler Worship in the Western Roman Empire', in: H. Temporini (ed.), *ANRW* 2 Principat 16/2 (1978), pp. 1201-1253.

Fitzgerald, J.T., *Cracks in an Earthen Vessel. An Examination of the Catalogues of Hardships in the Corinthian Correspondence* (SBLDS 99; Atlanta: Scholars Press, 1988).

Fitzmyer, J.A., *The Gospel according to Luke*, vol. 2 (AB; Garden City: Doubleday, 1985).

Foakes Jackson, F.J., 'Stephen's Speech in Acts', *JBL* 49 (1930), pp. 283-286.

——, Lake, K. (eds.), *The Beginnings of Christianity* 5 vols. (London: MacMillan, 1922-1939).

Fridrichsen, A., 'Zum Stil des Paulinischen Peristasenkatalogs 2 Cor. 11,23ff.', *SO* 7 (1928), pp. 25-29.

——, 'Peristasenkatalog und *res gestae*. Nachtrag zu 2 Cor. 11,23ff', *SO* 8 (1929), pp. 78-82.

Fusco, V., *Da Paolo a Luca. Studi su Luca-Atti* vol. 1 (SB 124; Brescia: Paideia, 2000).

Gager, J.G., *Moses in Greco-Roman Paganism* (Nashville, New York: Abingdon, 1972).

——, *Reinventing Paul* (Oxford: Oxford University Press, 2000).

Gasque, W.W., 'The Historical Value of the Book of Acts. An Essay in the History of New Testament Criticism', *EvQ* 41 (1969), pp. 68-88.

——, 'Tarsus', *ABD* vol. 6, pp. 333-334.

Gaventa, B.R., 'Ethiopian Eunuch', *ABD*, vol. 2, p. 667.

Georgi, D., *Die Gegner des Paulus im 2. Korintherbrief. Studien zur religiösen Propaganda in der Spätantike* (WMANT 11; Neukirchen-Vluyn: Neukirchener Verlag, 1964) [= *The Opponents of Paul in Second Corinthians* (Studies of the NT and its World; Edinburgh: Clark, 1987)].

Girlanda, A., 'De conversione Pauli in Actibus Apostolorum tripliciter narrata', *VD* 39 (1961), pp. 66-81.129-140.173-188.

Gladigow, B., 'Roman Religion', in: *ABD* vol. 5, pp. 809-816.

Gnilka, J., *Der Philipperbrief* (HThK; Freiburg etc: Herder, 1968).

——, *Das Evangelium nach Markus*, vol. 1 (EKK; Zürich [etc.]: Benziger; Neukirchen-Vluyn: Neukirchener Verlag, 1978).

——, *Das Matthäusevangelium*, vol. 2 (HThK; Freiburg [etc.]: Herder, 1988).

Goldenberg, R., *The Nations that Know Thee Not. Ancient Jewish Attitudes towards Other Religions* (BibS 52; Sheffield: Academic Press, 1997).

Goodenough, E.R., *Jewish Symbols in the Graeco-Roman Period* 13 vols. (BS 37; Princeton: Princeton University Press, 1953-1968), now edited and abridged by J. Neusner, Princeton, 1988.

Goodman, M., *Mission and Conversion. Proselytizing in the Religious History of the Roman Empire* (Oxford: Clarendon Press, 1994).

Goulder, M.D., *Paul and the Competing Mission in Corinth* (LPS; Peabody: Hendrickson, 2001).

Gressmann, H., 'Jüdische Mission in der Werdezeit des Christentums', *ZMR* 39 (1924), pp. 169-183.

Gundry, R.H., *Mark. A Commentary on his Apology for the Cross* (Grand Rapids: Eerdmans, 1993).

Gwyn Griffiths, J., *Apuleius of Madauros, the Isis-Book (Metamorphoses, Book XI)* (EPROER 29; Leiden: Brill, 1975).

Haacker, K., *Paulus. Der Werdegang eines Apostels* (SBS 171; Stuttgart: Katholisches Bibelwerk, 1997).

Haenchen, E., *Die Apostelgeschichte* (KEK; Göttingen: Vandenhoeck & Ruprecht, 5th ed., 1965, ¹1956).

Hahn, F., *Christologische Hoheitstitel: ihre Geschichte im frühen Christentum* (UTB 1873; Göttingen: Vandenhoeck & Ruprecht, 5th rev. and enl. ed. 1995, ¹1963).

——, *Das Verständnis der Mission im Neuen Testament* (WMANT 13; Neukirchen-Vluyn: Neukirchener Verlag, 1963).

——, 'Der Apostolat im Urchristentum. Seine Eigenart und seine Voraussetzungen', *KuD* 20 (1974), pp. 54-77.

Hainz, J., 'Kirche', in: M. Görg, B. Lang (eds.), *Neues Bibel-Lexikon*, vol. 2 (Zürich, Düsseldorf: Benziger, 1995), cols. 481-486.

Harnack, A., *Die Mission und Ausbreitung des Christentums in den ersten drei Jahrhunderten* 2 vols. (Leipzig: Hinrich, 2nd rev. ed. 1906, ¹1902).

Hartman, L., 'Baptism', *ABD* vol. I, pp. 583-594.

Hedrich, C.W., 'Paul's Conversion/Call: A Comparative Analysis of the Three Reports', *JBL* 100 (1981), pp. 415-432.

Hemer, C.J., 'The Name of Paul', *TynB* 36 (1985), pp. pp. 179-183.

Hengel, M., 'Die Synagogeninschriften von Stobi', *ZNW* 57 (1966), pp. 145-183.

——, *Judentum und Hellenismus. Studien zu ihrer Begegnung unter besonderer Berücksichtigung Palästinas bis zur Mitte des 2. Jahrhunderts vor Christus* (WUNT 10; Tübingen: Mohr, 1969, 2nd ed. 1973).

——, 'Die Ursprünge der christlichen Mission', *NTS* 18 (1971-72), pp. 15-38; [= *Between Jesus and Paul. Studies in the Earliest History of Christianity* (London: SCM, 1983), pp. 58-64].

——, 'Zwischen Jesus und Paulus', *ZTK* 72 (1975), pp. 151-206 [= *Between Jesus and Paul*, pp. 1-29].

——, *Zur urchristlichen Geschichtsschreibung* (CP; Stuttgart: Calwer, 1979).

——, *Between Jesus and Paul. Studies in the Earliest History of Christianity* (Philadelphia: Fortress, 1983).

——, 'The Interpenetration of Judaism and Hellenism in the pre-Maccabean Period', in: W.D. Davis, L. Finkelstein (eds.), *The Cambridge History of Judaism* vol. 2: *The Hellenistic Age* (Cambridge [etc.]: Cambridge University Press, 1989), pp. 167-228.

——, *The Pre-Christian Paul* (London: SCM Press, 1991) [= 'Der vorchristliche Paulus', in M. Hengel, U. Heckel (eds.), *Paulus und das antike Judentum* (WUNT 58; Tübingen: Mohr, 1991)].

——, Schwemer, A.M., *Paul between Damascus and Antioch. The Unknown Years* (London: SCM, 1997).

Herz, P., 'Bibliografie zum römischen Kaiserkult (1955-1975)', in: H. Temporini (ed.), *ANRW 2 Principat*, 16/2 (1978), pp. 833-910.

Hill, D., *The Gospel of Matthew* (NCB; London: Oliphants, 1972).

Hock, R.F., 'Paul's Tentmaking and the Problem of his Social Class', *JBL* 97 (1978), pp. 555-564.

——, 'The Workshop as a Social Setting for Paul's Missionary Preaching', *CBQ* 41 (1979), pp. 438-450.

——, *The Social Context of Paul's Ministry. Tentmaking and Apostleship* (Philadelphia: Fortress, 1980).

Holladay, C.R., *Fragments from Hellenistic Jewish Authors. Vol. 1: Historians* (TTPS 20; Chico: Scholars Press, 1983).

Hollander, H.W., *1 Korintiërs I* (T&T; Kampen: Kok, 1996).

——, Van der Hout, G.E., 'The Apostle Paul calling himself an Abortion: 1 Cor. 15:8 within the Context of 1 Cor. 15:8-10', *NT* 38 (1996), pp. 224-236.

Holleman, J., *Resurrection and Parousia. A Traditio-Historical Study of Paul's Eschatology in 1 Corinthians 15* (SNT 84; Leiden [etc.]: Brill, 1996).

Holtz, T., *Der erste Brief an die Thessalonicher* (EKK; Düsseldorf: Benziger; Neukirchen-Vluyn: Neukirchener, 1986).

Horsley, G.H.R. (ed.), *New Documents Illustrating Early Christianity*, (North Ryde: The Ancient History Documentary Research Centre, 1981-),vol. 4, pp. 114-115.

Horsley, R.A., Hanson, J.S., *Bandits, Prophets and Messiahs. Popular Movements in the Time of Jesus* (Harrisburg: Trinity Press, 1999 = 1985).

Howard, G., *Paul: Crisis in Galatia. A Study in Early Christian Theology* (SNTSMS 35; Cambridge [etc.]: Cambridge University Press, 2nd ed., 1990).

Howell, jr., D.N., 'Mission in Paul's Epistles: Genesis, Pattern, and Dynamics', in: W.J. Larkin jr., J.F. Williams (eds.), *Mission in the New Testament. An Evangelical Approach* (ASMS 27; Maryknoll: Orbis, 1998).

Hubbard, B.J., *The Matthean Redaction of a Primitive Apostolic Commissioning: An Exegesis of Matthew 28:16-20* (SBLDS 19; Missoula: SBL, 1974).

Hübner, H., 'Paulusforschung seit 1945. Ein kritischer Literaturbericht', in: W. Haase (ed.), *ANRW 2 Principat* 25/4 (1985), pp. 2649-2840.

Hultgren, A.J., 'Paul's Pre-Christian Persecutions of the Church: their Purpose, Locale, and Nature', *JBL* 95 (1976), pp. 97-111.

Jacobson, A.D., 'The Literary Unity of Q. Lc 10,2-16 and Parallels as a Test Case', in: J. Delobel (ed.), *Logia. Les paroles de Jésus/The Sayings of Jesus. Mémorial Joseph Coppens* (BETL 59; Leuven: Peeters/University Press, 1982), pp. 419-423.

Jellicoe, S., 'Aristeas, Philo and the Septuagint *Vorlage*', *JThS* ns 12 (1961), pp. 261-271.

Jeremias, J., *Die Abendmahlsworte Jesu* (Göttingen: Vandenhoeck & Ruprecht, 4th ed. 1967, ¹1935).

Jervell, J., *Die Apostelgeschichte* (KEK; Göttingen: Vandenhoeck & Ruprecht, 1998).

Jewett, R., *A Chronology of Paul's Life* (Philadelphia: Fortress, 1979).

——, *Dating Paul's Life* (Philadelphia: Fortress, 1979).

Jones, F.S., *'Freiheit' in den Briefen des Apostels Paulus. Eine historische, exegetische und religionsgeschichtliche Studie* (GTA 34; Göttingen: Vandenhoeck & Ruprecht, 1987).

Juster, J., *Les Juifs dans l'empire romain. Leur condition juridique, économique et sociale*, vol. 1 (Paris: Geuthner, 1914).

Kasting, H., *Die Anfänge der urchristlichen Mission. Eine historische Untersuchung* (BeTh 55; München: Kaiser, 1969).

Kim, S., *The Origin of Paul's Gospel* (WUNT 2-4; Tübingen: Mohr, 2nd ed., 1984, ¹1981).

Klein, G., *Der älteste christliche Katechismus und die jüdische Propaganda-Literatur* (Berlin: Reimer, 1909).

Klijn, A.F.J., 'Stephen's Speech – Acts VII.2-53', *NTS* 4 (1957/1958), pp. 25-31.

——, Reinink, G.J., *Patristic Evidence for Jewish-Christian Sects* (SNT 36; Leiden: Brill, 1973).

Kloppenborg, J.S., *The Formation of Q. Trajectories in Ancient Wisdom Collections* (SAC; Philadelphia: Fortress, 1987).

——, *Q-Parallels. Synopsis, Critical Notes & Concordance* (Sonoma: Polebridge, 1988).

Knauf, E.A., 'Zum *Ethnarchen* des Aretas 2 Kor 11,32', *ZNW* 74 (1983), pp. 145-147.

Knox, W.L., *The Acts of the Apostles* (Cambridge: University Press, 1948).

Koester, H., *Introduction to the New Testament, volume 1: History, Culture, and Religion of the Hellenistic Age* (New York, Berlin: W. de Gruyter, 1995).

—— (ed.), *Ephesos, Metropolis of Asia. An Interdisciplinary Approach to Archaeology, Religion, and Culture* (HTS 41; Valley Forge: Trinity, 1995).

Koukouli-Chrysantaki, C., 'Colonia Iulia Augusta Philippensis', in: C. Bakirtzis, H. Koester (eds.), *Philippi at the Time of Paul and after His Death* (Harrisburg: Trinity Press, 1998).

Kraabel, A.T., 'The Diaspora Synagogue: Archaeological and Epigraphical Evidence', in: W. Haase (ed.), *ANRW II Principat* 19/1 (1979), pp. 477-510.

Kreitzer, L., *2 Corinthians* (NTG; Sheffield: Academic Press, 1996).

Kuhn, K.G., 'Das Problem der Mission in der Urchristenheit', *EMZ* 11 (1954), pp. 161-168.

Labahn, M., 'Paulus – ein *homo honestus et iustus*. Das lukanische Paulusportrait von Act 27-28 im Lichte ausgewählter antiker Parallellen', in: F. W. Horn (ed.), *Das Ende des Paulus. Historische, theologische und literaturgeschichtliche Aspekte* (BZNW 106; Berlin, New York: De Gruyter, 2001), pp. 74-106.

LaGrand, J., *The Earliest Christian Mission to 'All Nations' in the Light of Matthew's Gospel* (Grand Rapids: Eerdmans, 1999 = University of South Florida: Scholars Press 1995).

La Piana, G., 'Foreign Groups in Rome during the First Centuries of the Empire', *HTR* 20 (1927), pp. 183-403.

Lake, K., 'Proselytes and God-Fearers', in: *Beginnings* vol. 5, pp. 74-77.

Lambrecht, J., 'Line of Thought in 1 Cor 15,1-11', *Gregorianum* 72 (1991), pp. 655-670.

Lane, E.N., 'Sabazius and the Jews in Valerius Maximus: a Re-examination', *JRS* 69 (1979), p. 37.

Lane Fox, R., *Pagans and Christians in the Mediterranean World from the Second Century AD to the Conversion of Constantine* (London: Penguin, 1986 = New York: Knopf, 1986).

Lang, F., *Die Briefe an die Korinther* (NTD; Göttingen: Vandenhoeck & Ruprecht, 1986).

Laufen, R., *Die Doppelüberlieferungen der Logienquelle und des Markusevangeliums* (BBB 54; Königstein/Bonn: Hanstein, 1980).

Le Grys, A., *Preaching to the Nations. The Origins of Mission in the Early Church* (London: SPCK, 1998).

Lerle, E., *Proselytenwerbung und Urchristentum* (Berlin: Evangelische Verlagsanstalt, 1960).

Levine, L.I., *The Ancient Synagogue. The First Thousand Years* (New Haven, London: Yale University Press, 2000).

Levinskaya, I., *The Book of Acts in its Diaspora Setting* (BAFCS 5; Grand Rapids: Eerdmans; Carlisle: Paternoster, 1996).

Liechtenhan, R., *Die urchristliche Mission. Voraussetzungen, Motive und Methoden* (ATANT 9, 1946).

Lienhard, J.T., 'Acts 6,1-6: A Redactional View', *CBQ* 37 (1975), pp. 228-236.

Lietaert Peerbolte, L.J., *The Antecedents of Antichrist. A Traditio-Historical Study of the Earliest Christian Views on Eschatological Opponents* (SJSJ 49; Leiden [etc.]: Brill, 1996).

——, 'The κατέχον / κατέχων' of 2 Thess 2:6-7', *NT* 39 (1997), pp. 138-150.

——, 'Man, Woman, and the Angels in 1 Cor 11:2-16', in: Gerard P. Luttikhuizen (ed.), *The Creation of Man and Woman. Interpretations of the Biblical Narratives in Jewish and Christian Traditions* (TBN 3; Leiden [etc.]: Brill, 2000), pp. 76-92

——, 'To Worship the Beast. The Revelation of John and the Imperial Cult in Asia Minor', in: M. Labahn, J. Zangenberg (eds.), *Zwischen den Reichen. Neues Testament und Römische Herrschaft* (TANZ 36; Tübingen, Basel: Francke, 2002), pp. 239-259.

——, 'Romans 15:14-29 and Paul's Missionary Agenda', in: P.W. van der Horst, M.J.J. Menken, G.C.M. van Oyen, J.F.M. Smit, *Persuasion and Dissuasion in Early Christianity, Ancient Judaism, and Hellenism* (CBET 33; Leuven, Paris, Dudley MA: Peeters, 2003).

Lietzmann, H., Kümmel, W.G., *An die Korinther I-II* (HNT; Tübingen: Mohr, 1949).

Lifshitz, B., 'L'origin du nom des chrétiens', *VigChr* 16 (1962), pp. 65-70.

Lindars, B., *New Testament Apologetic: the Doctrinal Significance of the Old Testament Quotations* (Philadelphia: Westminster Press, 1961).

Löhr, H., 'Zur Paulus-Notiz in 1 Clem 5,5-7', in: F. W. Horn (ed.), *Das Ende des Paulus. Historische, theologische und literaturgeschichtliche Aspekte* (BZNW 106; Berlin, New York: De Gruyter, 2001), pp. 197-213.

Lohmeyer, E., Schmauch, W. *Das Evangelium des Matthäus* (KEK; Göttingen: Vandenhoeck & Ruprecht, 1956).

Lohse, E., 'Die urchristliche Mission', in: R. Kottje, B. Moeller (eds.), *Ökumenische Kirchengeschichte. Vol. 1: Alte Kirche und Ostkirche* (Mainz: Grünewald; Munchen: Kaiser, 1970).

Lohse, E., 'St. Peter's Apostleship in the Judgment of St. Paul, the Apostle to the Gentiles. An Exegetical Contribution to an Ecumenical Debate', *Gregorianum* 72 (1991), pp. 419-435.

——, *Paulus. Eine Biografie* (München: Beck, 1996).

Luck, U., Das *Evangelium nach Matthäus* (ZB; Zürich: Theologischer Verlag, 1993).

Lüdemann, G., 'Acts of the Apostles as a Historical Source', in: J. Neusner, P. Borgen, E.S. Frerichs, R. Horsley (eds.), *The Social World of Formative Christianity and Judaism. Essays in Tribute to Howard Clark Kee* (Philadelphia: Fortress Press, 1988), pp. 109-125.

Lüdemann, G., *Paulus und das Judentum* (TEH 215; München: Kaiser, 1983).

——, *Das frühe Christentum nach den Traditionen der Apostelgeschichte* (Göttingen: Vandenhoeck & Ruprecht, 1987).

Lührmann, D., *Die Redaktion der Logienquelle. Anhang: Zur weiteren Überlieferung der Logienquelle* (WMANT 33; Neukirchen: Neukirchener Verlag, 1969).

——, *Der Brief an die Galater* (ZB; Zürich: Theologischer Verlag, 1978).

Luz, U. *Das Evangelium nach Matthäus*, vol. 2 (EKK; Zürich, Braunschweig: Benziger; Neukirchen-Vluyn: Neukirchener Verlag, 1990).

——, *Das Evangelium nach Matthäus*, vol. 3 (EKK; Zürich [etc.]: Benziger; Neukirchen-Vluyn: Neukirchener Verlag, 1997).

McCasland, S.V., 'The Way', *JBL* 77 (1958), pp. 222-230.

McGiffert, A.C., 'The Historical Criticism of Acts in Germany', in: *Beginnings*, vol. 2, pp. 363-395, esp. pp. 367-376.

McKnight, S., *A Light among the Gentiles. Jewish Missionary Activity in the Second Temple Period* (Minneapolis: Fortress Press, 1991).

MacMullen, R., *Christianizing the Roman Empire (A.D. 100-400)* (New Haven, London: Yale University Press, 1984).

Major, H.D.A., Manson, T.W., Wright, C.J., *The Mission and Message of Jesus. An Exposition of the Gospels in the Light of Modern Research* (New York: Dutton and Co., 1938).

Malherbe, A.J. (ed.), *The Cynic Epistles. A Study Edition* (SBLSBS 12; Atlanta: Scholars Press, 1977).
——, *Paul and the Thessalonians. The Philosophic Tradition of Pastoral Care* (Philadelphia: Fortress, 1987).
——, *Paul and the Popular Philosophers* (Minneapolis: Fortress, 1989).
Malina, B.J., *The New Testament World. Insights from Cultural Anthropology* (Louisville: Westminster John Knox Press, 3rd rev. ed., 2001, ¹1981).
——, Neyrey, J.H., *Portraits of Paul. An Archaeology of Ancient Personality* (Louisville: Westminster John Knox Press, 1996).
Manson, T.W., *The Sayings of Jesus* (London: SCM Press, 1949 [= 1937]).
Marshall, I.H., *1 and 2 Thessalonians* (NCB; London: Marshall, Morgan & Scott; Grand Rapids: Eerdmans, 1983).
——, 'Luke's Portrait of the Pauline Mission', in: P. Bolt, M. Thompson (eds.), *The Gospel to the Nations. Perspectives on Paul's Mission* (Leicester: Apollos; Downers Grove: Intervarsity, 2000), pp. 99-113.
Martin, R.P., *Carmen Christi. Philippians ii,5-11 in Recent Interpretation and in the Setting of Early Christian Worship* (SNTSMS 4; Cambridge: University Press, 1967) [also as: *A Hymn of Christ. Philippians 2:5-11 in Recent Interpretation and in the Setting of Early Christian Worship* (Downers Grove: Intervarsity, 1997)].
——, *Philippians* (NCB; London: Marshall, Morgan & Scott; Grand Rapids: Eerdmans, 1976).
——, *2 Corinthians* (WBC; Waco: Word Books, 1986).
Martyn, J.L., *Galatians: a New Translation with Introduction and Commentary* (AB; New York [etc.]: Doubleday, 1998).
Mason, S., *Flavius Josephus on the Pharisees* (SPB 39; Leiden etc: Brill, 1991).
Matill, A.J., 'The Value of Acts as a Source for the Study of Paul', *PRS* 5 (1978), pp. 76-98.
Mattingly, H.B., 'The Origin of the Name "Christians"', *JThS* 9 (1958), pp. 26-37.
Meeks, W.A., *The Prophet-King. Moses Traditions and the Johannine Christology* (SNT 14; Leiden: Brill, 1967).
——, *The First Urban Christians. The Social World of the Apostle Paul* (New Haven, London: Yale University Press, 1983).
Mengel, B., *Studien zum Philipperbrief. Untersuchungen zum situativen Kontext unter besonderer Berücksichtigung der Frage nach der Ganzheit oder Einheitlichkeit eines paulinischen Briefes* (WUNT 2.8; Tübingen: Mohr, 1982).
Menoud, P.H., 'Le sens du verbe ΠΟΡΘΕΙΝ (Gal 1.13,23; Act 9.21)', in: idem, *Jésus-Christ et la foi. Recherches néotestamentaires* (BT; Neuchatel, Paris: Dalachaux & Niestlé, 1975), pp. 40-47 [originally published in: W. Eltester, F.H. Kettler (eds.), *Apophoreta. Festschrift für Ernst Haenchen* (BZNW 30; Berlin: De Gruyter, 1964), pp. 178-186].
Merkelbach, R., *Isisfeste in griechisch-römischer Zeit. Daten und Riten* (BKP 5; Meisenheim: Hain, 1963).
——, *Isis Regina – Zeus Sarapis. Die griechisch-ägyptische Religion nach den Quellen dargestellt* (Stuttgard, Leipzig: Teubner, 1995).
Merklein, H., *Das kirchliche Amt nach dem Epheserbrief* (SANT 33; München: Kösel, 1973).

——, 'Die Ekklesia Gottes. Der Kirchenbegriff bei Paulus und in Jerusalem', *BZ* 23 (1979), pp. 48-70.

Metzger. B.M. (ed.), *A Textual Commentary on the Greek New Testament* (Stuttgart: Deutsche Bibelgesellschaft, United Bible Societies, 2nd ed., 1994, ¹1974).

Meyer, J.P., *A Marginal Jew. Rethinking the Historical Jesus* Vol. 2: *Mentor, Message, and Miracles* (ABRL; New York [etc.]: Doubleday, 1994).

Michel, O., *Der Brief an die Römer* (KEK; Göttingen: Vandenhoeck & Ruprecht, 1966).

Mora, F., *Prosopografia isiaca. Vol. 2: Prosopografia storica e statistica del culto isiaco* (EPROER 113; Leiden, København, Köln: Brill, 1990).

Müller, U.B., *Der Brief des Paulus an die Philipper* (ThHK; Leipzig: Evangelische Verlagsanstalt, 1993).

Munck, J., *Paulus und die Heilsgeschichte* (AJ 26,1; Koebnhavn: Munksgaard, 1954) [= *Paul and the Salvation of Mankind* (London: SCM, 1959)].

Mundle, W., 'Die Stephanusrede Apg 7: eine Märtyrerapologie', *ZNW* 20 (1921), pp. 133-147.

Murphy-O'Connor, J., *St. Paul's Corinth. Texts and Archaeology* (GNS 6; Delaware: Glazier, 1983).

——, *Paul. A Critical Life* (Oxford [etc.]: Oxford University Press, 1996).

Mussies, G., 'Jewish Personal Names in Some Non-Literary Sources', in: P.W. van der Horst, J.W. van Henten (eds.), *Studies in Early Jewish Epigraphy* (AGAJU 21; Leiden [etc.]: Brill, 1994), pp. 242-276.

Mussner, F., *Der Galaterbrief* (HThK; Freiburg [etc.]: Herder, 1974).

Neufeld, V.H., *The Earliest Christian Confessions* (NTTS 5; Leiden: Brill, 1963).

Neusner, J., *A History of the Jews in Babylonia. Vol. 1: the Parthian Period* (SPB 9; Leiden: Brill, 1965).

Nicholas, B., *An Introduction to Roman Law* (CLS 3; Oxford: Clarendon, 1962).

Nilsson, M.P., *Dionysiac Mysteries* (Lund: Gleerup, 1957).

——, *Geschichte der griechischen Religion.*Vol. 2: *Die hellenistische und römische Zeit* (HAW 5.2; München: Beck, 2nd ed., 1961, ¹1950).

Nock, A.D., *Conversion. The Old and the New in Religion from Alexander the Great to Augustine of Hippo* (Oxford: Clarendon, 1933).

——, 'Religious Developments from the Close of the Republic to the Reign of Nero', in: *The Cambridge Ancient History* vol. x (Cambridge: University Press, 1934), pp. 465-511.

——, *Essays on Religion and the Ancient World* (Oxford: Clarendon, 1972).

Noethlichs, K.L., *Das Judentum und der römische Staat. Minderheidenpolitik im antiken Rom* (Darmstadt: Wissenschaftliche Buchgesellschaft, 1996).

Ollrog, W.-H., *Paulus und seine Mitarbeiter. Untersuchungen zu Theorie und Praxis der paulinischen Mission* (WMANT 50; Neukirchen-Vluyn: Neukirchener Verlag, 1979).

Orr, W.F., Walther, J.A., *1 Corinthians* (AB; Garden City: Doubleday, 1976).

Panagopoulos, J., 'Zur Theologie der Apostelgeschichte', *NT* 14 (1972), pp. 137-159.

Penella, R.J., *The Letters of Apollonius of Tyana. A Critical Text with Prolegomena, Translation and Commentary* (MS 56; Leiden [etc.]: Brill, 1979).

Pesce, M., *Le due fasi della predicazione di Paolo. Dall'evangelizzazione alla guida della comunità* (SB 22; Bologna: Edizioni dehoniane, 1994).

Pesch, R., 'Voraussetzungen und Anfänge der urchristlichen Mission', in: K. Kertelge (ed.), *Mission im Neuen Testament* (QD 93; Freiburg [etc.]: Herder, 1982), pp. 11-70.

——, *Die Apostelgeschichte*, 2 vols. (EKK; Zürich: Benziger Verlag; Neukirchen-Vluyn: Neukirchener Verlag, 1986).

——, Gerhart, E., Schilling, F., '"Hellenisten" und "Hebräer". Zu Apg. 9,29 und 6,1', *BZ* 23 (1979), pp. 87-92.

Petersen, W.L., 'Ebionites, Gospel of the', in: *ABD* vol. 2, pp. 261-262.

Petzke, G., *Die Traditionen über Apollonius von Tyana und das Neue Testament* (SCHNT 1; Leiden [etc.]: Brill, 1970).

Popkes, W., *Christus Traditus. Eine Untersuchung zum Begriff der Dahingabe im Neuen Testament* (ATANT 49; Zürich: Zwingli Verlag, 1967).

Powers, D.G., *Salvation through Participation. An Examination of the Notion of the Believers' Corporate Unity with Christ in Early Christian Soteriology* (CBET 29; Leuven: Peeters, 2001).

Price, S.R.F., *Rituals and Power. The Roman Imperial Cult in Asia Minor* (Cambridge, London [etc.]: Cambridge University Press, 1984).

Räisänen, H., 'The "Hellenists": a Bridge between Jesus and Paul?', in: idem, *Jesus, Paul and Torah. Collected Essays* (JSNTSS 43; Sheffield: Sheffield Academic Press, 1992), pp. 149-202.

——, 'Die "Hellenisten" der Urgemeinde', in: W. Haase, *ANRW II Principat* 26/2 (1995), pp. 1468-1514.

Ramsay, W.M., 'Lycaonian and Phrygian Notes', *CR* 19 (1905), pp. 367-370.

Reinbold, W., *Propaganda und Mission im ältesten Christentum. Eine Untersuchung zu den Modalitäten der Ausbreitung der frühen Kirche* (FRLANT 188; Göttingen: Vandenhoeck&Ruprecht, 2000).

Repo, E., *Der "Weg" als Selbstbezeichnung des Urchristentums* (Helsinki: Suomalainen Tiedeakatemia 1964).

Rey-Coquais, J.-P., 'Syrie romaine, de Pompée à Dioclétien', *JRS* 68 (1978), pp. 44-73.

Reynolds, J., Tannenbaum, R., *Jews and God-fearers at Aphrodisias* (Cambridge: The Cambridge Philological Society, 1987).

Riesner, R., *Die Frühzeit des Apostels Paulus. Studien zur Chronologie, Missionsstrategie und Theologie* (WUNT 71; Tübingen: Mohr, 1994).

Robinson, J.M., Hoffmann, P., Kloppenborg, J.S., *The Critical Edition of Q. Synopsis including the Gospels of Matthew and Luke, Mark and Thomas with English, German, and French Translations of Q and Thomas* (Leuven: Peeters, 2000).

Roetzel, C.J., *Paul. The Man and the Myth* (Columbia: University of South Carolina Press, 1998).

Roloff, J., *Die Apostelgeschichte* (NTD; Göttingen: Vandenhoeck und Ruprecht, 1981).

Romm, J.S., *The Edges of the Earth in Ancient Thought: Geography, Exploration, and Fiction* (Princeton NJ: Princeton University Press, 1992).

Ross Taylor, L., *The Divinity of the Roman Emperor* (Middletown, Connecticut: American Philological Association, 1931).

Rothaus, R.M., *Corinth: The First City of Greece. An Urban History of Late Antique Cult and Religion* (RGRW 139; Leiden [etc.]: Brill, 2000).

Runesson, A., *The Origins of the Synagogue. A Socio-Historical Study* (CBNTS 37; Stockholm: Almqvist&Wiksell, 2001).

Rutgers, L.V., 'Roman policy toward the Jews: Expulsions from the city of Rome during the first century C.E.', in: K.P. Donfried, P. Richardson (eds.), *Judaism and Christianity in First-Century Rome.* (Grand Rapids [etc.]: Eerdmans, 1998), pp. 93-116.

Salac, A., 'Inscriptions de Kymé d'Eolide', *BCH* 51 (1927), 378-383.

Saldarini, A.J., *Pharisees, Scribes and Sadducees in Palestinian Society. A Sociological Approach* (Wilmington: Glazier, 1988).

Sanders, E.P., *Paul and Palestinian Judaism. A Comparison of Patterns of Religion* (London: SCM, 1977).

——, *Paul, the Law, and the Jewish People* (Philadelphia: Fortress, 1983).

——, *Jesus and Judaism* (London: SCM, 1985).

——, *Paul* (PM; Oxford: Oxford University Press, 1991).

Sandmel, S., *Philo's Place in Judaism. A Study of Conceptions of Abraham in Jewish Literature* (New York: KTAV, 1956; augmented edition, 1971).

Sandnes, K.O., *Paul – One of the Prophets? A Contribution to the Apostle's Self-Understanding* (WUNT 43; Tübingen: Mohr, 1991).

Schaberg, J., *The Father, the Son and the Holy Spirit. The Triadic Phrase in Matthew 28:19b* (SBLDS 61; Chico: Scholars Press, 1982).

Schäfer, P., *Judeophobia. Attitudes towards the Jews in the Ancient World* (London, Cambridge: Harvard University Press, 1997).

Schiffman, L.H., 'The Conversion of the Royal House of Adiabene in Josephus and Rabbinic Sources', in: L.H. Feldman, G. Hata (eds.), *Josephus, Judaism, and Christianity* (Detroit: Wayne State University Press, 1987), pp. 293-312.

Schille, G., *Anfänge der Kirche. Erwägungen zur apostolische Frühgeschichte* (BeTh 43; München: Kaiser, 1966).

——, *Die urchristliche Kollegialmission* (ATANT 48; 1967).

Schlier, H., *Der Brief an die Galater* (KEK; Göttingen: Vandenhoeck & Ruprecht, 4th ed., 1965).

——, *Der Römerbrief* (HThK; Freiburg [etc.]: Herder, 1977).

Schmithals, W., *The Office of Apostle in the Early Church* (Nashville, New York: Abingdon, 1969) [= *Das kirchliche Apostelamt* (Göttingen: Vandenhoeck& Ruprecht, 1961)].

——, *Die Apostelgeschichte des Lukas* (ZB; Zürich: Theologischer Verlag, 1982).

Schneider, G., *Apostelgeschichte*, 2 vols. (HThK; Freiburg [etc.]: Herder, 1980.1982).

Schoeps, H.-J., 'Ebionite Christianity', *JThS* 4 (1953), pp. 219-224.

——, *Paulus. Die Theologie des Apostels im Lichte der jüdischen Religionsgeschichte* (Tübingen: Mohr, 1959).

Schrage, W., *Der erste Brief an die Korinther (1 Kor 6,12-11,16)* (EKK; Düsseldorf: Benziger; Neukirchen-Vluyn: Neukirchener, 1995).

Schreiber, S., *Paulus als Wundertäter. Redaktionsgeschichtliche Untersuchungen zur Apostelgeschichte und den authentischen Paulusbriefen* (BZNW 79; Berlin, New York: De Gruyter, 1996).

Schulz, S., *Q. Die Spruchquelle der Evangelisten* (Zürich: Theologischer Verlag, 1972).

Schürmann, H., 'Mt 10,5b-6 und die Vorgeschichte des synoptischen Aussendungsberichtes', in: J. Blinzer, O. Kuss, F. Mußner (eds.), *Neutestamentliche Aufsätze* (FS J. Schmid; Regensburg: Pustet, 1963), pp. 270-282.

——, *Das Lukasevangelium*, vol. 2.1 (HThK; Freiburg [etc.]: Herder, 1993).

Schwankl, O., 'Auf der Suche nach dem Anfang des Evangeliums. Von 1 Kor 15,3-5 zum Johannes-Prolog', *BZ* 40 (1996), pp. 39-60.

Schweitzer, A., *Die Mystik des Apostels Paulus* (Tübingen: Mohr, 1930).

Schweizer, E., *Das Evangelium nach Matthäus* (NTD; Göttingen: Vandenhoeck &Ruprecht, 1973).

Scott, J.M., *Paul and the Nations. The Old Testament and Jewish Backgrounds of Paul's Mission to the Nations with Special Refernce to the Destination of Galatians* (WUNT 84; Tübingen: Mohr, 1995).

Scullard, H.H., *Festivals and Ceremonies of the Roman Republic* (London: Thames & Hudson, 1981).

Searle, P.J., 'Christian – Noun or Adjective?', *ET* 87 (1975/76), 307-308.

Segal, A.F., *Paul the Convert. The Apostolate and Apostasy of Saul the Pharisee* (New Haven, London: Yale University Press, 1990).

Sevenster, J.N., *The Roots of Pagan Anti-Semitism in the Ancient World* (SNT 41; Leiden: Brill, 1975).

Sherwin-White, A.N., *Roman Society and Roman Law in the New Testament* (Oxford: Clarendon, 1963).

Simon, M., *Verus Israel: étude sur les relations entre chretiens et juifs dans l'empire romain (135-425)* (Paris: Boccard, 2nd ed. 1964, ¹1948).

Smith, R.H., 'Matthew 28,16-20, Anticlimax or Key to the Gospel?', *SBL Seminar Papers* (Atlanta: Scholars Press, 1993), pp. 589-602.

Spencer, F.S., *The Portrait of Philip in Acts. A Study of Roles and Relations* (JSNTSS 67; Sheffield: Sheffield Academic Press, 1992).

Stanley, D.M., 'Paul's Conversion in Acts: Why the Three Accounts?', *CBQ* 15 (1953), pp. 315-338.

Stark, R., *The Rise of Christianity. A Sociologist Reconsiders History* (Princeton: Princeton University Press, 1996).

Steichele, H., *Vergleich der Apostelgeschichte mit der antiken Geschichts-schreibung. Eine Studie zur Erzählkunst in der Apostelgeschichte* (München, diss. 1971).

Stendahl, K., *Paul among Jews and Gentiles, and other Essays* (Philadelphia: Fortress Press, 1976).

Stern, M., *Greek and Latin Authors on Jews and Judaism*, 3 vols. (Jerusalem: Israel Academy of Sciences and Humanities, 1974-1984).

——, 'The Jews in Greek and Latin Literature', in: S. Safrai, M. Stern, *et al* (eds.), *The Jewish People in the First Century*, vol. 2: *Historical Geography, Political History, Social, Cultural and Religious Life and Institutions* (CRINT, 1,2; Assen, Amsterdam: Van Gorcum, 1976), pp. 1101-1159.

Stowers, S.K., 'Social Status, Public Speaking and Private Teaching', *NT* 26 (1984), pp. 59-82.

Strecker, G., 'Die Legitimität des paulinischen Apostolates nach 2 Korinther 10-13', *NTS* 38 (1992), pp. 566-586.

Strobel, A., 'Armenpfleger "um des Friedens willen"', *ZNW* 63 (1972), pp. 271-276.

Stuhlmacher, P., *Der Brief an Philemon* (EKK; Zürich: Benziger; Neukirchen-Vluyn: Neukirchener, 1975).

Suhl, A., 'Der Beginn der selbständigen Mission des Paulus', *NTS* 38 (1992), pp. 430-447.

——, 'Paulinische Chronologie im Streit der Meinungen', in: W. Haase, *ANRW II Principat* 26/2 (1995), pp. 939-1188.

Taylor, N., *Paul, Antioch and Jerusalem. A Study in Relationships and Authority in Earliest Christianity* (JSNTSS 66; Sheffield: Sheffield Academic Press, 1992).

Tcherikover, V.A., 'Jewish Apologetic Literature Reconsidered', *Eos* 48 (1956), pp. 169-193.

——, Fuks, A., *Corpus Papyrorum Iudaicarum*, 2 vols. (Cambridge, Mass.: Harvard University Press, 1957 and 1960).

Theissen, G., 'Legitimation und Lebensunterhalt: ein Beitrag zur Soziologie urchristlicher Missionare', *NTS* 21 (1974/75), pp. 192-221; also in Theissen, G., *Studien zur Soziologie des Urchristentums* (WUNT 19; Tübingen: Mohr, 1979, 2nd rev. ed. 1983), pp. 201-230.

Thiessen, W., *Christen in Ephesus. Die historische und theologische Situation in vorpaulinischer und paulinischer Zeit und zur Zeit der Apostelgeschichte und der Pastoralbriefe* (TANZ 12; Tübingen, Basel: Francke, 1995).

Thornton, T.C.G., 'To the end of the earth: Acts 8,1', *ET* 89 (1978), pp. 374-375.

Thrall, M.E., *The Second Epistle to the Corinthians* vol. 1 (ICC; Edinburgh: Clark, 1994).

Trebilco, P.R., *Jewish communities in Asia Minor* (SNTSMS 69; Cambridge [etc.]: Cambridge University Press, 1991).

Trilling, W., *Das wahre Israel. Studien zur Theologie des Matthäus-Evangeliums* (SANT 10; München: Kösel, 1964).

Van Unnik, W.C., 'Der Ausdruck ἕως ἐσχάτου τῆς γῆς (Apostelgeschichte 1:8) und sein alttestamentlichen Hintergrund', in: *Studia Biblica et Semitica Theodoro Christiano Vriezen Dedicata* (Wageningen: Veenman, 1966), pp. 335-349

——, 'Tarsus or Jerusalem. The City of Paul's Youth', in: *Sparsa Collecta. The Collected Essays of W.C. van Unnik*, vol. 1 (SNT 29; Leiden: Brill, 1973), pp. 259-320.

Versnel, H.S., *Inconsistencies in Greek and Roman Religion I: Ter Unus. Isis, Dionysos, Hermes, Three Studies in Henotheism* (SGRR 6; Leiden, New York, København, Köln: Brill, 1990).

Victor, U., *Lukian von Samosata: Alexandros oder der Lügenprophet* (RGRW 132; Leiden, New York, Köln: Brill, 1997).

Vielhauer, Ph., *Geschichte der urchristlichen Literatur* (Berlin, New York: De Gruyter, 1975).

Vincent, M.R., *A Critical and Exegetical Commentary on the Epistles to the Philippians and to Philemon* (ICC; Edinburgh: Clark, 1897).

Volz, P., *Die Eschatologie der jüdischen Gemeinde im neutestamentlichen Zeitalter* (Tübingen: Mohr Siebeck, 1934).

Von der Osten-Sacken, P., 'Die Apologie des paulinischen Apostolats', *ZNW* 64 (1973), pp. 245-262.

Von Dobschütz, E., 'Die Berichte über die Bekehrung des Paulus', *ZNW* 29 (1930), pp. 144-147.

Wagner, J. R., *Heralds of the Good News. Isaiah and Paul <in Concert> in the Letter to the Romans* (SNT 101; Leiden [etc.]: Brill, 2002).

Waitz, H., 'Die Quelle der Philippus-Geschichten in der Apostelgeschichte 8,5-40', *ZNW* 7 (1906), pp. 340-355.

Wanamaker, C.A., *The Epistle to the Thessalonians. A Commentary on the Greek Text* (NIC; Grand Rapids: Eerdmans; Exeter: Paternoster, 1990).

Wander, B., 'Warum wollte Paulus nach Spanien? Ein forschungs- und motivgeschichtlicher Überblick', in: F.W. Horn (ed.), *Das Ende des Paulus. Historische, theologische und literaturgeschichtliche Aspekte* (BZNW 106; Berlin, New York: De Gruyter, 2001), pp. 175-195.

Watson, F., *Paul, Judaism and the Gentiles. A Sociological Approach* (SNTSMS 56; Cambridge [etc.]: Cambridge University Press, 1986).

Wedderburn, A.J.M., *Baptism and Resurrection* (WUNT 44; Tübingen: Mohr Siebeck, 1983).

——, *The Reasons for Romans* (Edinburgh: Clark, 1988).

——, 'The "Apostolic Decree": Tradition and Redaction', *NT* 35 (1993), pp. 362-389.

Wehnert, J., *Die Wir-Passagen der Apostelgeschichte. Ein lukanisches Stilmittel aus jüdischen Tradition* (GTA 40; Göttingen: Vandenhoeck&Ruprecht, 1989).

Weiser, A., *Die Apostelgeschichte*, 2 vols. (OTKNT; Gütersloh: Mohn, 1981.1985).

Wellhausen, J., *Das Evangelium Marci* (Berlin: Reimer, 1903).

Wendland, P., *Die Hellenistisch-Römische Kultur in ihren Beziehungen zum Judentum und Christentum* (HNT 2; Tübingen: Mohr, 1912, 4th. ed. 1972).

Wengst, K., *Christologische Formeln und Lieder des Urchristentums* (SNT 7; Gütersloh: Mohn, 1972).

——, *Didache (Apostellehre), Barnabasbrief, Zweiter Klemensbrief, Schrift an Diognet* (Darmstadt: Wissenschaftliche Buchgesellschaft, 1984).

Wernle, P., *Paulus als Heidenmissionar* (Leipzig, Tübingen: Mohr, 1899).

Wikenhauser, A., 'Doppelträume', *Biblica* 29 (1948), pp. 100-111.

Wilckens, U., *Die Missionsreden der Apostelgeschichte. Form- und traditionsgeschichtliche Untersuchungen* (WMANT 5; Neukirchen-Vluyn: Neukirchener Verlag, 3rd ed., 1974, [1]1961).

——, *Der Brief an die Römer* 3 vols. (EKK; Düsseldorf: Benziger; Neukirchen-Vluyn: Neukirchener, 1978.1980.1982).

Wilson, A.N., *Paul. The Mind of an Apostle* (London [etc.]: Sinclair-Stephenson, 1997).

Wilson, S.G., *The Gentiles and the Gentile Mission in Luke-Acts* (Cambridge: University Press, 1973).

Windisch, H., 'Die Christusepiphanie von Damascus und ihren religionsgeschichtlichen Parallellen', *ZNW* 31 (1932), pp. 1-9.

Winger, M., 'Tradition, Revelation and Gospel. A Study in Galatians', *JSNT* 53 (1994), pp. 65-86.

Witt, E.R., *Isis in the Ancient World* (London: Thames & Hudson; 1997) [= *Isis in the Graeco-Roman World* (Ithaca: Cornell University Press, 1971)].

Zerwick, M., *Biblical Greek. English Edition adapted from the Fourth Latin Edition by J. Smith S.J.* (Rome: Pontifical Institute, 1963, 3rd repr. 1987).

Zmijewski, J., *Der Stil der paulinischen "Narrenrede". Analyse der Sprachgestaltung in 2 Kor 11,1-12,10 als Beitrag zur Methodik von Stiluntersuchungen neutestamentlicher Texte* (BBB 52; Köln, Bonn: Peter Hanstein, 1978).

INDICES

INDEX OF MODERN AUTHORS

INDEX OF REFERENCES TO ANCIENT SOURCES

BIBLE

7,32	261, 263	1,8	101, 102, 118n130, 120, 153,
7,33	282, 283		156
8,16	282, 283	1,8a	101n65
8,17	189	1,8b	101n65
8,18	282, 283	1,25	273
9,16	113n113	1,26	274, 276
8,26	282, 283	2,22	113
8,29	282, 283	2,23	102n66, 152n58
8,42	261, 269	2,33	118n130
9,4	282, 284	2,37	274, 276
9,7	261, 273	2,38	118n130
10,36	261, 270	2,40	119n133
10,41	113n113	2,41	115
11,3	261, 263	2,42	276
11,42	261, 270	2,42-43	274
11,47	113n113	2,43	276
11,50-51	92	3,1	119
12,18	113n113	3,3	119
12,37	113n113	3,4	119
12,44	284	3,11	119
12,44-45	282	3,20	261, 270
12,45	284	3,26	261, 270
12,49	282, 284	4,13	119
13,16	274, 282, 284	4,19	119
13,20	282, 284	4,28	102n66
14,24	282, 284	4,29	119n133
14,26	282, 284	4,33	274, 276
15,21	282, 284	4,35	276
15,26	282, 284	4,35-37	274
16,5	282, 284	4,36	130, 187, 229, 276
16,7	282, 284	4,37	276
17,3	261, 270	5,2	274, 276
17,8	261, 270	5,12	274, 276
17,18	261, 266, 270	5,13	113
17,21	261, 270	5,18	274, 276
17,23	261, 270	5,21	118n130, 261, 263
17,25	261, 270	5,29	274, 277
18,24	261, 263	5,33	152n58
19,13	140n7	5,36	103n71, 152n58
19,17	140n7	5,37-38	101, 158
19,20	140n7	5,38-39	152
20,21	261, 270, 282, 285	5,40	274, 277
20,30	113n113	5,42	114n117, 130
21,8	153n62	6,1	106, 107, 140n7
		6,1-7	106n84, 107
Acts		6,2	107
1,2	274, 276	6,3	118, 126
1,5-6	106n84	6,5	111, 118, 119

16,14	229
16,15	229, 234n115
16,19	234n113
16,21	229, 230
16,22	230
16,23	217n41, 229
16,25	192n43
16,25-27	196

1 Corinthians

1,1	161, 177, 204n6, 229, 274, 280
1,1-2	160
1,2	183n21, 213n36, 214, 217n41, 218, 234n107
1,4	213n36, 245n146, 246
1,7	250n159
1,9	183n21
1,10-3,23	210
1,11	229
1,12	81n1, 228
1,13	133
1,13-17	115n121
1,14	229
1,16	212, 230
1,17	114n119, 116, 165n98, 184, 206, 212, 261, 267
1,18	252
1,21	169
1,23	92n38, 97, 112, 207
1,24	183n21
1,26	183n21, 218
1,30	213n36, 214
2,2	92n38, 97
2,4	254
3,1	213n36, 214
3,4	81n1, 228
3,5	81n1, 228
3,5-9	206, 210, 211
3,6	81n1, 228
3,6-7	211
3,9	230n87, 232n95
3,10	212, 245n145
3,10-17	211
3,13	169
3,13-15	206n12
3,16	216
3,21-23	210n28

3,22	81n1, 228
4,6	81n1, 228
4,9	274, 278
4,10	213n36, 214
4,11-12	222
4,12	144, 225n65
4,15	213n36, 214
4,17	213n36, 216, 217n41, 230, 282
4,19	245
5,1	250n159
5,5	252
5,5-6	98n53
5,8	250
6,4	217n41
6,11	216
6,13-15	224
6,14	92n38
6,15	219n52
7,15	183n21
7,17	183n21, 217n41
7,20	183n21
7,21	183n21
7,22	183n21
8,5-6	93, 96, 98n53
8,7	240
8,11	91, 92n38
9,1	17, 76, 162, 163, 182, 205, 206, 227n78, 240n128, 278
9,1-2	274
9,1-23	224
9,2	179n4, 274, 278
9,3	162
9,5	182, 274, 278
9,5-6	182
9,6	76, 187, 229
9,12	193n46, 224
9,15-18	227n78
9,16	114n119, 165n98, 200n64, 206, 224
9,18	165n98, 206, 224
9,19	76, 224
9,19-23	224, 225, 241
9,20	104
9,22	259
9,23	104n75
9,27	112n103, 207
10,2	115n121

NON-BIBLICAL SOURCES

JEWISH

PAGAN

CHRISTIAN

PRINTED ON PERMANENT PAPER • IMPRIME SUR PAPIER PERMANENT • GEDRUKT OP DUURZAAM PAPIER - ISO 9706

N.V. PEETERS S.A., WAROTSTRAAT 50, B-3020 HERENT